P9-DUI-573

Locational Analysis in Human Geography

Second Edition
Volume II

Locational Methods

Peter Haggett
Professor of Urban and Regional Geography, University of Bristol

Andrew D. Cliff
University Lecturer in Geography and Fellow of Christ's College, Cambridge

Allan Frey
Senior Lecturer in Geography, University of Bristol

Edward Arnold

Copyright © Peter Haggett, Andrew Cliff and Allan Frey 1977

First published 1977 by
Edward Arnold (Publishers) Ltd
25 Hill Street, London W1X 8LL

The first edition of
Locational Analysis in Human Geography
© Peter Haggett 1965
was first published in 1965 by
Edward Arnold (Publishers) Ltd
and reprinted 1966; 1967; 1968; 1969; 1970; 1971.

ISBN Cloth 0 7131 5899 9
vol. I paper 0 7131 (Chapters 1–7) 5955 3
vol. II paper 0 7131 (Chapters 8–16) 5956 1

All rights reserved. No part of this publication may be reproduced, stored in a retrieval system, or transmitted in any form or by any means, electronic, photocopying, recording or otherwise, without the prior permission of Edward Arnold (Publishers) Ltd.

This book is published in two editions. The paperback edition is sold subject to the condition that it shall not, by way of trade or otherwise, be lent, re-sold, hired out or otherwise circulated without the publisher's prior consent in any form of binding or cover other than that in which it is published and without a similar condition including this condition being imposed upon any subsequent purchaser.

Filmset by Keyspools Limited, Golborne, Lancs.
Printed in Great Britain by J. W. Arrowsmith Ltd., Bristol

Contents

[1] A detailed contents list appears at the beginning of each of the chapters. Starred sections (*) indicate areas which demand a fuller statistical background than is assumed in the remainder of the book.

Volume II: Locational Methods

Preface to the Second Edition

Locational studies have changed over the last fifteen years in ways hardly foreseen when the first edition[1] was being written. Then, geography stood on the edge of changes in both emphasis and style which came, in the mid-1960s, to be bundled together as yet another 'new' geography of the sort which periodically besets the discipline. The times were those of J. F. Kennedy's New Frontier; universities and their individual subjects were expanding; the mood was optimistic. Perhaps individual disciplines catch the feeling of society as a whole, for now the mid-1970s find geography in a more sombre mood. The first edition described itself as 'a report from an active battlefront'. Even with three authors, rather than one, peering through the smoke, the lines of development remain as hard to see. But, if we retain the military metaphor, then the cavalry charge described in the early 1960s seems now to have slowed to grinding trench warfare. To be sure, the current geographer is better armed but he faces a tougher battle. As capabilities rise, so too do expectations, and certain locational problems are now revealed as starkly difficult. To overcome them will take much more time and effort and a higher order of application than had been imagined a decade or so ago.

As with any architectural renovation, the present book is an odd blend of old and new. Retained is the basic distinction between locational concepts

[1] Few books are more exasperating than those which refuse to die gracefully! Since the first edition of this book was written, dozens of more substantive works on locational analysis by other pens have been published. Thus it was the expectation (even hope) of the original author that the first edition of this book would be the only one. Left unchanged and unrevised it might be expected to slip peacefully from the bookshelves, to be recalled—if at all—as a nostalgic 'period piece'. Unpredictably, the book stubbornly refused to go out of print and although outdated was translated into an increasing number of foreign languages. Given soaring printing costs, to revise a few points here and there and to update references would have added hugely to the published costs of any 'new' version, while doing little to come to terms with the changes in human geography as a whole. A more radical revision was called for. I was fortunate in that, at a time when my own timetable was having to be drastically curtailed, two of my colleagues (both then at Bristol) agreed to help with the task. Andrew Cliff took especial interest in the sections concerned with formal statistical and mathematical modelling (especially Chapters 7, 10–13, 15–16), while Allan Frey concentrated on methodological and conceptual questions. Without their efforts and enthusiastic cooperation, a second edition would have remained long unwritten. It is our joint view of locational analysis and its role in human geography that this second edition now presents.

P.H.

(Part One), and ways of testing and extending them (Part Two); added is a concern with regional applications (Part Three). Within Part One, the spatial format—from 'flows' to 'surfaces'—is maintained, and a new chapter on diffusion has been added. Part Two is heavily revised and contains much new material to allow a fuller examination of the statistical models needed in locational analysis. Part Three extends the work of the first edition on region building by considering optimization and forecasting methods. Given the increasing importance of regional planning at present, we would expect greater emphasis to be given to Part Three in any future revisions. Decisions on whether to retain or to dispense with old favourites in the material contained in the first edition caused occasional heart searching. Inevitably, what was seen as 'sound timber' by the original author, sometimes appeared as 'dry rot' to his colleagues. But we were agreed that many of the debates on the philosophy of geography (for example, on exceptionalism, the place of quantification in the subject, and the neglect of the geometric tradition) had now grown stale. New issues, like the value of a phenomenological approach and the radical role of science, have taken their place in Chapter 1. Likewise, the notion of a natural scale of geographical magnitude (the G-scale of the first edition) has been revised to bring the scale into line with Haggett (1965a).

Inevitably, problems of what to cut out were incomparably more difficult than what to include. We were tempted to add the subtitle 'a macrogeographical approach', to the book's main title to indicate the emphasis we squarely place on aggregate behaviour patterns and macroscale geographical phenomena. Major developments in human microgeography—in space/time trajectories, in perception, and in the theory of decision making—have taken place over the last decade, associated particularly with the research of workers such as Torsten Hägerstrand, Yi-Fu Tuan and Julian Wolpert. We debated whether or not to include an extended treatment of such material in this edition. In the end, the pressures of space and our consciousness of the fact that others could write with more authority in this area, restricted us to very limited cross-references. We view this work in microgeography with optimism, and look forward to the enrichment it promises for the somewhat formal areas of aggregate model building reported here.

Given its restricted compass, the book will be seen by some critics as narrow and positivist in its philosophy. Certainly, the Neyman–Pearson, rather than the Bayesian, approach to statistical analysis is followed in Part Two, where the emphasis is on the critical and sceptical scrutiny of locational ideas. Where these notions of human spatial organization come from remains a matter of intuition and imagination, and research on the topics reported in Part One leaves plenty of scope for creativity. Together, Parts One and Two form the two halves of Medawar's (1969) hypothetic-deductive method, still the conventional approach to most scientific problem solving. If this 'cycle' of construction and testing seems too academic, then in Part Three we begin to consider the utility of ideas in terms of their regional applications.

Throughout, our joint aim has been to direct this second edition, like the first, to the audience we know best—the second and third year undergraduate at an English university. Most of the chapters are thus based on lecture and classroom material. However, many locational models are now part of the English school curriculum, while statistical methods form an essential part of the first and second year geography undergraduate's training. A higher level of mathematical understanding is therefore assumed than was the case with the first edition. Important textbooks like those of King (1969b) and Wilson and Kirkby (1975) are now available, and we expect undergraduates to be familiar with these basic works. Sections in the book which are of greater statistical or mathematical difficulty have been starred and it is suggested that they could be omitted at a first reading. A glossary of notation appears at the end of the book which summarises the main notational conventions used, and a small selection of statistical tables is also included. Our hope is that the book may prove useful to the reader wanting a general outline of locational analysis while, at the same time, containing enough challenging material to attract those wishing to pursue study at greater depth.

Acknowledgement was paid in the first edition to a number of sources of help. These debts incurred by the original author have been compounded over the intervening years and remain heavier than ever, especially in both Cambridge and the West Country. All three of us have also benefitted from generous help on both sides of the Atlantic during periods of research or teaching in other institutions. We have also gained from critical comments by the editors of translated versions of the first edition, especially from the French (Philippe Pinchemel), German (Dietrich Bartels), and Russian editions (Yuri Medvedkov and Mark Bandman). Three other acknowledgements are in order. First, to Keith Ord of the Statistics Department at Warwick University, goes a special word for his unstinting advice and help with the more mathematical sections of the book. Second, we are grateful to our publisher, Edward Arnold, and to their Geography Editor, John Davey, not only for support in producing this volume, but for innovative leads given in geography publishing in this country. Third, we wish to thank Arin Bayraktaroglu and Sue Flint in the Statistics Laboratory at Cambridge, whose continued good humour enabled them to survive the typing of a lengthy manuscript made no easier by three varieties of handwriting, standardized only in illegibility.

Our children now span the age range from diapers, through pop music, to latch keys. It was not in their nature to suffer in silence while this edition was being hammered out at home, but we appreciated the occasional demodulation. That these brief episodes occurred at all was due, as always, to the three whose names grace an earlier page. We dedicate this book to them with affection.

Chew Magna, Somerset   Peter Haggett
Bonfire Night, 1975.   Andrew Cliff
                                                                Allan Frey

Note: The paperback edition of this book is presented in two volumes. These are self-contained and may be used individually. So that they may be read and used together, cross-references from volume I to volume II and vice versa are retained, and both volumes contain complete Contents pages, References and Indexes. The pagination of volume II continues from volume I. There is thus a jump in pagination between the final chapter of the latter and the References.

Acknowledgements

The authors and publishers gratefully acknowledge permission received from the following to modify and make use of copyright material in diagrams and tables:[1]

Full citations to books, journals and authors may be found in the references; sources of material are given in the captions.

American Geographical Society for figs 6.18, 6.19; American Statistical Association for fig. 9.8 and table 9.1; Association of American Geographers for figs 4.11(b), 6.23, 9.20, 9.21, 13.15, 13.16 and tables 9.9, 15.2; Cambridge University Press for figs 2.9, 2.10, 2.12, 4.2, 4.3, 8.5, 8.9, 8.10, 11.5, 11.7, 11.16, 12.2, 12.3, 14.7, 14.8, 14.9, 15.3 and tables 2.4, 2.5, 14.4, 14.5; Centre for Urban and Community Studies, University of Toronto for fig. 3.15; Clark University for table 6.5; Colston Research Society, University of Bristol, for figs 12.26, 12.27; Department of the Navy, Arlington, Va. for fig. 14.3; to the Escher Foundation, Collection Haags Gemeentemuseum, the Hague for fig. 1.5; Dr P. Fores for fig. 9.24; W. C. Found for table 6.8; Geografiska Annaler for figs 5.13, 9.16, 9.17 and table 9.3; Charles Griffin & Co. Ltd for fig. 13.6 and tables 7.2, 8.5, 8.6, 10.5, 13.2, 13.3; Güven Gülöksüz for fig. 4.11(c); Harper & Row Inc. for fig. 1.3 and tables 1.1, 8.4; Heinemann Educational Books Ltd for fig. 9.6; Holden-Day Inc. for fig. 12.13(c) and (d); Institute of British Geographers for figs 1.4, 6.10, 16.3 and tables 10.2, 10.3, 16.1; Johns Hopkins University Press for table 8.7; Journal of Asian Studies for fig. 5.14; Liber Grafiska Map Service Division for fig. 7.2; Methuen & Co. Ltd for fig. 4.16; Northwestern University Press for fig. 7.4; Ohio State University for figs 4.20, 5.6, 12.5, 12.14, 12.15, 12.16 and 16.1; Oliver and Boyd, Dr F. Yates, the literary executor of the late Sir Ronald Fisher and the McGraw-Hill International Book Co. for statistical tables; Operations Research Society of America for fig. 14.18; Oxford University Press for fig. 14.1; Pergamon Press Ltd for figs 2.6, 6.20, 14.14 and tables 4.6, 4.9; Pion Ltd for figs 7.9, 11.2, 12.6, 12.12, 13.1, 13.2, 13.3 and tables 10.1, 10.4, 11.2, 11.4, 13.1; Pitman & Sons, London and Dr Frederick Croxton for fig. 8.2; Prentice-Hall Inc. for figs 6.3, 6.22, 15.7; J. N. Rayner and R. G. Golledge for figs 12.17, 12.18, 12.19, 12.20(a), 12.21, 12.23; Royal Statistical Society for table 14.6; R. S. Spooner for fig. 4.21; P. J. Taylor for table 2.1; University of

---

[1] Numbers refer to figures and tables in this book.

Chicago Press for fig. 10.5; University of Minnesota Press for fig. 7.8; University of Washington Press for fig. 14.21; James E. Vance Jr. for fig. 2.11; Wayne State University Press for fig. 14.20; John Wiley & Sons Inc. for table 12.1; Yale Law Journal Company and Fred B. Rothman & Co. for fig. 14.19.

Acknowledgement is also made to the copyright holders in the figures below which have been redrawn or modified from the first edition:
The American Association of Petroleum Geologists for fig. 12.1; The American Geographical Society for figs 3.21, 3.23, 4.10, 4.18 and 4.19; The Association of American Geographers for figs 1.9, 2.7, 6.14, 6.15, 6.21, 8.12, 9.2, 10.9 and 14.15; Department of Regional Science, University of Pennsylvania for figs 3.20, 5.3, 14.22 and 14.23; *Economic Geography* for figs 2.21, 5.1 and 6.11, The Free Press, Glencoe, for fig. 10.8; *Geografiska Annaler*, Sweden, for fig. 4.6; C. W. K. Gleerup Publishers, Sweden, for figs 2.3, 2.5, 3.8, 4.7, 5.11, 5.18, 5.19 and 7.1; K. A. Gunawardena for fig. 5.1; Hafner Publishing Co. for figs 2.2 and 4.10; Holt, Rinehart & Winston Inc for fig. 14.16; Hutchinson & Co. Ltd for figs 3.9 and 6.5; The Institute of British Geographers for figs 12.1 and 14.4; *Liverpool and Manchester Geological Journal* for fig. 8.3; The Ministry of Transport for figs 2.10 and 3.10; MIT Press and the author for figs 2.20, 5.9 and 5.26; Thomas Nelson & Sons Ltd and the editors for fig. 9.22; Peat, Marwich, Caywood, Schiller & Co. for figs 3.6 and 3.17; Princeton University Press for figs 3.4 and 3.18; *Professional Geographer* for figs 5.2, 9.3, 13.10 and 14.17; *Przeglad Geograficzny* for figs 14.12 and 14.13; Regional Science Research Institute for figs 9.11 and 15.2; The Research Center in Economic Development and Cultural Change, Chicago, for figs 4.12 and 4.13; The Royal Geographical Society for figs 8.6 and 12.4; The State University of Iowa, Dept. of Geography, for fig. 5.22; *Tijdschrift voor Economische en Sociale Geografie* for figs 4.2 and 7.1; *The Times* and T. H. Hollingsworth for fig. 2.21; The University of Chicago Press for figs 2.2, 3.16, 3.19, 3.20, 3.22, 6.16, 6.17, 9.12, 9.13, 9.14 and 9.15; The University of Michigan for fig. 7.7; The University of Michigan Press for figs 4.3, 4.4, 5.17 and 6.4; The University of Toronto Press for fig. 2.13; University of Wales Press for fig. 9.7; The US Conservation Foundation and the authors for fig. 8.11; The US Department of Agriculture for figs 8.3, 8.4 and 8.10; Yale University Press for figs 2.14, 2.16, 3.2, 3.3, 4.17, 5.4 and 5.10.

For Brenda, Margaret, and Val

Part Two:

Methods of Locational Analysis

Only when a regularity has already been recognized or suspected can the planning of an experiment begin: until that time the mere multiplication of experiments is comparatively fruitless . . . and the accumulation of observations in large numbers will be as much a waste of energy in physics as in cartography. (STEPHEN TOULMIN, The Philosophy of Science, 1953, pp. 111–12.)

8 Data Collecting

8.1 Introduction

Further development of the locational models outlined in Chapters 2–7 depends largely upon our ability to test them against observed geographical patterns. More theoretical models can and will be developed on deductive bases, but we are unlikely ever to know how useful these are unless an adequate feedback of information in the form of empirical data can be ensured. The next six chapters of this book are concerned with the ways in which geographical information can be gathered, measured, classified, and described; not simply to add to the present jumble of regional information that we already have to hand, but in order that our existing concepts may be critically examined. It is all too easy to collect information in human geography, all too hard to collect information which is significant and relevant to specific locational questions. To this extent, the organization of Part Two of the book follows the well-established paths of experimental design, moving from the collecting of evidence, through to the testing of hypotheses about spatial patterns.

In this opening chapter of Part Two, we look at the problem faced by geographers in coping with information on a vast spatial scale. At the global level, this 'coverage' problem is simple and immediate. The earth's surface is so staggeringly large that, even if we caricature the difficulty, each of the geographical profession's 3,000 nominal practitioners (Meynen, 1960) might be assigned an area of some five thousand square miles for individual study. If we agree with Hartshorne, that the purpose of geography is '... to provide accurate, orderly and rational description and interpretation of the variable character of the earth's surface' (Hartshorne, 1959, p. 21) then this is a gross measure of the magnitude of the task we set ourselves.

This can hardly be regarded as a new difficulty. At least from the time of Eratosthenes, the size of the problem has been apparent and it may well be that our predecessors were more keenly aware of its importance. Many a doubtful isopleth now strays self-importantly across areas that our more honest forbears might have filled with heraldic doodles labelled '*Terra Incognita*' or '*Hic Dracones*'!

This chapter approaches the problem by regarding any geographical area— global or local—as the potential source of a statstical *population* (a term defined below) of interest to the locational analyst. Our problem is then reduced to a twofold one: (i) drawing representative samples from the population using sampling theory, and (ii) improving the quality of the populations from which we draw our sample. We look at each of these aspects in turn.

8.2 Geographical Populations

8.2.1 *Sources of geographical information*

One of the difficulties that has beset the collection of locational data in the past is the heavy dependence on secondary sources. Of the categories shown in Table 8.1, none is more important than that labelled 'archival sources', which includes both information recorded directly on an areal framework (e.g. maps and air photographs), as well as information which could be transferred to an areal framework (e.g. census records). It is difficult to make precise estimates, but a rapid check of locational research published in geographical periodicals over the last few years suggests that this source still accounts for over 95 per cent of our work.

Table 8.1   Sources of locational information in human geography

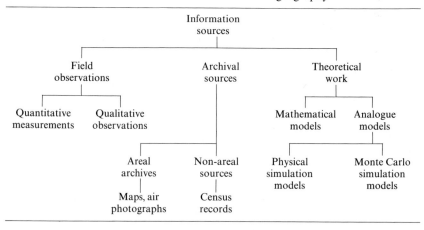

This dependence on secondary sources has three main consequences: (i) locational analysis is using data which have been collected primarily for non-geographical purposes, and these data are usually oblique in varying degrees to the direct research needs of geographers; (ii) we are dependent on the original accuracy of the survey, an accuracy which may be surprisingly low [cf. Morgenstern's (1963) critique of economic data], and which is in any case outside our direct control; (iii) data are released in 'bundles' (i.e. for administrative areas) which are inconvenient and anchronistic, and pose extremely acute problems in mapping and interpretation. Although there are ways of outflanking some of these problems (Section 8.3) and we shall continue to make use of by-product sources for the foreseeable future, there is considerable need to explore the alternative sources of geographical information.

Much of this chapter is concerned with the possibilities of using sampling methods to collect significant information according to our particular research needs. Insofar as this implies field collection, this represents a return to a tradition which was a hallmark of nineteenth-century geography and persisted strongly in the Land Utilization Survey in Britain in the 1930s (Board, in Chorley and Haggett, 1965, Chapter 10). Less traditional is the possibility of information being produced by theoretical work in which locational conditions are simulated by mathematical or physical models, as in the studies of diffusion processes discussed in Chapter 7. Of the two alternative sources, that of fieldwork offers the best immediate solution in that it promises to give, at least when linked to rigorous experimental designs, directly relevant information on the applicability of existing locational models. At the same time, it provides data which can be tested, extended, and manipulated in theoretical work.

The whole problem of information in geography is a complex one which has been somewhat clouded by traditional attitudes (e.g. the difficulties of handling apparently 'complete' rather than sample data) and a tendency to view problems as being uniquely geographical. Many of our difficulties are common to most sciences, and we are likely to gain in perspective by viewing them in a more eclectic framework.

8.2.2 *Types of geographical populations*

A statistical *population* (also sometimes called a *universe*) may be defined as any finite or infinite collection of individual objects, some of whose characteristics we wish to study (Kendall and Buckland, 1960). A geographical population is therefore a collection of objects with some geographical characteristic in common. Thus we might conceive of the counties of the co-terminous United States as a geographical population, in which there are a large but finite number (3,074) of individuals. Although, as we shall see later in this chapter, the definition of *individuals* in this population gives difficulty, the definition of populations is a process which is governed by the research objectives. As Krumbein (1960, p. 349) has argued, once the objects of the study have been defined, the population has been defined.

In general, the population will be too large for us to have either the time or the money to examine every individual. We therefore select from the population some sub-set of individuals for study. The sub-set of individuals selected is known as the *sample*, and the selection procedure as *sampling*. The sampling procedures of geographical interest are described in Section 8.3. All of them are designed to make the characteristics of the sampled individuals as representative as possible of the characteristics of the population as a whole. The object of the exercise is to enable the researcher to make inferences about the characteristics of the population on the basis of the characteristics of the sampled individuals. Sampling theory is concerned with (i) designing procedures which will make these inferences as precise as possible, and (ii) enabling us to make probability statements about the degree of confidence we can place in the inferences.

Sampling and statistical inference. Conventional statistical hypothesis testing has been developed around this population/sample model; we test hypotheses about means, correlation, and so on, for sample data, as a basis for inferences about the population as a whole. In some circumstances, the population may be small, and we might then be tempted exhaustively to sample it (i.e. to sample all the individuals in the population). If this is done, so that we are prepared to argue that the individuals sampled comprise the population, we cannot proceed with statistical inference in the usual manner. The model we apply to the data then either fits or it does not, for there is no larger population about which to make inferences.

If the situation described above should occur, we must look for a different framework from the population/sample model within which to work. Two alternatives are open to us. We could proceed as in time series analysis, and argue that the data to be analyzed represent one possible outcome of some stochastic generating process (as with the models described in Chapter 7). We would then try to make statements about the process itself using data from a realization of that process. Otherwise, we could proceed using randomization methods (as in Section 11.3.2); that is, we would take the observed spatial configuration of data as given, and ask if it is significant in some way in the set of all possible spatial configurations which could be formed with the *same* data values. For example, suppose we know the unemployment rates for each of the n English counties in 1976. Under the time series approach, we would argue that these rates are but one realization of economic processes which control levels of unemployment, and these processes might produce very different levels on other occasions. Under randomization, we would recognize that the observed spatial allocation of unemployment rates to counties constitutes but one of $n!$ possible spatial arrangements of the rates among the counties, and we would be interested in determining whether there is anything 'significant' about the actual configuration observed.

Although the choice of model (population/sample; stochastic process/ realization; randomization) makes little difference to the *mechanics* of carrying out a statistical test, the philosophical issues involved are very important, and the choice of an appropriate framework will depend on the nature of the geographical problem in hand. It is the purpose of this chapter to look at the structure of the population/sample framework in more detail.

Sampling schemes. The distinction between a *finite* and *infinite* population is thus an important one in terms of the statistical theory of sampling (Stuart, 1962, pp. 36–42). In the case of a finite population, say the 50 states of the United States, we implicitly assume that a given state is chosen only once in any sample drawn. If we draw New Hampshire as the first state in a sample of six, then we automatically exclude it from being a further member of the sample. This is called sampling *without replacement*. We may contrast this with the situation in which we replace the selected state after each selection. This is called sampling *with replacement*, and New Hampshire could appear more than once in our sample.

Sampling with replacement seems inefficient, since we may duplicate information, and we could even have six New Hampshires in a sample of six, albeit with a very small probability of occurrence $[(\frac{1}{50})^6$, if each state of the Union, is assumed to be equally likely to occur in our sample]. Nevertheless, it is useful where we do not wish to worry about checking duplications in a sample, and, much more important, it produces major simplifications in the theory of sampling and in the ease of making inferences from a sample to a population. Sampling with replacement allows us to draw a sample of any size we please, since at any stage we always have 50 states still to choose from. As Stuart (1962, p. 39) argues, the population has now become inexhaustible and thus the effective size of the population is now infinite. Note that this fundamental inexhaustibility, on which so much statistical theory is built, is imposed on the population by the sampling method—with or without replacement. An apparently finite population (e.g. the states of the U.S.A.) can be converted into an infinite population by sampling with replacement; likewise, an apparently infinite population (e.g. point samples of land use over southern England) can be converted into a finite (but very large) population by sampling without replacement.

A less vital distinction may be made in some geographical research between (i) the *target population* which is the conceptual or ultimate total population, and (ii) the *sampled population* which is the actual population from which samples may be drawn (Cochran, Mosteller, and Tukey, 1954). If we wish to test the validity of a locational concept, say the rank–size distribution of cities (Section 4.3), our target population about which we wish to generalize or predict may be the world. However, the population that we are in fact able to sample from is less than this, since for reasons of census shortcomings or political caution, not all countries in the world release appropriate data. Thus Ginsburg (1961), in his *Atlas of economic development*, defined a target population of 140 'countries or equivalent administrative units'. However, for most of his forty-seven indices, the sampled population was only about one hundred countries. Even for population density, the most widely available index, the sampled population (139 countries) fell just short of the target population.

In relatively few research problems are the target and sampled population synonymous. We must often face the fact that we are dealing with the accessible sub-population only, and '... it becomes a matter of judgement whether the sampled and target populations are nearly enough identical that inferences about the sampled population can be applied without qualification to the target population' (Krumbein, 1960, p. 353).

8.2.3 *Problems of operational definition*

Definition of the individuals that make up a geographical population poses very complex, but essentially local, difficulties which must be solved by adopting operational definitions. An *operational definition* is a set of arbitrary rules or criteria by which individuals that belong to a population can be clearly recognized. Although general discussions of the problem exist (e.g. Morgenstern, 1963), it may be more helpful to illustrate a specific case. Urban settlements form a typical problem case.

Nature of the problem. Alexander (1963, p. 528) has shown that the concept of an 'urban settlement' varies considerably from country to country: Denmark counts as urban all settlements with 250 or more inhabitants, while Spain and Switzerland count as urban only those with 10,000 or more. For the United States, the Bureau of the Census publish data for four different types of 'urban-like areas'. These are, in rough order of size: (i) the *urban place* which includes all places of 2,500 inhabitants or more; (ii) the *incorporated city* or city of 2,500 inhabitants or more which has a separate political entity; (iii) the *urbanized area* which is centred on one city of 50,000 or more inhabitants and includes the urban fringe around each city; and (iv) the *standard metropolitan area*: this is based on a group of counties which contains at least one city of 50,000 or more inhabitants, but with most of its area non-urban in character. These categories, (i)–(iv), are not mutually exclusive. However, each gives a somewhat different picture of urban land in the United States and each has special value in special circumstances. Indeed, since the historical record for each varies, this frequently determines which type will in fact be used. Data for incorporated cities are in the main available since 1900; data for standard metropolitan areas were organized after World War II, and for urbanized areas only after 1950. In Britain, the problem of city definitions is equally acute, and Dickinson (1963, p. 68) has shown, for example, that Liverpool may be either larger or smaller than Manchester depending on how each city is demarcated.

Davis and his group (International Urban Research, 1959, pp. 6–7) have suggested that there are a number of ways in which the 'natural' city (i.e. the urbanized area) may be misrepresented by the census records; these are shown diagrammatically in Figure 8.1, in which the 'natural' city is shaded and the statistical units of the census are marked with a solid line. The first of these three types is described as the 'underbounded' city, in which the statistical boundary is smaller than the urban area. In consequence, parts of the urban area may be either left without any demarcation between them and surrounding rural districts, or else divided up among other statistical cities (Figure 8.1A). Such underbounded types are common in Australia where large urban areas are commonly divided into municipalities, shires, councils, etc. Thus Sydney proper had a population of only 193,100 in 1955 while the whole Sydney urban area had a population of 1,869,000. The second type, the 'overbounded' city, is one in which the statistical boundary is larger than the urban area and may contain more than one urban area (Figure 8.1B). In the Philippines, the political–statistical boundaries of most 'cities' include both huge areas of rural land and towns of various sizes. The third possibility, the 'truebounded' city, where the political and geographical boundaries coincide, is ideal but rare (Figure 8.1c). Pakistani cities appear to approach this ideal most nearly.

✳✳✳✳

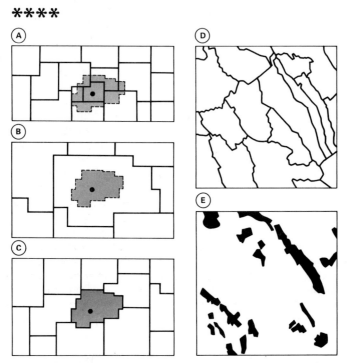

Figure 8.1   A, B, C Alternative relations between statistical units and the urbanized area of a city. **D** Civil parish boundaries in a sample quadrat of the central Chilterns, southern England. **E** Farmland misclassified by using the boundaries shown in **D**. Source: Coppock, 1960, p. 318.

Attempted solutions. The problem of standardizing definitions of cities has not been solved. Among the partial solutions put forward, one of the most complex is that used by the United States Census Bureau in its definitions of Standard Metropolitan Areas (SMA). These they define in terms of (i) density, (ii) function, and (iii) integration (Office of Statistical Standards, 1958). SMAs must contain at least one city of 50,000 or more inhabitants as a core. To this are added adjacent counties which are 'metropolitan' in character (i.e. they contain 10,000 non-agricultural workers, or 10 per cent of the non-agricultural workers of the SMA, or have at least 50 per cent of their population residing in civil divisions with a population density of 150 or more per square mile and contiguous to the central city). In addition, non-agricultural workers must constitute at least two-thirds of the total employed population of the county. To these stringent rules are added criteria of integration between the central-city county and outlying counties, based on percentage of commuting (e.g. 15

per cent of workers in the outlying county must work in the central-city county) and telephone communication (calls per month to central-city county at least four times that of the number of the subscribers in the outlying county).

Although even with these rules, exceptions had to be made (e.g. for New England, with its historically distinct 'town system'), this careful attempt by the United States Census Bureau has placed the problem of city definition on a new level. It has led directly to work such as that of the International Urban Research group at Berkeley which has produced the most complete tally of world cities on a comparable basis yet achieved. Their definition of a 'metropolitan area' runs to twelve closely argued pages (including two on 'hard cases') (International Urban Research, 1959, pp. 20–32).

Understandably, other and less complex solutions have been proposed. Grytzell (1963) has used a 'sliding-scale' of population density, illustrating his method of demarcation for five major cities (New York, London, Paris, Stockholm, and Copenhagen). He argues that fixed population densities obscure important regional variations in the density of urban areas, and that it is the relative density of the city which distinguishes it from surrounding areas.

While the definitional problem has been discussed here with reference to urban areas, it extends to all geographical populations. Overlap of alternative definitions of city has similarities to the farm boundary/parish boundary problem discussed by Coppock (1955) and illustrated for the Chiltern area of southern England. Here, as Figure 8.1D suggests, the outline of the areal unit for which agricultural statistics appear to be collected (i.e. the parish) and the areal unit to which they in fact relate (i.e. the land belonging to *farms located in that parish*) may show considerable divergence. As a result, a significant proportion of the farmland lies outside the boundaries for which it has been mapped (Figure 8.1E).

8.3 Spatial Sampling Procedures

Sample studies have long been used in both research and teaching in geography. Platt (1942, 1959) was acutely aware of the '. . . old and stubborn dilemma of trying to comprehend large regions while seeing at once only a small area' (1942, p. 3) and he skilfully used sample field studies to build up an outstandingly clear series of pictures of the regions of Latin America. Similarly Highsmith (Highsmith, Heintzelman, Jensen, Rudd, and Tschirley, 1961) has used a world-wide selection of sample studies as the basis for an extremely useful teaching manual in economic geography.

There is an important difference, however, between these attempts to use sampling to circumvent the coverage problem, and the way in which sampling is now used in research. This essential difference is between *purposive* and *probability* sampling. In purposive or 'hunch' sampling, individuals are selected which are *thought* to be typical of the population as a whole; thus Platt (1942) chooses one *fazenda* as representative of the São Paulo coffee belt. The validity of the choice depends on the skill of the selector, and is usually open to debate. In probability sampling (Table 8.2) the samples are drawn on the basis of rigorous mathematical theory and, once the design is adopted, individuals are drawn from the population by established rules. In this introductory account of sampling procedures we shall confine our attention solely to matters of geographical interest and leave many areas of sampling theory unexplored. Two outstanding introductions to sampling methods, Stuart's *Basic ideas of scientific sampling* (1962) and Cochran's *Sampling techniques* (1953), provide a comprehensive coverage of its philosophy and theory. Yates's *Sampling methods for censuses and surveys* (1960) is the classic manual of practical survey design.

Table 8.2   A model of sampling designs

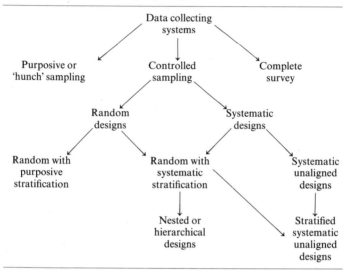

Source: Haggett. In Chorley and Haggett, 1965a, p. 166.

8.3.1 *Basic considerations: the Central Limit Theorem*

Suppose that the variate, X, defined for a geographical population, is normally distributed with mean, μ, and finite variance, σ^2. If repeated independent samples of size n are drawn from this population, and the mean of each of these samples, $\bar{x}_1$, $\bar{x}_2$, ..., is calculated, then the distribution of these sample means (i.e. the *sampling distribution* of sample means) will also be normal with a mean equal to the population mean, μ, and a standard deviation equal to $\sigma/\sqrt{n}$. See Figure 8.2A, B. Indeed, the *Central Limit Theorem* states that as $n \to \infty$, the same result holds *whatever the distribution of the population from which the samples are drawn*. See Figure 8.2c. It is this theorem which lies at the heart of sampling theory. In practice, for repeated samples of a given size, the sample means are approximately normally distributed about the population mean when $n > 30$, whatever the form of the population distribution. It is the generality of this large sample result which is so remarkable, for its validity does not depend in the least on the form of the population we are sampling from. Provided our sample size is large enough, the population may be extremely irregular, or very regular, and the sample means will still be approximately normally distributed about the population mean. Yates (1960, p. 190) has referred to this as the *normal law of error*.

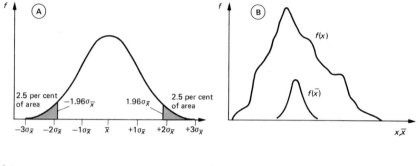

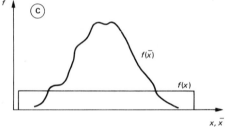

Figure 8.2   Central Limit Theorem. **A** Theoretical sampling distribution of sample arithmetic means from a normally distributed population. **B** Observed distribution $[f(\bar{x})]$ of 100 sample means $(\bar{x})$ for samples of size $n = 10$ drawn from a normal population $[f(x)]$ of $N = 972$ individuals. **C** Observed distribution of 1000 sample means $(\bar{x})$ for samples of $n = 4$ drawn from a rectangular population of $N = 122$. Source: Croxton, Cowden, and Klein, 1968, pp. 540–5.

Figure 8.2A shows a typical normal distribution with its familiar bell-shaped curve. Its density function, which gives the frequency with which deviations from the mean occur in the elemental range x to $x + dx$, is defined as

$$f(x)dx = \frac{1}{\sigma\sqrt{2\pi}} e^{-\frac{1}{2}(x-\mu)^2/\sigma^2} dx, \quad -\infty < x < \infty, \tag{8.1}$$

where the parameters of the distribution are the mean, μ, and the variance, σ^2. We can therefore determine, using (8.1), the frequencies with which deviations *greater* than a given magnitude may be expected to occur; these frequencies are listed in Appendix Table A1 for various values of $(x-\mu)/\sigma$, the deviates of the standard normal curve. The operation, $(x-\mu)/\sigma$, is a standardizing transformation, and if applied to normally distributed data, it ensures that the transformed data will also be normally distributed but with mean zero and unit variance (standard deviation). Hence, Table A1 tells us that for such a standard normal curve, only five per cent of the observations will lie outside

± 1.96 standard deviations from the mean, and only one per cent outside ± 2.58.

With this information, 'if we know that an estimate is subject to the normal law of error, we can assign probable limits of error to this estimate' (Yates, 1960, p. 191). We know from our earlier discussion that, for a sample of size n, the sampling distribution of sample means is normally distributed about the population mean with a standard error of $\sigma/\sqrt{n}$, where we can estimate σ^2 by

$$\sigma^2 = \frac{1}{(n-1)} \sum_{i=1}^{n} (x_i - \bar{x})^2. \tag{8.2}$$

Thus if we draw a sample of n observations which has a mean of $\bar{x}$, the above discussion and Table A1 imply that we can say with 95 per cent confidence that the mean of the population from which the sample is drawn will lie within ± 1.96 standard errors of the sample mean, or with 99 per cent confidence, within ±2.58 standard errors, and so on. To obtain these confidence bands, we simply scale the deviation values for the standard normal distribution, which are computed for a normal distribution with a standard deviation of one, by the standard error of our sampling distribution.

In interpreting the Central Limit Theorem, we should note three important reservations:

(1) Although the form of the population distribution does not affect the normality of the sampling distribution of sample means, we stress again that irregularity of the population distribution will affect the rapidity with which the approximation begins to hold. 'The more irregular the [population] distribution is, the larger the sample size we shall need for the sampling distribution of the sample average to approximate to the normal.' (Stuart, 1962, p. 32.)

(2) The Central Limit Theorem rests on the assumption of random sampling. A random sample is any sample selected by a chance mechanism with *known* chances of selection; as Section 8.3.2 shows, the chances of selection need not be equal for all samples so long as they are known. Once selection bias, either purposive bias (e.g. sampling only 'convenient' locations near highways or systematic sampling) or accidental bias (e.g. spatial autocorrelation—see Chapter 11—among the sampled observations), is allowed to intrude, then the whole apparatus of inference from sample to population falls to the ground, in that the determination of probable limits of error in estimating population parameters, as described above for the mean, becomes impossible (Yates, 1960, Chapter 7).

(3) The normal law of error embodied in the Central Limit Theorem applies to other parameters, such as totals and variances, as well as to the sample mean. However, larger sample sizes are generally necessary for the normal approximation to be valid.

8.3.2 *Spatial configuration of the samples*

Different spatial sampling designs are used to investigate particular geographical problems. Here we choose to illustrate the range of designs available for the study of a single but very important locational distribution, land use. This is a distribution which we can regard as continuous and which has tended to be studied in the past by direct and complete survey, rather than by sampling. Various types of sampling design have been evolved for this kind of distribution (Table 8.2): six of them—simple random sampling, stratified sampling, systematic sampling, stratified systematic unaligned sampling, nested or multistage sampling, and multifactor sampling—are discussed here.

The treatment is based on that of Krumbein (1960), Berry (1962), and Quenouille (1949).

(i) In *simple random sampling*, a sample of *n* individuals is drawn from the areal population at a series of randomly chosen co-ordinate positions. If both axes of the co-ordinate grid ranged over the interval [0, 100] say, two random

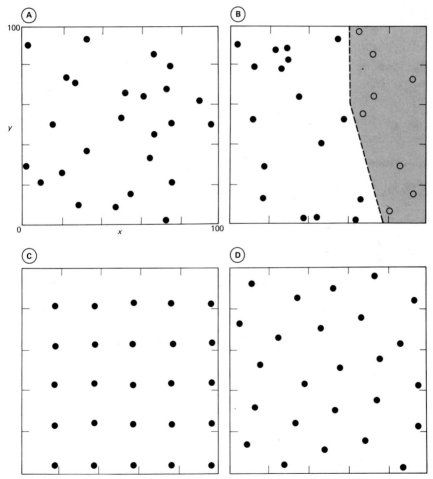

Figure 8.3 Alternative sampling designs: random (**A**), stratified random (**B**), systematic (**C**), and stratified systematic unaligned sample (**D**). Sources: Krumbein, 1960, p. 361; Berry, 1962, p. 7.

numbers in the range $[0, 100]$, corresponding to the y and x co-ordinates, would be drawn to determine each location. See Appendix Table A6. For example, the random numbers, 98 and 26, would give a location 98 units north by 26 units east, or a grid reference of 9826 in terms of a standard reference system. Figure 8.3A shows the location of 24 points drawn by simple random sampling for a hypothetical study area.

(ii) In *stratified random sampling*, the study area is divided into natural segments or *strata* (such as cropland and woodland) and the individuals in the sample are drawn independently from each segment. Within each segment, the location of the points is determined by the same randomization procedure as in simple random sampling. Figure 8.3B shows such a sample for 24 points. In this case, the number of individuals chosen from each segment (the so-called *sampling fraction*) has been made proportional to its area; 16 points in the left-

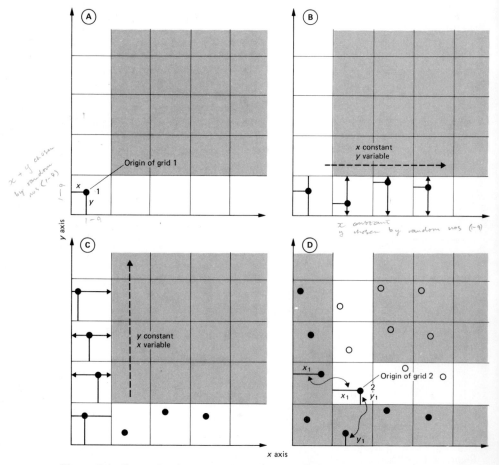

Figure 8.4 Stages in the generation of a stratified systematic unaligned sample. Source: Berry, 1962, p. 7.

hand segment (two-thirds of the area) and 8 points in the right-hand segment (one-third of the area). This method has been used frequently in geographical research, notably by Wood (1955) in a study of land use in eastern Wisconsin, United States.

(iii) In *systematic sampling*, a grid of equally spaced locations is defined with one individual at each location. Figure 8.3c shows a simple case for 25 individuals. Here the grid is square and at right angles to the sides of the study area. The origin of the grid is decided by randomization of the original grid point.

✳✳✳✳

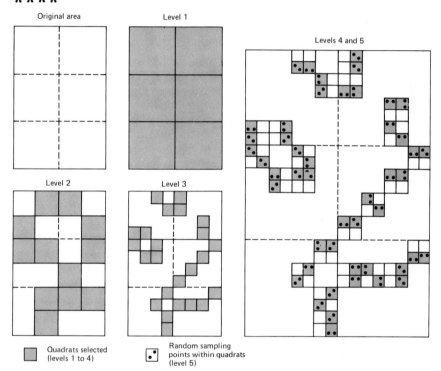

Original area   Level 1

Levels 4 and 5

Level 2   Level 3

▨ Quadrats selected (levels 1 to 4)

⊡ Random sampling points within quadrats (level 5)

Figure 8.5   Stages in the development of a five-level nested design in the Tagus–Sado basin, central Portugal.

(iv) A *stratified systematic unaligned sample* (Figure 8.3D) is a composite design derived from the preceding sampling designs by Berry (1962, p. 7) with the theoretical advantages of (a) randomization, and (b) stratification, together with the useful aspects of (c) systematic samples. By avoiding alignment of the sample points, it avoids the possibility of error caused by periodicities in the phenomena of interest, which is a risk with systematic samples. Its construction is shown in Figure 8.4 where the study area is sytematically divided into a regular checkerboard of sub-areas. Beginning with the corner sub-area, the location of a point, 1, is determined by random numbers (Figure 8.4A), the x- and y-axes of the sub-area being numbered zero to nine, so that two random numbers between zero and nine give the co-ordinate position with respect to both the axes as in a simple random sample. Figure 8.4B shows the completion of the lower row of the plan: the x co-ordinate is kept constant all along the row, but the y co-ordinate is varied using a random numbers table. As these numbers, 2, 9, 8, ..., are drawn, the points move up and down with respect to the y-axis but remain in the same position with respect to the x-axis. Figure 8.4c shows the completion of the left-hand column. The same principle is followed, but here it is the y co-ordinate which remains fixed and the x co-ordinate which alters. When both the first row and column are completed, a new corner point must be generated, point 2. As Figure 8.4D shows, its location is determined from the points drawn in the previous stage. The random x co-ordinate x_i, of point i, and the random y co-ordinate, y_j, of point j, are combined to locate point 2. This point is then the starting point for a new row and a new column, which in their turn, are used to generate a new corner point, point 3. This process continues until all columns and rows are full. Open circles in Figure 8.4D show the completed quadrangle.

(v) In *nested*, *hierarchic*, or *multistage sampling* we divide the study area into a hierarchy of sampling units that nest within one another as in Figure 8.5. Random numbers are used to select the large first-stage units, the smaller second-order units within these, and so on. The final location of points within each small unit is also randomly determined. Nested sampling has prime advantages in reducing field costs (if each sample point has to be visited in order to collect data) and in investigating scale variations (see Section 12.3) but the design has higher sampling errors.

(vi) In *multifactor sampling*, the study area is divided into strata which represent combinations of factors assumed to be affecting a given land-use pattern. Figure 8.6 shows ways in which the spatial overlap of three factors may give rise to a series of factor-combination regions. Random sampling within each region may allow the effect of each factor, and interactions between factors, to be assessed using appropriate analysis of variance designs (Haggett, 1964; see also Section 12.3).

8.3.3 *Efficiency of alternative spatial designs*

How do we know which of the various sample designs to use? One attempt to answer this question has been made by Berry (1962, pp. 10–11), who carried out field testing of the various designs to determine their relative efficiency in land-use sampling. For a ten square mile area (Coon Creek) he successively tested stratified systematic unaligned samples (randomly oriented with respect to each other), and stratified random samples against the variance of a simple random sample. The results (Table 8.3) show the high relative efficiency of the stratified systematic unaligned sample. Its margin over the simple random sample is 21.5, and over the stratified random sample, 5.6.

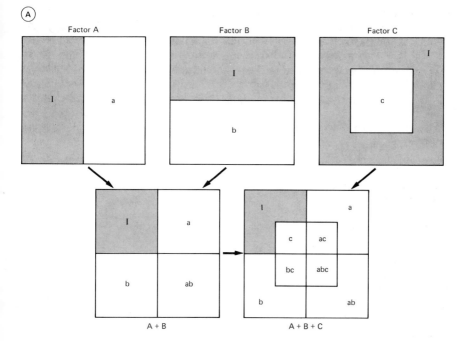

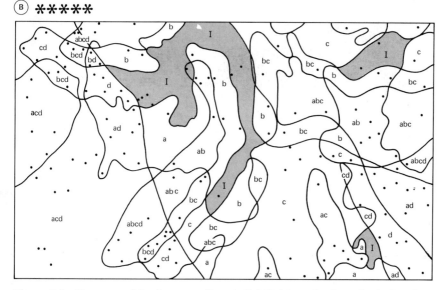

Figure 8.6 Factor-combination sampling. **A** Subdivision of a hypothetical region using combination of three factors, *a*, *b*, and *c*, measured on a presence–absence scale. Areas where factors are absent are denoted by I. Factors *b* and *c* are successively superimposed on *a*. **B** Location of sampling points within factor-combination regions in the Fortaleza Basin, Taubaté county, Brazil. Source: Haggett, 1964, p. 368.

Comparative tests were extended to a second area of about 45 square miles (Montfort). Here the differences were less impressive, but the same order of efficiency was maintained: (i) stratified systematic unaligned, (ii) stratified random, (iii) simple random. Differences in the magnitude of the results in the two areas may well be linked to the different type of areal pattern analysed—woodland in large blocks in the Coon Creek cases and cultivated land in small blocks in the Montfort case. Haggett and Board (1964) have shown that the accuracy of sample-based estimates of land-use areas varies with both the proportion of the area covered by the phenomenon under survey and its fragmentation, and this factor might well have operated in Berry's case.

Table 8.3   Comparative efficiency of sampling designs

Field areas:	Coon Creek	Montfort
Characteristic of field areas:		
Area in square miles	10	46
Pattern under investigation	Woodland	Cultivated land
Proportion of total area	40.8%	55.4%
Number of sample points	660	184
Relative efficiency of sampling designs (variance):		
Simple random sample	3.66	13.4
Stratified random sample	0.96	11.3
Systematic sample	—	12.8
Stratified systematic unaligned	0.17	10.2

Source: Berry, 1962, pp. 10–11.

The stratified sampling designs are also likely to be superior to other designs if spatial autocorrelation is present among the variate values of either (i) neighbouring points or (ii) points located at regular distance harmonics across the map. If (i) is the problem, simple random sampling designs will suffer, while if (ii) is the case, systematic designs will suffer because the positive correlation among the observations makes them worth less in information content than independent observations.

In this discussion of sampling designs, a *point* sampling unit has been

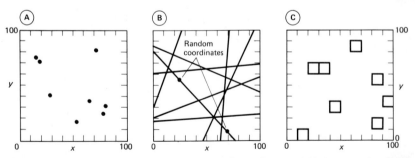

Figure 8.7   Alternative simple random sampling schemes. **A** Point samples. **B** Line samples. **C** Quadrat samples. In each case, eight sampling units have been selected by random number co-ordinates in the *x* and *y* axes; each line sample is drawn through a pair of random number co-ordinates.

assumed. Two other geometrical forms are equally applicable—the area sampling unit or *quadrat*, and the linear sampling unit or *line transect*. See Figure 8.7 and also Chapter 13. Haggett (1963) compared the efficiency of point, quadrat, and transect methods in determining the proportion of woodland cover from Ordnance Survey maps for the West Midlands. In this area of low woodland cover (about five per cent of the land area), the accuracy of the transect method (i.e. measuring the length of intercept of woodland along traverse lines) was considerably higher than the other two. Further investigation of the value of sampling from traverse lines on both maps and in the field seems justified. Both transects and quadrats have traditionally been used in qualitative geographical studies, notably by Platt (1959), but their main development in field sampling has been in botany. Quadrats, the most common form of sampling unit in botany, are usually square in shape and vary in size from a few centimetres to several metres. As Figure 8.8 shows, this

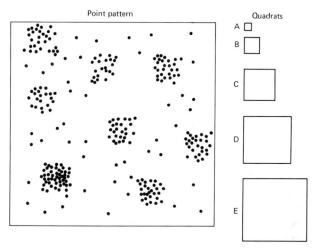

Figure 8.8   Relations between the size of quadrats and spatial pattern. Sampling with smaller quadrats (**A** and **B**) will suggest slight clustering, intermediate quadrat (**C**) strong clustering, and large quadrats (**D** and **E**) regularity. The reason why quadrat **C** will suggest strong clustering is because its size and that of the point clusters are approximately the same. In contrast, **E** is sufficiently large to include more than one cluster. See Section 13.4. Source: Kershaw, 1964, p. 104.

variation in quadrat size has had a notorious effect on the results obtained (Kershaw, 1964, p. 30, and Section 13.4.4) but fluctuations in the result may be harnessed to yield important information about the scale of the pattern being investigated (Grieg–Smith, 1964, pp. 54–93). Similar techniques in the breakdown of geographical patterns into scale components are discussed in Chapter 12.

8.3.4 *Space-time sampling*

The sampling designs discussed so far are useful if we are trying to measure some aspect of environmental quality that varies over *space*. How do geographers cope with qualities that are also varying over *time*? Let us pose as an example the problem of measuring traffic flow within a city. This will vary over space between the different parts of the city, but it will also vary from day to day and from hour to hour. A complete survey would require a rather dense pattern of recording stations across the city, each continuously monitoring traffic flow. Since we must assume a finite budget, there is a limit to the number of such stations that a city can afford. Sampling theory indicates where a small but representative number of stations can be located.

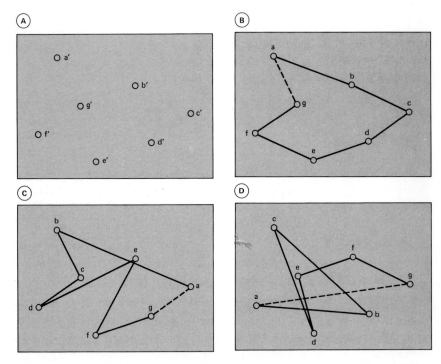

Figure 8.9   Sampling in a space-time framework. **A** Sampling sites; **B** Monday (*a″*); **C** Tuesday (*b″*); **D** Wednesday (*c″*). Compare with Table 8.4.

One of the ways in which this can be done is shown in Figure 8.9. Here the traffic throughout the city is sampled by a series of seven occasional recording stations (*a′–g′*). The number seven in this case is suggested by the need to measure flow levels on each day of the week (related to different automobile patterns and their concentration in different parts of the city). Table 8.4 shows how the time can be divided into seven equally spaced days (*a″–g″*) and equally spaced hours within each day (*a–g*). By visiting the seven out-stations in a different but predetermined sequence each day (Figure 8.9B–D), the observer can build an unbiased picture of traffic fluctuations. Note that by arranging the recording sequence in this symmetric square design—a Latin square in the language of statistics—each day's average is composed of a balanced mix of locations and hours, each hour's average is made up of a balanced mix of locations and days, while each location's average is a balanced mix of hours and days. As a further bonus, the total recording effort is reduced to one-seventh, plus the time taken by an observer to move from one temporary station to the next.

Table 8.4   Balanced Latin square design for space-time sampling.

		Location of sampling sites				
	a'	b'	c'	d'	e'	f'	g'
		Times of the day					
Days of the week:							
Monday, a"	a	b	c	d	e	f	g
Tuesday, b"	b	e	a	g	f	d	c
Wednesday, c"	c	f	g	b	d	a	e
Thursday, d"	d	g	e	f	b	c	a
Friday, e"	e	d	b	c	a	g	f
Saturday, f"	f	c	d	a	g	e	b
Sunday, g"	g	a	f	e	c	b	d

Source: Haggett, 1975a, p. 543.

8.3.5 Sample size considerations

Calculation of the size of sample required to attain a given level of accuracy is straightforward in the case of simple random samples. As noted in Section 8.3.1 estimates of population parameters such as the mean, variance, totals and proportions are subject to the normal law of error in simple random samples. In particular, the standard errors of these estimates are inversely proportional to the square root of the sample size, n. This means that, given a limited budget, the probable accuracy of any sample survey can be estimated; or vice versa, given a fixed limit of desired accuracy, the time–cost estimates required to collect the necessary sample size can be made. The square root relationship implies a quadrupling of the sample size every time the standard error of the estimate of the population parameter is to be halved.

Figure 8.10 shows this relationship very clearly. This chart plots the proportion of a sample with a given characteristic (on the x-axis) against the sample size on the y-axis. Note that the y-axis is on a log scale. Let us assume that a simple random sample of $n = 200$ observations of land use in an area have been taken, and that 80 of them are found to be woodland. The proportion of woodland in the population as estimated from this sample is $P = 80/200 = 0.4$ on the x-axis of the Figure 8.10. Superimposed on the graph are a series of lines which give the 95 per cent confidence bands which must be placed about the sample estimate in order to obtain the population proportion limits; the principle is exactly the same as that employed in Section 8.3.1 to place confidence bands about the sample mean. The intersection of lines drawn from $n = 200$ and $P = 0.4$ in the woodland example is approximately on the ± 0.07 line. Thus at the 95 per cent confidence level, the true (population) proportion of woodland cover will lie between 33–47 per cent. By increasing the sample size, these limits creep inwards. Thus, if we assume that in the sample, P remains fixed at 0.4, when $n = 550$, the limits are ± 0.04, and with $n = 2200$, the limits are ± 0.02 (the square root relationship).

There is, of course a danger in estimating proportions where either (i) the sample size is too small, or (ii) the estimated proportion is too small. In Figure 8.10, the shaded area in the lower left-hand section of the graph shows the danger area (for the 95% confidence level), where the lower confidence limit would drop our estimate of the population proportion below zero. Since this is an impossibility (areas cannot have negative amounts of woodland), the sample size must be increased or a lower confidence level accepted. As Cochran (1953) has pointed out, the use of random sampling for determining the proportion of rare characteristics (like built-up areas in a land use survey of a rural district) is like looking for a needle in a haystack. Here, other and more complex sampling procedures may be more appropriate.

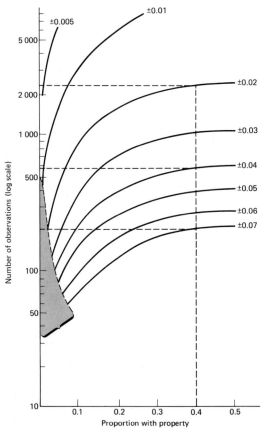

Figure 8.10   Ninety-five per cent confidence bands for proportions for simple random sample. The diagram is symmetric about a vertical axis drawn through the value of 0.5 on the horizontal axis. Source: Berry, 1962, p. 3.

Any sampling design which is more appropriate than the simple random sample for a given geographical problem will either, for the same sample size, yield estimates of population parameters with smaller standard errors, or yield the same level of accuracy (i.e. same standard errors for the estimates) as the simple random sample but with a much smaller sample size. To illustrate the contention, we quote an example from Yates (1960, Section 3.7) on the wheat acreage of farms in Hertfordshire in 1939. The population comprised 2496 farms which were sampled using the following designs:

(i) a 20% simple random sample (499 farms);

(ii) a stratified random sample with a uniform sampling fraction of $\frac{1}{20}$ from each stratum;

(iii) a stratified random sample with a variable sampling fraction. We would expect the wheat acreage grown on any farm to vary with farm size and geographical district. In Hertfordshire, stratifying farms by size has the effect of also stratifying by district, and we give in Table 8.5 the number of farms sampled in each stratum for designs (ii) and (iii). Table 8.6 gives the estimated wheat acreages for each design, the standard errors of the estimates, and the actual errors. The sample size required to attain the same level of accuracy (as given by the sampling standard error) with different sampling designs is, from our above discussion, approximately proportional to the squares of the standard errors. These sample sizes are shown in the column 'relative variance', with the simple random sample being given the base point of 100.

Table 8.5   Farm size groups (strata) and sampling fractions used with designs (ii) and (iii).*

Size groups (acres) or strata	Design (ii)		Design (iii)	
	Sampling fraction	No. of farms in sample	Sampling fraction	No. of farms in sample
1–5	$\frac{1}{20}$	87	nil	0
6–20	$\frac{1}{20}$	104	$\frac{1}{200}$	3
21–50	$\frac{1}{20}$	71	$\frac{1}{60}$	6
51–150	$\frac{1}{20}$	104	$\frac{1}{20}$	26
151–300	$\frac{1}{20}$	80	$\frac{1}{10}$	40
301–500	$\frac{1}{20}$	43	$\frac{1}{5}$	43
501 +	$\frac{1}{20}$	10	$\frac{1}{3}$	17
		499		135

Source: Yates, 1960, p. 32.   *Hertfordshire farms.

Thus stratification by size reduces the number of farms required by about a factor of four, and the variable sampling fraction results in a further reduction by a factor of about two and a half.

Table 8.6 also illustrates that the actual errors of the estimates are never markedly larger than the standard errors. Note that the simple random sample gives the most accurate estimate of acreage.

This is an illustration of the fact that an inaccurate method of sampling will sometimes by chance given an accurate estimate. The accuracy of a sampling procedure must never be judged by the magnitude of a single discrepancy; a large discrepancy provides some evidence that a method is inaccurate, but a single small discrepancy provides practically no evidence that it is accurate.

Yates (1960, p. 34).

Yates (1960, p. 98) has suggested the following general rules about choice of sample size and sampling design:

Table 8.6   Comparison of sample designs.*

| Sample type | Wheat acreage | | | |
	Estimate	Standard error	Actual error	Relative variance
(i)	46,020	±7960	+1340	100
(ii)	40,220	±4110	−4460	27
(iii)	42,765	±2550	−1915	10

(i) Simple random sample; (ii) Stratified random sample with fixed sampling fraction; (iii) Stratified random sample with variable sampling fraction.
Source: Yates, 1960, p. 33.
*Hertfordshire farms.

(i) the use of stratification, a variable sampling fraction or supplementary information will generally decrease standard errors of the estimates. 'Consequently the calculation of the [sample size] required in the case of a simple random sample gives an upper limit to the [sample size] required in any reasonable form of sampling using the same sampling units.'

(ii) Stratification increases accuracy substantially only if there are marked differences between strata.

(iii) A variable sampling fraction can greatly increase accuracy if the units sampled vary substantially in size.

(iv) Detailed stratification requires large samples, but produces increases in accuracy with increases in sample size more rapidly than is indicated by the square root law.

(v) If multi-stage sampling is used, more final stage units will have to be sampled than will be the case with single-stage sampling of the final stage units.

8.4 Data Coverage Problems

8.4.1 *Spatial variations in data quality*

More locational information is available about the human occupation of the earth's surface today than at any previous time. The trickle of maps and census reports available at the beginning of the century has now risen to a torrent which is rising dramatically with succeeding decades. Increases have not, however, been uniform, so that regional contrasts in information are tending to become more acute. Indeed Berry (in Ginsburg, 1961, p. 110) has shown that a poor standard of data is one of the concomitants of under-development, so that there appears to be a direct relationship between economic development and information. We return to this point in more detail below. Even for population density, the evidence for Brazil (Section 2.7.3) suggests that densely peopled areas have a fine mesh of subdivisions for which data are released, compared to the broad mesh of the relatively empty areas.

Comparisons over time also run into difficulties. The very fact of improving information may make comparisons with earlier periods invalid. Figure 2.19 shows the subdivision of an area of rapid population increase over successive thirty-year time periods. Although far more is known in detail about the area in the final period (1960) than in the initial period (1870), the degree of *comparable* detail is controlled by the largest areal denominator, i.e. the 1870 period. Dickinson (1963) has illustrated similar problems of subdivision and boundary change in England and Wales, while Hall (1962) has noted the problems in tracing the industrial growth of London from census data. We can illustrate the degree of variability in coverage for different types of environmental information by examining the situation in Latin America (Table 8.7). For vertical aerial photographs at the scales of 1 : 10,000 to 1 : 30,000, the overall coverage is around 10 per cent of the sub-continent, but individual countries reveal variations in coverage of from less than 0.5 per cent (Bolivia) up to 30 per cent (Brazil). For topographical maps with scales between 1 : 50,000 and 1 : 100,000, the continental average is 18 per cent, and there are variations from as low as two per cent (Bolivia) up to complete coverage for El Salvador and Haiti. Geological maps at scales of 1 : 50,000 to 1 : 250,000 are much more restricted than the two preceding types of information. The average for Central and South America is only 2 per cent, with individual countries ranging from a trace to half the country covered. Finally, soil maps have an overall average of 3.5 per cent coverage. No country has more than one-third of the area covered and nearly one-third of the countries have less than two per cent.

Table 8.7   National variations in the levels of spatial information.

	Percent of surface area covered by medium-scale maps and photographs			
	Vertical aerial photographs	*Topographic maps*	*Geological maps*	*Soil maps*
Latin America	36	18	2	3.5
Sample countries:				
Brazil	63	7	30	1
Argentina	68	50	18	5
Venezuela	68	38	11	7
Costa Rica	90	30	5	5
Bolivia	72	3	48	2

Source: Herfindahl (1969), p. 76, Table 8.

When information relates to rather static phenomena such as terrain qualities, surface geology, and soil cover, the area of map coverage is a reasonable way of measuring the quality of the records. For estimating certain flow resources, however, information must be gathered continuously over time. Thus, estimates of the probability of drought hazards or the likely size and frequency of floods are based on statistical analysis of historical records. Other things being equal, the longer the climatic or hydrologic record, the greater is its value. Here the difference in information between advanced and developing countries is even more marked.

Sets of information like those for Central and South America are helpful insofar as we can generalize about patterns of environmental information. First, information availability is inversely related to *map scale*. More information is published on small scales with low degrees of resolution than on large scales with high degrees of resolution. For example, all the data given in Table 8.7 refer to maps or photographs on medium scales. For the four types of information, the coverage at smaller scales is much greater. For the larger scales the relevant proportions are either the same or lower.

The definition of what constitutes an adequate scale of mapping is continually being refined as the demand for information grows. To illustrate this point, Figure 8.11 shows the response to that demand in the United States. Topographic map production since 1900 has increased not only in total volume but manifests a growing share of large-scale maps.

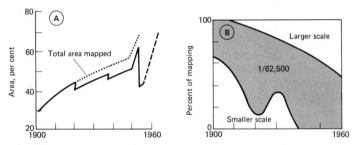

Figure 8.11   Mapping progress in the United States, 1900–60, showing percentage of total area considered to be adequately mapped when judged on scale and age grounds (**A**), and changing scales of map production (**B**). Source: Langbein and Hoyt, 1952, p. 56.

As noted at the beginning of this sub-section, environmental information is also directly related to the level of economic development of the area. It is difficult to justify high unit costs per square kilometre for surveys of areas expected to have low development potential. At the national level, the statistics for indicators such as map production or census reports reveal that information is available in greater quantity and detail for countries with a high degree of development like Japan or Sweden than for those with a low degree of development like Nigeria or Thailand. Nevertheless, countries like Canada may have large empty areas on the map despite a high gross national product, whereas some small underdeveloped countries like El Salvador may have rather high quality data. In general, the relationship between environmental information and level of economic development holds, largely because information is costly and its generation demands a considerable level of resources and investment.

The relationship between environmental information and *time* is complex. If the curve of total information is plotted against historical time, it appears to be an exponential curve in which information doubles over a steadily decreasing number of years. We can conceive of a map having a useful life related either to the change in the area it portrays or to external changes in information standards. For a rapidly developing metropolitan area the degree of change is intense and the life of a map is short. Conversely, maps of an unpopulated arctic area may change little over similar periods and have relatively longer periods of usefulness. Considerable survey activity is obviously necessary to maintain (let alone expand) the mapped area of the earth's surface.

A vitally important supplement to such 'archival' data in maps and censuses is the growth of air-photo coverage. Although this has a history going back at least to 1858, the effect of World War II and the 'cold war' that followed has been virtually to complete and/or revise the air-photo coverage of the whole earth's surface. Rapid improvements have been made in both lenses and cameras, in vehicles (through to the U2 and satellites), in mapping with electronic plotters, and in interpretation with electronic scanners. More revolutionary changes are foreshadowed in 'completely automated terrain-sensing systems' in which information about the earth's surface may be recorded by satellite, relayed back to base, and made available on magnetic tape. It seems possible that continuous recording of certain simple locational information may replace discontinuous mapping within the foreseeable future (Haggett, 1975a, Chapter 20).

8.4.2 *Area standardization problems*

In Chapter 2, we noted the great variety in both the size and shape of territories. Whether as states at one spatial level or parishes at another, these territorial units form the most common type of statistical population in locational research. The distorting effect of these oddly assorted collecting areas upon statistical analysis is discussed in detail in Section 10.6.1. The problem posed for the spatial model builder is analogous to that faced by an econometrician seeking to model a time series in which data are only available at irregular time periods—say, the reigns of monarchs, or the lives of Parliaments.

Table 8.8   Size and variability of administrative subdivisions*

Administrative subdivision:	Major (state)	Minor (county)
Number of subdivisions	48	100†
Area parameters in square miles:		
Arithmetic mean	60,757	1,356
Standard deviation	46,861	2,486
Coefficient of variation	67%	183%
Mean separation distance, d	118	16

Source: McCarty, Hook, and Knos, 1956, pp. 13–15.
       * United States, 1940.   † Random sample.

Extent of variation. Of course, the degree to which irregular collecting areas distort regional comparisons is directly related to their variability. McCarty (McCarty, Hook, and Knos, 1956, pp. 8–19) examined size variations for the two main statistical units in the continental United States (i.e. states and counties). The results are summarized in Table 8.8. For states, the range was from Texas with 71,289 square miles to Rhode Island with 289 square miles, with considerable bunching of the area values about the mean of some 61,000 square miles. County values were obtained by (i) arranging states alaphabetically, and (ii) numbering all 3,074 counties serially to obtain the *sampling frame*, and then (iii) drawing one hundred counties as a simple random sample. Within this sample, the variation between the largest and smallest was less extreme than in the case of states; San Bernardino county, California (20,160 square miles), is only about two hundred times the size of the smallest, Ohio county, West Virginia (109 square miles). The comparable ratio for states is nearer three hundred. On the other hand, the counties are less strongly grouped around the mean value and the coefficient of variation, $c = 100s/\bar{x}$, where s is the sample standard deviation, is over twice as great.

By using the values for areal collecting units in correlation studies, areas are treated as *points*. Thus we may use US state data for one variable, X (e.g. steel mills), and for a second variable, Y (e.g. automobile plants). It is relevant, therefore, to attempt to measure the degree of 'shrinkage' that is entailed in regarding areas as points. A tentative measure of shrinkage was evolved by McCarty who assumed that all his areal units were square. The average distance, d, between all possible pairs of points within a square figure is given by the expression $d = 0.52\sqrt{l}$ where l is the length of one side of the square (McCarty, *et al.*, 1956, p. 14). Table 8.8 (last line) summarizes the findings obtained by applying this formula to the United States. It suggests that we can regard states as points if we are prepared to accept the fact that our hypothetical steel mills and automobile plants will be about 120 miles apart on average and will still be considered to be identical. For counties the degree of tolerance is less, around 16 miles.

Chisholm (1960) has used an alternative type of separation index for studies of movement to work in northwestern Europe. If a circle of exactly the same area as any administrative subdivision is constructed, then the diameter, d', of the circle is given by $d' = 2\sqrt{A/\pi}$ where A is the area of subdivision. Chisholm has shown for each of the seven *Länder* of West Germany that the mean diameter of their subdivisions (*Gemeinde*) varies from only 3.1 to 4.3 kilometres, but that this conceals more considerable variations. For one *Land*, Schleswig–Holstein, the diameters of individual subdivisions varied from three to sixteen kilometres.

Aggregation solutions. Where the collecting units are many and irregular, one counter-measure is to group them into fewer but more regular areas. Such a technique was adopted by Coppock (1960) in a study of parish records in the Chilterns. Here, not only were parishes irregular in shape and size, and ran orthogonally across the major geological boundaries, but the farms for which the data were collected had land outside the parishes for which their acreages were recorded. Grouping parishes in this case produced more regular mapping units and reduced the farm overlap problem (Figure 8.1D) since, with larger units, the farm area outside the combined parish boundaries was proportionally much lower. There are some cases, however (notably with the strip parishes of the Chilterns which run orthogonally across major physiographic zones), where bundling together yields very little advantage, and, as discussed in Section 10.6, may actually hinder statistical analysis.

In the cases we have discussed, the problem is to gain the maximum uniformity in collecting areas, while, at the same time, preserving as much of the original data as possible. Haggett (1964) has suggested that the coefficient of variation may be used as an indication of both loss of detail and of gains in uniformity, and that only when the latter exceeds the former is the loss of detail justified. Table 8.9 shows a case in point in an analysis of county data in southeastern Brazil. Here the original 126 counties were grouped into 24 'super-counties' but the 82 per cent loss in detail was less than the 89 per cent gain in uniformity as measured by comparisons of the coefficient of variation. Where units are in any case very regular, as with county units in the American Middle West (Weaver, 1956), the method is hardly justified.

Table 8.9   Aggregation of administrative units*

Areal unit:	*County* *(municipio)*	*Super- county*
Characteristics:		
Number of units	126	24
Mean area, sq. miles	133	699
Coefficient of variation	74.20%	7.91%

Source: Haggett, 1964, p. 373.
  *Southeast Brazil, 1950.

Aggregation and testing will be very much speeded up when computer programs are developed which can rapidly check a large proportion of the possible number of ways in which contiguous units can be combined and recombined. In view of the enormously large number of possible combinations it is uncertain that the combinations used so far are the optimum ones in terms of uniformity of size.

Table 8.10   Elimination solution to irregular-areas problem*

Number of counties eliminated	0	1	4
Coefficient of variation of remaining counties	183	130	119

Source: McCarty, Hook, and Knos, 1956, p. 13.
  *United States: sample of 100 counties.

Elimination solutions. Problems of the unevenness of areal statistical units might be remedies by eliminating the aberrant areas. As Table 8.10 demonstrates, the coefficient of variation for McCarty's 100-county sample (McCarty *et al.,* 1956, p. 13) was reduced by elimination of the largest county, San Bernardino county, California. When the four largest counties (all having areas of more than 500 square miles) were removed, the remaining 96-county sample showed a coefficient of variation of only 119. These results suggest that material improvements can be made by eliminating large aberrant areas (see Section 11.4.2 for a particular application of this principle), but that the trend (so far as McCarty's results go) is one of diminishing returns. In other words, the gains made from this method fall off rather rapidly once outstanding values have been removed. How far the gains from standardization are matched by the losses of sample size is a matter for individual decision.

Grid-type solutions. One difficulty in dealing with aggregated collecting areas is that they are themselves highly irregular in shape if not in size. Attempts have therefore been made to collect information not for areal units but on regular frames or grids. An outstanding example of this type of work is the *Atlas of the British Flora* (Perring and Walters, 1962), where field data on the occurrence of British vascular plants were collected for the 100 square kilometre grid-squares of the British National Grid System. This grid system was also used by Johnson (1958) in a study of the location of factory population in the West Midlands. Grid systems are extremely well adapted for mapping, and the flora maps (Figure 9.22) were all mechanically tabulated (Walters, 1957). This has very considerable merit in an era where more maps are being produced directly as computer output, as in Figure 16.1 (Davis and McCullagh, 1975), and allows a very ready comparison between the original data and the distribution of controlling factors. It also allows microanalysis by breaking down the original squares into smaller ones, or macro-analysis by combining such squares into larger units on the lines of nested sampling discussed earlier in this chapter.

***

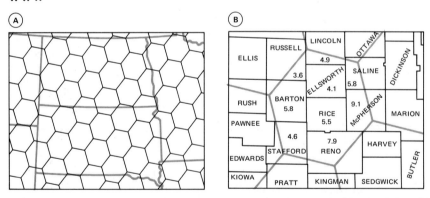

Figure 8.12   **A** Hexagonal grid used in northern Great Plains, United States. **B** Detail of the grid in central Kansas showing relation of the grid to county boundaries. Source: Robinson, Lindberg, and Brinkman, 1961, p. 214.

In both the examples cited, data were either collected on a regular grid pattern or were precisely located and could therefore be assigned to a grid. Where data only exist for irregular administrative areas the transfer to a grid is more complex. Robinson, Lindberg, and Brinkamn (1961, p. 214) used a regular hexagonal grid in a study of population trends in the Great Plains of the United States (Figure 8.12). County data were transferred to the grid by measuring how much of the area of each hexagon was contributed by any one county, and multiplying this share by the population density of the county. The sum of all the county parts gave the average value for the hexagonal unit. Figure 8.12B shows how the hexagon centred in Rice county, Kansas, includes the whole of that county and the adjoining Ellsworth county. It also includes parts of another seven adjacent counties. By assuming that the county averages for rural farm population (the figures shown on the map) exist uniformly throughout the county, this value could be multiplied by a proportion equal to the portion of the hexagon's area that the county contributed. For example McPherson county has a density of 9.1 per square mile and makes up 0.12 of the hexagon's area: its contribution to the resultant density is thus 9.1×0.12, or 1.09. The county products were summed to give a density for the whole hexagon of 5.94 (Table 8.11).

Table 8.11   Computation of mean population density for hexagon*

County	Rural farm population density (a)	Proportion of hexagon (b)	Product (ab)
Rice	5.5	0.17	0.93
Ellsworth	4.1	0.17	0.70
Reno	7.9	0.16	1.26
Barton	5.8	0.13	0.75
Stafford	4.6	0.12	0.55
McPherson	9.1	0.12	1.09
Saline	5.8	0.06	0.35
Lincoln	4.9	0.04	0.20
Russell	3.6	0.03	0.11
Total	—	1.00	5.94

Source: Robinson, Lindberg, and Brinkman, 1961, p. 214.
    *Centre of hexagon in Rice county, central Kansas, United States, 1950.

This principle was first used by Thiessen in 1911 for calculating the average rainfall over watersheds, and its accuracy clearly hinges on two principles: (i) the degree to which population density (or any similar measure) can logically be regarded as uniform over the county, and (ii) the number of counties which make up the regular hexagonal unit. Where each hexagon contains a number of undivided counties, the assumptions under (i) become less limiting as the 'split' counties contribute less to the total value. Again the problem is one of optimizing, possibly through linear programming, the reliability of each grid-unit (by increasing the hexagon size) and increasing the number of such grid-units (by decreasing the hexagon size).

Grid-free solutions. Clearly the foregoing methods (aggregation, elimination, and grid-type solutions) must involve some loss in detail, in that the revised units are fewer than the original. Attention may also be directed to the way that generalized maps can be made, via *trend surface analysis* (see Section 12.2), which retain *all* the original control points. This 'best-fit' polynomial surface uses all the available records, and builds them into a generalized picture, and is of particular importance where there are gaps in the areal spread of records.

8.5 Conclusions

In this opening chapter of Part Two we have been concerned with ways in which locational information is assembled. The basic method is that of sampling from a geographical population. However, such populations may be ambiguously defined, and the data may be variable in quality over both time and space. Because of their concern for spatial detail and an insistence on working at levels which range all the way up to the global scale, geographers are particularly vulnerable these data quality problems. On their solution hangs much of our ability to test and refine the models described in Part One of this book.

9 Map Description

9.1 Introduction

We consider in this chapter some of the methods used by geographers to describe locational data in map form. Mapping procedures form such a central part of geographical training that to attempt to compress them into a single chapter must be presumptuous. A review by Robinson and Sale (1969) is recommended to place the methods discussed here in a wider geographical context. We concentrate on the twofold difficulties of (a) using conventional maps to portray locational data and (b) interpreting existing maps to draw inferences about spatial processes. This second theme, which is introduced here, reappears throughout the remaining chapters in this second section of the book.

9.2 Mapping and Measurement Levels

The types of maps that geographers can draw are directly controlled by the level of the measurements that they can collect. The notion of 'levels of measurement' is one that has fundamental applications in statistics, but its importance in mapping has been generally overlooked. Basically, the theory of measurement states that there are four scales—the nominal, ordinal, interval, and ratio scales—with radically different properties (Siegel, 1956, pp. 21–30).

Measurement is at its weakest at the nominal (or classificatory) level where numbers or symbols are used to identify an object. When we identify a piece of country as 'woodland', we are using a symbol to represent a type of land use. The only formal property of members of such a class is *equivalence* ($\equiv$) and the range of cartographic operations we can perform is very limited; the nominal map is commonly only a mosaic of differently coloured or shaded areas in which each shade represents a definite class.

At the *ordinal* (or ranking) scale of measurement, numbers or symbols are used both to identify objects and to describe their relations to other objects. When we identify a 'Class B road' in Britain, we are using a symbol not only to identify a class of road, but we are putting it in some kind of relationship to other roads which are higher (e.g. 'Motorways' and 'Class A roads') or lower (e.g. minor roads) on our scale. The formal difference between the ordinal and the previous scale is that it not only has (i) equivalence ($\equiv$) but also (ii) the relation, 'greater than' or 'less than' ($>$ or $<$). Ordinal scales are common in mapping conventions where we use symbols of different sizes to indicate settlements on a size scale (e.g. city–town–village–hamlet); or railways of different classes; or zones of varying agricultural productivity (e.g. Class I, Class II, ... Class n).

The difference between the two highest scales, the *interval* scale and the *ratio* scale, is important in certain statistical operations, but since most locational data are measured on ratio scales it has less direct significance for mapping. The fundamental difference between the two scales is that in the interval scale there are no absolute zeros whereas ratio scales have absolute zeros. If we compare two points on a time scale (e.g. AD 1900 and AD 1950) and on a distance scale (e.g. 1,900 and 1,950 miles from London) we can see that while

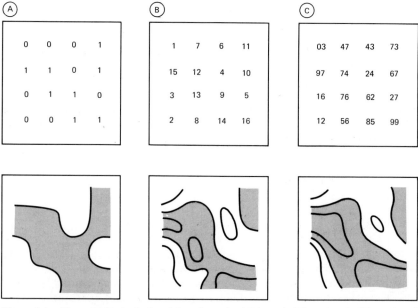

Figure 9.1 Hypothetical relationships of nominal (**A**), rank (**B**), and ratio (**C**), scales of measurement to contour patterns on the map. Areas above the mean are shaded.

the differences between the two are the same, fifty years and fifty miles, there is a fundamental difference in the ratios. For the measure of distance we can say that 1,950 miles is 1.02 times as great as 1,900 miles from London; however, a similar statement is not possible about AD 1900 and AD 1950 since the base for the time scale is a quite arbitrary zero. On mathematical (though clearly not on theological) grounds, the base might just as well be at AD 1800 which would make the second date 1.5 times as large as the first. Thus in the interval scale the ratio of any two points is dependent on the unit of measurement; in the ratio scale it is independent of the unit of measurement. In formal terms both scales have the property of (i) equivalence, of (ii) rank, and (iii) the known ratio of any two intervals (i.e. the ratio of AD 1850 to AD 1875 in relation to AD 1900 to AD 1950 is 1:2). Only the ratio scale has the additional property, (iv), the known ratio of any two scale values.

Most locational data are found to be measured on the highest (ratio) scale and are represented cartographically by isarithmic maps of features like population density; or flow maps of traffic volume; or settlement maps in which the symbol is directly related to the population of the unit. The history of geographical exploration is also the history of improving levels of measurement, e.g. the substitution of exact height contours for the hachured 'highs' and 'lows' (ordinal scale) of early maps.

A practical illustration of the effect of three of the measurement levels on cartographic method is shown in Figure 9.1 in which the distribution of a type of land use (e.g. woodland) is shown over a 16 unit area. At the nominal scale, the distribution of woodland is shown by one or zero denoting 'presence' or 'absence' (Figure 9.1A). In the ordinal and ratio scales this information is related to the 16 sub-regions into which the area may be divided. In the first, the sub-regions are ranked by the amount of woodland within their boundaries, with contours drawn at ranks 4.5, 8.5, and 12.5; areas over 8.5 are shaded (Figure 9.1B). In the second, the percentage of woodland in each sub-region is measured (the ratio scale) and contours are drawn at 25, 50 and 75 per cent; areas over 50 per cent are shaded (Figure 9.1C). As the level of measurement is raised, so the corresponding isarithmic map increases in both complexity and accuracy; viewed the other way round (i.e. from right to left) the impact of falling levels of measurement and the error inherent in them can also be seen.

9.3 Single Component Maps

Most locational data, whether it be originally linear, point, or areal in nature, can be converted through density ratios into a continuous form, and plotted as an isarithmic map. Once in that form we may regard it, as does Robinson (1961), simply as a statistical surface in which height (e.g. rural population density) varies over area in much the same way as the terrain varies on topographic maps. Viewing locational data in this way immediately suggests that much of morphometric analysis (conventionally restricted to topographic studies) may be applicable to the 'topography' of all isarithmic surfaces.

Although such isarithmic maps are three-dimensional in the sense that a distribution (measured in the z-dimension) varies continuously over an area (measured in the xy-plane), we refer to it here as a *single component* map in the sense that only one component is being 'mapped' on to the reference plane. In such maps the most common method of showing variations in the z-dimension is through the use of contours. Clearly such maps are based on the assumption that the distribution is a continuous variable, but as Warntz (1959) has shown, there are considerable theoretical and operational gains to be had by regarding such variations as continuous, even if, in practical terms, they appear discontinuous. Indeed, whether one regards population as discrete 'quanta' or as a continuous 'potential' is not a question of reality, but rather of scale and of the particular model being tested.

There may, however, be cases in which it is prudent to retain the data in their discontinuous form. The non-overlapping cells or counties are then mapped as *choropleth* maps with appropriate values ('height') assigned to each cell. See Section 10.6 for a discussion of the effect of continuous/discontinuous data upon statistical analysis.

9.3.1 *Number and spacing of class intervals* (*contours*)

Although there is no definitive answer to the number of contours (on an isarithmic map) or class intervals (on a choropleth map) that might be used in constructing a map, it seems logical that there should be some systematic relation to the number of control points or counties. For example, a finely contoured map based on few control points gives an impression of accuracy unwarranted by the information on which it is based; conversely, it seems wasteful to use very few contours when in fact we know a great deal about rises and falls in the surface we investigate.

One rough guide may be suggested from comparison with a parallel problem in statistics. Here Brooks and Carruthers (1953, p. 13) have suggested that the number of classes in a histogram should not be more than five times the logarithm of the number of observations. In cartographic terms this would mean that a map based on, say, 500 control points or counties should not be divided into more than thirteen classes. To show these thirteen classes we would clearly need twelve contours. As Brooks and Carruthers argue, there is nothing sacred about the relationship proposed; it merely gives a sensible relationship between accuracy and the available data, and so provides a rough rule-of-thumb which might be more widely used. One logical outcome of this sort of rule, if adopted, is that the number of control points is determined by the contour interval. If then we need a ten contour map we might argue, by the inverse rule, that we need at least 150 control points on which to base it.

In topographic maps, contours are normally plotted at equal height intervals, at least over the lower and intermediate altitudes. In statistical maps of locational data, equal interval contours may be less useful. Jenks and Coulson (1963) have studied an area of central Kansas, where the range of rural population densities is from 1.6 to 103.4 persons per square mile, and where the marked areal concentration of the high values makes equal step maps uninformative. On such a map with seven equal steps (intervals at 16.0,

30.6, 45.1, 59.7, 74.2, and 88.7 persons per square mile) only four classes were actually represented on the map while over 90 per cent of the map area was in one of the classes.

✳✳✳✳

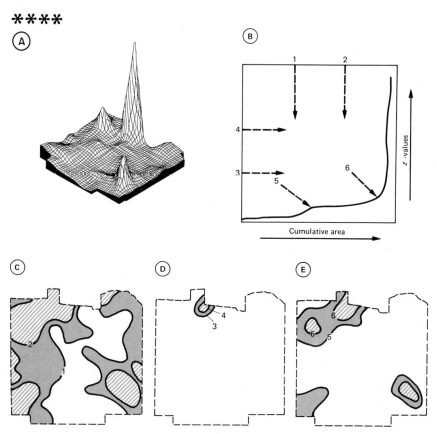

Figure 9.2 **A** Smoothed statistical surface. **B** Graphic array of z-values against area. The numbers 1 to 6 refer to contours on the three lower diagrams. **C** Contour map with equal area spacing. **D** Contour map with equal z-value spacing. **E** Contour map with spacing determined by critical breaks in the graph **B**. Source: Jenks, 1963, pp. 16, 19.

Problems of representing small pockets of high value readings within great expanses of low value readings are very common in human geography and have provoked considerable cartographic attention. Robinson and Sale (1969) have suggested that selection of appropriate contour intervals may be aided by cumulative frequency graphs in which the first component (area, xy) is plotted against the second component (values, z). To do this the collecting units (e.g. counties) are placed in order of their z-values (e.g. county population density), and their areas are progressively summed to give the cumulative frequency curve (Figure 9.2B). There are broadly three choices that can be made on the contour intervals: (i) to divide the z-values into equal divisions; (ii) to divide the xy-values (i.e. area) into equal divisions; or (iii) to divide the z-values into sections of uniform slope on the curve. The first method (Figure 9.2D) has the advantage of uniformity and ease of comparison with other areas; the second method (Figure 9.2C) has the advantage of a very even 'spread' of information over the map, but lacks comparability with other areas. The third method, using significant breaks in the cumulative frequency graph (Figure 9.2E) gives the sharpest picture of local variations in detail, but lacks either the comparability or the evenness of the first two choices.

Perhaps the most useful approach to contour interval decisions is to regard the mapped distribution as a statistical frequency distribution in which the locational concentration (i.e. skewness in statistical terms) may be met by an appropriate transformation. Transformed z-values may take the form of geometrical sequences (e.g. 2, 4, 8, 16 ...) in cases of extreme locational concentrations of high values, or an arc-sine sequence (e.g. 3, 12, 25, 42, 59, 75, 88, 97 per cent) where values are crowded at both lower and upper values of a sequence (Fisher and Yates, 1957, p. 70). In each case the transformation is appropriate to the form of the distribution and, since it gives a contour interval based on a known mathematical distribution, ready comparison with other cases is allowed.

9.3.2 *Arrangement of control points*

Map accuracy clearly depends on the original accuracy of the readings and the number of readings in any given area. Blumenstock (1953) has discussed the problem at length for meteorological maps, and his analysis is of wider significance for all maps of geographical phenomena. There are, however, as Mackay (1953) has shown, problems in accuracy which spring not from the original data but from the locational pattern of the recording points or 'control' points. Where choropleth maps of discrete counties are concerned, the framework of control areas is fixed; where isarithmic maps are being generalized from point observations, the framework problem may be more complex. Figure 9.3A shows the original four values on a grid for which

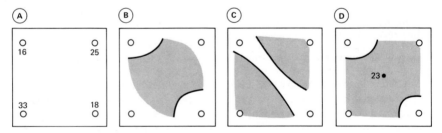

Figure 9.3   Indeterminacy problems in contour interpolation between a regular grid of four control points. Source: Mackay, 1953.

contour lines have to be interpolated. Unless other information is available it is assumed that the gradient between two points is linear and contour lines are geometrically interpolated. Geometrical interpolation is merely a matter of proportional allocation: if a 20 per cent contour is to be drawn between control points with values of 16 and 25 per cent respectively, then this contour would be placed four-ninths of the way along the line joining the lower and higher control points. The method is not, however, entirely foolproof. Figures 9.3B and 9.3C show two alternative interpretations of the 20 per cent contour in which the areas above 20 per cent (shaded) are shown as a diagonal ridge across the map and then as two ridges separated by a narrow col. Both interpretations are valid from the geometrical interpolation method.

Solution of this indeterminate case is possible if we assume a secondary control point at the centre of the square with a value equal to the mean of the four corner values, i.e. 23 per cent. Using this value the contours drawn in previous figures can be checked and the continuous 'ridge' confirmed (Figure 9.3D). It should be emphasized that such indeterminate cases spring from the use of *square* lattices for control point location (the common National Grid type of reference frame), and where an alternative control-point arrangement can be chosen, there is considerable value in adopting a *triangular* arrangement that eliminates this problem. Whether such a solution is worth the more complex arrangement of collecting areas, i.e. the rhombic, hexagonal, or 'staggered-rectangle' forms, is a matter for debate. Certainly the hexagonal system has been used effectively in a study of population densities in the Great Plains of the United States (Robinson *et al.*, 1961).

9.3.3 *Measures of map complexity*

Maps, like fingerprints or faces, come in a virtually infinite variety of spatial patterns. Even if we have an artificially simple map consisting of only four cells and two values, high and low (Figure 9.4A) there are six alternative patterns. If we double the map dimensions to a 4×4 matrix, again with half the cells with high values and half with low values, then the number of alternative maps jumps to 12,870 (Figure 9.4B). If we allow each of the sixteen cells to have a different value, rather than simply being either high or low, the number of alternative maps is 2.09×10^{13}. The diversity of maps is given by the usual combinatorial equation,

$$C(n, k) = \binom{n}{k} = \frac{n!}{k!(n-k)!},$$ (9.1)

where C is the number of combinations (i.e. maps), n is the number of cells in the map, and k is the number of different values that any given cell can take on.

Visual comparison of the simple maps shown in Figure 9.4 shows some intuitive differences in spatial pattern. In some, the high values are clumped together; in others, high and low values follow each other in a checkerboard pattern. Suppose we wish to try to match map patterns by placing similar ones together and separating those which are different. [Hodge and Gattrell (1975) suggest cases where this procedure may be required in studies of the location of urban public facilities.] While we can use an eyeball method where the maps are few and the differences are clear, this approach breaks down as the number of maps and their complexity increases. Attempts have therefore been made to measure pattern complexity in a quantitative way to give a more reliable yardstick of differences.

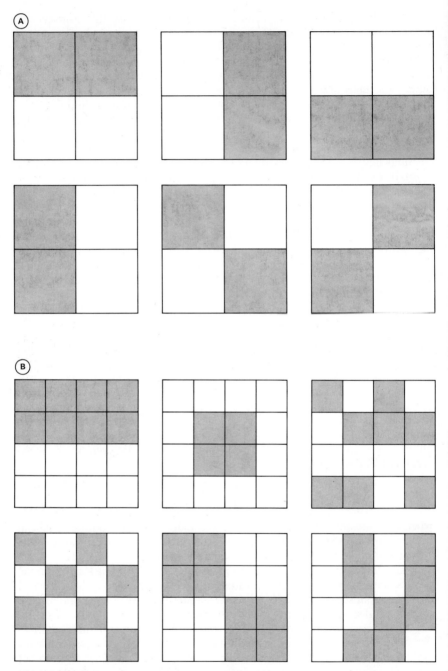

Figure 9.4 Combinations of high (shaded) and low value cells give alternative map patterns. **A** 2 × 2 matrix with complete set of map patterns. **B** 4 × 4 matrix with a sample from 12,870 different map patterns.

One of the simplest measures of map pattern is the fragmentation index, F, of Monmonier (1974), namely

$$F = (n-1)/(n_k - 1) \qquad (9.2)$$

where n is the number of map cells and n_k is the number of discrete map regions. A map region is defined as a set of non-overlapping but contiguous cells, each with the same value from the range of k values that a cell can take on; it is effectively a two-dimensional runs statistic analogous to the one-dimensional runs statistic commonly encountered in time-series analysis.

Gattrell (1975) has proposed a measure of map redundancy by recording in a square matrix of order k the number of joins or adjacencies between pairs of contiguous map cells with similar values. Entries in the matrix are converted into probabilities by dividing each element by the total number of joins, and their distribution is used by Gattrell as an index of map pattern. For example, high probabilities along the diagonals indicate strong clustering into a few regions; high off-diagonal probabilities suggest a very dispersed pattern. Both Monmonier and Gattrell's approaches may be regarded as special cases of the general spatial autocorrelation statistics developed by Cliff and Ord (1973). Detailed consideration of these measures is undertaken when autocorrelation in space is discussed in Chapter 11. We may note at this stage that, apart from the statistics considered in Cliff and Ord (1973), most measures proposed so far relate to first-order spatial patterns, in the sense that they relate to the joins or contacts between physically contiguous pairs of cells. However, it is possible to conceive of patterns which generate similar first-order measures, but which differ in their higher-order (i.e. more distant) spatial relations. A proper description of map pattern requires study over the full range of adjacencies possible. The relationships between map scale and pattern may be examined via correlogram analysis (Section 11.5) or by the methods discussed in Chapter 12 (trend surface, analysis of variance and spectral analysis).

9.3.4 *Measures of geographical association*

Map complexity (Section 9.3.3) considers the problem of comparing maps without regard to their absolute location, i.e. Map A may describe the density of rural settlement in Iowa and Map B rural settlement in Illinois. Where two maps are of different phenomena in the *same* location, the problem of comparison is simpler, and it can be handled by descriptive indices. One of the most frequently encountered in the geographical literature is the *coefficient of geographical association*, *G*. It has appeared under various guises as the 'coefficient of linkage' or the 'coefficient of similarity' since its first use in industrial location studies by Hoover (1936) some forty years ago, and its great attraction would seem to spring from very easy computation. Basically it is a measure of the association between any two phenomena over a set of geographical regions.

A simple illustration of the use of the *G* coefficient is given in Figure 9.5A. Here, the two distributions being compared are (i) the woollen industry and (ii) all industry, over the eleven 'standard regions' of Britain. In each case, the distribution is measured by the number of workers, and this is broken down into the percentages in each region. Thus the first region, A, on Figure 9.5A, has 0.90 per cent of Britain's woollen industry workforce and 25.20 per cent of all the workforce employed in all industry, where the national total for both the woollen industry and all industry is 100 per cent. The percentage shares are plotted on Figure 9.5A with the heavy line showing the woollen industry and

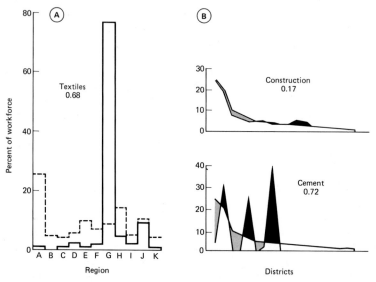

Figure 9.5   Computation of locational coefficient for sample industries in England and Wales (**A**) and Portugal (**B, C**).

the broken line all industry. Gaps between the two lines indicate the difference (f_i) for each region, i.

The G coefficient is given by the formula

$$G = \left\{ \sum_i |f_i| \right\} / 100 \tag{9.3}$$

where the summation is over either the positive or the negative deviations. The sum of either sign may be used in the computation, as both are equal. In the case of Figure 9.5A there is only one region with a positive deviation, region G, the East and West Ridings of Yorkshire, in which the share of the woollen industry (76.5 per cent) exceeds the share of all industry (8.8 per cent) by 67.7 per cent. The value of the G coefficient is therefore 0.677. The coefficient has a range from zero to one with low values when the two distributions being compared are similar, and high values when the two distributions are very unlike. Figure 9.5 also shows curves for two contrasting industries in Portugal: the building industry (Figure 9.5B) tends to be very dispersed, in the sense that it follows the general distribution of the industrial workforce, and has a G coefficient of only 0.17; conversely the cement industry (Figure 9.5C) is highly localized and has a G coefficient of 0.72. Clearly the index has considerable value in describing locational patterns along a continuous range, and workers like Chisholm (1962, p. 93) have used it with considerable success in agricultural studies. For England and Wales in 1956, Chisholm found that he could place the distribution of 29 horticultural crops along a continuum ranging from 0.39 for lettuce, with its widespread distribution around urban peripheries, to 0.61 for celery, with its strong concentration on the deep, well-drained soils of the Fens and parts of Norfolk.

The prime drawback of the G coefficient lies in its critical dependence on the size and number of the collecting areas. With a few large areas, values of G are characteristically low; with many small areas, values are characteristically high (see Section 10.6.1) so that direct comparisons with coefficients calculated for distributions in other countries are invalidated.

McCarty *et al.* (1956) have compared unfavourably the reliability of G and a true measure of association, the Pearson product moment correlation coefficient, r. He finds that not only is G very dependent on the actual magnitudes of the values being compared, but that it gives no indication of the existence of strong *inverse* association (i.e. when high values of one distribution are strongly associated with low values of another). In one case studied, the G coefficient showed a value of 0.256, implying similarity, for two distributions which Pearson's r suggested were almost completely uncorrelated ($r = 0.006$).

Although modifications of the original index have been attempted (Thompson, 1957), there is a need to treat the ubiquitous G with considerable caution. It certainly provides a useful, if erratic, description of locational concentration *within* an area but provides little basis for comparison between different areas, or between the same areas in different times (save only in the case of unchanged internal boundaries). Similar strictures must be placed on the use of a less common by-product of the coefficient of geographical association, the *locational quotient* (L_Q). The locational quotient gives a region-by-region description of the situation shown in Figure 9.5A by comparing values of the two distributions. Thus region A, London and the southeast, with 0.9 per cent in the woollen industry but 25.2 per cent in all industry, has a locational quotient of 0.9/25.2 or $L_Q = 0.04$. Quotients above one indicate a regional 'surplus' of the industry with, for example, the East and West Ridings of Yorkshire (G) showing a value of 8.64.

9.4 Multicomponent Maps

Where we have to deal with not one value varying regionally (the single component map) but a whole series of such values, the cartographic problems become much more severe. There are certainly a number of ingenious ways in which simple contour maps may be superimposed—by the use of super-imposed coloured contours or intervisible plastic overlays—but the point is quickly reached where the fall-off in comprehension outweighs any gains in completeness. Even the most successful of such maps, like those of Learmonth and Pal (1959) on disease in India, are rarely able to show more than two factors independently. As a result, research has turned towards ways of breaking down the complexities of multidimensional systems *before* the mapping stage is reached. By doing this, statistical complexities have been substituted for cartographic complexities, but the complications described above have been outflanked. Four of the more successful methods are described here.

9.4.1 *Percentage data: facies mapping*

Where the phenomena being mapped can be broken down into not more than three percentage components, we can make use of facies triangles or 'ternary' diagrams. Research on facies triangles was developed in geology, where the sedimentary rocks could be broken down into three components or 'end members' (sand, shale, and non-clastics) in terms of their percentage contribution to the total weight of the sample. A parallel problem in land use studies would be the breakdown of an area into woodland, cropland, and other land use types, in which each type was measured as a percentage of the total area.

Figure 9.6A shows a facies triangle in which the three vertices represent 100 per cent of each of the three components, A, B, and C, and points within the triangle represent combinations of these three. For example point x indicates a mixture of 60 per cent A, 20 per cent B, and 20 per cent C; and point y indicates a mixture of 10 per cent A, 30 per cent B, and 60 per cent C. Clearly the nearer the point lies to the middle of the triangle, the greater the mixing, and the nearer the point lies to one of the vertices of the triangle, the greater the dominance of a single component.

Facies triangles have been occasionally used in the non-geological literature to describe composition. Clark (1940), in the *Conditions of economic progress*, suggested that the breakdown of a country's employment into primary, secondary, and tertiary industry might provide a sensitive index of economic growth, and that the changing composition of areas might be plotted on facies triangles. However, less use has been made of the method than its potential suggests. Forgotson (1960) has reviewed a number of uses of the method in geology which might be taken up in our own compositional studies. One of the simplest uses of the facies triangle was developed by Pelto (1954), in which a *classifying function* was used to divide the triangle into seven classes: three single-component sectors (A, B, and C), three two-component sectors (AB, AC, and BC), and one three-component sector (ABC). Within each class, the ratio lines are drawn to indicate the relative strength of a component. In this system, point x falls within class A and point y within class BC (Figure 9.6B). A second method, also introduced by Pelto, attempted to establish quantitative facies boundaries rather than classes, through the concept of an *entropy function*. Here entropy refers simply to the degree of mixing of the components, with high entropy values occurring near the centre of the triangle and low values near the three end members. In Figure 9.6C, contours for the 70 and 60 entropy ratios are plotted: both x and y have rather similar entropy functions and Pelto suggests that in mapping these ratios, distinctive shading might be superimposed on the contours to indicate the three end members.

Krumbein (1955a) has suggested a simple *facies departure* method to map the relation of points on the triangle to a given control point. This control point might be, say, the average composition, or the optimum combination for

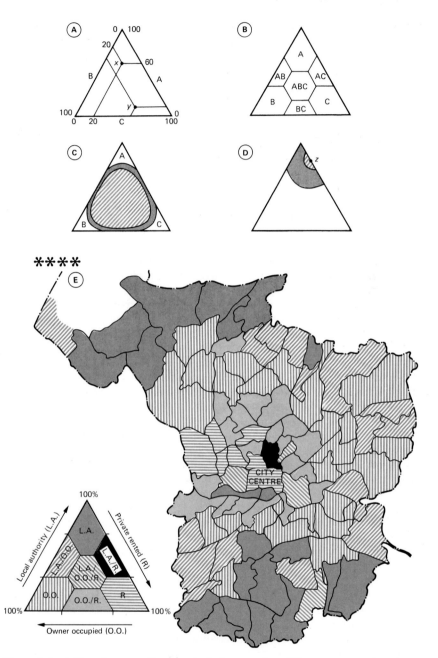

Figure 9.6 **A** Use of ternary diagrams in facies mapping of three-component systems. **B** Classifying-function method. **C** Entropy-function method. **D** Facies-departure method. **E** shows an application of the classifying function method to household tenure in the city of Bristol, England. Sources: Forgotson, 1960, pp. 88–95; Bassett and Hauser, 1975, p. 44.

the area, depending on the problem in hand. In Figure 9.6D, z is chosen as the control point; here A is 80 per cent, B is 0 per cent, and C is 20 per cent. Contours are drawn as concentric circles to show departures from the control point. The disadvantage of the method is that, although it shows the amount of regional departures, it does not show the direction of departure, and it needs, therefore, to be compared to maps based upon the classifying function method. An application of the classifying function method to household tenure data for the city of Bristol, England, appears in Figure 9.6E. Little use has as yet been made in geography of this type of analysis. Board has, however, explored the use of a more complex derivative, the tetrahedron, to show four component analyses of South African land use.

9.4.2 *Percentage data: combination mapping*

A typical problem in multi-component mapping is faced by the geographer working with zonal data. In agricultural zones, he may have to investigate a range of a dozen or so crops which are grown in different rotational combinations in the different parts of his study area. How can such diversity be shown on a single map? One suggestion put forward by Weaver (1954) is the *crop combination index*, which sorts out the major crop combinations, and thereby enables minor crops to be eliminated. Although Weaver worked on the crop distributions of the American Middle West, and his method has been mainly used for crop studies in other areas (e.g. Thomas, 1963, on the agriculture of Wales during the Napoleonic Wars), the index is not intrinsically limited to agricultural studies: it can be applied to any distributional data expressed in terms of percentage components and it is therefore described here simply as a *combination index*.

Calculation of the combination index is a simple procedure which is illustrated in Figure 9.7. Here, the sample problem is to determine the appropriate combination index for a Breconshire parish which in 1801 had six crops—wheat, oats, barley, peas, potatoes, and turnips—whose percentage contributions to the total cropland (100 per cent) were respectively 32.0, 31.5, 17.1, 11.7, 4.4, and 3.3 (Thomas, 1963, p. 81). These percentages are plotted in Figure 9.7, the points being joined by a broken line.

The problem in mapping is to calculate how many of the six crops need to be included. Is this parish to be mapped as, say, a one-crop unit (wheat) or as a four crop unit (wheat–oats–barley–peas)? Weaver's answer to this problem is to suggest a series of model situations. He argued that in a model one-crop area, 100 per cent of the cropland would be in one crop and 0 per cent in the others; in a model two-crop area, 50 per cent of the cropland would be in each of two crops, and 0 per cent in the others; in a model three-crop area, 33.3 per cent of the cropland would be in each of the three crops, and 0 per cent in the others; and so on. These ideal curves are shown in Figure 9.7 by the heavy unbroken lines.

Using these ideal curves as standards, Weaver then compared each ideal curve with the actual curve to find which of them the latter most closely resembled. To measure this comparison, he used the method of least squares: that is the deviations (shown by the vertical lines in Figure 9.7) were measured

(f), were then squared (f^2), and were finally summed (Σf^2). The closest correspondence between the model and the actual curves is given by the minimum least squares value. In Thomas's case, the successive values for Σf^2 show a characteristic U-shaped curve with high values for the one-crop and six-crop extremes. The lowest value, $\Sigma f^2 = 356$, suggests that we can regard this parish as a four-crop unit and disregard the two smallest crops.

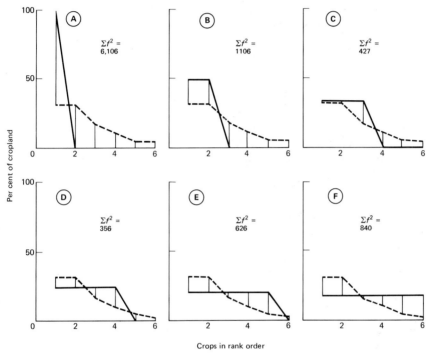

Figure 9.7 Stages in the computation of combination indices. Source: Thomas, 1963, p. 81.

Combination indices may be mapped by shading the number of activities, with the sequence 1, 2, 3, 4 ... n indicating a combination continuum from monoculture to diversity. In practice, the crop components are coded by letters (e.g. W for wheat, O for oats, B for barley), and the combination letters (e.g. WOB) overprinted on the shading, or else separate maps of the leading combinations are prepared. Holmes and Haggett (1975) have suggested refinements to the Weaver method which allow more accurate estimates of combinations to be made in situations where a large number of crops make up a small proportion of the total cropland.

The role of any such combination index is to reduce the confusion in multiple component mapping, by sorting the dominant elements from the recessive. It is perhaps at its most useful where a few items are important, and least successful where a very even balance is found among a large group of times. Similar problems are met with in plant ecology, in the comparison and description of complex plant communities, and there would seem to be a number of worthwhile botanical indices, described by Greig–Smith (1964, pp. 1–19, 131–57), that might usefully be tested on comparable geographical problems.

9.4.3 *Mapping multivariate data*

Assume we have data available for a large range of locational phenomena for a given area. Two mapping strategies are open. First, we can produce single maps for each of the features being mapped. In this case, our mapping problem is simply one of preserving comparability between the class intervals or contours on the different maps. Some measurements may range from 1 to 10^6, others may range from 0.98 to 1.02, and there is clearly some need to reduce these ranges to a single comparative level. Ranking the counties in order from the highest to the lowest (rank 1, 2, 3, ... n) on any given measure provides such a common yardstick. The problem with ranking, however, is that it throws away so much of the information gained in the measurement process: 10.7, 6.2, 6.1, and 0.004 become simply 1, 2, 3, and 4 despite the great differences in the original measurements. Retaining the relative differences between counties along a common yardstick may demand their reduction to z-scores in the manner described below (Section 9.5.1; see especially equation 9.4).

A second strategy is to reduce the measurements to a smaller number of indices using one of the appropriate multivariate techniques such as principal components or factor analysis. Ginsburg's *Atlas of economic development* (1961) provides an example of the two mapping strategies. In the first part of the atlas, 43 separate indicators of economic development are presented as separate maps scaled by ranking system. In the second part, these indicators are reduced to only four component maps, together accounting for 94 per cent of the original variation between the countries. Harman (1960) is the standard handbook on the methods employed.

9.5 Probability Mapping

9.5.1 *Probability maps based on the normal distribution*
Most maps use the conventional devices of contours, or the shading of counties, to show the distribution of some phenomenon over a geographical area. While this method is useful as a simple spatial description of the data, it may have drawbacks if one wishes to make inferences about the distribution of the phenomenon. Where the variate values $\{y_i\}$ of counties are being mapped, it may be more revealing to plot these as standard scores, $\{z_i\}$. Recall from Section 8.3.1 that the standard score is given as

$$z_i = (y_i - \bar{y})/s(y), \tag{9.4}$$

where $\bar{y}$ and $s(y)$ are the mean and standard deviation, respectively, of the observations on Y, taken over all n counties. If we can assume that Y is normally distributed, then expressing the observations in terms of the standard normal deviate allows inferences to be drawn on the relative rarity of individual observations. For example, as discussed in Section 8.3.1, a value equal to or greater than $+2.58$ may be expected to occur in less than one per cent of cases if the variate under study follows a Gaussian distribution (Table A1). See also Section 10.5. Thomas (in Berry and Marble, 1968, p. 332) has used standardized regression residuals of the form $(\hat{y}_i - y)/\mathrm{S.E.}(y)$, where $\hat{y}_i$ is the calculated regression value for the ith county and $\mathrm{S.E.}(y)$ is the standard error of the estimate for all counties. This expression gives the magnitude of the difference between estimated and observed values in term of the variation within the whole set of observations.

9.5.2 *Probability maps based on the Poisson distribution*

Whether a particular observation on a map has special significance, in the sense of being either 'surprisingly high' or 'surprisingly low', can be measured only in terms of *a priori* expectations. Choynowski (1959) and White (1972) have proposed the use of the Poisson probability distribution for the map study of rare medical events.

✱✱✱

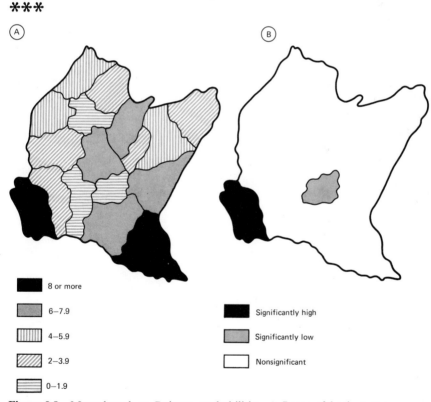

Figure 9.8 Maps based on Poisson probabilities. **A** Rates of brain tumours per 100,000 in 17 counties of the Rzeszow district of Poland. **B** Probabilities of observed rates. Source: Choynowski, 1959, pp. 181–2.

Suppose that a study area can be subdivided into counties of the same size. If events occur at random among the counties (a not unreasonable assumption for isolated events), so that each county has an equal and independent chance of having an event occur in it, then the Poisson law describes the probability $P(X = x)$, of x events occurring in a specific county; i.e. the probability of observing the number of cases, x, recorded in a particular county. Clearly, these probabilities could be mapped for each county to provide a basis for determining areas of surprisingly high or low incidence of the medical event under study.

Figure 9.8 shows Choynowski's findings based on the incidence of brain tumours in the Rseszow district of Poland. The average rate for the whole area was 5.17 cases per 100,000 people, but observed rates for individual counties ranged from zero to 11.8. How significant are these county-to-county variations? Two counties have 'high' rates of incidence on the first map, but only one is 'significantly' higher than expected as judged by the 95 per cent probability level in the second map. Note that Gorlice county, with nine cases in a population of 83,000 and a rate of 10.8 per 100,000 was insignificant at this level (Table 9.1). Lesko county with only two cases, but in a population of only 17,000, was estimated as significant even though its observed rate (11.8 per 100,000) is only slightly greater than that for Gorlice. White (1972) has extended Choynowski's use of Poisson probability maps for medical data, with special reference to the problem of aggregating observations over both time and space. We return to the use of the Poisson distribution, and other members of the Poisson family, for map analysis in much more detail in Chapter 13.

Table 9.1   Number of brain tumours and resulting probabilities in seventeen counties of the Rzeszow District chosen for illustration.

County	Population in thousands	No. of tumours for 100,000	Number of tumours		Probability
			Expected	Observed	
Brzozow	70	0.0	3.6	0	0.03
Debica	110	3.6	5.7	4	0.33
Gorlice	83	10.8	4.3	9	0.03
Jaroslaw	102	5.9	5.3	6	0.43
Jaslo	101	4.0	5.2	4	0.40
Kolbuszowa	60	1.7	3.1	1	0.18
Krosno	101	2.0	5.2	2	0.10
Lesko	17	11.8	0.9	2	0.22
Lubaczow	40	2.5	2.1	1	0.39
Lancut	91	6.6	4.7	6	0.33
Mielec	73	5.5	3.8	4	0.52
Nisko	67	3.0	3.5	2	0.33
Przemysl	88	6.8	4.6	6	0.31
Przeworsk	57	3.5	2.9	2	0.43
Rzeszow	182	7.1	9.4	13	0.16
Sanok	56	7.1	2.9	4	0.33
Tarnobrzeg	67	4.5	3.5	3	0.52

Source: Choynowski, 1959, p. 388.

9.6 The Shape of Map Distributions

9.6.1 *The shape of discrete areas*

That insights into spatial processes may be gained from a study of spatial form is one of the themes running through Part One of this book. Study of the distinctive shape of a distribution occupied distinguished biologists like D'Arcy Wentworth Thompson, Huxley, and Medawar, who saw in changing forms clues to biological growth and evolution. Scholars in all the disciplines that have tried to formulate process–form arguments have found it necessary to devise adequate means of describing shape. Since the English language has a limited, if evocative, shape vocabulary (e.g. the 'hook-like' shape of Cape Cod or the 'tear-drop' shape of Ceylon) it has proved necessary to develop quantitative means of describing the shape of map distributions. The number of such shape indices is now very large (see the bibliography by Boots and Lamoureaux, 1972) and we indicate here only some of the most commonly used measures (Table 9.2).

Table 9.2 Elementary measures for measuring the shape of geographic areas.

Elongation ratio	L/L'	Werrity, 1969
Form ratio	A/L^2	Horton, 1932
Circularity ratio	$(4A)P^2$	Miller, 1953
Compactness ratio	$(2\sqrt{\pi A})/P$	Richardson, 1961
	A/A'	Cole, 1964
	$1.273A/L^2$	Gibbs, 1961
Ellipticity index	$L/2\{A/[\pi(L/2)]\}$	Stoddart, 1965
Radial shape index	$\sum_{i=1}^{n} \|(100d_i / \sum_{i=1}^{n} d_i) - (100/n)\|$	Boyce and Clark, 1964
	$A / \sqrt{2\pi \int d_i^2 dx dy}$	Blair and Bliss, 1967

A = area, L = longest (major) axis, L' = secondary (minor) axis, P = perimeter, A' = area of smallest circle to enclose figure, d_i = distance of ith area from centroid of the figure.

Source: For individual papers, see Boots and Lamoureaux, 1972.

In trying to measure a shape, two questions have to be answered: (a) what characteristics do we measure, and (b) how do we combine them into an effective index? In addressing the first, we assume that the shape of each spatially discrete area is being separately studied. Figure 9.9 summarizes the characteristics commonly measured. Going up the dimensional scale, these are:

(i) *Points within the closed figure.* Two sets of points may be measured, i.e. externally given centres (like the CBD of a town or the administrative centre of a province), and internally given centres (most commonly the centroid or centre of gravity of the distribution).

(ii) *Lines within the closed figure.* The perimeter of the figure, its longest axis (the distance between the two most distant points on the perimeter of the figure), and distances between points within the figure are typically used.

(iii) *Area of the closed figure.* The area of the figure itself may be supplemented by measurements of the areas of the smallest internal and external enclosing circles (see Figure 9.9).

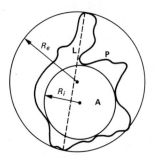

Parameters

A	Area
P	Perimeter
L	Longest axis
R_i, R_e	Radii of internal and external enclosing circles

Figure 9.9   Shape parameters.

Combination of measurements into appropriate indices will depend on the distribution being studied. Where the shape of a simple plane figure is under study, very elementary ratios may prove useful. Thus Gibbs (1961) has used an index which may be reduced to

$$S_{(1)} = (1.273A)/L^2, \quad 0 \leqslant S_{(1)} \leqslant 1, \tag{9.5}$$

to describe the degree to which the shape of a city has a circular form. Here A is the area of the figure and L is the length of its longest axis. Values range from zero for a completely linear city to one for a completely circular city. Cole (1960) has proposed an equally simply measure of shape for the study of civil divisions (e.g. parishes) in political geography, which may be stated as:

$$S_{(2)} = (A/A'), \quad 0 \leqslant S_{(2)} \leqslant 1, \tag{9.6}$$

where A' is the area of the smallest circle to enclose the figure. In both the indices, the circle is used as a standard of compactness, with higher index values indicating more compact city or parish shapes. There is, however, no reason why other shapes should not be used as standards if they are appropriate to the research purpose in hand. Thus, Lee and Sellee (1970), in a study of Sudanese village shapes, made comparisons with several standard shapes. Let A denote the area of the figure and let A_s denote the area of the standard shape with an area equal to that of the feature under study. Using the terminology of set theory, they compared the intersection of the two areas, $(A \cap A_s)$, with the union, $(A \cup A_s)$, in the measure,

$$S_{(3)} = \frac{A \cap A_s}{A \cup A_s}, \quad 0 < S_{(3)} \leqslant 1. \tag{9.7}$$

As Figure 9.10 shows, the area of overlap between the two shapes is made as great as possible. The method is useful in handling punctured or fragmented shapes, which cause difficulties for the simpler indices.

Although studies of shape *per se* are of interest in work on morphological evolution [e.g. Marsden's (1960) time series study of the growth of Brisbane since 1861], they have proved of greatest applied use in spatial allocation studies, where ensuring a compact shape for administrative or electoral areas may be a major goal of boundary reorganization (see Sections 14.5.2 and 15.4.3). In these cases, information is available not only on the shape of any area, but also on the distribution of phenomena (say, population) within it.

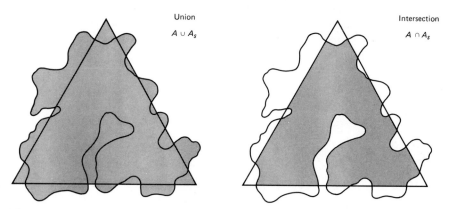

Figure 9.10 Comparison of the area of an observed figure (A) with a given standard shape of the same area (A_s).

Massam and Burghardt (1968) and Massam and Goodchild (1971) have looked at the shape efficiency of various systems of administrative areas in southern Ontario. Their measures of shape efficiency are defined in terms of the distances, d_{ij} and d_{ik}, travelled by the population p_i, located in each of the $i = 1, 2, ..., n$ townships within an area, to two central points, *viz.* the *actual* administrative centre at location j and some supposed *optimally located* administrative centre at position k. The latter may be crudely estimated by the mean or median of the population for an area (see Section 9.6.2) or resolved by the linear programming methods discussed in Chapter 15. Given the location of k, then a useful measure of shape efficiency is

$$S_{(4)} = \frac{\sum\limits_{i=1}^{n} p_i d_{ik}^2}{\sum\limits_{i=1}^{n} p_i d_{ij}^2}, \quad 0 \leqslant S_{(4)} \leqslant 1. \tag{9.8}$$

This index is simply the ratio of the moments of inertia about an optimal (k) and an actual (j) centre of administration for an area. The closer the two centres, the higher the ratio, and the greater the efficiency. Clearly, the index may be readily extended by measuring distance in more meaningful terms (e.g. in time or cost of journey) and by using a distance-decay exponent suited to the problem under study. Further discusssion of shape measures in relation to the efficient design of social administration areas is given by Massam (1975, Chapter 2).

9.6.2 *'Centrographic' measures of shape*

In the previous section, we have referred to the 'centroid' of a geographical distribution. A series of measures of centricity have been developed from formal statistical theory, and are characterized by the extension of familiar statistical parameters of location and dispersion into the two dimensional plane. This idea is not, of course, a new one. As early as 1892, Johnson discussed the deviations of bullet marks around a target as a probability density surface (Johnson, 1892) and by 1937 Sviatlovsky and Eells could publish an extensive review of geographical work, done largely in Russia, employing what came to be called 'centrographic methods'.

**

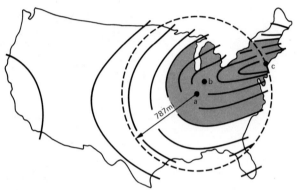

Figure 9.11   Potentials of population in the United States with the mean (*a*), median (*b*), and mode (*c*) of the distribution. Source: Warntz and Neft, 1960, p. 62.

Warntz and Neft (1960) have shown how three familiar statistical measures of *central tendency*, the mean, median, and mode, may be translated into areal dimensions. The mean centre of a distribution they define as the point where

$$\int D^2 . G(dA) \tag{9.9}$$

is minimized; while the median centre is defined as the point where

$$\int D . G(dA) \tag{9.10}$$

is minimized. In both equations, G is the density of population over a very small part (element) of area, dA, and D is the distance from each small part to the mean or median point in question. In the same way, the mode can be defined in terms of the position of the high point on the density surface. Figure 9.11 shows for the United States a smoothed density surface for its 1950 population potential with contours at intervals of 50 units, and values above 300 units shaded. Here, the mean centre is located in Southern Illinois, the median centre in central Indiana, and the modal centre in New York City. The location of the three points shows the greater sensitivity of the mean centre to distant outlying centres of population, in this case on the Pacific coast of the United States.

Paralleling the measures of central tendency in statistical descriptions of frequency distributions are the measures of *range* or *dispersion*. Figure 9.11 shows the dynamic radius (Stewart and Warntz, 1958) of the United States population in 1950: it is plotted as a circle with a radius of 787 miles about the Illinois mean centre. It is defined by the expression,

$$\sqrt{\sum_{i=1}^{n} p_i d_{ij}^2 \bigg/ \sum_{i=1}^{n} p_i}, \tag{9.11}$$

where p_i is the population of the ith sub-area, and d_{ij} is the distance from the ith sub-area to the mean centre at j. Warntz and Neft (1960, p. 66) point out that the historical westward movement of the mean along the thirty-ninth parallel has been accompanied by a widening dynamic radius. This means that, although the gap between the spatial locations of the mean and the mode has been widening, the distribution has not become more skewed.

The extensive literature on centrographic analysis has been summarized by Bachi (1963). Most attempts to translate formal statistical measures of centrality and dispersion into the two-dimensional spatial plane are hindered by their dependence on the orientation of the coordinate grid upon which measurements are made. Court and Porter's (1964) debate on the measurement of spatial medians illustrates the practical difficulties in estimating centroid positions. One feasible, but tedious, trial-and-error method employs an annular graticule which is used to sum populations at specified distance bands from the trial centre (Hart, 1954); other computer-based algorithms using Newton–Raphson procedures were discussed in relation to plant location in Section 5.6.1 above.

9.7 Maps as Graphs

Frequently, the spatial pattern examined in locational analysis consists of linear elements. These may be naturally occurring link systems (like the transport patterns analyzed in Chapter 3) or artificially created linear patterns like the link structures used to describe the contiguity relations of county systems. We examine here some of the ways in which we can reduce such linear maps to a convenient, easily handled format.

9.7.1 *Conventional topological measures from graph theory*

One approach to networks has been suggested by Garrison (1960) and Kansky (1963) based upon graph theory. Some fourteen measures of network structure, of varying complexity, are proposed by Kansky; we examine here only a few judged either to be fundamental in illustrating the basis of graph theory, or alternatively suggested by empirical analysis to be rather closely associated with other aspects of regional development.

Transportation networks may be reduced to rather abstract terms which enable basic properties to be recognized that might elude a 'head-on' study of the transport network as such. This process of simplification was touched on in Section 3.5.1, when the way was illustrated in which the original railroad network of Sardinia could be reduced to a simple pattern of points connected by lines (see Figures 3.20B and C).

Figure 9.12A illustrates a simple case of such an abstract network. It consists of two isolated networks (*sub-graphs*), g_1 and g_2, which are each made up of a series of routes (*edges*), e_1, e_2, ..., e_n, and which connect a series of nodes (*vertices*), v_1, v_2, ..., v_n. We also know the distance along each route in miles (*edge distance*), $d_1, d_2, ..., d_n$. These four measures, g, e, n, and d, form the basic elements which, in various combinations, form the more complex indices proposed by Kansky. For convenience these measures are grouped here simply as (i) measures of centrality, (ii) measures of connectivity, and (iii) measures of shape.

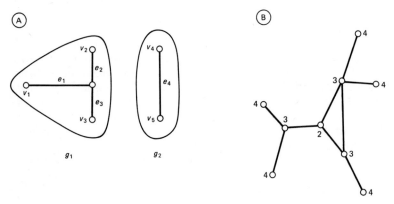

Figure 9.12 **A** Fundamental measures of networks in terms of vertices (v), edges (e), and sub-graphs (g). **B** Measure of centrality of vertices by König numbers. Source: Kansky, 1963, pp. 11, 28.

(i) The first measure of *centrality* was developed by König in 1936 and is here termed the König number (Kansky, 1963, pp. 28–9). Let $s(i,j)$ denote the number of edges in the shortest path from vertex i to vertex j. Then the König number for vertex i is defined as

$$\text{Max}\{s(i,j)\}, \qquad (9.12)$$
$$_{j \neq i}$$

that is, the longest shortest-path originating from vertex i. It is shown for each point in Figure 9.12B. It is thus a measure of topological distance in terms of edges, and suggests that vertices with low König numbers (e.g. the vertex with a number of 2 in Figure 9.12B) occupy a central place in the abstract transport system.

This measure becomes more meaningful if we realize that in many traffic movements (e.g. road transport) the nodes represent delay points; and centres with low König numbers might be realistically 'near' the centre of the system.

In any case, distance, d, can be introduced either as mileage or time into the calculations, and nodes with low König numbers re-examined in order to select the central location.

(ii) The simplest measure of the degree of *connectivity* of a transport network is given by the *Beta* index (β). This relates two of the four fundamental properties as $\beta = E/n$, where E is the total number of edges and n is the total number of vertices in the network (Kansky, 1963, pp. 16–18). In Figure 9.13, the number of vertices remains constant at seven, while the number of connecting edges is progressively increased from six in Figure 9.13A to nine (Figure 9.13D). As the number of edges increases, the connectivity between the vertices rises and the Beta index changes progressively from 0.86 to 1.00, 1.14, and finally 1.28. Values for the index range between extremes of zero and three, with values below one indicating trees and disconnected graphs, values of one indicating a network which has only one circuit (Figure 9.13B), and values between one and three indicating a complex network. Practical examples of variations in the index for the railway networks in eighteen countries are given in Figure 3.19A.

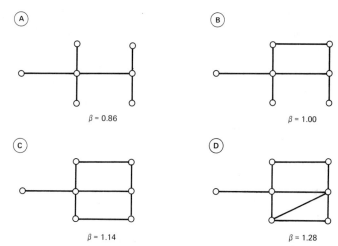

Figure 9.13 Comparison of network connectivity through the β index. Source: Kansky, 1963, p. 11.

(iii) The *shape* of a network is a more difficult concept to grasp. Here we begin with the concept of 'diameter' (itself a weak index for measuring transportation networks), and move on from this to the more complex, but more useful, measures of network shape. δ is an index measuring the topological length or extent of a graph by counting the number of edges in the shortest path between the most distant vertices. Thus, in Figure 9.14, the values of the diameter vary from two to four, rising as the 'extent' of the graph increases, but falling as improved connections are made between the vertices. Hence, the third and fourth graphs in the series have different diameters even though their extent is the same.

Using this concept of diameter, we can move on to relate it to the actual dimensions of the network by defining the index, $\pi = m_T/m_\delta$, where m_T is the total mileage of the transportation network and m_δ is the total mileage of the network's diameter (Kansky, 1963, pp. 21–3). In Figure 9.15A, we have a network where the total mileage, m_T, is 150. Inspection of the graph's diameter in terms of the preceding diagram shows that the value of δ is four. There is, however, no unique diameter but six alternative paths that fulfil the minimum diameter criterion: the locations and lengths of these paths are shown in Figure 9.15B. The mean length of the six diameter paths is 55 miles, so that the shape index, π, is $150/55 = 2.73$.

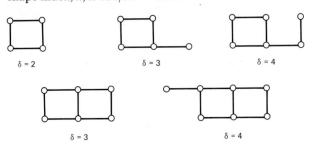

$\delta = 2$ $\delta = 3$ $\delta = 4$

$\delta = 3$ $\delta = 4$

Figure 9.14 Derivation of a measure of network diameter (δ). Source: Kansky, 1963, p. 13.

In practice, shape indices vary considerably. Developed countries like France may have indices approaching 30, while underdeveloped countries like Bolivia may have values of about one for their railway networks; there is considerable evidence that π is a sensitive index of the economic state of a transport network (see Figure 3.19B).

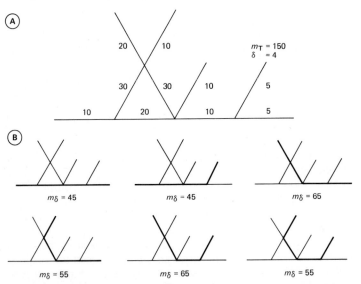

Figure 9.15 Derivation of a shape index for a hypothetical route network. Source: Kansky, 1963, p. 23.

9.7.2 *The S-I index*

Conventional indices of graph structure (Table 9.3) have the advantage of simplicity and ease of computation. Unfortunately, the measures are limited in so far as they may confound graphs which intuitively display a different pattern of edges. Figure 9.15 shows typical examples. To overcome this problem, a measure has been proposed which uses the frequency distribution of shortest paths, $s(i, j)$, in the graph under consideration (James, Cliff, Haggett, and Ord, 1970). As before, we define $s(i,j)$ as the number of links or edges which comprise the shortest path between nodes i and j. Then $F\{s(i,j)\}$ is a discrete distribution which summarizes the frequency of occurrence, f_l, of shortest paths of length $l = 0, 1, 2, 3, \ldots$ links within the graph. Using $F\{s(i,j)\}$, we can compute a measure, the so-called *S-I* index (Ord, 1967), which provides a way of determining which theoretical discrete frequency distribution based upon the hypergeometric series that $F\{s(i,j)\}$ most closely approximates. In order to define the *S-I* index, we must first obtain the first three moments of $F\{s(i,j)\}$. The first moment, or mean μ'_1, is given by

$$\mu'_1 = \overline{l} = \frac{1}{N} \sum_{l=0}^{\delta} f_l l \tag{9.13}$$

where

$$N = \sum_{l=0}^{\delta} f_l.$$

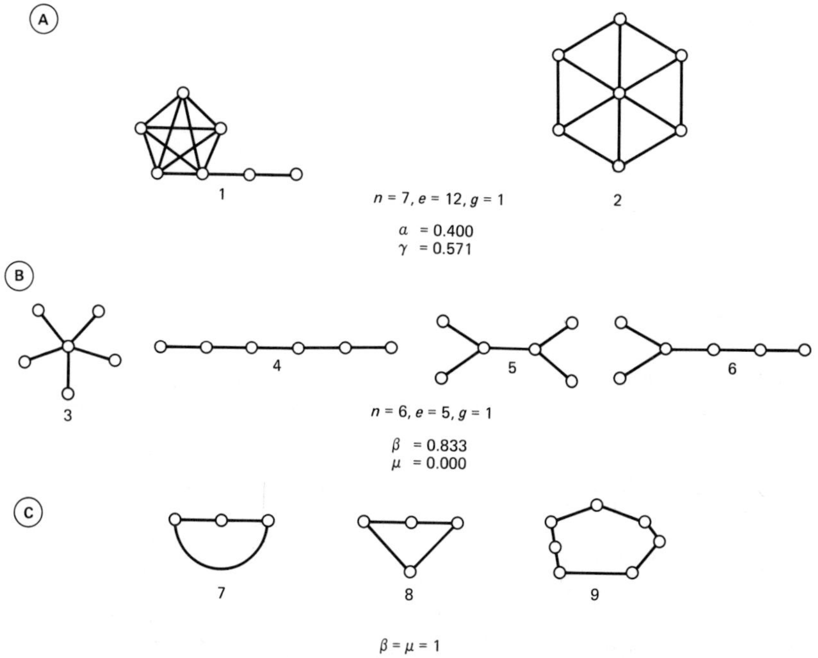

Figure 9.16 Some examples of graphs confounded by the indices α, β, γ, μ. Source: James *et al.*, 1970, p. 15.

The second and third central moments of $F\{s(i,j)\}$, μ_2 and μ_3, respectively, are given by

$$\mu_2 = \frac{1}{N} \sum_{l=0}^{\delta} f_l(l-\bar{l})^2 \tag{9.14}$$

$$\mu_3 = \frac{1}{N} \sum_{l=0}^{\delta} f_l(l-\bar{l})^3. \tag{9.15}$$

From (9.13)–(9.16), we have

$$S = \mu_3/\mu_2 \tag{9.16}$$

and

$$I = \mu_2/\mu_1'. \tag{9.17}$$

Table 9.3   Some indices of graph structure

Index and Identity Number	Bounds	Interpretation
(1) $\beta = e/n$	$0 \leqslant \beta \leqslant (n-1)/2$	Ratio of edges (e) to vertices (n).
(2) $\mu = e - n + g$	$0 \leqslant \mu \leqslant \dfrac{(n-1)(n-2)}{2}$	The cyclomatic or first Betti number. Gives the number of fundamental loops within a graph.
(3) $\alpha = 2\mu/(n-1)(n-2)$	$0 \leqslant \alpha \leqslant 1$	Ratio of the observed number of circuits to the maximum possible number (proportion redundant).
(4) $\gamma = 2e/n(n-1)$	$0 \leqslant \gamma \leqslant 1$	Ratio of actual number of edges to maximum possible (degree of connectivity).
(5) $\delta = \max_{ij}\{s(i,j)\}$	$1 \leqslant \delta \leqslant n-1$	Diameter of graph.
(6) $D(G) = \sum_i \sum_j s(i,j)$	$n(n-1) \leqslant D < \dfrac{n^2(n-1)}{2}$	Dispersion of graph. Only defined for $g = 1$.
(7) $A(G) = D(G)/n(n-1)$	$1 \leqslant A < n/2$	Average path length

Source: James, et al.,1970, p. 14.

Using the *S-I* index, the complete set of theoretical discrete distributions based on the hypergeometric series can be mapped on to the *S-I* plane (Figure 9.17A). To examine the structure of any graph, the values of S and I are computed, and their position is plotted on the *S-I* chart.

The special value of the *S-I* index lies in its ability to discriminate between networks which have the same conventional graph theoretic parameters. All the graphs shown in Figure 9.16 are clearly differentiated in the *S-I* plane. James *et al.* (1970, p. 20) go on to show that basic graph types—from simple chains to completely connected graphs—tend to lie in distinct and characteristic regions of the *S-I* chart (Figure 9.17B). In general, the index provides a powerful means of classifying network patterns on maps in terms of the distribution of shortest path lengths in the graph. Forer (1974) has made effective use of *S-I* measures in studying the evolution of New Zealand's domestic airline network between 1939 and 1970.

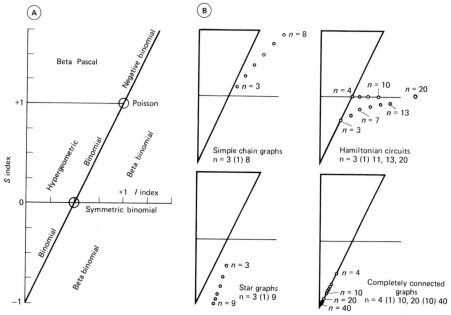

Figure 9.17 A *S-I* diagram. **B** characteristic values for some basic graph types. Source: James *et al.*, 1970, pp. 19–20.

9.7.3 *Computation of the shortest path distribution*

To illustrate the steps involved in the computation of the shortest-path distribution, $F\{s(i,j)\}$, we consider the example shown in Figure 9.18.

Step 1. Reduce the graph to a binary connection matrix, C, by setting the typical element of C, c_{ij}, equal to one if there is a direct link between nodes i and j, and $c_{ij} = 0$ otherwise. Reproduce C in the first order shortest-path matrix, S_1 (Figure 9.18).

Step 2. Calculate C^2. Each element, $c_{ij}^{(2)}$, $i, j = 1, 2, ..., n$, in C^2 gives the total number of *two* step links between nodes i and j. For example, in Figure 9.18 $c_{33}^{(2)} = 4$, and so there are four two step links which start and finish at node $3(3 \rightarrow 1 \rightarrow 3; 3 \rightarrow 4 \rightarrow 3; 3 \rightarrow 2 \rightarrow 3; 3 \rightarrow 5 \rightarrow 3)$. In addition, $c_{36}^{(2)} = 1$, implying that there is a two step link between nodes 3 and 6 $(3 \rightarrow 5 \rightarrow 6)$.

As far as the shortest-path distribution is concerned, $c_{36}^{(2)}$ is a genuine two-step link, whereas $c_{33}^{(2)}$ is redundant information. To obtain S_2 first put $S_2 = S_1$. Next, compare C^2 and S_2 element by element. If $c_{ij}^{(2)} \neq 0$ *and* $s_{ij}^{(2)} = 0$, $(i \neq j)$, put $s_{ij}^{(2)} = 2$; otherwise do not alter $s_{ij}^{(2)}$. The '2' serves to indicate that there is a two-step link between i and j.

Step 3. Calculate C^3. Copy the element values of S_2 across into S_3. Compare C^3 and S_3 element by element. If $c_{ij}^{(3)} \neq 0$ *and* $s_{ij}^{(3)} = 0$, $(i \neq j)$ put $s_{ij}^{(3)} = 3$ to indicate that there is a three-step link between i and j.

Step 4. Repeat step 3 by raising **C** to successively higher powers until there are no zero values left in the off-diagonal elements of the shortest-path matrix. In Figure 9.18, this is achieved with $\mathbf{C}^3$, and so we note that the matrix powering procedure is continued up to the diameter of the graph.

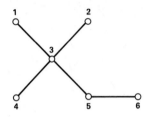

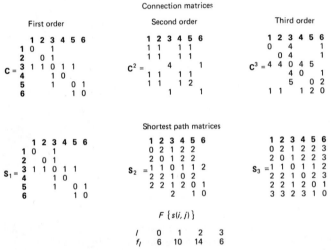

Figure 9.18 Computation of the shortest path distribution using matrix powering methods. Blank cells in the off-diagonal positions of the matrices are zero.

The following points about $F\{s(i,j)\}$ are evident from Figure 9.18:
(1) $f_0 = n$, the number of vertices in the graph.
(2) $f_1 = 2E$.
(3) $f_1/f_0 = 2\beta$.
(4) Max $(l) = \delta$.
(5) A high modal value for $F\{s(i,j)\}$ indicates that a large proportion of nodes are linked only indirectly and that the graph is tree-like. Conversely a low modal value is suggestive of a well connected graph; indeed, if $c_{ij} = 1$ for all i, j in **C**, the mode is 1.

9.7.4 *Latent structure in networks*

Graph theoretic measures and the *S-I* index are only two of a wide variety of methods available to extract significant generalization from network maps. A typical pioneering study is that of Garrison and Marble (1962), who dissected the pattern of internal airline links in Venezuela (Figure 9.19). Here, the system of 59 cities linked by 104 routes was displayed as a binary connection matrix. The matrix was reduced through principal components analysis to produce a set of four leading components (Table 9.4). Component I scaled the nodes in terms of their direct connections with other nodes, producing a nearly linear scaling of the cities by size. This basic component accounted for 19 per cent of the total observed variation. Component II showed up as a 'field' effect, centrying on the leading city of Caracas, C; this raised total variance accounted for by a further seven per cent. Somewhat similar in importance, component III described a major regionalization effect centred on Maracaibo, Mo, and Santa Barbara, B, as opposed to the 'eastern' system centred on Caracas and Maturin, Ma. The fourth component showed a weak but detectable minor regionalization effect.

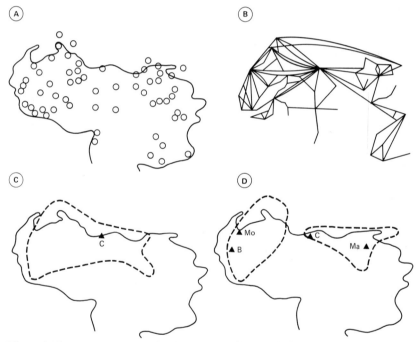

Figure 9.19 Latent structure in the pattern of internal airline links in Venezuela. **A** vertices. **B** Links between vertices. **C** Component II fields. **D** Component III fields. Source: Garrison and Marble, 1962.

More recently, Gould (1967) has extended this type of analysis to the road networks of Uganda and Syria. In the first country, the focus of the first component was the leading node of Kampala, with a field effect decreasing away from the capital. In the second country, Syria, Aleppo, Damascus, and Homs, all break-of-bulk towns at the base of the mountains paralleling the coast, were identified by component I. Tinkler (1972) has critically reviewed the earlier studies which used principal components methods to analyze binary connection matrices. His comparison of alternative ways of decomposing such matrices does, however, support the view that distinct physical interpretations may be placed upon the major components (the eigenvectors) extracted.

Table 9.4   Principal components analysis of latent structure in Venezuelan airline routes

Components:	Variation explained		Interpretation
	Per cent	Cumulative per cent	
I	18.7	18.7	Size axis
II	7.5	26.1	Caracas 'field' axis
III	6.6	32.7	East–West 'field' axis
IV	5.2	38.0	Minor regionalizing axis

Source: Garrison and Marble, 1962, p. 69.

The way in which graph structure can allow some cities to dominate a particular network has been studied by Reed (1970). Consider the graph of the five-node system shown in Figure 9.20A. As described in Section 9.7.3, a matrix of the shortest paths between all pairs of nodes can be constructed from this graph. The quantity, $\bar{s}(i,j)$, $i = 1, 2, ..., n$, the average length of the shortest paths from node i to all other nodes, j, in the network can then be computed.

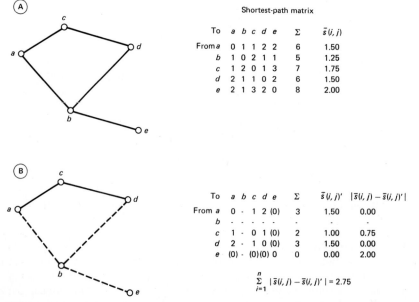

Figure 9.20   Effect of removal of nodes on the connectivity of a graph. Source: Reed, 1970, p. 771.

To find any node's degree of control over the network, it is 'edited out' by removing all its direct links. For each remaining node in the revised (reduced) graph, $\bar{s}(i, j)$ is again calculated [called $\bar{s}(i, j)'$] (Figure 9.20B), and the absolute difference between each of these values and the corresponding nodal $\bar{s}(i,j)$ value in the original graph is noted. Nodes which, when removed, produce the largest changes in the $\bar{s}(i,j)$ values of other nodes exercise the greatest degree of control (i.e. potential disruptive effect) within the network.

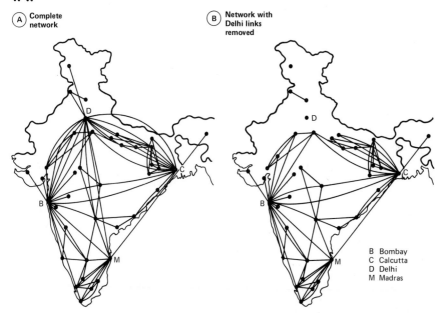

Figure 9.21 Hierarchies of urban dominance in India measured by domestic airline network connections. **A** Links between 40 cities with a 1961 population of 100,000 or greater. **B** Effect of removing Delhi. Source: Reed, 1970, pp. 775–7.

The absolute difference approach to nodal dominance was tested by Reed for India's major domestic airline services in the late 1960s. This complex network includes all cities with a 1961 population of 100,000 or more, plus three smaller cities at the end of airlines. The map (Figure 9.21A) shows direct links as defined by the exchange of one or more planes per week; links indicate only the existence of such a service, without considering the volume of flow. To examine the impact of individual nodes on the connectivity of the network, their direct links were removed city by city from the full system. Figure 9.21B shows the effect of removing Delhi, thus reducing strong north–south components in the network and cutting off four northern cities from the rest of the airline system. Table 9.5 gives the results for the first seven nodes in order of importance. Bombay is clearly the critical city in network dominance (final column of table), even though it looks similar to Delhi and Calcutta on simpler measures (first three columns). Reed's method allows the separation of India's urban hierarchy into four levels: national, regional, sub-regional and route endings.

Table 9.5   Impact of individual cities on the connectivity of a network*

	Number of direct links	Number of links to reach all cities by shortest paths	Average link distance to reach all cities	Mean change in link distance of other cities with given city removed
Bombay	18	60	1.54	.412
Calcutta	16	61	1.56	.256
Delhi	17	60	1.54	.206
Madras	10	68	1.74	.115
Hyderabad	8	75	1.92	.052
Visakhapatram	4	92	2.36	.023
Bangalore	7	85	2.18	.019

Source: Reed, 1970, pp. 776, 779.

* India's domestic airline system, March 1967.

Although we have limited consideration in this book to the study of network maps, it is evident that the methods described are generally applicable to all networks, non-spatial as well as spatial. Extensive use has been made of graph theory in the study of structural relations between sectors within a regional economy (Ponsard, 1969; Storey, 1972).

9.8 Co-ordinate Systems for Map Data

9.8.1 *Coding of geographical data*

Developments in computer technology have had considerable significance for the processing of locational data. Such data may now be readily stored on punched cards, magnetic tape, etc., and 'translated' into a map of any desired characteristic by an automated plotter (Figure 9.22). An outstanding early example of machine mapping from coded geographical data is the *Atlas of the British Flora* (Perring and Walters, 1962). The basis of the atlas was a deck of punched card records for each of the 2,000 British vascular species for every ten kilometre square cell of the National Grid. Details of location, species (presence or absence), habitat, date, collector, and other relevant information were coded, and the 1,500,000 pieces of information sorted mechanically. At a late stage in the analysis, data were fed into a mechanical tabulator which printed a dot (if the species was present) in the location indicated by the digits of the ten kilometre reference system (Figure 9.22).

In the case of the Perring and Walters atlas, the problem of geographical co-ordinates was simply solved through the use of the existing *xy* co-ordinate system of the National Grid. Similar systems are available in a number of countries, notably Sweden where census data are being coded on a ten-metre grid on the 1:10,000 map series (Hägerstrand, 1955). For world-wide studies, the more complicated spheroidal reference systems of latitude and longitude must be substituted for rectangular co-ordinate systems. The difficulties of automated computation of distances, areas, and directions on a spherical reference system are further complicated by the departure of the earth's form from that of a true sphere: lengths of a degree of a meridian range from 68.703 statute miles (at zero to one degree latitude) to 69.407 statute miles (at eighty-nine to ninety degrees latitude). Therefore, increasing use is being made of the Transverse Mercator projection to provide a conformal projection base for topographic map series. The prime advantage of this projection is that scale departures are uniform along lines parallel to the standard great circle, allowing the build-up of an xy co-ordinate rectangular system in which a given x-value will have a uniform scale characteristic at any y-value. It has been widely used by the United States in its UTM system (Universal Transverse Mercator) for building up a series of identical projections for mid-latitudes, each unit covering an area of six degrees of longitude by 800 kilometres.

***

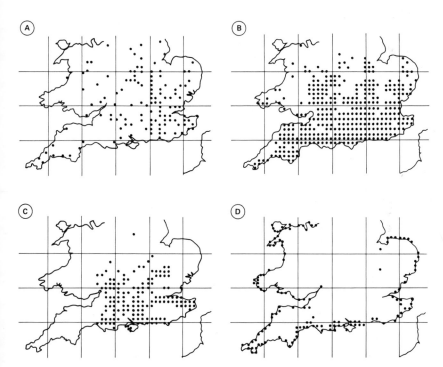

Figure 9.22   Computer maps of distribution of four plant species by 10×10 kilometre quadrats in southern England. Source: Perring and Walters, 1962.

Outside these standard systems, interesting use has been made of azimuthal projections. For example, in the migration studies reviewed in Chapter 2, information is stored in terms of *distance* and *direction* from the source of migration. Other systems with time and direction might prove useful in mapping traffic studies (Bunge, 1962, p. 55).

9.8.2 *Multidimensional scaling of co-ordinates*

A second approach to co-ordinates is to try and make them fit the characteristics of the data being plotted. For example, geographers are frequently concerned with discovering map structure from a matrix of interpoint distances. We may have information on travel costs between a set of locations, migration flows between regions, or capital flows between countries. Direct plotting of these data in terms of, say, travel cost space or migration flow space is rarely possible. Consider the problem of plotting the following

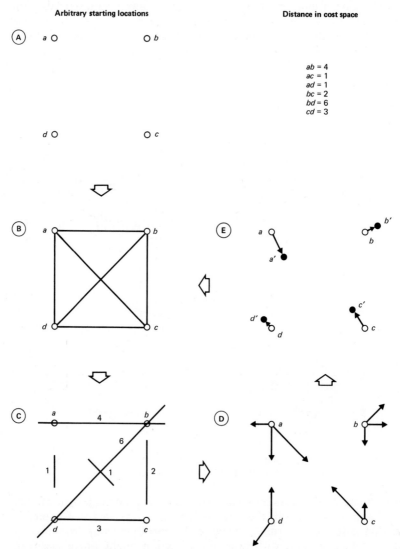

Figure 9.23 Tobler's multilateration method for multidimensional scaling.

interpoint data for four locations (a, b, c, d). Suppose that the distance from a to b (ab) is 4 units, $ac = 1$, $ad = 1$, $bc = 2$, $bd = 6$, and $cd = 3$. A few minutes experimenting with pencil and compass will show that there is no way that the four points (a, b, c, d) can be plotted on to the two-dimensional plane of a map sheet so as to retain the precise values of the interpoint distances.

One solution to this problem is to try to obtain a best-fit approximation to their locations. For example, we can regard this as a multilateration problem, in which we have to find the spatial co-ordinates of points so that the map distances calculated from these co-ordinates agree as closely as possible with the given distances. Figure 9.23 shows a six-stage graphical multilateration sequence given by Tobler (in Gollege and Rushton, 1972, pp. 14–17):

Step 1. Locate the *n* points arbitrarily.

Step 2. Draw straight lines through each pair of points.

Step 3. On each line, centre a segment of length equal to the given distance. This step is omitted if an observation is missing.

Step 4. Draw vectors from each point to the ends of the segments representing the given distances.

Step 5. Relocate each point in the new position defined by the average of the local vectors.

Step 6. If no points have moved in Step 5, stop; otherwise use the new positions to begin a fresh cycle starting at Step 2.

✳✳

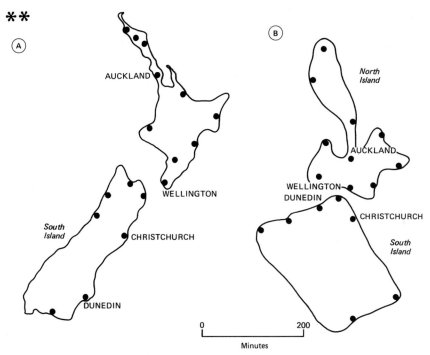

Figure 9.24 Use of multidimensional scaling in translating time distance for airline links between major New Zealand cities into map format. **A** Conventional geographic space. **B** Time-space map for 1970 journey times. Source: Forer, 1974, p. 287.

Whenever the researcher is confident of the metric properties of his data (e.g. exact travel times, or travel costs, between pairs of cities) then the true distances will be as given. Where there is doubt about the accuracy or appropriateness of the original data, then non-metric rather than metric scaling is recommended. In non-metric scaling, the distances 'fitted' are monotonically transformed distances; the transformation commonly used is the rank ordering from shortest to longest.

In practice, the mapping is achieved through a series of multidimensional scaling programs developed for computer use by investigators like Torgerson and Kruskal. Golledge and Rushton (1972) provide an extensive review of the major non-metric multidimensional scaling (MDS) methods and comment on their applicability for map analysis. Figure 9.24 illustrates a recent geographical application of MDS by Forer (1974) to show the location of New Zealand's cities in terms of time space. Kendall (1971) has used MDS techniques to construct county base maps when only incomplete information on contiguities between counties is available, and Tobler and Winerburg (1971) have explored its use in archaeological reconstructions.

9.9 Conclusions

It will be evident from this review, partial though it is, that the traditional importance of mapping procedures within geography has not been reduced by the last few decades of quantitative work. Indeed, one could argue that the emphasis on locational and spatial arrangements has given a renewed emphasis to map information. Developments in both statistical methodology (e.g. spatial autocorrelation and multidimensional scaling) and in computer technology have tended to open up new avenues for map analysis.

10 Hypothesis Testing

10.1 **Introduction.** 10.2 **Spatial Independence: The Problem:** 1 Spatial distortion and the *t*-test; 2 Spatial distortion in regression models; 3 Spatial distortion in other statistical models. 10.3 **Spatial Independence: Solutions:** 1 Allowing for correlated observations; 2 Removing the correlation; 3 Spatial variate differencing. 10.4 **Spatial Stationarity:** 1 Concepts of stationarity; 2 Formal definitions of stationarity; 3 Consequences of non-stationarity. 10.5 **Normality:** 1 Problem of non-normality; 2 Transformations to normality; 3 Distribution-free procedures. 10.6 **Irregular Collecting Areas:** 1 Impact on statistical measures; 2 Standardization of collecting areas. 10.7 **Conclusions.**

10.1 Introduction

The testing of hypotheses is of special importance in geography, in that one of the essential roles it plays is to subject 'systematic' ideas to 'regional' tests. Indeed, the building, testing, and rebuilding of hypotheses is the slow path by which inductive theory construction proceeds, and the research cycle demands the death of old hypotheses and the birth of new ones. Since the first edition of this book appeared, the use of conventional statistical models and tests of inference such as X^2, the *t*-test, the *F*-test, correlation and regression, and so on, has become commonplace in human geography. It is not the purpose of this chapter to outline the procedures for carrying out such analyses. Standard accounts of the methods exist, such as those of King (1969b), Hammond and McCullagh (1974) and Yeates (1974), who are all geographers; elementary texts by statisticians are those of Hoel (1966), Freund (1967), and Wetherill (1967). A collaborative text by the geologist, Krumbein, and a statistician, Graybill, is especially useful (Krumbein and Graybill, 1965). Rather, the aim of this chapter is to examine those properties of geographical data which make their analysis using statistical methods of the sort cited more difficult than might at first appear. The problems and their consequences for tests of inference and other statistical models are considered, and possible remedies are suggested.

10.2 Spatial Independence: the Problem

Suppose that data have been collected for a set of $i = 1, 2, ..., n$ points or areas, and that the variate for the *i*th location is denoted by X_i. However, while statistical methods are traditionally developed from assumptions which include a statement like 'let X_i $(i = 1, 2, ..., n)$ be n independent, identically distributed variates' (Cliff and Ord, 1975a), such spatially located data generally exhibit systematic spatial variation, or *spatial autocorrelation* (see Chapter 11), thus breaking the independence assumption quoted above.

It is evident from the literature that geographers have been quite clear that the assumption of independence cannot be sustained for spatial data. Thus Tobler (1970) has referred to 'the first law of geography: everything is related to everything else, but near things are more related than distant things', while Gould (1970, pp. 443–444) stated:

> Why we should expect independence in spatial observations that are of the slightest intellectual interest or importance in geographic research I cannot imagine. All our efforts to understand spatial pattern, structure, and process have indicated that it is precisely the lack of independence—the interdependence—of spatial phenomena that allows us to substitute pattern, and therefore predictability and order, for chaos and apparent lack of interdependence—of things in time and space.

We are faced, therefore, with the problem that much statistical theory demands independent observations, while geographical theory demands spatially interdependent phenomena. This problem has a long history. In anthropology, it is referred to as Galton's problem (Naroll, 1961; Strauss and Orans, 1975), in recognition of comments by Galton on a paper by Tylor (1889), in which he argued that the historical links between societies through migration (Chapter 2) and diffusion (Chapter 7) make the assumption of statistical independence inapplicable. Galton comments:

> It was extremely desirable for the sake of those who may wish to study the evidence for Dr Tylor's conclusions, that full information should be given as to the degree in which the customs of the tribes and races which are compared together are independent. It might be, that some of the tribes had derived them from a common source, so that they were duplicate copies of the same original. Certainly, in such an investigation as this, each of the observations ought, in the language of statisticians, to be carefully 'weighted'. It would give a useful idea of the distribution of the several customs and of their relative prevalence in the world, if a map were so marked by shadings and colour as to present a picture of their geographical ranges.

In this section (10.2), we discuss the difficulties which spatial dependence causes in the attempt to apply standard statistical tests to geographical data. In the next (10.3), we try to show how the troublesome effects of this 'spatial distortion' may be reduced.

10.2.1 *Spatial distortion and the t-test*

If we apply a statistical model which assumes independent data to spatially autocorrelated observations, quite misleading results may be obtained. We can illustrate this with reference to Student's *t*-test for the difference between means. This material is summarized from Cliff and Ord (1975a).

Suppose that we have drawn samples of sizes N_1 and N_2 respectively from populations X_1 and X_2 which are $N(\mu_1, \sigma_1^2)$ and $N(\mu_2, \sigma_2^2)$ respectively.[1] If we take the simplest model and assume that $\sigma_1^2 = \sigma_2^2 = \sigma^2$, then under the null hypothesis, H_0, of no difference between the population means, μ_1 and μ_2, the quantity

$$t = \frac{\bar{x}_1 - \bar{x}_2}{\hat{\sigma}_{\bar{x}_1 - \bar{x}_2}} \qquad (10.1)$$

will follow Student's t distribution with $N_1 + N_2 - 2$ degrees of freedom, *provided that the samples are independent* (see Table A2). Here, $\bar{x}_1$ and $\bar{x}_2$ are the means of the samples drawn from populations 1 and 2, while $\hat{\sigma}_{\bar{x}_1 - \bar{x}_2}$, the estimated standard error of the differences between sample means, is given by

$$\hat{\sigma}_{\bar{x}_1 - \bar{x}_2} = \sqrt{\frac{N_1 s_1^2 + N_2 s_2^2}{N_1 + N_2 - 2}} \sqrt{\frac{N_1 + N_2}{N_1 N_2}}, \qquad (10.2)$$

where s_1^2 and s_2^2 are the variances of samples 1 and 2. Figure 10.1 shows a typical situation. A Monte Carlo experiment may be constructed to determine whether (10.1) is distributed as t if the data are not independent.

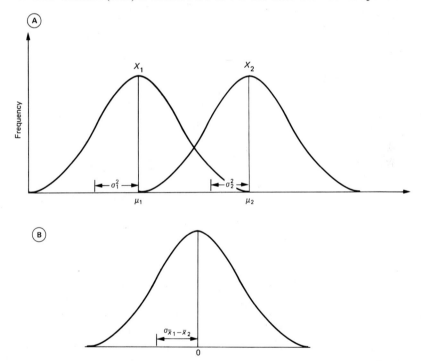

Figure 10.1   Form of Student's t test for the difference between means. **A** Population distributions. **B** Sampling distribution of differences between sample means.

[1] The notation $N(\mu, \sigma^2)$ means a normally distributed population with mean μ and variance σ^2.

However, in order to do this, we must first show how normally distributed variables with a specified degree of spatial autocorrelation in them can be constructed.

Suppose that we wish to construct a variable in which the values of that variable in contiguous counties of an n county system are correlated by an amount ρ. We use the matrix, $\mathbf{W}$, to specify the structure of the county system by setting the typical element of $\mathbf{W}$, w_{ij}, equal to one if counties i and j are contiguous, and $w_{ij} = 0$ otherwise. The $\{w_{ij}\}$ are scaled so that $\sum_{j} w_{ij} = 1$, where the summation is over the counties contiguous to i, $i = 1, 2, ..., n$.

(A) $\rho = 0.0$

0.02	0.37	2.78	−3.24	0.11
−2.34	0.00	2.27	2.89	2.33
1.79	2.04	2.13	−1.87	1.90
−0.18	1.56	−1.18	4.08	−0.64
4.93	−1.86	2.08	4.40	−4.00

(B) $\rho = 0.9$

4.70	6.67	9.35	4.69	6.79
3.73	6.95	10.56	10.28	10.16
8.59	9.97	10.26	7.40	9.04
8.97	9.43	8.20	11.62	6.24
12.50	7.83	10.40	11.69	2.29

(C) $\rho = -0.9$

7.17	−6.68	10.09	−11.83	8.02
−9.22	6.22	−5.87	10.52	−5.75
9.52	−5.90	9.33	−10.45	8.36
−10.65	10.21	−9.78	9.93	−5.35
15.17	−12.11	8.78	−0.43	2.63

Figure 10.2 Effects of spatial autocorrelation on a geographical distribution. **A** Map of original observations which are spatially independent. Maps of same observations **(B)** positively autocorrelated by the amount $\rho = 0.9$ and **(C)** negatively autocorrelated by the amount $\rho = -0.9$. In **(B)**, note the similarity among the observation levels compared with **(A)** and in **(C)** the alternating pattern characteristic of negative spatial autocorrelation.

Cliff and Ord (1973, p. 147) have shown that n spatially located observations, $\mathbf{x}' \equiv \{x_1, x_2, ..., x_n\}$, which are normally distributed and ($1 \times n$) correlated by an amount ρ, can be generated by the matrix equation

$$\underset{n \times 1}{\mathbf{x}} = \underset{n \times n}{(\mathbf{I} - \rho\mathbf{W})^{-1}} \underset{n \times 1}{\mathbf{u}} . \tag{10.3}$$

Here, $\mathbf{u}$ is a vector obtained by random sampling from an $N(\mu, \sigma)$ population, in addition to previously defined terms. What (10.3) does is to take a vector of independent observations, $\mathbf{u}$, and then to use the operator $(\mathbf{I} - \rho\mathbf{W})^{-1}$ to correlate them (a) by the pre-specified amount ρ, and (b) between those counties for which $w_{ij} \neq 0$. $\mathbf{x}$ is the vector of autocorrelated observations (see Figure 10.2).

Returning to the t-test example, the required Monte Carlo experiment has the following steps.

Step 1. Specify the county systems from which the data are to be collected. Cliff and Ord (1975a) assumed that X_1 and X_2 were both measured on lattices of square cells, mapped on to a torus.[2] In the lattices, $w_{ij} = 1$ if cells i and j had a common edge, and $w_{ij} = 0$ otherwise. 3×3, 5×5, 7×7 and 10×10 lattices were tried.

Step 2. Indicate the level of autocorrelation to be introduced into X_1 and X_2 by ρ_1 and ρ_2 respectively.

Step 3. Evaluate the correlating operators,

$$(\mathbf{I} - \rho_1\mathbf{W})^{-1},$$

and

$$(\mathbf{I} - \rho_2\mathbf{W})^{-1}.$$

Step 4. Generate the vectors $\mathbf{u}$ and $\mathbf{v}$ by random sampling from $N(\mu_1, \sigma_1^2)$ and $N(\mu_2, \sigma_2^2)$ populations respectively. Cliff and Ord took $\mu_1 = \mu_2 = 0.0$ and $\sigma_1^2 = \sigma_2^2 = 1.0$ without loss of generality; that is, equal means and variances, because of the model postulated by equations (10.1) and (10.2).

Step 5. Calculate the autocorrelated variate values, $\mathbf{x}_1$ and $\mathbf{x}_2$, as

$$\mathbf{x}_1 = (\mathbf{I} - \rho_1\mathbf{W})^{-1}\mathbf{u}$$

and

$$\mathbf{x}_2 = (\mathbf{I} - \rho_2\mathbf{W})^{-1}\mathbf{v}.$$

Step 6. Evaluate t.

Step 7. Repeat steps 4–6 m times (see below). This experiment generates the sampling distribution of (10.1) under the null hypothesis of no difference in the population means, and for degrees of autocorrelation, ρ_1 in X_1 and ρ_2 in X_2. Cliff and Ord tried the following pairs of values of ρ_1 and ρ_2: 0.0 and 0.0; 0.0 and 0.5; 0.0 and 0.9; 0.5 and 0.5; 0.5 and 0.9; 0.9 and 0.9; -0.5 and -0.5; -0.9 and -0.9; 0.5 and -0.5; 0.9 and -0.9. In step 7 above, m must be chosen large

---

[2] A torus is a solid ring of circular cross section. This doughnut-shaped geometrical figure is frequently used in statistical experiments to avoid the complications of edge effects. We return to the difficulties caused by edge effects in Section 12.2.2.

enough for the generated sampling distribution to be representative, especially in the tail areas which are used for hypothesis testing. Cliff and Ord took $m = 1200$. The empirical percentage points for the $\alpha = 0.10, 0.05, 0.025, 0.01$ and 0.005 significance levels (one-tailed test) were then determined in the generated sampling distributions, and compared with the tabulated percentage points for t with $N_1 + N_2 - 2$ degrees of freedom as given in Table A2. Some of the results for the 7×7 lattice (upper tail only) appear in Table 10.1.

Several points can be made on the basis of this table. First, when $\rho_1 = \rho_2 = 0.0$, X_1 and X_2 are uncorrelated and the assumptions of the t-test outlined for equations (10.1) and (10.2) are met. We would therefore expect a high degree of correspondence between the tabulated and empirical percentage points. As Table 10.1 shows, this is the case except for extreme values of α. We need not worry unduly about lack of correspondence in such instances, since only a few wild random number values in the experiment can produce severe fluctuations when α is extreme. Second, positive autocorrelation in both X_1 and X_2 will result in *overstatement* of the significance of any analysis if the conventional t-test formulae and tables are used; that is, the probability of a Type I error (the probability of rejecting H_0 when it is in fact true) exceeds the nominal level. The overstatement increases as the level of autocorrelation increases. When the autocorrelation is negative, the situation is reversed and *understatement* of the significance of results occurs; that is, the true Type I error probability is too small. Third, when one of the variables is positively autocorrelated, and the other is negatively autocorrelated, the effects are not self-cancelling; the true probability of a Type I error again exceeds the nominal level.

These difficulties with the t-test arise because positively autocorrelated observations produce a downwards bias (understatement) in the estimated standard error which appears in the denominator of t [equation (10.2)]. Negatively autocorrelated observations bias the estimate of the standard error upwards (overstatement).

10.2.2 *Spatial distortion in regression models*

These sorts of results are well known to econometricians (cf. Johnston, 1972, Section 8.2) from their work on regression models. A basic assumption of the regression model,

$$\mathbf{Y} = \mathbf{X} \quad \boldsymbol{\beta} + \boldsymbol{\varepsilon} , \qquad (10.4)$$
$$n \times 1 \quad n \times k \; k \times 1 \quad n \times 1$$

is that the error terms, $\boldsymbol{\varepsilon}$, are independent. For data with a geographical ordering, this requirement implies that the errors must be spatially independent. If ordinary least squares are used to estimate the model, the consequences of failure to meet this assumption are as follows (Johnston, 1972, pp. 246–49). We assume that the errors are positively autocorrelated:

(1) the sampling variances of the regression coefficients, var $(\hat{\boldsymbol{\beta}})$, will be seriously underestimated;

(2) the variance of the errors, σ_ε^2, will be underestimated. Since this esti-

Table 10.1 Tabulated percentage points for t (one-tailed test), and empirical percentage points with various levels of correlation in X_1 and X_2.

Empirical percentage points for t with ρ_1 and ρ_2 =

α	*t tabulated**	0.0, 0.0	0.0, 0.5	0.0, 0.9	0.5, 0.5	0.5, 0.9	0.9, 0.9	−0.5, −0.5	−0.9, −0.9	0.5, −0.5	0.9, −0.9
		Independent observations	*Positively autocorrelated observations*					*Negatively autocorrelated observations*		*Mixed autocorrelation*	
0.10	1.29	1.30	1.88	7.30	2.39	7.21	8.51	0.77	0.37	1.77	5.50
0.05	1.66	1.61	2.53	9.20	3.01	9.08	10.98	0.99	0.47	2.25	7.08
0.025	1.98	1.97	2.94	10.90	3.63	11.05	12.88	1.17	0.56	2.65	8.12
0.01	2.36	2.23	3.40	13.22	4.05	13.38	14.99	1.35	0.65	3.14	10.02
0.005	2.62	2.42	3.71	14.69	4.47	16.63	16.35	1.47	0.73	3.53	11.48

*See Appendix, Table A2.

Source: Cliff and Ord, 1975a, p. 731.

mate, $\hat{\sigma}_{\varepsilon}^2$, appears in the denominator of the t and F tests used to examine the significance of the regression [Johnston, 1972, equations (2–30) and (2–36)], overstatement of the significance of the regression is likely. In addition, an inflated value for F means that the coefficient of multiple correlation, R^2, will also be inflated [Johnston, 1972, equation (5–60)]. If the error terms are negatively correlated, the reverse occurs (understatement of the significance of any regression). Johnston (1972, Section 8.2) has shown additionally, that the level of spatial autocorrelation in the $\{X\}$ variables in the regression is important as well. Positive (or negative) autocorrelation in those variables works in the same direction as positive (or negative) autocorrelation in the errors, thus compounding the problems noted. Johnston (p. 245) also indicates that if the $\{X\}$ variables are spatially independent, 'then even if [the $\{\varepsilon\}$ are] autocorrelated the bias is not likely to be serious.'

10.2.3 *Spatial distortion in other statistical models*

What happens with other models? Cliff, Martin and Ord (1975b) have demonstrated for a particular application of the X^2 goodness-of-fit test, that failure to meet the asumption of independent observed frequency counts will generally lead to substantially increased risks of a Type I error. For principal components and factor analysis, where again independence is assumed, the picture is more complicated. Cliff and Ord (1975b) have shown that if the variables in the analysis are equi-correlated, then the same results will be obtained, scale factors apart, as if the independence assumption were met. Whether this conclusion is of practical value remains unexplored; we have little idea of the relative levels of spatial autocorrelation in geographical variables.

The general lesson to be learned from the above discussion is, however, clear. If geographers continue to apply the usual forms of many of the basic statistical models to spatially autocorrelated data, then a very severe risk is run of reaching misleading conclusions. In addition, it means that the substantive results reported in studies to date which have not taken this problem into account should be interpreted with great caution.

10.3 Spatial Independence: Solutions

What approaches are available which enable the difficulty outlined in the preceding section to be overcome? An appropriate strategy might be:

(1) determine *before* carrying out any analysis whether there is any spatial autocorrelation in the data. If there is not, that is if the data are spatially independent, proceed with the analysis using the conventional models. In the next chapter, a series of measures of spatial autocorrelation are described which enable a decision to be reached on whether independence is present or not, in a data set.

(2) If we conclude that the independence assumption cannot be sustained, two basic alternatives are open to us. We can either modify the appropriate technique to allow for the correlated observations, or we can try to remove the

correlation from the data—make them spatially independent—so that the conventional models may be applied.[3] We now consider these alternatives in turn.

10.3.1 *Allowing for correlated observations*

Gould (1970) has argued that understanding the pattern of autocorrelation over space in geographical variables is so basic an aim of geographical inquiry that any analysis should allow for this fact. He believes that 'cleaning up' the data to make them independent 'represents a throwing out of the baby with the bathwater.' However, we should be quite clear that modifying the models to allow for the autocorrelation is an extremely lengthy procedure. Thus Cliff, Martin and Ord (1975b) considered an application of the X^2 test in evaluating the goodness-of-fit between the observed and expected frequencies (counts) of contiguities between sub-areas of different colours in a choropleth map (see Section 11.3.1). The expected counts were derived under the null hypothesis of no spatial pattern among sub-areas of a particular colour in the map. The way in which the counts were obtained meant that the requirement in the X^2 test of independence among the observed counts was not satisfied. The authors considered only the simplest case of regular lattices mapped on to a torus, and contiguities between cells with an edge in comon (the so-called *rook's case*, by analogy with chess). The revised formula for X^2 was

$$X^2 = \mathbf{a}'\mathbf{V}^{-1}\mathbf{a}, \tag{10.5}$$

where $\mathbf{a}$ is a column vector of (observed-expected) counts, and $\mathbf{V}$ is a matrix of covariances among the observed counts. The distribution of X^2 for the problem examined lay between $\chi^2_{(2)}$ and $\chi^2_{(3)}$. Each element of $\mathbf{V}$ involved the solution of an equation of 28 terms; in addition, $\mathbf{V}$ is lattice specific so that general tables to test the significance of (10.5) could not be constructed. A straightforward hand calculation thus developed into a computer problem in all cases studied. If irregular lattices are considered the situation is even more complicated.

Correction procedures are also available for regression models (see Johnston, 1972, Chapter 8). Provided that the pattern and extent of spatial autocorrelation is fully known, generalized least squares can be employed to allow for the correlated observations; again, however, this cannot be done for practical examples without computer programs. Finally, we note that ways of modifying the difference between means *t*-test to allow for spatially autocorrelated data are considered in Cliff and Ord (1975a). See also Section 11.6.

10.3.2 *Removing the correlation*

Given the practical difficulties of modifying existing models to allow for spatially autocorrelated data, it is of value to consider whether the data can be

---

[3] As Cliff and Ord (1975a) have noted, the formally correct procedure is always to use modified methods. However, the strategy outlined is much simpler if the independence assumption is met, and the loss of efficiency resulting from application of the strategy will generally be slight.

transformed in some way to remove the correlation. Then conventional models may be employed. This idea is discussed in Johnston (1972, Chapter 8) in the time series case, and it has been considered by Martin (1974) for spatially located data. (See also Student, 1914, and Curry, 1971). Denote the value of X in county i by x_i, and let us suppose that the $\{x_i\}$ values are spatially autocorrelated according to the first order scheme

$$x_i = \rho \sum_j w_{ij} x_j + u_i, \quad i = 1, 2, ..., n, \qquad (10.6)$$

where ρ and the $\{w_{ij}\}$ are as defined for equation (10.3), the summation is over the j counties contiguous to i, and the $\{u_i\}$ are error terms. This is the spatial equivalent of the time series model,

$$x_t = \rho x_{t-1} + u_t, \quad t = 2, 3, ..., T, \qquad (10.7)$$

where we use t to denote the typical time period, and T is the number of time periods. Equation (10.6) implies that the values of X are spatially autocorrelated among contiguous counties, while (10.7) implies that the observation at t is correlated only with the value in the immediately preceding time period.

For a scheme such as (10.7), the correlation can be removed, and the variate values made independent, by applying the difference operator,

$$\Delta_\rho x_t = x_t - \rho x_{t-1}, \quad t = 2, 3, ..., T. \qquad (10.8)$$

These variate differences can then be analyzed using conventional statistical models. However, for the spatial scheme, (10.6), the definition of an operator such as (10.8) is not obvious. Whereas in the time series case, the dependence can extend in one direction only—backwards—in the spatial case, the dependence is multilateral; that is, it can extend in all compass directions. See Whittle (1954) and Cliff and Ord (1973, Chapter 1) for a discussion of this problem.

10.3.3 *Spatial variate differencing*

Multilateral dependence means that spatial difference operators can be constructed in several different ways. One of the most commonly used (Lebart, 1969; Martin, 1974) is to define

$$\Delta x_i = x_i - \sum_j w_{ij} x_j. \qquad (10.9)$$

This difference filter is most effective in eliminating spatial autocorrelation when the autocorrelation parameter, ρ, in equation (10.6) is approximately one. Figure 10.3 shows a simple example of this difference operator applied to a set of contiguous counties.

Variate differencing may be used as a means of satisfying the independence assumption in analyses where either estimation or hypothesis testing is the aim. In hypothesis testing, the limited results available to date suggest that the following guidelines may be employed (see, for example, Cliff and Ord, 1975a):

(a) as noted earlier, if $\rho \leqslant 0$, use of the original observations will result in tests of hypotheses which are conservative, in the sense that the true risk of a Type I error will be less than the nominal (tabulated) value;

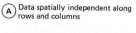

(A) Data spatially independent along rows and columns

-2.59	-3.59	-4.94	-4.76	3.31
-1.04	3.88	0.54	0.97	-4.54
1.32	1.67	4.14	-0.35	1.15
2.37	-3.43	-4.71	-2.89	-3.61
2.00	-3.88	2.95	-2.53	4.19

(B) Autocorrelated along rows and columns by amount $\rho = -0.8$

1.49	-6.04	0.51	-10.16	12.24
-4.15	7.19	-4.20	7.51	-12.15
3.00	-2.17	8.53	-6.15	8.78
0.04	0.50	-9.39	4.21	-10.32
5.23	-8.12	10.13	-9.61	12.16

(C) $\rho \sum_j w_{ij} x_j$ for Rook's case

4.08	-2.45	5.44	-5.40	8.92
-3.11	3.31	-5.75	6.53	-7.61
1.68	-3.84	4.38	-5.80	7.63
-2.33	3.93	-4.68	7.10	-6.11
3.23	-4.24	7.23	-7.08	7.97

(D) $\Delta x_i = x_i - \rho \sum_j w_{ij} x_j$

-2.59	-3.59	-4.94	-4.76	3.31
-1.04	3.88	0.54	0.97	-4.54
1.32	1.67	4.14	-0.35	1.15
2.37	-3.43	-4.71	-2.89	-3.61
2.00	-3.88	2.95	-2.53	4.19

Figure 10.3   The use of difference operators to reduce spatial autocorrelation in a set of observations. See equation (10.9).

(b) if ρ is slightly greater than zero, use of the original observations will result in a slightly liberal test, whereas variate differences may produce a very conservative test;

(c) as ρ approaches 1, the use of data which have been differenced may result in a slightly conservative test, but the conclusions will be much more reliable than those based upon the original observations. Tests based upon the original observations will carry a risk of a Type I error which is greatly in excess of the nominal level. Thse guidelines imply that, in hypothesis testing, a strategy which will always tend to err on the safe side in terms of the risk of a Type I error, is to use the original observations when $\rho \leqslant 0$, and to use variate differences when $\rho > 0$.

Table 10.2 Effect of spatial autocorrelation upon the variance of $\hat{\beta}$, the estimated regression coefficient, in a simple linear regression, for a 5×5 regular lattice.

Level of spatial autocorrelation		Estimated coefficient,	Estimated variance,	True variance,
in X, λ	in errors, ρ	$\hat{\beta}$	$\text{vâr}(\hat{\beta})$	$\text{var}(\hat{\beta})$
0.0	0.0	0.515	0.127	0.136
	0.2	0.577	0.126	0.139
	0.4	0.534	0.131	0.145
	0.6	0.436	0.190	0.217
	0.8	0.514	0.246	0.381
	1.0	0.631	0.504	1.197
0.4	0.0	0.534	0.113	0.124
	0.2	0.481	0.113	0.153
	0.4	0.479	0.119	0.159
	0.6	0.488	0.154	0.207
	0.8	0.433	0.251	0.552
	1.0	0.481	0.635	1.264
0.8	0.0	0.519	0.071	0.080
	0.2	0.538	0.077	0.099
	0.4	0.568	0.079	0.124
	0.6	0.502	0.088	0.140
	0.8	0.495	0.153	0.402
	1.0	0.476	0.454	0.965

Source: Martin, 1974, p. 190.

The only paper in which spatial variate differencing is used, and in which substantial empirical results are given, is that of Martin (1974). His findings illustrate many of the points we have made. Martin postulated the simple population regression model,

$$Y_i = 1.0 + 0.5X_i + \varepsilon_i \qquad i = 1, 2, ..., n, \quad (10.10)$$
$$= \alpha + \beta X_i + \varepsilon_i.$$

He assumed that X and the errors were autocorrelated spatially according to the first order schemes

$$X_i = \lambda \sum_j w_{ij} X_j + v_i, \tag{10.11}$$

and

$$\varepsilon_i = \rho \sum_j w_{ij} \varepsilon_j + \mu_i, \tag{10.12}$$

where λ and ρ are parameters expressing the level of autocorrelation in the same way as ρ_1 and ρ_2 in Section 10.2.1. The standard assumptions were made about v and μ. Using a Monte Carlo experiment similar to that described in Section 10.2.1, Martin empirically estimated the regression (10.10) using ordinary least squares for 5×5, 6×6 and 7×7 regular lattices and varying values of λ and ρ. Some of the results he obtained are shown in Table 10.2. It is immediately evident that the formulae led to underestimation of the true variance of $\hat{\beta}$. We use var($\hat{\beta}$) to denote this true variance, and vâr($\hat{\beta}$) to denote the estimated variance. This confirms the discussion in Section 10.2.2 and theoretical work in Johnston (1972, Chapter 8). Martin repeated his analysis after applying the operator (10.9) to (10.11) and (10.12). The revised results are given in Table 10.3. They show that vâr($\hat{\beta}$) is much closer to var($\hat{\beta}$) when $\rho, \lambda \geqslant 0.4$. It is for such values of ρ and λ that the errors in vâr($\hat{\beta}$) are worst in Table 10.2.

Table 10.3 Effect of spatial autocorrelation upon the variance of $\hat{\beta}$; regression estimated using first spatial differences for $\{X\}$ and $\{\varepsilon\}$.

Level of spatial autocorrelation		Estimated coefficient,	Estimated variance,	True variance,
in X, λ	in errors, ρ	$\hat{\beta}$	vâr($\hat{\beta}$)	var($\hat{\beta}$)
	0.0	0.547	0.132	0.147
	0.2	0.559	0.107	0.145
0.0	0.4	0.510	0.106	0.144
	0.6	0.450	0.100	0.130
	0.8	0.470	0.085	0.086
	1.0	0.489	0.082	0.082
	0.0	0.555	0.172	0.236
	0.2	0.507	0.138	0.179
0.4	0.4	0.479	0.117	0.145
	0.6	0.516	0.116	0.140
	0.8	0.496	0.104	0.138
	1.0	0.506	0.104	0.103
	0.0	0.495	0.185	0.191
	0.2	0.536	0.157	0.163
0.8	0.4	0.532	0.142	0.143
	0.6	0.482	0.130	0.131
	0.8	0.481	0.127	0.127
	1.0	0.500	0.124	0.123

Source: Martin, 1974, p. 191.

The discussion in this section would therefore suggest that, provided simple and reliable spatial variate differencing schemes can be defined, this approach may prove to be more practical than the methods discussed in Section 10.3.1. Finally, we note that for hypothesis testing, a procedure which may be employed, instead of either the correctly modified methods or variate differencing, is that discussed in Cliff and Ord (1973, p. 81), namely:

(1) generate m sample values of the test statistic such as t or X^2 under H_0 for the appropriate level of spatial dependence in the data;

(2) reject H_0 at the $100 \left(\dfrac{j+1}{m+1} \right)$ per cent level (one-tailed test) if the observed value of the test statistic exceeds at least all but the j largest generated values.

10.4 Spatial Stationarity

10.4.1 *Concepts of stationarity*

Most of the basic data examined by the human geographer are values of social and economic variables measured at various points, or collected for different areas, located in the plane. A fundamental property of such data is that they are generally non-stationary. Granger (1969) has described (wide sense) *stationarity* as 'an assumption that the relationship between values of the

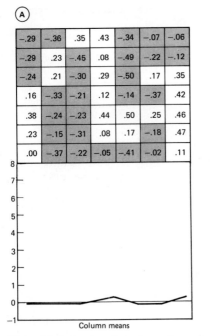
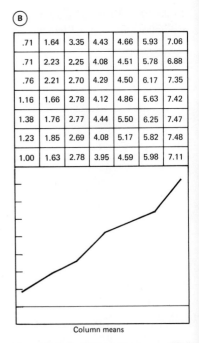

Figure 10.4   Regional configurations of variate values typical of (**A**) stationary and (**B**) non-stationary spatial series. The non-stationarity is manifested as a steady increase (trend) in the mean of the process from west to east across the map.

processes [generating the data] is the same for *every* pair of points whose *relative* positions are the same. Thus, for example, if direction did not matter, the degree to which those variables were related would depend only on the distance between the points. The relationship between values measured at Oxford and London will be the same as between values measured at two Lincolnshire villages 55 or so miles apart.' Clearly, this assumption is unrealistic for social and economic variables, and runs counter to traditional geographical concepts such as the region. Figure 10.4 illustrates a typical situation.

An example given by Granger (1969) will reinforce the above discussion. Granger took seasonally adjusted monthly unemployment figures for the period August 1958–March 1965 for seven regions of the UK, and computed the average coherence (a measure of correlation arising in spectral analysis— see Section 12.4.4) between all pairs of the series. The results he obtained are reproduced in Table 10.4.

Table 10.4   Average coherences between regional unemployment time series in the UK.

	London and South-East	East and South	South-West	Wales	North-West	North	Scotland
London and South-East	—						
East and South	0.819	—					
South-West	0.774	0.819	—				
Wales	0.654	0.629	0.631	—			
North-West	0.712	0.597	0.588	0.549	—		
North	0.686	0.673	0.581	0.432	0.514	—	
Scotland	0.644	0.553	0.534	0.483	0.566	0.583	—

Source: Granger, 1969, p. 23.

If spatial stationarity were present in these data, we would expect roughly the same coherences between contiguous regions across the country, whereas the figures in fact suggest a stronger relationship between areas in the South then in the North. As Granger comments, the Northern series seem to be more related to the London series than to each other, a result which is highly suggestive of spatially non-stationary data, and which may reflect the role of the South-East in determining the economic prosperity of the country.

Before we can proceed further and discuss the consequences of spatially non-stationary data for statistical modelling and hypothesis testing, we must make our definition of stationarity a little more precise.

10.4.2 *Formal definitions of stationarity*

Cliff and Ord (1975b) have made the following definitions. Suppose that data have been collected for a set of points or areas. Let $i = 1, 2, ..., n$ index the n members of the set. Denote the variate for the ith location by Y_i, and we assume that Y_i can be decomposed into a stochastic component, X_i, and a deterministic component, m_i, such that $E(X_i) = 0$, or $E(Y_i) = m_i$.

Definition 10.1 X_i is said to describe a spatially stationary process in the wide sense, or to be weakly spatially stationary, if the quantities,

$$E(X_i X_j) = \sigma(i,j), \tag{10.13}$$

depend only upon the relative positions of locations i and j. This is essentially the definition given by Granger (1969) and discussed above.

Definition 10.2 If X_i satisfies equation (10.13) and, in addition, the correlation between X_i and X_j depends only upon the distance between their locations and not upon the orientation of the chord between i and j, then the process is said to be weakly isotropic.

Definition 10.3 If the joint distribution of the $\{X_i\}$ depends only upon the relative positions of the locations, then the spatial process is strictly stationary.

Definition 10.4 The process is strictly isotropic if it is both strictly stationary and direction-invariant.

10.4.3 *Consequences of non-stationarity*

It is worth noting, to reinforce the discussion of the previous sections, that while geographical data may be highly spatially autocorrelated and yet stationary, non-stationarity and spatial dependence can be related. If the $\{X_i\}$ all have identical marginal distributions, then non-stationarity implies that the data are spatially dependent. However, many statistical models employed by geographers are based more generally upon the assumptions of either wide or strict sense stationarity. For example, the Poisson process, which forms the benchmark for the assessment of the degree of randomness in spatial point patterns (see Chapter 13), is a strictly stationary and strictly isotropic process.

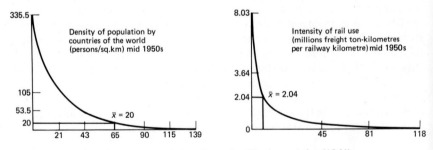

Figure 10.5   Examples of skewed data from the Ginsburg Atlas (1961).

Comparison with the Poisson is, therefore, only really valid if these assumptions can be sustained for the data set being analysed. Similarly, spectral methods, which are considered in Chapter 12, assume wide sense stationarity if serious distortion of the power and cross-spectra is to be avoided (see Granger, 1969), while estimation of many of the forecasting models described in Chapter 16 also depends upon a stationarity assumption. Indeed, it is difficult to make any progress at all in modelling spatial data if non-stationarities are present (Cliff and Ord, 1975b). However, stationarity can often be introduced into the data by de-trending with a difference filter of the sort given in equation (10.9). For a further discussion of this problem, see Kendall (1973).

10.5 Normality

10.5.1 *Problem of non-normality*

A further fundamental assumption of many statistical models is that the population or process generating the data is *normal*. While we know all too little about which distributions best describe geographical data, it is clear from the few studies already made that very little geographical data is normally distributed. For example, almost all the indices plotted as cumulative curves in the Ginsburg Atlas (1961) are strongly skewed (see Figure 10.5). Statistical models vary considerably in their robustness to the normality assumption, and we now consider two examples to illustrate a broad statement which may be followed. This is:

> ... that whereas tests on population means (i.e. Student's *t*-tests for the mean of a normal population and for the difference between means of two normal populations with the same variance) are rather insensitive to departures from normality, tests on variances (i.e. the X^2 test for the variance of a normal population, the *F*-test for the ratio of two normal population variances, and the modified LR [Likelihood Ratio] test for the equality of several normal variances ...) are very sensitive to such departures. Tests on means are robust; by comparison, tests on variances can only be described as frail. (Kendall and Stuart, 1967, pp. 465–66).

As our examples we take first, from Kendall and Stuart (1967, pp. 466–67), the difference between means test, *t*, given in equation (10.1). In addition to the sort of independence discussed in Section 10.2, *t* will only follow Student's *t* distribution if the numerator and denominator of (10.1) are independent, which holds for normal parents. However, Kendall and Stuart show that the correlation between the numerator and denominator is, asymptotically,

$$\rho = \frac{\kappa_3}{\{\kappa_2(\kappa_4 + 2\kappa_2^2)\}^{1/2}} \frac{(N_1 N_2)^{1/2}}{N_1 + N_2 - 2} \left(\frac{1}{N_1} - \frac{1}{N_2} \right). \tag{10.14}$$

Here $\kappa_2 = \mu_2$, $\kappa_3 = \mu_3$ and $\kappa_4 = \mu_4 - 3\mu_2^2$, where μ_r is the *r*th moment about the mean (*r*th central moment); in addition to previously used notation κ is called the *r*th *cumulant*. Equation (10.14) implies that the correlation between the numerator and denominator, ρ, will be equal to zero whenever κ_3 is zero— that is, the populations are symmetric—*whatever kurtosis is present in the data.* Similarly, if $N_1 = N_2$, $\rho = 0$. Thus 'if sample sizes are equal, even skewness in the parent is of little effect in disturbing normal theory. If the parent is symmetrical, the test will be robust even for differing sample sizes' (Kendall and Stuart, 1967, p. 467).

For tests on variances, however, the kurtosis in the populations is critical. We reproduce in Table 10.5 the findings given in Kendall and Stuart (1967, p. 468), and which are based on work by Box (1953). In Table 10.5, k is the number of samples whose variances are to be compared, and $\gamma_2 = \kappa_4/\kappa_2^2$. In a normal population, $\gamma_2 = 0$. $\gamma_2 > 0$ generally implies a 'peaked', compared with a normal, population, while $\gamma_2 < 0$ generally denotes a squashed or flattened population. What Table 10.5 shows is that when $\gamma_2 > 0$, the probability of a Type I error is dramatically increased; if $\gamma_2 < 0$, the risk of a Type II error is increased.

Table 10.5   True probability of exceeding the asymptotic normal theory critical value for α (size of test) $= 0.05$.

γ_2	$k = 2$	$k = 3$	$k = 5$	$k = 10$	$k = 30$
−1	0.0056	0.0025	0.0008	0.0001	0.0000001
0	0.05	0.05	0.05	0.05	0.05
1	0.110	0.136	0.176	0.257	0.498
2	0.166	0.224	0.315	0.489	0.849

Source: Kendall and Stuart, 1967, p. 468.

Given that we have established that, in some circumstances, parental normality is critical, we now ask how the problem may be overcome. This is considered in Sections 10.5.2 and 10.5.3.

10.5.2   *Transformations to normality*

The first possibility is to transform the data in such a way that the observations are brought close to normality. As far as we know, a common feature of geographical data is a positive skewness, and the correction most frequently used by geographers in that situation is the logarithmic transformation. For example, King (1961) used it for the values of urban environments in a study of city-spacing in the United States, Haggett (1964) for rural environments in a study of forest distribution in Southeast Brazil, and Cliff and Ord (1969) in a study of patterns of dairy farming in Eire.

Kendall and Stuart (1967, p. 469) point out that transformations designed to stabilize a variance, that is, to make it independent of some population

Table 10.6   Transformations used to normalize or stabilize data.

Distribution	Transformation	Remarks
Normal	None	—
Log-normal	Log X	Normalizes data
Binomial	Arc sine	Stabilizes variance
Poisson	$\sqrt{X}$	Stabilizes variance
Gamma	$\sqrt{X}$ or log X	Stabilizes variance (?)

Source: Krumbein, 1955b, p. 8.

parameter, also frequently serve to normalize the distribution to which they are applied. Such transformations are commonly used in analysis of variance (Ord, 1972a). Krumbein (1955b) discusses such applications in the analysis of land-use data, and he gives the table reproduced as Table 10.6. Figure 10.6 shows the effect of converting percentage data on forest distribution in Portugal into *angular* units through the arc-sine transformation. Tables for this conversion are given in Fisher and Yates (1957, Table X, p. 20).

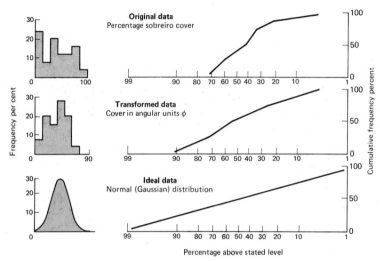

Figure 10.6   Use of arc-sine transformation for land-use data. Source: Haggett, 1961.

Frequently, however, there may be considerable doubt as to which transformation is appropriate, or indeed if a transformation is needed at all. Plotting alternative transformations on probability paper on which a normal distribution appears as a straight line is a useful trial-and-error method. Jeffers (1959) has presented a short-cut method for determining the appropriate transformation by comparing the sample variance and the sample mean on double logarithmic paper. See Figure 10.7. One, although by no means the

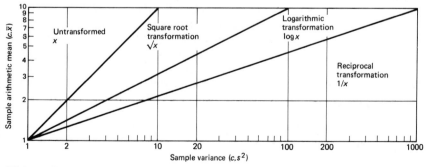

Figure 10.7   Graphical determination of appropriate data transformations to normality. On the diagram, c is an arbitrary scaling constant.

only, formal method of testing whether sample data can reasonably be assumed to have come from a normal population is to evaluate the moment ratios

$$b_1 = \frac{m_3^2}{m_2^3},$$ (10.15)

and

$$b_2 = \frac{m_4}{m_2^2}.$$ (10.16)

Here m_r is the rth sample moment about the sample mean. b_1 is a measure of skewness, while b_2 is a measure of kurtosis. Tests for departures for normality, plus tables, based on b_2, $\sqrt{b_1}$, and a combination of both ratios, are given in D'Agostino and Pearson (1973), while the power of b_2 in detecting non-normality is considered by Bowman (1973).

Thus transformation will allow non-normal data to be corrected. Against this, however, it must be remembered that once the transformed data have been analysed, *the results of the analysis and therefore their interpretation apply only to the transformed data*; it is all too easy to interpret the results as if they applied to the original data. Appreciating the implications of the results of statistical analyses of transformed data for the original forms may be extremely difficult, and individual workers must balance the theoretical gains against the practical losses for each problem. Krumbein (1957) has, however, reminded us that our concern for preserving certain forms of measurement (e.g. per cent scales in land use measurement) is often based more on convention than on any unique or immutable qualities of this form as against others: we are, for example, prepared to accept the pH scale of acidity despite the fact that differences between points on it are logarithmic and not arithmetic.

10.5.3 *Distribution-free procedures*

The second approach, instead of using normal theory methods (either because they are robust to non-normality or because transformations of the observations will make the data approximately normal) is to abandon them altogether. In their place, we can use so-called *distribution-free* methods which do not depend on the form of the parent distributions at all, provided that they are continuous. Kendall and Stuart (1967, Chapter 31) give an account of such methods, while an elementary text is that of Siegel (1956). We do, however, pay a penalty for using distribution-free, rather than normal, methods; namely, their power against the equivalent normal methods is always less when the assumptions of the latter can be approximately sustained.

10.6 Irregular Collecting Areas

In general, the results of statistical tests using area based data are affected by the sizes and shapes of the territorial units for which the data are collected. In

Section 2.7 something was seen of the great variety in both the sizes and the shapes of *territories*. Whether as states, counties, or parishes, these territories form the most common source of locational data. It is true that a few countries, such as Sweden and the USA, record some population data on regular grid systems (see, for example, Hägerstrand, 1955, and Passonneau and Wurman, 1966), but a very high proportion of essentially locational data is likely to be available for territorial units only, at least for the next few decades (Coates and Rawstron, 1971). In this section, we therefore look at the implications of these irregular collecting areas for locational analysis, and the ways in which observations based on them may be standardized.

10.6.1 *Impact on statistical measures*

The clearest illustration of the yoking of statistical quantities to the characteristics of the collecting area arises with measurements of density. Duncan studied an apparently simple question: what is the density of population in an area of downtown Chicago centred on 31st Street and Indiana Avenue? (Duncan, Cuzzort and Duncan, 1961, p. 35). If the 'immediate vicinity' is defined by a census tract of 0.024 square miles, the answer is 91,300 people per square mile. However, by widening the term, 'vicinity', to include the local community area of about one and a half square miles, the population density is halved. Clearly there is an inescapable indeterminacy about density ratios dependent on variable collecting units. For comparable densities, e.g. comparisons between cities, the situation becomes still more difficult. As Table 10.7 shows, Chicago may be either more or less densely populated than Detroit depending on the areal definition used for the two cities. Still more striking contrasts are shown with comparisons over time; the population of the United States appears to be becoming more concentrated on the evidence of the counties, but more dispersed on the evidence of the states (Figure 10.8).

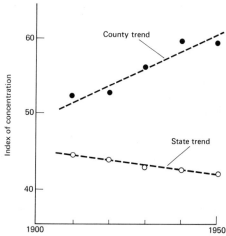

Figure 10.8   Indices of population concentration for the United States by counties and states. Source: Duncan, Cuzzort and Duncan, 1961, p. 86.

Table 10.7   Urban population densities under alternative census boundaries.

Areal definition	Chicago (C)* (inhab./sq. ml.)	Detroit (D)* (inhab./sq. ml.)	Ratio (D/C)
City	17,450	13,249	0.76
Urbanized area	7,713	6,734	0.86
Standard metropolitan area	1,519	1,535	1.01

Source: Duncan, Cuzzort, and Duncan, 1961, pp. 35–6.
* 1950.

Robinson (1956) makes clear the problem inherent in density comparisons with a simple hypothetical example. Figure 10.9A shows a study region which has been partitioned into six sub-regions, each of equal area, $A = 2$, units. The values of two variables, X and Y, in each sub-region are also shown. Figures 10.9B and 10.9C are obtained from 10.9A by various combinations of the original six sub-regions. Using the values for X and Y, the sample Pearson product moment correlation coefficient, r, was computed, yielding $r = 0.715$ (Figure 10.9A), $r = 0.875$ (Figure 10.9B) and $r = 0.500$ (Figure 10.9C). Clearly, the value of r varies with the subdivision used, not withstanding the identical distribution of values of X and Y in the study region.

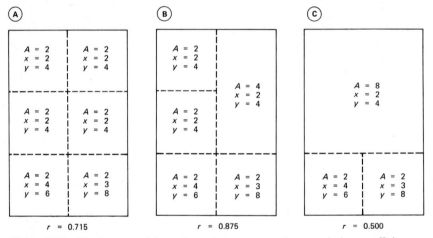

Figure 10.9 The impact of boundary changes upon the correlation coefficient, r. Source: Robinson, 1956, p. 234.

The dependence of the correlation coefficient upon the territorial base is well known to statisticians. Thus, Yule and Kendall (1957, pp. 310–13) illustrate this problem by computing the correlation between the yields per acre of wheat and potatoes in the 48 counties of England and Wales in 1936. They obtained $r = 0.22$. The 48 counties were grouped into 24. The yield of each pair of combined counties was defined as the unweighted arithmetic mean of the yields of the two counties grouped together. The revised r value was 0.30. Repeating the process for 12, 6 and 3 counties, they obtained, successively, $r = 0.58$, $r = 0.76$ and $r = 0.99$.

Similar difficulties arise with comparison of movements. For example, Table 10.8 shows the differences between Belgium and the Netherlands in the proportion of out-commuters in 1947 (Chisholm, 1960, p. 187). The difference is, at first sight, striking. But when (i) the subdivisions on which the figures are calculated and (ii) the census definition of a commuter are considered, the differences begin to look less conclusive. The Dutch basic unit for the calculations, the *Gemeente*, had an area on average three times as great as the Belgian unit, the *Commune*. Moreover, because of the census definition of a commuter (i.e. a worker moving outside the territorial unit in which he resides), the smaller the collecting unit, the greater the apparent amount of commuting. Some models which enable estimates to be made of the probability that an individual's journey-to-work will take him outside the territorial unit in which he resides, conditional upon the size of that unit, are considered in Kulldorff (1955).

Table 10.8   Apparent contrasts in commuting.

Country:	Belgium (1947)	Netherlands (1947)
Commuters, percentage	40.0	15.2
Administrative unit, mean size in hectares*	1,880	6,670

Source: Chisholm, 1960, p. 187.
   * Weighted according to inhabitants in each administrative unit.

Unless great care is taken, such 'mirage' effects are likely to become more common as more quantitative studies are made by geographers using secondary statistical sources. Indeed, one statistician, M. G. Kendall, has warned that with certain coefficients of geographical association, we can get any coefficient we choose by juggling with the collecting boundaries (Florence, 1944, p. 113). It is an open question whether detailed medical maps (e.g. Murray, 1962) in which mortality indices are most carefully standardized for age and sex should not equally well be standardized for the size of the collecting areas for which they are computed. We need to be reassured that some of the apparently 'unhealthy' areas, representing small pockets of disease in Lancashire and Yorkshire, owe nothing to the fragmented system of local government areas.

Thus, the dependence of statistical measures upon the data base makes any inter-regional comparisons very difficult. The difficulties are increased by the fact that, in the analysis of regional values, we are frequently transforming what are essentially continuous data into discontinuous point data.

10.6.2 *Standardization of collecting areas*

(a) *Area-weighting solutions.* Dangers in leaving the size of census tracts out of account in correlation studies have led several geographers to consider the possibility of weighting the observations, in the definition of the correlation coefficient, by the size of area for which they are collected (Robinson, 1956; Thompson, 1957; Robinson, Lindberg and Brinkman, 1961; Thomas and

Anderson, 1965). However, as Yule and Kendall (1957) state, there is as yet no complete answer using this approach. To have generality, any weighting procedure must take into account the form of the autocorrelation function among observations. The area weighting solutions proposed to date work only for spatially independent observations.

(*b*) *Other solutions.* A series of other attempts by various geographers to solve the problems have been noted in Section 8.4.2. Most of them are smoothing operations of one sort or another, such as aggregating many and irregular collecting units into fewer but more regular areas; eliminating aberrant areas; and transforming the units into a regular grid by, for example, trend surface mapping. The drawback is that once this has been done, it is difficult to determine how much of the pattern in the data over space is due to genuine relationships, and how much is due to the smoothing operation employed.

In summary, we have to recognize that the analysis of areal data *is* conditional upon the size and shape of the data collection units, and that the results of such analyses should be interpreted with this in mind. Work on the aggregation of economic variables may be useful in this context (Theil, 1971), while a further alternative might be to use the trend surface model or the nested analysis of variance described in Chapter 12 to determine which scale (size) of areal units is most important. See also Harvey (1968a). An alternative but pie-in-the-sky solution would be for *all* data to be collected on the same sized regular grid, so that distortions due to this source could be regarded as a constant. Such a solution would have the added advantage of making all spatial modelling very much easier. The irregularly spaced and discontinuous nature of most spatial data is a severe handicap to modelling (Granger, 1969; Cliff and Ord, 1975b). It implies that, wherever possible, we should try to develop models conditionally upon the structure of the data collection units. This restricts the inferences that can be made from the analyses, but it means that some progress is possible. As discussed in Cliff and Ord (1975b), the spatial autocorrelation models considered in Chapter 11 provide an example of this approach.

10.7 Conclusions

In this chapter, we have looked at several properties of spatial data which make difficult their analysis using conventional statistical methods. Locational data are generally spatially autocorrelated, non-stationary, non-normal, irregularly spaced, and discontinuous. The consequences of these properties for statistical analysis have been outlined, and possible remedies have been proposed. Thus, to overcome the lack of independence, we have considered as alternatives, the modification of the statistical models to allow for dependent data, and variate differencing filters. In the case of non-normality, the possibilities are transforming the data, or the use of distribution-free methods. Finally, the great variety of grids upon which spatial data are measured implies that, wherever possible, methods must be developed conditional upon the lattice used.

11 Spatial Autocorrelation

11.1 Introduction

The analysis of spatially located data is one of the principal concerns of the geographer. Such data arise in two basic forms. First, we may have collected variate values at a series of points, or for a series of areas, in a study region. It can then be argued that the locations of the points or areas to which the data refer will provide some information about the spatial pattern of variation in the data. That is, the locations of the observation units are taken as given, and attention is focussed upon the spatial pattern in the variate values of these units. Second, however, we may be more interested in the spatial pattern formed by the locations of the units themselves (i.e. their relation to each other) than in the variate values.

These two sorts of spatial data are analysed in quite different ways. For example, appropriate techniques for the analysis of spatial pattern in variate values are the spatial autocorrelation and trend surface models, while the evaluation of pattern in locations might proceed by nearest neighbour, quadrat count or Thiessen polygon methods. It is the purpose of this and the next two chapters to examine, with examples, some of the models in the two categories. The literature on the analysis of spatial pattern in variate values is vast, and we have divided our coverage into two parts. The first, which is the theme of this chapter, is concerned with evaluating the level of dependence among spatially located observations. We shall see that the same techniques can also be used in the time domain. The second, covered in the next chapter, is concerned with those methods which help to identify the spatial (and temporal) scale levels at which geographical processes are operating. Finally, the literature describing ways of studying the patterns formed by locations is considered in Chapter 13.

11.2 Concepts of Autocorrelation

11.2.1 *Spatial autocorrelation*

Consider a study area which has been exhaustively partitioned into n non-overlapping sub-areas, such as the counties of England and Wales, or the states of the United States. Suppose that a random variable, X, has been measured in each of the sub-areas, and that the value of X in the typical sub-area, i, is x_i. X could describe either (1) a single population, from which repeated drawings are made to give the x_i; (2) n separate populations, one for each county; or (3) a partition of a finite population among the n counties. The underlying population model used will depend upon the conceptualisation of the problem in hand. For example, the incidence of lung cancer in the English counties might be considered under (1), gross national product of the countries of Western Europe under (2), and the distribution of the Democrat vote by states in a US Presidential Election under (3). Although the examples we have given are for area-based data, variate values collected at points could equally well be analysed using the methods to be described. Thus we might be interested in the spatial variability of rainfall or temperature at meteorological stations.

A basic property of such spatially located data is that the set of values, $\{x_i\}$, are likely to be related over space. This idea underlies the concept of the region in geography, and as discussed in Section 10.2, has been reiterated by Tobler (1970), Gould (1970) and Cliff and Ord (1973). If the $\{x_i\}$ display interdependence over space, we say that the data are *spatially autocorrelated*. Following Cliff and Ord (1973, Appendix 1), a plausible model of the spatial interdependence among the $\{x_i\}$ is the scheme,

$$x_i = \rho \sum_j w_{ij} x_j + u_i, \quad i = 1, 2, \ldots, n. \tag{11.1}$$

Here, the $\{u_i\}$ are independent and identically distributed variates with common variance, σ^2. The set of weights, $\{w_{ij}\}$, as in Section 10.2, are any set of non-negative constants that specify which j sub-areas in the study area have variate values directly spatially related with x_i. We assume that the $\{w_{ij}\}$ are scaled so that $\sum_j w_{ij} = 1$, $i = 1, 2, \ldots, n$. The constant, ρ, is a measure of the overall level of spatial autocorrelation among the $\{x_i x_j\}$ pairs for which $w_{ij} > 0$. For example, suppose that $w_{ij} = 1$ (unscaled) if j is physically continuous to i, and $w_{ij} = 0$ otherwise. Then (11.1) reduces to the model used in the Monte Carlo experiment of Section 10.2.1, and in equation (10.6). More general sets of weights may, however, be constructed, and the reader is referred to Cliff and Ord (1973, Section 1.4.2) and to Cliff and Ord (1975c) for a further discussion of the choice of weights. For example, Tobler's 'first law of geography' given at the beginning of Section 10.2, might be captured by

$$w_{ij} = d_{ij}^{-\alpha} \tag{11.2}$$

where d_{ij} is the distance between points or areas, i and j, and α is a 'friction of distance' parameter as used in many gravity and interaction models (see Section 2.4.2). Finally, when $\rho > 0$ in model (11.1), we say that there is *positive* spatial autocorrelation among the $\{x_i\}$, while $\rho < 0$ implies *negative* spatial autocorrelation. The former case is characterized by similar $\{x_i\}$ values in sub-areas with non-zero $\{w_{ij}\}$ values, and the latter by very different (for example $+/-$) relationships (cf. Figure 10.2). If $\rho = 0$, there is said to be no spatial autocorrelation in the study area on X.

11.2.2 Space–time autocorrelation

As noted in the discussion of equation (10.7), model (11.1) is the spatial equivalent of the time series model,

$$x_t = \rho x_{t-k} + u_t, \quad t = 1, 2, ..., T, \tag{11.3}$$

where terms are as defined in Section 10.3.2. Economists have long recognized that economic time series display temporal autocorrelation. But the fundamental difference between (11.3) and (11.1) is that dependence in time can only extend backwards, whereas in the spatial case the dependence is multi-directional (Whittle, 1954). Frequently, however, the locational analyst is concerned with understanding the processes which have produced regional patterns in economic data. That is, as Bennett (1974) has noted, he is not concerned solely with the analysis of cross-sectional (spatial) data. His task is to unravel the complex patterns of autocorrelation in both time *and* space to gain some insight into the functional dependencies between areas implied by the presence of autocorrelation. Thus we might postulate that

$$x_{it} = f(x_{i,t-k}, x_{j,t-k}), \quad k = 1, 2, ...; j \neq i. \tag{11.4}$$

If our time–space matrix is as shown in Figure 11.1, model (11.4) would imply a complex 'cone' of dependencies between regions going back through time. In addition, the time interval between our data recording points is often

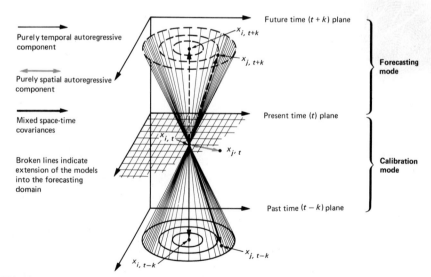

Figure 11.1   Pattern of dependencies between regions in time and space (cf. Figure 16.2).

sufficiently long, compared with the rate of operation of the geographical process, that what appear as simultaneous effects beween regions may occur. In terms of the forecasting models to be discussed in Chapter 16, the dependency of x_{it} on $x_{i,t-1},...,x_{i,t-k}$ in equation (11.4) is, as shown in Figure 11.1, a purely *temporal* autoregressive element; the simultaneous effects represent a purely *spatial* autoregressive component; while the remaining terms in the historical part of the 'cone' of Figure 11.1 represent general space-time covariances. The cone of dependencies which stretches from the present into the past will also project into the future. That part of the cone shows which regions, j, will be affected by area i in the future as multiplier effects work themselves through the time–space system. Although the coefficients to be developed in the next section are defined in the context of *spatial* autocorrelation, we shall see that they are analogous to time series measures of autocorrelation, and that they can be used for that purpose.

11.3 Testing for Autocorrelation*

11.3.1 *Some alternative measures*

The simplest way in which the set of observations, $\{x_i\}$ can be measured is on a binary nominal scale. Conventionally, we put $x_i = 1$ if an event has occurred in the ith sub-area, and $x_i = 0$ if it has not. Moran (1948) has called the former black, B, sub-areas, and the latter white, W, sub-areas, thus creating a two-colour choropleth map. Two measures of spatial autocorrelation among the B and W sub-areas are the test statistics

$$BB = \tfrac{1}{2}\sum_{(2)} w_{ij}x_i x_j,$$ (11.5)

and

$$BW = \tfrac{1}{2}\sum_{(2)} w_{ij}(x_i - x_j)^2.$$ (11.6)

Here

$$\sum_{(2)} = \sum_{\substack{i=1 \\ i \neq j}}^{n} \sum_{j=1}^{n}.$$

BB and BW are the (weighted) numbers of BB and BW links in the study area. BW also reduces to the 'number of runs' statistic in one dimension (Siegel, 1956, pp. 52–58), and is a test of randomness in a time series (see Kendall, 1973). Cliff and Ord (1973, Chapter 1) discuss the extensions in the literature of (11.5) and (11.6) to k colour choropleth maps.

If X is ranked or interval scaled, BB and BW will not be efficient measures of spatial autocorrelation since information will be lost in reducing the data to a binary classification. Instead of doing this, we might use one or other of the coefficients

$$I = \left(\frac{n}{W}\right)\frac{\sum_{(2)} w_{ij}z_i z_j}{\sum z_i^2},$$ (11.7)

or

$$c = \frac{n-1}{2W} \frac{\sum_{(2)} w_{ij}(x_i - x_j)^2}{\sum z_i^2}, \tag{11.8}$$

where $z_i = x_i - \bar{x}$ and $W = \sum_{(2)} w_{ij}$. Cliff and Ord (1973, Chapter 1) discuss the origins and development of (11.7) and (11.8). Both coefficients are in the classic form for a measure of correlation; that is, I and c are ratios of covariance and squared differences respectively, to variance, among the variate values.

In terms of temporal autocorrelation, we note that I reduces in one dimension to the usual serial correlation coefficient; c corresponds in form (a) to the Durbin and Watson d statistic (Durbin and Watson, 1950, 1951, 1971) used to search for temporal autocorrelation in regression residuals, and (b) to the von Neumann ratio.

So far, we have descriptive measures of the degree of spatial autocorrelation in a map, and Table 11.1 summarizes (in qualitative terms), the kinds of values that each statistic (11.5)–(11.8), will take on for various values of ρ in model (11.1).

Suppose, however, that we wish to test formally $H_0: \rho = 0$ against $H_1: \rho \neq 0$ in (11.1). We now indicate how this can be done.

Table 11.1 Values of autocorrelation coefficients for values of ρ.

	Coefficient			
ρ	BB	BW	I	c
<0	low	high	low	high
>0	high	low	high	low

11.3.2 Distribution theory

Cliff and Ord (1973, Section 2.4) have shown that BB, BW, I and c are all asymptotically normally distributed as $n \to \infty$ when $\rho = 0.0$ in (11.1), provided that in the weights matrix, $\mathbf{W} \equiv \{w_{ij}\}$, no definite set of sub-areas dominates the study region as, for example, does the articulation point in a star lattice. See also Sen (1976). Thus to test $H_0: \rho = 0$ against $H_1: \rho \neq 0$, we may treat

$$z = \{s - \mu'_1(s)\}/\sigma(s) \tag{11.9}$$

as (approximately) a standard normal deviate (Table A1), where $\mu'_1(s)$ and $\sigma(s)$ denote the mean and standard deviation under H_0 of the statistic, s, which might be any one of those given in equations (11.5)–(11.8). The null hypothesis is rejected whenever the observed value of z falls in the critical region [that is, for a two-tailed test, if $|z| \geqslant z_\alpha$, where $P(|z| \geqslant z_\alpha | H_0) = \alpha$, and α is the size of the test]. Serious inferential error is unlikely unless $n \lesssim 20$, when certain correction factors should be used (Cliff and Ord, 1973, Chapter 2).

We now require expressions for $\mu_1'(s)$ and $\sigma(s)$ for the various measures of autocorrelation under the null hypothesis of no spatial autocorrelation in the study area. We assume initially that X represents an 'original data' variate, rather than derived data such as regression residuals. Given this assumption, the location and scale parameters, μ_1' and σ respectively, for BB and BW under H_0 have been derived under two assumptions (Cliff and Ord, 1973, Chapter 1).

(1) free sampling (with replacement), where the individual sub-areas are independently coded B or W with probabilities p and $(1-p)$ respectively; or

(2) non-free sampling (without replacement), where we assume that each sub-area has the same probability, *a priori*, of being B or W, but colouring is subject to the overall constraint that there are n_1 sub-areas coded B and n_2 coded W, where $n_1 + n_2 = n$. These assumptions will be violated if the coding process is not independent for each county (that is, if there exist interactions between counties), *or* if counties have different probabilities of B or W coding.

For I and c, there are also two models for H_0:

(1) assumption N, normality, that the $\{x_i\}$ are the result of n independent drawings from a normal population or populations; and

(2) assumption R, randomization: whatever the underlying distribution of X, we consider the position of the observed value of I (or c) in the set of values obtained if I (or c) was evaluated for every possible spatial arrangement of the $\{x_i\}$ in the county system. There are $n!$ such values. In effect, we are asking if the observed pattern of $\{x_i\}$ values, as judged by I or c, is in any sense unusual in the set of all possible patterns that the $\{x_i\}$ could have formed. Again, departures from assumptions N or R may indicate either interactions between counties or non-identical distributions.

We now record the first two moments of the various measures under the different assumptions. Full details are given in Cliff and Ord (1973, Chapters 1 and 2).

Definitions As subscripts, $N =$ assuming normality, $R =$ under randomization,

$$S_1 = \tfrac{1}{2}\textstyle\sum_{(2)}(w_{ij}+w_{ji})^2,$$

$$S_2 = \sum_{i=1}^{n}(w_{i.}+w_{.i})^2,$$

b_2 defined in equation (10.16)

$$w_{i.} = \sum_{j=1}^{n} w_{ij}, \qquad w_{.j} = \sum_{i=1}^{n} w_{ij},$$

$$n^{(k)} = n(n-1)\dots(n-k+1).$$

In the equations for BB and BW links, we have used the general notation, p_r and p_s, to denote the probability that a county is of colour r or s (say B or W), and n_r and n_s to denote the number of counties coloured r or s (B or W, for example).

Choropleth maps

(a) Free sampling

BB

$$\mu'_1 = \tfrac{1}{2}Wp_r^2,$$ (11.10)

$$\mu_2 = \tfrac{1}{4}[S_1 p_r^2 + (S_2 - 2S_1)p_r^3 + (S_1 - S_2)p_r^4].$$ (11.11)

BW

$$\mu'_1 = Wp_r p_s,$$ (11.12)

$$\mu_2 = \tfrac{1}{4}[2S_1 p_r p_s + (S_2 - 2S_1)p_r p_s(p_r + p_s) + 4(S_1 - S_2)p_r^2 p_s^2].$$ (11.13)

(b) Non-free sampling

BB

$$\mu'_1 = \frac{Wn_r^{(2)}}{2n^{(2)}},$$ (11.14)

$$\mu_2 = \tfrac{1}{4}\left[\frac{S_1 n_r^{(2)}}{n^{(2)}} + \frac{(S_2 - 2S_1)n_r^{(3)}}{n^{(3)}} + \frac{(W^2 + S_1 - S_2)n_r^{(4)}}{n^{(4)}} - W^2\left(\frac{n_r^{(2)}}{n^{(2)}}\right)^2\right].$$ (11.15)

BW

$$\mu'_1 = \frac{Wn_r n_s}{n^{(2)}},$$ (11.16)

$$\mu_2 = \tfrac{1}{4}\left[\frac{2S_1 n_r n_s}{n^{(2)}} + \frac{(S_2 - 2S_1)n_r n_s(n_r + n_s - 2)}{n^{(3)}}\right.$$
$$\left. + \frac{4(W^2 + S_1 - S_2)n_r^{(2)} n_s^{(2)}}{n^{(4)}} - 4W^2\left(\frac{n_r n_s}{n^{(2)}}\right)^2\right].$$ (11.17)

The coefficient I

$$E_N(I) = E_R(I) = -(n-1)^{-1},$$ (11.18)

$$E_N(I^2) = \frac{n^2 S_1 - nS_2 + 3W^2}{W^2(n^2 - 1)},$$ (11.19)

$$E_R(I^2) = \frac{n[(n^2 - 3n + 3)S_1 - nS_2 + 3W^2] - b_2[(n^2 - n)S_1 - 2nS_2 + 6W^2]}{(n-1)^{(3)}W^2}.$$ (11.20)

The coefficient c

$$E_N(c) = E_R(c) = 1,$$ (11.21)

$$\mu_2 = \operatorname{var}_N(c) = \frac{(2S_1 + S_2)(n-1) - 4W^2}{2(n+1)W^2},$$ (11.22)

$$\operatorname{var}_R(c) = \{(n-1)S_1[n^2 - 3n + 3 - (n-1)b_2]$$
$$- \tfrac{1}{4}(n-1)S_2[n^2 + 3n - 6 - (n^2 - n + 2)b_2]$$ (11.23)
$$+ W^2[n^2 - 3 - (n-1)^2 b_2]\}/n(n-2)^{(2)}W^2.$$

11.3.3 *Comparison of measures*

Cliff and Ord (1973, Chapter 7) have made a fairly extensive comparison of the relative power of the various measures of spatial autocorrelation described above. (We define the power of a statistical test of a hypothesis as the probability that the test will reject the alternative hypothesis, H_1, when the alternative is false. The power is thus greatest when the probability of a Type II error is least.) Both Monte Carlo and analytical methods were used. Their general ranking of the coefficients from best to worst was I, c, BW, and BB. They also showed that the likelihood ratio test approaches I as $\rho \to 0$. Thus, for alternatives near H_0, and large samples, I is the best statistic available. Further, empirical studies (Cliff and Ord, 1973, Chapter 7) indicate that the ranking noted above applies for small samples even when ρ is not near zero. These findings suggest the general rule: use I with interval and ranked data; use BW for choropleth maps.

11.4 Autocorrelation in Regression

11.4.1 *Testing regression residuals for autocorrelation*

As noted in Section 10.2.2, a basic assumption of the classic ordinary least squares regression model,

$$\mathbf{Y} = \mathbf{X}\boldsymbol{\beta} + \boldsymbol{\varepsilon} \tag{11.24}$$

is that the $(n \times 1)$ vector of error terms, $\boldsymbol{\varepsilon}$, should satisfy the equations

$$E(\boldsymbol{\varepsilon}) = \mathbf{0} \tag{11.25}$$

and

$$\mathrm{var}(\boldsymbol{\varepsilon}) = \sigma^2 \mathbf{I}, \tag{11.26}$$

where $\mathbf{I}$ is the identity matrix. Equations (11.25) and (11.26) imply, among other things, that the errors should have mean zero and be pairwise uncorrelated. If the errors are not pairwise uncorrelated—that is, if they are autocorrelated—then inflation of R^2, t and F will result when the autocorrelation is positive, and overstatement of the significance of any results obtained will occur. With spatially located data, autocorrelated errors are common, and so it is very important to be able to test whether assumption (11.26) has been satisfied. Appropriate allowances can then be made as the examples to be discussed in Section 11.4.2 will show. Although any of the coefficients (11.5)–(11.8) may be used as *measures* of spatial autocorrelation in regression residuals, they may *not* be tested for significance with the distribution theory given in Section 11.3.2. Durbin and Watson (1950, 1951) and Theil (1965) have shown that the residuals from a *calculated* regression are not independent, even under H_0, as required by the assumptions outlined in Section 11.3.2.

Denote the calculated residual for the ith sub-area by

$$e_i = y_i - \sum_{j=1}^{k} x_{ij} b_j, \quad i = 1, 2, ..., n. \tag{11.27}$$

Here y_i is the value of the dependent variable, Y, x_{ij} denotes the value of the jth regressor variable, X, for area $i(x_{i1} = 1$ for all $i)$, and b_j are the least squares estimators of the parameters, β_1, β_2, ..., β_k. We assume that there are k regressor variables. Then, following Cliff and Ord (1973, Chapter 5) the first two moments in the regression case of the statistic,

$$I = (n/W) \sum\nolimits_{(2)} w_{ij} e_i e_j / \sum_{i=1}^{n} e_i^2, \tag{11.28}$$

are, under assumption N,

$$E(I) = -I_{1x}/(n-k), \tag{11.29}$$

where

$$I_{1x} = (n/W) \sum\nolimits_{(2)} w_{ij} d_{ij},$$

$$d_{ij} = \mathbf{x}_i'(\mathbf{X}'\mathbf{X})^{-1}\mathbf{x}_j,$$

$$\mathbf{x}_i' = (x_{i1}, ..., x_{ik}), \quad \mathbf{X} = \{x_{ij}\},$$
$$(n \times k)$$

and

$$\text{var}(I) = \frac{n}{(n-k)W^2} \left[\frac{n^2 S_1 - n S_2 + 3W^2}{n^2} + \frac{1}{n} \sum_{i=1}^{n} \sum_{j=1}^{n} (w_{i.} + w_{.i})(w_{j.} + w_{.j})d_{ij} \right.$$

$$+ 2\left(\sum\nolimits_{(2)} w_{ij} d_{ij}\right)^2 - \left\{ \sum\nolimits_{(3)} (w_{ik} + w_{ki})(w_{jk} + w_{kj})d_{ij} + \sum\nolimits_{(2)} (w_{ij} + w_{ji})^2 d_{ii} \right\}$$

$$\left. + \frac{1}{n} \sum\nolimits_{(3)} (w_{ij} + w_{ji})(w_{ik} + w_{ki})(d_{ii} d_{jk} - d_{ij} d_{ik}) \right] - (n-k)^{-2}. \tag{11.30}$$

A test of significance may be carried out as before to determine significant departure from H_0.

11.4.2 *Causes of and solutions for spatially autocorrelated residuals*

We have noted above that detection of spatial autocorrelation among regression residuals implies the fitted model is inappropriate in some way, and enables remedial action to be taken. The following examples, taken from Cliff and Ord (1973, Chapter 6) have been chosen to illustrate the principal causes of autocorrelated residuals and the kinds of solutions which may be employed.

Cliff and Ord (1973) examined three regressions given by O'Sullivan (1968) in a paper on the spatial structure of the Eire economy. The three regressions were as follows:

Regression (1)
$\quad Y =$ 1961 population as percentage of 1926 population by county;
$\quad X =$ accessibility of each county on the arterial road network (ARA).
$\qquad$ (a) $y = 133.45 - 0.0103x \quad R^2 = 0.40$,
$\qquad$ (b) $\log y = 4.19 - 0.6210x \quad R^2 = 0.52$.

Regression (2)
  Y = value of retail sales (£000) by county;
  X = total personal income (£000) by county.
$$y = -2393.8 + 0.5405x \quad R^2 = 0.99.$$

Regression (3)
  Y = the percentage, in value terms, of the gross agricultural output of each county consumed by itself;
  X = ARA.
$$y = -8.49 + 0.0053x \quad R^2 = 0.70.$$

Regression (1) was an attempt to relate the rate of rural depopulation to accessibility. Regression (3) is in the same spirit, and tried to relate accessibility to a measure of the level of subsistence.

The authors tested the residuals from each of these regressions for spatial autocorrelation using equations (11.28)–(11.30) and the following forms of **W**:

1. $w_{ij} = 1$ if counties i and j had a length of county boundary in common, and $w_{ij} = 0$ otherwise (binary weights);

2. $w_{ij} = d_{ij}^{-1} \beta_{i(j)}$, where d_{ij} was the distance between the geographical centroids of counties i and j, and $\beta_{i(j)}$ denoted the proportion of the perimeter of county i in contact with county j.

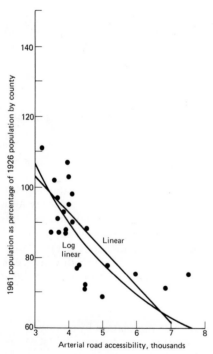

Figure 11.2   Graph of data and regression lines for O'Sullivan's regressions 1(a) and 1(b). Source: Cliff and Ord, 1973, p. 110.

Table 11.2   Results of tests for spatial autocorrelation in regression residuals from O'Sullivan (1969).

Value of autocorrelation coefficient, I	Binary weights: regression				Unstandardized boundary length/county centre distance weights: regression				Standardized boundary length/county centre distance weights: regression			
	1(a)	1(b)	2	3	1(a)	1(b)	2	3	1(a)	1(b)	2	3
I	0.190	0.130	0.230	0.397	0.247	0.189	0.228	0.454	0.155	0.080	0.293	0.436
$E(I)$	−0.056	−0.058	−0.042	−0.056	−0.058	−0.060	−0.042	−0.058	−0.059	−0.062	−0.042	−0.059
$\sigma(I)$	0.114	0.113	0.117	0.114	0.144	0.143	0.146	0.144	0.139	0.139	0.144	0.139
Standard deviate	2.17	1.67	2.32	3.98	2.12	1.74	1.85	3.56	1.54	1.02	2.32	3.56
	*	*	*	**	*	*	*	**			*	**

*significant at $\alpha = 0.05$ level (one tailed test).
**significant at $\alpha = 0.01$ level (one tailed test).
Source: Cliff and Ord, 1973, p. 108.

3. $w_{ij} = w_{ij}/\sum_j w_{ij}$, where the summation is over the j counties contiguous to i. The results of the analysis are given in Table 11.2.

Non-spatial adjustments. In the case of regression (1), whatever the form of **W**, the positive spatial autocorrelation among the residuals from regression 1(a) is stronger than that among the residuals from regression 1(b). One of the causes of autocorrelated disturbances is an incorrect specification of the form of the relationship between y and x. For example, as Johnston (1972) states, if we specify a linear relation between y and x when the true relation is a quadratic, then the disturbance term associated with the linear relation will contain a term in x^2. If there is any autocorrelation in the x^2 values, then we shall obtain autocorrelation in the composite disturbance term. As Figure 11.2 shows, in the case of regression (1), the true relation between y and x is probably best described by a power curve of the form

$$y = \alpha x^\beta + \gamma, \tag{11.31}$$

with $\beta < 0$. By using equation 1(a), rather than (11.31), the disturbances will contain a term in x^β. In addition, Cliff and Ord also found that x was highly spatially autocorrelated. If γ in equation (11.31) is assumed to be equal to zero, a relation of the form of (11.31) can be reduced to a linear form by taking logs of both sides, as done by O'Sullivan in regression 1(b). The term in x^β will no longer pass through to the residuals, and this is reflected in the drop in the level of spatial autocorrelation in the residuals in regression 1(b) compared with 1(a). See Table 11.2.

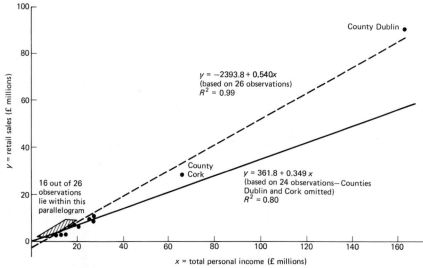

Figure 11.3 Plot of y against x for O'Sullivan's regression (2). Note how the pecked regression line based on 26 observations bisects the extreme values for Co. Dublin and Co. Cork. Sixteen out of 26 observations lie above the calculated regression line. If Dublin and Cork are omitted, the revised regression (solid line) has twelve observations above and twelve below the line. R^2 falls from 0.98 to 0.80, but the regression residuals become random.

Turning to regression (2), we note, despite the very high R^2 value, that the residuals displayed a high degree of spatial autocorrelation. First, the y variable (gross value of retail sales) is a commonly used surrogate variable for x (gross personal income), and this accounts in part for the inflated value of R^2. Second, the regression provides an example of the way in which the position of a regression line fitted by least squares can be dominated by a few very large and/or very small y and x values. See Figure 11.3. When this happens, a high R^2 is obtained, while the regression equation may be a poor estimator of the relationship between non-extreme y and x values. The limited usefulness of the equation as a predictor of retail sales in non-extreme counties is revealed in the autocorrelated residuals. When this sort of problem arises, the difficulty can be mitigated by using a criterion to fit the regression line which places less emphasis upon extreme observations. Minimum absolute deviations, where the line is fitted to minimize $\sum |e_i|$ rather than $\sum e_i^2$, and linear programming techniques are possibilities (Wagner, 1959, 1962). (See also Chapter 15.) Alternatively, the regression may be calibrated in the usual way, but omitting extreme data points (Tukey, 1962). In this particular example, the latter strategy was adopted. The extreme values for Counties Cork and Dublin were dropped. The revised regression equation, based on 24 observations, was

$$y = 361.8204 + 0.3489x \quad R^2 = 0.80.$$

The residuals from this regression were tested for spatial autocorrelation using binary weights. The following results were obtained: $I = 0.0425$, $E(I) = -0.0587$ and $\sigma(I) = 0.1166$, yielding the non-significant standard deviate of 0.87. Following Geary's (1954) arguments, the revised regression would be judged, because the residuals are uncorrelated, to have accounted for all the systematic spatial variation in y. Conversely, the original regression with the correlated residuals would, by definition, have left unaccounted for some systematic spatial variation in y. The revised regression might therefore be regarded as more successful from a geographical point of view, despite the lower R^2.

Spatial adjustments. If we now consider regression (3), it is evident from Table 11.2 that the residuals are highly autocorrelated with all forms of **W**. Although a common cause of autocorrelated residuals is the omission of an important regressor variable from the estimating equation, Cliff and Ord (1973) were unable to find any other variable which would eliminate the autocorrelation. They therefore suggested that the autocorrelation was so pervasive as to indicate the need for a spatial autoregressive model. They specified the model

$$y_i = \alpha + \beta x_i + \varepsilon_i \tag{11.32}$$

and

$$\varepsilon_i = \rho L \varepsilon_i + u_i, \quad i = 1, 2, ..., n. \tag{11.33}$$

Here L is the spatial lag operator

$$L\varepsilon_i = \sum_j w_{ij} \varepsilon_j, \quad i, j = 1, 2, ..., n, i \neq j,$$

implying a first order spatial Markov scheme among the errors, given the forms of **W** used in Table 11.2. We assume that the errors have zero mean and variance σ^2. Equations (11.32) and (11.33) yield, following Cliff and Ord (1973, p. 128), the transformed relationship

$$y_i = \gamma_1 + \gamma_2 x_i + \gamma_3 L y_i + \gamma_4 L x_i + u_i, \qquad (11.34)$$

where $\gamma_1 - \gamma_4$ are parameters to be estimated, and this estimation is subject to the constraint

$$\gamma_4 + \gamma_2 \gamma_3 = 0. \qquad (11.35)$$

Model (11.34) is of great interest from a geographical point of view in that y_i appears on both sides of the equation. Apart from the specific problem considered here, this situation would also arise if we developed directly (Figure 11.1) a spatial autoregression to handle the 'simultaneous effects' among regions on a single variable. For example, we might postulate

$$y_{ij} = \beta_0 + \beta_1 y_{i-1,j} + \beta_2 y_{i+1,j} + \beta_3 y_{i,j-1} + \beta_4 y_{i,j+1} + \varepsilon_{ij}, \qquad (11.36)$$

as in Figure 11.4. This sort of model is also useful to interpolate missing data points, which is a common problem in historical geography. See Section 16.6. From Cliff and Ord (1973, Sections 5.7 and 5.8), the critical thing about models of the form of (11.34) and (11.36), which contain purely *spatial* autoregressive elements, is that the parameters *cannot validly be estimated using ordinary least squares* (Whittle, 1954). Instead, a maximum likelihood method based on results by Mead (1967) and Ord (1975) must be used. For (11.34), the procedure is as follows (Cliff and Ord, 1973, p. 104):

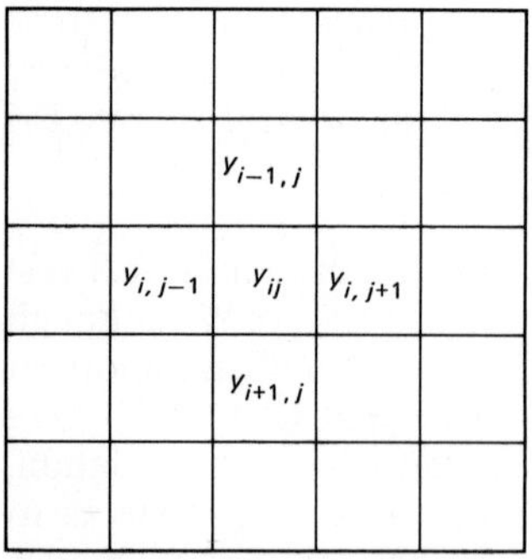

Figure 11.4   A first order spatial autoregressive process. The subscripts i and j refer to row i and column j, respectively, of the lattice.

Step 1: compute the OLS residuals, $\{e_i\}$, say, for (11.32).
Step 2: estimate ρ in $e_i = \rho L e_i + u_i (i = 1, 2, \ldots, n)$ by $\tilde{\rho}$, where $\tilde{\rho}$ is that value of ρ which minimizes

$$|\mathbf{I} - \rho \mathbf{W}|^{-2/n} \Sigma [e_i - \bar{e} - \rho (L e_i - \bar{e}_L)]^2, \qquad (11.37)$$

and $|\mathbf{I} - \rho \mathbf{W}|$ is the determinant of the matrix enclosed by the lines. See

Johnston (1972, pp. 78–85) for a discussion of the properties of determinants. In equation (11.37), $n\bar{e}_L = \Sigma L e_i$.

Step 3: construct the new variables,

$$\tilde{y}_i = y_i - \tilde{\rho} L y_i \quad \text{and} \quad \tilde{x}_i = x_i - \tilde{\rho} L x_i. \tag{11.38}$$

Step 4: calibrate the OLS regression of the $\{\tilde{y}_i\}$ on the $\{\tilde{x}_i\}$, yielding $\tilde{\beta}$ as the estimate for β in (11.32). Construct the OLS residuals in the usual way. Return to step 2 and repeat steps 2–4 until the process converges to a steady value of ρ. In the case of O'Sullivan's regression (3), this procedure yielded eventually $\tilde{y} = -1.32 + 0.00378\tilde{x}$.

Apart from the applications of spatial autoregressive models noted above, it is worth commenting that pervasive serial correlation in regression residuals, implying the need for such models, frequently arises in industrial and agricultural situations where inertia is now the principal locating factor (see, for example, Section 5.5.2).

11.5 Autocorrelation and Correlogram Analysis

11.5.1 *Correlograms in time*

It is common in time series analysis to determine the serial correlation structure among the variate values at lags of 1, 2, 3, ... time periods; that is, we consider the autocorrelations between the values of X_t and X_{t-1}, X_t and X_{t-2}, and so on. This approach is called *correlogram analysis*, and it is frequently very suggestive of the sorts of processes operating. Consider, for example, a recent study of epidemics in an English county (Cliff, Haggett, Ord, Bassett and Davies, 1975, Chapters 6 and 8). Here, the data set analysed was the number of measles cases reported in each week for the 27 General Register Office districts (GROs) in Cornwall over more than four years from 1966 (week 40) to 1970 (week 52). See Figure 11.5. The number of weeks, T, was 222, and the authors thus had a 222 element time series for each of the GROs. Earlier literature suggests two basic empirical regularities in measles series for large communities (population in excess of 250,000). First, the *time* series appear to be cyclic—measles is a recurrent epidemic—and to have a periodicity of about 2 years (Bartlett, 1957). More precisely, periodicity seems to be inversely related to the density on the ground of the population at risk. Second, *spatially*, measles epidemics appear to spread in a very contagious fashion (Haggett, 1972), not only at the individual spatial level but also between adjacent geographical areas. However, the population of the largest Cornish GRO is under 40,000 (1971), and of the smallest, under 4,000, and the purpose of the study was to investigate how far these two empirical regularities held for such small communities.

For each GRO, the coefficient I, given in equation (11.7) was used to determine the degree of serial correlation in the weekly infection rate. This rate was measured by the measles cases reported per 1,000 children aged 15 or under, since 97 per cent of all measles cases occur in that age band. That is, the temporal autocorrelation between x_t and x_{t-1}, x_t and x_{t-2} ... x_t and x_{t-k} was calculated for $k = 1(1)212$. The upper limit of 212 for k was chosen to prevent

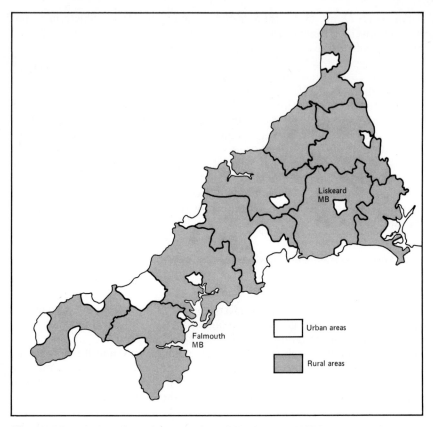

Figure 11.5   The locations of the Cornish GROs. Source: Cliff, Haggett, Ord, Bassett and Davies, 1975, p. 165.

the sample size from becoming too small. As it is, some authorities such as Box and Jenkins (1970) would argue that the upper limit for k should not exceed $\frac{1}{4}T$, where T is the number of weeks in the series, if large standard errors for the estimated autocorrelations are to be avoided. A series of correlograms was produced by plotting $I(k)$ in z-score form against k for each GRO. The correlograms fell into two clear groups:

Group (1): a set of 13 GROs for which the raw data displayed a major measles outbreak at the beginning and the end of the period studied, and a minor outbreak roughly half-way between. The representative correlogram for Falmouth MB is reproduced in Figure 11.6A.

Group (2): the remainder, which differed from group (1) in that they all missed one or other of the major outbreaks referred to above. The representative correlogram for Liskeard appears in Figure 11.6B.

Both sets of correlograms displayed high serial correlation over short lags, which is indicative of strong temporal clustering in the incidence of measles cases. From somewhere around lag 4–20 (depending upon the GRO), the group (1) correlograms moved along largely in random fashion (no significant autocorrelation) until lags 151–194, when a major new peak in the autocorrelation function appeared (see Figure 11.6A). This peak represented the cycle length of about three and a half years between the two major epidemic outbreaks. The group (2) correlograms (Figure 11.6B) did not have this cyclical peak because those GROs missed one of the major epidemic outbreaks.

Although Bartlett's (1957) regularity appears to hold for large communities, the above results imply a more complicated situation in small communities. First, cyclical periodicity was always in excess of three, rather than two, years, and some communities 'missed' an epidemic altogether. Second, although the authors tried, they were unable to establish any clear statistical relationship between periodicity and density of the susceptible population; but, in general, periodicity was found to be longer in rural, than in urban, GROs. It is important to note, however, that the theory developed by Bartlett assumes that the communities studied form closed populations; that is, there is assumed to be no interaction between communities. This is unlikely to be true in the present example, and it may account for some of the differences between fact and theory.

11.5.2 Correlograms in space: theory

It is of interest to geographers to extend the sort of analysis described in Section 11.5.1 into the spatial domain. Clearly the matrix powering procedure outlined in Section 9.7.3 can be used to determine first, second, ... spatial lags. Define the spatial lag operator, L, as

$$L^0 x_i = x_i$$

and for the typical spatial lag $g(>0)$ from sub-area i as

$$L^g x_i = \sum_{j \in g} w_{ij} x_j, \quad \sum_{j \in g} w_{ij} = 1,$$

where the notation, $j \in g$, is used to denote summation over the j sub-areas at spatial lag g from i. Putting $z_i = x_i - \bar{x}$, the gth order spatial autocorrelation, $I(g)$, is

$$I(g) = (n/W) \sum_{i=1}^{n} z_i L^g z_i \bigg/ \sum_{i=1}^{n} z_i^2 = (n/W) \sum_{i=1}^{n} \sum_{j \in g} w_{ij} z_i z_j \bigg/ \sum_{i=1}^{n} z_i^2. \quad (11.39)$$

Here $L^g z_i = L^g x_i - \bar{x}$ (Cliff and Ord, 1973). Defining $L^g z_i$ in this way, rather than as $L^g z_i = L^g x_i - \overline{L^g x}$, where $n\overline{L^g x} = \sum_{i=1}^{n} L^g x_i$, means that comparability between the $\{I(g)\}$ at different spatial lags is retained, although the correlogram is damped (Box and Jenkins, 1970, p. 32). One form of correlogram is just the plot of $I(g)$ against g for $g = 1, 2, ...$

We now use the function

$$r_{gs} = \sum_{i=1}^{n} L^g z_i L^s z_i \bigg/ \left\{ \sum_{i=1}^{n} L^g z_i^2 \sum_{i=1}^{n} L^s z_i^2 \right\}^{\frac{1}{2}} \quad (11.40)$$

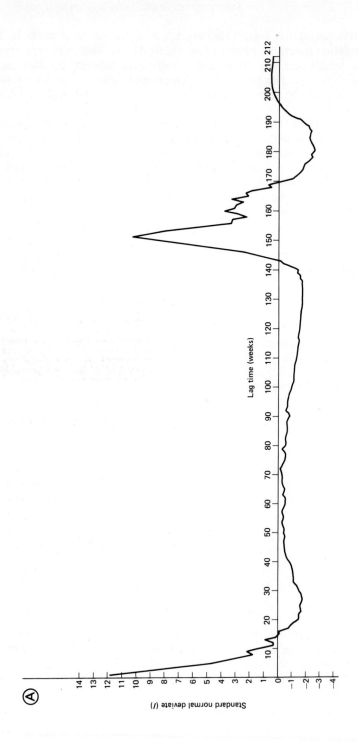

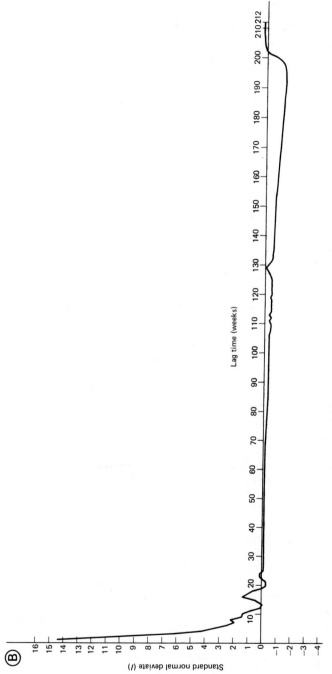

Figure 11.6 **A** Group 1 correlogram (Falmouth MB). **B** Group 2 correlogram (Liskeard MB). Source: Cliff, Haggett, Ord, Bassett and Davies, 1975, pp. 175–7.

to denote the sample correlation between the spatially lagged variables, $L^g z_i$ and $L^s z_i$, $0 \leqslant g < s \leqslant m$, where m is the diameter of the study area in a graph theoretic sense. Working with this function, Cliff *et al.* (1975, Chapter 8) have shown how partial spatial correlograms can be constructed, just as they can in the time domain (Box and Jenkins, 1970, pp. 64–66). The sample partial *correlation* between the variables X_1 and X_3, given X_2, is

$$r_{13.2} = (r_{13} - r_{12}r_{23}) / \{(1 - r_{12}^2)(1 - r_{23}^2)\}^{\frac{1}{2}}. \tag{11.41}$$

Higher order partial correlations are defined in terms of the partial correlations of the next lower order. Thus

$$r_{14.23} = (r_{14.2} - r_{13.2}r_{34.2}) / \{(1 - r_{34.2}^2)(1 - r_{34.2}^2)\}^{\frac{1}{2}}. \tag{11.42}$$

The sample partial *spatial autocorrelations* are found by computing $r_{12}, r_{13.2}$, $r_{14.23}$, and so on, from (11.40), and then substituting into expressions like (11.41) and (11.42). For this substitution to work, we have to redefine r_{gs} in (11.40) as $r_{gs} = \text{corr}(x_g, x_s)$, where x_g and x_s correspond to the $(g-1)$th and $(s-1)$th order lagged variables, $L^{g-1}x_i$ and $L^{s-1}x_i$, respectively.

In addition to distinguishing the effects of several variables, the method may be used to explore spatial patterns. As an example, Cliff *et al.* supposed that $\mathbf{W}_1$ was the weights matrix for urban–rural links in a study, and $\mathbf{W}_2$ the corresponding matrix for rural–rural links. The variables $\mathbf{X}_1 = \mathbf{W}_1 \mathbf{X}$ and $\mathbf{X}_2 = \mathbf{W}_2 \mathbf{X}$ were defined. The evaluation of the partial autocorrelation between X and X_2 given X_1 would indicate the degree of rural–rural interaction, after allowing for urban–rural dependence.

11.5.3 *Correlograms in space: regional applications*

We can illustrate the spatial correlogram approach by returning to the same Cornish epidemic data discussed in Section 11.5.1. The GRO map shown in Figure 11.5 may be converted into a weighting matrix, $\mathbf{W}$, by putting the typical element of $\mathbf{W}$, w_{ij}, equal to one if the ith and jth GROs are contiguous, and $w_{ij} = 0$ otherwise. The map is thus reduced to a binary planar graph, and the non-zero elements of $\mathbf{W}$ represent those GROs which are first nearest neighbours (one spatial lag apart) in the sense of Section 11.5.2. Using the matrix powering routine described in Section 9.7.3, second, third ... eighth spatial lags were determined (the diameter of the graph was eight). Having defined the spatial lags, Cliff *et al.* then tested for spatial autocorrelation between GROs at $g = 1, 2, ..., 8$ spatial lags using $I(g)$ given in (11.39). This was done for each of the 222 weeks. Binary only weights were used, since this produces a smoothly declining correlogram if distance is the only factor determining the spatial pattern of outbreaks. To summarize the results, the average value of $I(g)$ in z-score form at each spatial lag for the first and second epidemic waves (i.e. weeks 1–50 and weeks 186–204 respectively) is reproduced in Figure 11.7. These periods covered the two epidemic outbreaks in the study area. No clear spatial autocorrelation pattern was found at other times.

From Figure 11.7, for the first epidemic it is evident that although many of the I values individually were not significant, positive autocorrelation predominated at spatial lags 1, 6, and 8, and negative autocorrelation at lags 2–4. The positive spatial autocorrelation at lag 1 and negative autocorrelation at lags 2–4 suggests that measles outbreaks are clustered spatially (cf. Haggett, 1972). The interesting feature of the average correlogram for the first epidemic is the positive autocorrelation at lags 6 and 8. To help interpret this, Cliff *et al.* determined the numbers of urban–urban, rural–rural and urban–rural links at each spatial lag, 1–8. These counts, along with the expected numbers in brackets under the assumption of independence between link type and spatial lag, are reproduced in Table 11.3. This table shows that spatial lags 1 and 2 are dominated by urban–rural and rural–rural links, whereas lags 4–8 are dominated by urban–urban links. In addition, lags 6–8 include predominantly those GROs on the main transport routes. A picture therefore emerged of similar levels of measles cases in (1) non-contiguous urban areas and (2) contiguous rural–urban and rural–rural districts. A possible interpretation of this pattern offered by the authors is to postulate initial outbreaks of measles in an epidemic in urban areas (a central place effect), followed by spread of the disease from the towns into surrounding rural areas by a spatial diffusion process (cf. the discussion on hierarchical and contagious diffusion in Section 7.4).

Turning to the second epidemic wave, the spatial clustering of measles outbreaks was again confirmed by the positive autocorrelation at lags 1–3, but there was negative autocorrelation at lags 4–8. This suggests that the central place effect was less important in the second epidemic than in the first.

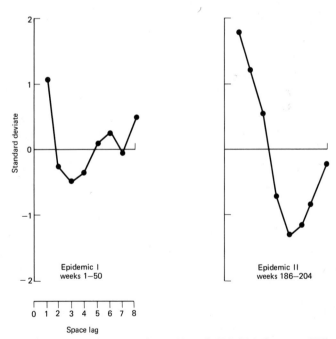

Figure 11.7   Average correlograms for *I*, weeks 1–50 and 186–204. Source: Cliff, Haggett, Ord, Bassett and Davies, 1975, p. 171.

In summary, the work of this section has been given to show how (auto) correlogram analysis can be used to identify the structure of a time–space process (cf. Figure 11.1). The results are suggestive of a mixed hierarchical/contagious diffusion process for the spatial spread of measles epidemics, and a cyclical recurrence, with some misses, through time. As we shall see (Section 16.5), the sort of analysis undertaken here can be extended to provide a basis for the formal identification of time–space forecasting models.

Table 11.3   Observed and expected numbers of links at different spatial lags in maps of epidemic data.*

Link Type	Spatial Lag								Totals
	1	2	3	4	5	6	7	8	
Urban–Urban	1(13.6)	20(28.4)	33(32.3)	31(24.5)	20(17.9)	18(13.2)	11(5.8)	3(1.2)	137
Rural–Rural	13(4.5)	14(9.3)	7(10.6)	6(8.1)	4(5.9)	1(4.3)	0(1.9)	0(0.4)	45
Urban–Rural	21(16.9)	39(35.3)	43(40.1)	26(30.4)	22(22.2)	15(16.4)	4(7.2)	0(1.4)	170
Totals	35	73	83	63	46	34	15	3	352

Source: Cliff, Haggett, Ord, Bassett and Davies, 1975, p. 172.
Expected numbers given in brackets.   *Cornwall, 1966–72.

11.6 Autocorrelation and Hypothesis Testing*

Given the deleterious consequences noted in Section 10.2 of failure to meet the independence assumption of many of the statistical tests of hypotheses, we can consider what insights into this problem can be gained from the work of Section 11.3. First, the tests given in equations (11.5)–(11.8) provide a means of verifying whether the independence assumption is tenable. If H_0 is accepted, we may proceed with the conventional tests. If H_0 is rejected, the kinds of action discussed in Section 10.3 should be considered.

Cliff and Ord (1975a) have also shown that the autocorrelation measure, I, given in equation (11.7) can be used to provide an approximate correction procedure for the difference-between-means t test, and the remainder of this section is based on their work. Repeating the equation for t given in equation (10.1), namely

$$t = \frac{\bar{x}_1 - \bar{x}_2}{\hat{\sigma}_{\bar{x}_1 - \bar{x}_2}}, \qquad (11.43)$$

we note that, when the variates X_1 and X_2 are first-order spatially autocorrelated by the amounts ρ_1 and ρ_2 respectively, the estimated standard error, $\hat{\sigma}_{\bar{x}_1 - \bar{x}_2}$, is given by

$$\hat{\sigma}_{\bar{x}_1 - \bar{x}_2} = s \sqrt{\frac{1}{N_1(1 - \tilde{\rho}_1)^2} + \frac{1}{N_2(1 - \tilde{\rho}_2)^2}} \qquad (11.44)$$

where

$$s^2 = \{(\mathbf{x}_1 - \bar{x}_1 \mathbf{1})'\mathbf{V}_1^{-1}(\mathbf{x}_1 - \bar{x}_1 \mathbf{1}) + (\mathbf{x}_2 - \bar{x}_2 \mathbf{1})'\mathbf{V}_2^{-1}(\mathbf{x}_2 - \bar{x}_2 \mathbf{1})\}/(N_1 + N_2 - 2).$$
$$(11.45)$$

In (11.44) and (11.45), the notation of Section 10.2.1 has been followed. In addition, $\tilde{\rho}_1$ and $\tilde{\rho}_2$ are the estimates of ρ_1 and ρ_2 respectively, while $\mathbf{V}_i^{-1}$ is given by

$$\mathbf{V}_i^{-1} = (\mathbf{I} - \tilde{\rho}_i \mathbf{W}_i')(\mathbf{I} - \tilde{\rho}_i \mathbf{W}_i), \quad i = 1, 2. \tag{11.46}$$

The elements of $\mathbf{W}_i$ are assumed to be scaled so that $\sum_j w_{ij} = 1$. Thus, if we assume, without loss of generality, that the variates X_1 and X_2 are both $N(0, 1)$, then $\mathbf{V}_1$ and $\mathbf{V}_2$ are simply the (spatial) variance-covariance matrices for X_1 and X_2 respectively [cf. equation (10.3)]; that is, they specify the spatial covariance structure among the variate values, and so equation (11.44) is feeding this information explicitly into the t-test formula. It is evident that, when $\tilde{\rho}_1$ and $\tilde{\rho}_2$ in (11.44) are both zero, (11.44) reduces to (10.2), as it should since both sets of variate values are then spatially uncorrelated.

Strictly speaking, the estimates, $\tilde{\rho}_1$ and $\tilde{\rho}_2$, in the above equations should be obtained by maximum likelihood (ML). However, I, given in equation (11.7) can be used to provide an acceptable approximation. As an estimator of ρ, I is inconsistent. Its great virtue, compared with maximum likelihood, is that it can be evaluated very simply. A further problem in using I is that the coefficient does not range over $[-1, +1]$ as does the ML estimator. However, $\max |I|$ can be calculated for any given lattice (Cliff and Ord, 1969, p. 53) as

$$\max |I| = \left\{ \operatorname{var}\left(\sum_j w_{ij} z_j \right) \middle/ \operatorname{var}(z_i) \right\}^{\frac{1}{2}}, \tag{11.47}$$

and so we can estimate ρ_i by

$$\tilde{\rho}_i = I/\max |I|, \tag{11.48}$$

which provides a more reasonable assessment on the usual $[-1, +1]$ interval. The bias present in (11.48) as an estimator is evident from Table 11.4, which suggests $|\tilde{\rho}| \leqslant |\rho|$. To obtain Table 11.4, an X variate autocorrelated by a known amount, ρ, was generated, using equation (10.3), for each of the lattices shown. $\tilde{\rho}$ was then calculated. The experiment was repeated 600 times for each value of ρ and each lattice to yield a mean value for $\tilde{\rho}$ (say $\bar{\tilde{\rho}}$) as $\sum \tilde{\rho}/600$. Table 11.4 also shows that despite the bias, (11.48) is a reasonable approximation provided that $n \gtrsim 25$.

Table 11.4   Comparison of $\bar{\tilde{\rho}}$ and ρ for various lattices.

Degree of autocorrelation in the pattern analysed, ρ	*Average* estimate of the degree of autocorrelation, $\bar{\tilde{\rho}}$*			
	3 × 3 lattice	*5 × 5 lattice*	*7 × 7 lattice*	*10 × 10 lattice*
−0.9	−0.72	−0.81	−0.83	−0.86
−0.5	−0.52	−0.49	−0.47	−0.48
0.0	−0.26	−0.06	−0.03	0.00
0.5	0.00	0.34	0.42	0.47
0.9	0.05	0.61	0.76	0.83

Source: Cliff and Ord, 1975a, p. 000.

*Based on 600 experiments.

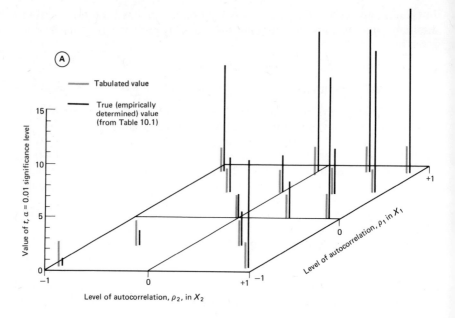

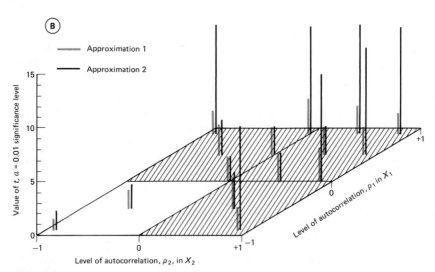

Figure 11.8 Impact of spatial autocorrelation upon Student's *t*-test for differences between means. **A** Comparison of tabulated percentage point with true percentage point for various levels of autocorrelation in X_1 and X_2. Note the highly variable, cirque-shaped pattern of true values in contrast to the (by definition) horizontal plane of the tabulated values. **B** Values of *t* yielded by Approximation 1 [equations (11.44), (11.48), and (11.49)] and Approximation 2 [equations (11.44), (11.45), and (11.48)]. Shaded area, where either or both of ρ_1 and ρ_2 is positive, indicates where a test of significance based on Approximation 1 should be used; unshaded area where Approximation 2 should be used.

We may simplify approximation (11.44) even further by taking s in that equation as given in the usual form of the t test, namely

$$s = \sqrt{\frac{N_1 s_1^2 + N_2 s_2^2}{N_1 + N_2 - 2}}. \tag{11.49}$$

See equation (10.1). Adapting the Monte Carlo experiment described in Section 10.2.1, approximation (11.44) was evaluated with s given by both (11.45) and (11.49). $\tilde{\rho}_i$ was calculated from (11.48). The results Cliff and Ord obtained for the 7×7 lattices and significance level $\alpha = 0.01$ (one-tailed test) are reproduced in Figure 11.8 (cf. Table 10.1). This figure suggests two general conclusions:

(1) If either or both of $\tilde{\rho}_1$ and $\tilde{\rho}_2$ is positive, take the statistic t given in equation (11.43), with $\hat{\sigma}_{\bar{x}-\bar{x}_2}$ given by equations (11.44), (11.48) and (11.49), to follow Student's t-distribution given in Table A2 with $(N_1 + N_2 - 2)$ degrees of freedom (approximation 1, say—shaded area in Figure 11.8B).

(2) if both $\tilde{\rho}_1$ and $\tilde{\rho}_2$ are negative, take t with $\hat{\sigma}_{\bar{x}_1-\bar{x}_2}$ given by equations (11.44), (11.45) and (11.48) to follow Student's t-distribution with $(N_1 + N_2 - 2)$ degrees of freedom (approximation 2, say). The use of these rules will provide a test of significance which is unlikely to result in serious inferential error. Cliff and Ord (1975a) have shown that the test thus modified can, in fact, be safely applied to any lattice for which N_1 and N_2 both exceed 25.

11.7 Conclusions

In this chapter, we have defined a series of tests for autocorrelation in variate values located in time and space. The utility of these measures in unravelling the structure of time–space processes has been illustrated with reference to the spread of measles epidemics in Southwest England. We have also shown how the measures can suggest ways in which (a) the specification of regression models may be improved and (b) statistical tests of hypotheses which assume independent observations may be approximately modified to allow for spatially intercorrelated data.

12 Scale Components

12.1 Introduction

In this chapter, we consider a series of methods which break down the variation in spatially and temporally located variate values into scale components. We can best illustrate the concept of scale components by two examples, one from a spatial series and one from a time series. In Southwest England, unemployment rates generally worsen as one moves from Bristol towards Land's End, although high peaks of unemployment above this generally rising surface frequently occur in coastal and mining areas. We may thus recognize two separate scale components in the map: a broad *regional* trend of increasing unemployment levels as one moves southwestwards from Bristol, disturbed by *local* irregularities. Similar time-scale components can be identified in a time series of unemployment rates for a given locality. Thus, one would expect to find strong seasonal variations in unemployment in a coastal resort town, possibly superimposed upon a general tendency for overall unemployment rates to rise or fall in response to changes in national economic factors.

The methods we describe here—trend surface analysis, analysis of variance and spectral analysis—can all be used to separate the variability in time series or spatial data into such trend, cyclical and local components of variation as they may contain. Knowledge of the proportion of the total variability in the data which may be attributed to the different components identified is important because each component commonly reflects different causal processes at work at different spatial and/or temporal scales. For example, in the time series unemployment example given above, the seasonal component would reflect local dependence of the labour force on the tourist industry,

378

while the long term rising or falling trend might reflect long term structural changes in the national economy. The methods thus begin to provide us with a means of identifying the important scales of analysis in a data set, which, given the scale-dependence of many statistical models noted in Section 10.6.1, is a necessary step in any problem tackled.

12.2 Polynomial Trend Surface Analysis

We assume that the value of a variable, Y, say, has been measured at several spatial locations, and that the X_1 and X_2 cartesian co-ordinates of the locations are known. The philosophy behind trend surface analysis is that the locations of the points provide some information about the spatial pattern of variation in Y. Various mathematical functions have been proposed to model the map of values of Y in terms of the X_1, X_2 locations: here we look at one of the simplest, polynomial functions. The polynomial trend surface model is formed by entering various power functions of the X_1 and X_2 cartesian co-ordinates as independent variables in a regression in which Y is the dependent variable. The model takes the simple linear form,

$$Y = \sum_{i=0}^{m} \sum_{j=0}^{n} \beta_{ij} X_1^i X_2^j + \varepsilon. \tag{12.1}$$

Here, the error terms or residuals, ε_i, are assumed to be independently normally distributed with mean zero and variance σ^2, and the model is estimated and treated like any other multiple regression equation (King, 1969b, pp. 152–3).

12.2.1 *Spatial form of the surface*

The spatial form of the surface generated by (12.1) depends upon the order of the fitted model. If we consider terms of up to the third order, we may recognize the following surfaces:

Surface

Linear	$\beta_{00} + \beta_{10} X_1 + \beta_{01} X_2$	(12.2)
Quadratic	$\beta_{00} + \beta_{10} X_1 + \beta_{01} X_2 + \beta_{20} X_1^2 + \beta_{11} X_1 X_2 + \beta_{02} X_2^2$	(12.3)
Cubic	$\beta_{00} + \beta_{10} X_1 + \beta_{01} X_2 + \beta_{20} X_1^2 + \beta_{11} X_1 X_2 + \beta_{02} X_2^2$	
	$+ \beta_{30} X_1^3 + \beta_{21} X_1^2 X_2 + \beta_{12} X_1 X_2^2 + \beta_{03} X_2^3$	(12.4)

Figure 12.1 shows schematically the general shape of the surface produced by the first, second and third order models, and, in addition, the corresponding equations and curves for two, rather than three, dimensions. It is apparent from these diagrams that the number of inflexions which can be handled by any equation is one less than the order of the equation.

Cliff, Haggett, Ord, Bassett and Davies (1975, Section 4.3) have examined in more detail the specific spatial contribution of each β coefficient in equations (12.2)–(12.4) to the form of the final surface. The procedure they adopted was as follows. The spatial array shown in the top right-hand diagram of Figure 12.2 was constructed. The observed co-ordinate values x_1 and x_2 were allowed to range over the integers $[-3, +3]$, thus defining the 49 locations shown by the dots. The cubic equation, (12.4), was then taken, exclusive of the coefficient β_{00}. The spatial pattern generated by individual coefficients was determined by arbitrarily setting the value of the particular coefficient under consideration equal to 1 in the trend surface equation, and by setting all other coefficients equal to zero. Simple substitution of the observed x_1 and x_2 co-ordinates into

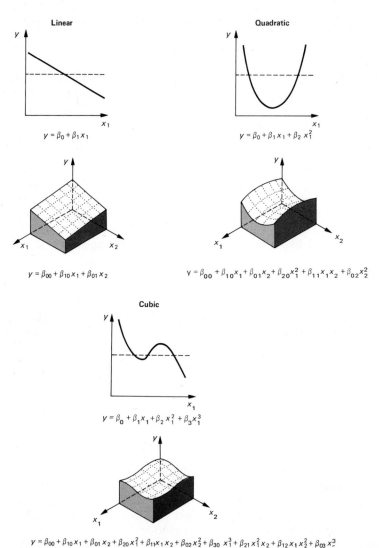

Linear

$$y = \beta_0 + \beta_1 x_1$$

$$y = \beta_{00} + \beta_{10} x_1 + \beta_{01} x_2$$

Quadratic

$$y = \beta_0 + \beta_1 x_1 + \beta_2 x_1^2$$

$$y = \beta_{00} + \beta_{10} x_1 + \beta_{01} x_2 + \beta_{20} x_1^2 + \beta_{11} x_1 x_2 + \beta_{02} x_2^2$$

Cubic

$$y = \beta_0 + \beta_1 x_1 + \beta_2 x_1^2 + \beta_3 x_1^3$$

$$y = \beta_{00} + \beta_{10} x_1 + \beta_{01} x_2 + \beta_{20} x_1^2 + \beta_{11} x_1 x_2 + \beta_{02} x_2^2 + \beta_{30} x_1^3 + \beta_{21} x_1^2 x_2 + \beta_{12} x_1 x_2^2 + \beta_{03} x_2^3$$

Figure 12.1   Relationship between two dimensional functions and their corresponding three dimensional surfaces. Source: Chorley and Haggett, 1965; Krumbein, 1956.

the equation then gave the y value, for each of the 49 locations, produced by the non-zero β coefficient. For each coefficient, the quantities, μ_y and σ_y, were calculated and a contour map of the $\{y\}$ surface was drawn. The contour interval selected was σ_y. The maps obtained are reproduced in Figure 12.2.

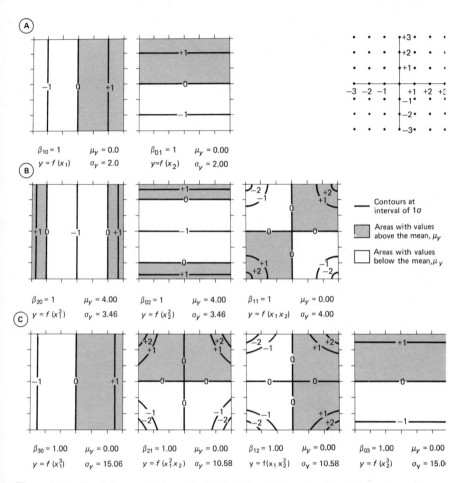

Figure 12.2   Spatial contribution of individual β coefficients in the cubic trend surface equation. **A** Linear terms; **B** Quadratic terms; **C** Cubic terms. Source: Cliff, Haggett, Ord, Bassett and Davies, 1975, p. 53.

Clearly, the nine maps show considerable spatial variation in the patterns produced by individual coefficients. These range from simple shed roof surfaces for the β_{10} and β_{01} coefficients (sloping east to west, and north to south respectively), through more complex 'saddle' type forms (for example, for the quadratic coefficient β_{11}), to convoluted forms 'recalling a plunging neckline' (the cubic β_{21} coefficient). Cliff *et al.* (1975, Chapter 4) have gone on to explore the patterns produced when more than one of the β coefficients is allowed to take on a non-zero value. Thus, in Figure 12.3, they allowed β_{20} and β_{02} of the quadratic terms to take on values of either ± 1. Four alternative forms can be generated; a pair of circular surfaces (a bowl or a dome) and a pair of less regular forms. The authors showed that if sets of 3, 4, ..., 9 coefficients were considered, then over 2,000 maps, each with a different and distinctive surface, could be generated.

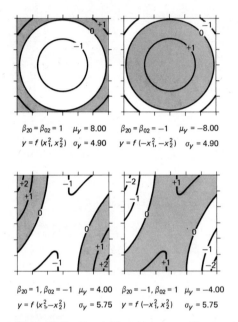

$\beta_{20} = \beta_{02} = 1$ $\mu_y = 8.00$ $\beta_{20} = \beta_{02} = -1$ $\mu_y = -8.00$
$y = f(x_1^2, x_2^2)$ $\sigma_y = 4.90$ $y = f(-x_1^2, -x_2^2)$ $\sigma_y = 4.90$

$\beta_{20} = 1, \beta_{02} = -1$ $\mu_y = 4.00$ $\beta_{20} = -1, \beta_{02} = 1$ $\mu_y = -4.00$
$y = f(x_1^2, -x_2^2)$ $\sigma_y = 5.75$ $y = f(-x_1^2, x_2^2)$ $\sigma_y = 5.75$

Figure 12.3   Spatial forms generated by quadratic terms in the trend surface equation. Shading as in Figure 12.2. Source: Cliff, Haggett, Ord, Bassett and Davies, 1975, p. 54.

12.2.2 *Limitations of the trend surface model*

Although, in principle, the idea of fitting surfaces to spatial data is attractive, care must be exercised. As the order of the surface increases, so does our ability to model local extremes. However, in increasing the complexity of the model, we increase our problems in interpreting the trends described. As the fitted surface more and more closely approximates the real world, so we lose the simplifying value of the model in pulling out the generalized trends in the data. Norcliffe (1969) has argued that many applications of polynomial trend surface methods in geography have simply been curve fitting explorations, followed by *a posteriori* justifications as to why good fits have been obtained. Norcliffe suggests that the technique should only be used in situations where the geographer has some *a priori* theoretical notions about the kind of surface which should describe a particular data set. For example, the known conical arrangement of land values, rents and population within a city (see Section 6.2.2) implies that a moderately good fit should be obtained with a quadratic surface. If poor fits of models are obtained in situations where we would expect good fits from our knowledge of the processes involved, the residuals may be highly suggestive of weaknesses in our pre-existing theoretical notions. Similar arguments are advanced by Chorley and Haggett (1965b) and Whitten (1974).

At a more technical level, we note that, since the model is a least squares regression, the assumptions of that method of analysis must be met if valid inferences are to be made (Johnston, 1972). The inter-regional comparison of trend surfaces is also not easy. Haggett and Bassett (1970) show that the estimated values of *individual β* coefficients, and their percentage explanation, are not invariant of the origin and orientation of the co-ordinate grid. However, the *overall* percentage explanation by terms of a given order (e.g. all linear or all quadratic) is unchanged. In addition, the coefficients of model (12.1) are not independent, which complicates any attempt to group surfaces on the basis of the numerical values of the coefficients (Cliff *et al.*, 1975, Section 4.5.2).

A final topic which has attracted some attention in the literature is the effect of spatially clustered data and boundary problems upon the fitting of trend surfaces. Davis (1973, pp. 349–52) has shown empirically that even extremely clustered data are unlikely to distort the fitted surface unduly, while to mitigate edge effects, he recommends calibration of the model over study regions which are larger than the area which is eventually to be mapped (cf. the use of toruses in Section 10.2.1). Further critical accounts of the trend surface model appear in Watson (1971, 1972) and Whitten (1974).

12.2.3 *Trend surfaces and scale components*

Apart from general surface fitting, a particularly important application of the trend surface model is to identify which spatial scale accounts for most of the point-to-point variation in a map. Thus Krumbein (1956, p. 2164) has used the technique to explore the relationships between trend and residual features of the data and geological processes operative at regional and local scales. Krumbein suggests that in the description of facies maps, for example, the first category of processes might include 'widespread regional controls on shelf, basin and geosynclinal deposition—the tectono-environmental complex that affected the entire depositional area, plus broad post-depositional structural and erosional changes [modellable by, say, the linear trend surface of equation (12.2). Local scale processes are] illustrated by smaller scale features, such as local variations in the sedimentary environment, growth of structures within the broad depositional area, and by localized post-depositional disturbances and erosion [modellable by high order surface terms].' If we argue that total map variance can be decomposed into three components: trend, local covariation, and specific variation at the datum point (such as measurement error), the trend surface model can be used to isolate the percentage of the total attributable to the various components. However, as Robinson (1970) has pointed out, local covariation and specific variation are often confounded in the error term of (12.1), although testing for autocorrelation in the residuals may help to separate out their effects. As we have noted, in view of the dependence of many statistical tests of hypotheses upon size of the observation units (see Section 10.6), isolation of the most important spatial scale (in terms of variance attributable)—whether regional, local or specific—for further analysis can be crucial.

Haggett (1964) has used a linear trend surface to separate regional and local components in forest distribution in southwest Brazil. The original distribution is shown in Figure 12.4A, with contours at ten-unit intervals and areas below the mean value for the whole region shaded. The general trend shown by this forest distribution map is that the linear surface (Figure 12.4B) falls off inland, dipping orthogonally to the coastline. Areas which rise above this plane, the positive residuals (Figure 12.4C), include the heavily forested parts of the Serra do Mar and the Serra da Mantiqueira escarpment. Negative residuals occur in the dry Taubaté basin and in the northwest part of the map (Figure 12.4D). Haggett (1965) has suggested fitting a (second) trend surface to the residuals from a trend surface, in an attempt to identify spatial pattern in them. The fitting would have to be done using generalized least squares, since the residuals will be correlated (see the discussion in Sections 10.2.1 and 11.4.1).

✳✳✳

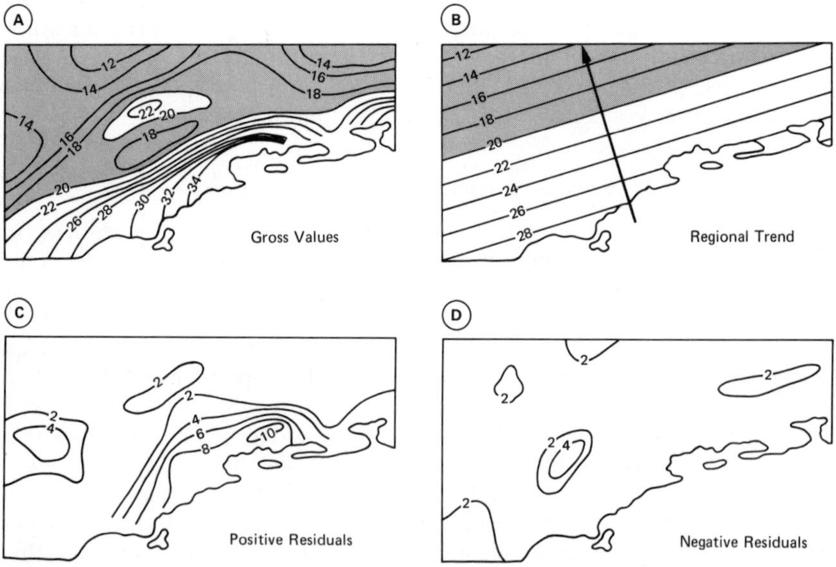

Figure 12.4   Forest distribution in the Brazilian Sudeste in terms of simple regional trend and local anomalies. Source: Haggett, 1964, p. 372.

12.3 Analysis of Variance*

We have stressed in this chapter the importance of identifying the appropriate geographical scale in any analysis that we undertake. As McCarty, Hook and Knos (1956, p. 16) have argued, 'Every change in scale will bring about the statement of a new problem, and there is no basis for presuming that associations existing at one scale will also exist at another.' Although trend surface methods can give some insights into the scale problem, an alternative model is nested analysis of variance, which we now consider.

12.3.1 Nested analysis of variance model

The principles behind the model to be described have been discussed in ecology (Greig Smith, 1957, 1964), geology (Olson and Potter, 1954; Krumbein, 1956), and political science (Stokes, 1965). Use of the model in geography has been considered by Chorley, Stoddart, Haggett and Slaymaker (1966), Moellering and Tobler (1972), and Cliff and Ord (1972). The idea of nested designs has also been introduced in Section 8.3.2 in connection with multi-stage sampling. See especially Figure 8.5.

Following the notation of Scheffé (1959, Sections 5.3 and 7.6) and of Moellering and Tobler, let X_{ijk} denote the variate, X in the kth 'district' of the jth 'county' of the ith 'region' of the study area (Figure 12.5, level 3). Then put

$$X_{ijk} - \mu = \alpha_i + \beta_{ij} + \gamma_{ijk}, \tag{12.5}$$

where $\alpha_i \sim IN(0, \sigma_\alpha^2)$, $\beta_{ij} \sim IN(0, \sigma_\beta^2)$ and $\gamma_{ijk} \sim IN(0, \sigma_\gamma^2)$. We are therefore postulating that the quantities $\{\alpha_i\}$, $\{\beta_{ij}\}$ and $\{\gamma_{ijk}\}$ are independent drawings from zero mean, normally distributed populations with variances $\sigma_\alpha^2, \sigma_\beta^2$ and σ_γ^2 respectively. In (12.5), μ is the overall (grand) mean, and the $\{\alpha_i\}$, $\{\beta_{ij}\}$, and $\{\gamma_{ijk}\}$ represent 'regional', 'county', and 'district' scale effects respectively, as in the Model II analysis of variance or *components of variance* model (Kendall and Stuart, 1966, Chapter 36; Cliff and Ord, 1972). 'The model represents the random variable $[X_{ijk}$ at the district level] as the sum of "effects" [from] each level of the hierarchy in which the ... area falls. ... The primary interest focusses upon the relative importance of the different levels in the hierarchy' (Cliff et al., 1975, Chapter 10) as judged by the amount of variance in X_{ijk} which may be ascribed to variability at the local, regional and county spatial scale levels. We have, from (12.5),

$$E[(X_{ijk} - \mu)^2] = \sigma_\alpha^2 + \sigma_\beta^2 + \sigma_\gamma^2. \tag{12.6}$$

Variability in X at the district level is thus assumed to be generated as the sum of independent variability from each spatial scale level, and we wish to estimate $\sigma_\alpha^2, \sigma_\beta^2$ and σ_γ^2.[1]

Rewriting equation (12.5) in terms of X yields the sums of squares

$$\sum_{(3)}(x_{ijk} - \bar{x}_{...})^2 = \sum_{(3)}(\bar{x}_{i..} - \bar{x}_{...})^2 + \sum_{(3)}(\bar{x}_{ij.} - \bar{x}_{i..})^2$$
$$+ \sum_{(3)}(x_{ijk} - \bar{x}_{ij.})^2, \tag{12.7}$$

or

$$SS_{total} = SS_\alpha + SS_\beta + SS_\gamma, \tag{12.8}$$

---

[1] This is in contrast to the more usual fixed effects Model I Analysis of Variance, where equation (12.5) would be subject to $\sum_i \alpha_i = \sum_j \beta_{ij} = \sum_k \gamma_{ijk} = 0$, and the chief purpose would be to estimate the $\{\alpha_i\}$, $\{\beta_{ij}\}$ and $\{\gamma_{ijk}\}$. The estimators are $\hat{\mu} = \sum_i \sum_j \sum_k x_{ijk}, \hat{\alpha}_i = \bar{x}_{i..} - \bar{x}_{...}, \hat{\beta}_{ij} = \bar{x}_{ij.} - \bar{x}_{i..}$ and $\hat{\gamma}_{ijk} = x_{ijk} - \bar{x}_{ij.}$. In these equations, the dot notation is used to indicate the mean of the variate values obtained by summing over the subscripts which are dots.

with degrees of freedom, respectively,

$$(N-1), (I-1), \sum_{i=1}^{I} (J_i - 1), \sum_{i=1}^{I} \sum_{j=1}^{J_i} (K_{ij} - 1). \tag{12.9}$$

Here,

$$\sum_{(3)} = \sum_{i=1}^{I} \sum_{j=1}^{J_i} \sum_{k=1}^{K_{ij}},$$

in addition to previously used notation, and N is the total number of x_{ijk} observations. I is the number of α level areas (that is, regions), J_i is the number of β level areas in the ith α level area (number of counties in the ith region), and K_{ij} is the number of γ level areas in the jth β level area of the ith α level area (number of districts in the jth county of the ith region). Figure 12.5 shows how the notation works out spatially. Thus (12.7) indicates that, before squaring and summing each term,

X_{ijk} − overall mean = deviation of regional mean from grand mean
+ deviation of county mean from regional mean
+ district deviations from county mean.

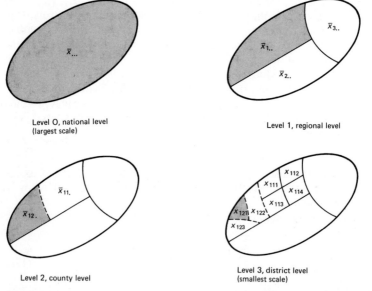

Level O, national level
(largest scale)

Level 1, regional level

Level 2, county level

Level 3, district level
(smallest scale)

Figure 12.5   Scale analysis in an irregular hierarchy. The dot notation attached to $\bar{X}$ at levels 0, 1 and 2 indicates that the mean was obtained from the level 3 X values by summing over the subscripts which are dots. Source: Moellering and Tobler, 1972, p. 42.

Although we have outlined a three level hierarchy, the number of levels is restricted only by the data available; we can have as many levels as we care to postulate. The usual analysis of variance table can be constructed from equations (12.7)–(12.9) as shown in Table 12.1. If the nested design is *balanced* (that is, all $K_{ij} = K$, all $J_i = J$, etc.), then the estimates of the unknown variances, σ_α^2, σ_β^2 and σ_γ^2, are given by

$$\hat{\sigma}_\gamma^2 = MS_\gamma$$

$$\hat{\sigma}_\beta^2 = \frac{1}{K}(MS_\beta - MS_\gamma), \qquad (12.10)$$

$$\hat{\sigma}_\alpha^2 = \frac{1}{JK}(MS_\alpha - MS_\beta).$$

Table 12.1   Nested analysis of variance computational formulae

Level	Source of variation	Sum of Squares	Degrees of freedom	Mean square (MS)
Regional	α	$SS_\alpha = \sum_i \sum_j \sum_k (\bar{x}_{i..} - \bar{x}_{...})^2$	$I - 1$	$MS_\alpha = SS_\alpha/(I-1)$
County	β	$SS_\beta = \sum_i \sum_j \sum_k (\bar{x}_{ij.} - \bar{x}_{i..})^2$	$\sum_{i=1}^{I}(J_i - 1)$	$MS_\beta = SS_\beta / \sum_{i=1}^{I}(J_i - 1)$
District	γ	$SS_\gamma = \sum_i \sum_j \sum_k (x_{ijk} - \bar{x}_{ij.})^2$	$\sum_{i=1}^{I}\sum_{j=1}^{J_i}(K_{ij} - 1)$	$MS_\gamma = SS_\gamma / \sum_{i=1}^{I}\sum_{j=1}^{J_i}(K_{ij} -$
		$SS_{total} = \sum_i \sum_j \sum_k (x_{ijk} - \bar{x}_{...})^2$	$N - 1$	

Style follows Scheffé, 1959, p. 186.

Similar formulae can be worked out for the unbalanced case (unequal numbers of counties in each region and/or unequal numbers of districts in each county) (Scheffé, 1959, pp. 256–7). *F* ratios may be calculated as follows (Scheffé, 1959, p. 254):

$$H_0: \sigma_\alpha^2 = \sigma_\beta^2 = 0 \quad F_{(I-1),\,\sum_i\sum_j(K_{ij}-1)} = MS_\alpha/MS_\gamma$$
$$H_0: \sigma_\beta^2 = 0 \quad F_{\sum_i(J_i-1),\,\sum_i\sum_j(K_{ij}-1)} = MS_\beta/MS_\gamma. \qquad (12.11)$$

As Tukey (1961) has noted, the fact that the $\{\sigma^2\}$ in the above analysis represent the variance components at each spatial scale makes the model conceptually very similar to Fourier and spectral analysis which is considered in the next section. A criticism of nested analysis of variance, as opposed to trend surface methods, for scale components analysis, is that the structure of the former assumes a 'clean break' in the variability at each scale boundary, as opposed to the continuous variability implied in the structure of the latter.

12.3.2 Examples of use of Model II in scale analysis

A few examples of the use of this kind of model exist. Thus Haggett (1961) has employed it to examine variability in the distribution of woodland in the

Tagus-Sado basin in central Portugal, while Chorley, Stoddart, Haggett and Slaymaker (1966) have considered the scale components in surface sand facies in the Breckland area of eastern England.

The particular example which we now look at in more detail is taken from Moellering and Tobler (1972). These authors examined the data set shown in

✱✱✱✱✱

(A)

```
2 2 2 1 0 1 0 0 1 2 0 0 0 0 1 2 0 1 0 1 2 2 0 1 1 2 0 1 1 1 1 2 1 1 2 0 1 2 0 2
0 2 0 1 2 0 1 1 1 2 2 0 1 1 0 0 0 1 0 1 0 2 2 0 1 2 2 1 2 1 0 0 1 0 1 0 2 0 1 2
1 0 1 1 0 0 1 0 1 1 1 0 1 0 1 1 0 1 2 0 2 0 0 1 3 0 1 2 1 0 2 1 1 2 0 0 1 0 2 2
0 1 1 1 0 2 0 1 2 0 0 0 2 2 0 0 0 1 0 0 1 2 0 0 0 1 0 0 0 1 0 9 0 0 0 1 1 1 1 1
1 2 0 0 0 0 0 0 0 0 1 0 2 0 2 2 0 1 2 1 0 1 1 1 0 3 0 1 2 0 1 1 1 1 0 0 1 0 3 1
1 3 1 0 1 0 1 0 0 0 0 0 2 2 0 2 0 0 1 0 0 1 0 0 0 0 1 2 1 1 1 2 1 0 2 1 3 1 1 1
0 1 0 0 0 1 0 1 0 1 2 0 1 3 1 1 4 1 3 1 0 1 1 0 0 0 0 0 0 0 2 2 2 0 1 2 0 3 0 1
0 0 1 0 0 1 0 0 1 3 0 0 1 0 0 1 0 0 1 0 2 2 0 2 0 0 1 2 1 2 2 2 0 0 1 1 0 0 1 0
0 1 1 0 1 1 0 1 1 3 1 1 3 0 1 0 2 0 1 0 0 0 1 3 3 2 0 0 0 0 1 0 1 0 1 0 0 0 1 0
0 0 0 0 0 1 1 2 0 0 1 5 2 0 0 0 0 2 0 0 2 1 0 1 0 0 2 0 0 0 1 0 0 1 0 0 0 1 2 0
0 2 0 0 1 1 1 0 1 1 1 0 2 1 4 2 1 0 1 2 2 0 1 1 2 1 0 0 0 0 1 2 2 0 0 0 0 0 0 0
0 0 0 1 1 0 1 0 0 0 0 1 2 2 2 0 0 0 1 0 1 3 1 2 0 0 0 0 0 2 1 2 0 0 0 2 0 1 1 1
0 1 0 0 1 2 0 0 0 0 0 0 0 1 1 0 1 1 1 2 1 1 1 3 0 1 0 1 1 0 1 4 1 1 2 0 1 0 2
0 0 0 1 1 1 1 0 1 1 0 0 0 0 1 2 0 1 1 1 1 3 0 2 1 0 0 0 0 2 0 0 0 3 0 2 0 1 1 2
0 1 1 0 0 0 1 1 2 0 0 1 0 0 1 0 0 2 0 0 0 1 0 0 0 1 1 1 0 0 0 0 2 0 0 2 1 0 0
3 4 1 1 0 3 1 0 0 0 2 0 0 0 1 0 1 2 1 0 0 1 4 1 0 0 2 2 0 0 0 1 0 1 1 1 0 4 4 0
0 0 1 0 0 1 1 1 1 1 0 0 1 0 2 0 3 2 0 2 2 3 1 0 0 1 1 0 1 3 0 0 1 1 0 1 1 1 0
1 1 0 1 0 1 0 0 2 1 0 0 2 2 0 0 2 1 5 2 0 0 0 0 0 0 0 0 1 0 0 1 2 2 0 0 2 1 0 1
0 3 0 1 0 0 0 2 0 0 0 2 0 0 0 0 1 0 2 0 0 0 0 1 1 0 0 2 0 0 0 0 0 0 1 3 0 0 1
0 1 1 0 2 0 1 0 0 0 0 0 1 1 0 0 1 0 1 0 0 0 1 1 2 1 1 0 0 0 0 1 1 0 1 0 0 2 1 2
1 0 0 0 1 1 0 0 1 1 0 0 2 1 0 0 0 0 1 3 0 2 2 1 4 0 1 0 0 0 3 0 0 1 1 0 1 0
0 2 1 1 0 1 1 0 0 0 1 1 0 0 3 1 1 0 0 1 0 2 5 2 1 1 0 1 2 0 0 1 1 0 1 2 0 0
0 0 0 0 0 2 0 1 1 1 2 0 0 1 2 1 1 0 1 0 0 3 2 1 4 5 0 2 1 1 1 1 2 0 2 0 0 0 1 0 1
0 0 1 1 2 0 0 1 0 0 1 1 0 0 0 0 0 2 0 0 1 2 2 1 0 0 3 3 1 1 0 1 0 0 0 0 0 0 1 0
1 0 1 1 0 0 1 1 2 2 1 0 0 0 0 0 1 0 0 2 1 1 0 0 0 1 1 0 1 1 0 0 2 0 2
0 0 1 1 1 1 1 0 0 0 2 2 1 2 0 0 0 2 1 0 0 0 0 0 1 1 0 3 0 0 1 2 0 7 1 0 2 0 0 2
0 1 1 1 1 2 2 2 0 2 0 3 1 0 1 0 0 1 0 0 1 1 3 1 0 1 0 2 1 2 1 0 0 0
0 2 1 0 0 0 2 1 2 0 0 0 0 1 0 3 0 1 1 0 0 0 1 0 0 0 1 0 0 0 2 2 1 1 0 1 0 1 1 0
0 0 0 0 1 0 0 2 0 0 0 0 0 0 0 1 1 0 0 1 1 0 1 0 0 1 1 0 1 1 0 1 1 1 2 0 1 0 2 1
2 0 0 1 2 0 0 0 0 0 1 0 0 1 1 2 1 3 2 0 0 0 0 0 0 0 0 0 1 0 0 0 1 1 1 1 0 2 1 0
```

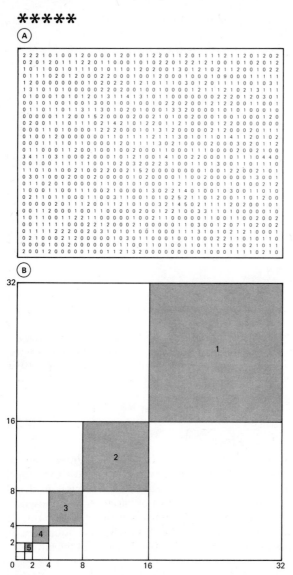

Figure 12.6   A Quadrat counts of houses from Matui's data for the Hukuno area of Japan. (Source: Cliff and Ord, 1973, p. 61.) **B** Amalgamation scheme for the hierarchical design. The identity numbers indicate the scale levels. Level 0 is the single cell composed of 1024 level 5 units.

Figure 12.6A. It gives the number of isolated houses per 1000 metre^2 quadrat in Hukuno Town, Tonami Plain, Japan (Matui, 1932). Moellering and Tobler took this quadrat size as their smallest spatial scale (level five), and looked at the variance component at this scale, and for various higher scales obtained by amalgamating quadrats in a balanced design. To do this, they deleted the last eight columns of data from the original 30×40 matrix shown in Figure 12.6A and repeated rows one and two of the matrix at the bottom. This resulted in a 32×32 matrix for analysis, and the amalgamation scheme appears in Figure 12.6B. Their results are given in Table 12.2. As they state, 'the importance of the scale-variance components diminishes quickly as the cell size gets larger. The interpretation is clearly that the distribution of population in Western Hukuno is attributable to local site conditions.' As we shall see (Sections 13.4.2 and 13.4.3), this conclusion is consistent with that of Cliff and Ord (1973, Section 3.3) who analysed these data using quadrat count methods.

Table 12.2   Scale variances from Matui's data.

Scale† Level	Source of variation	Sum of squares	Percent of TSS	df	Mean square
5	ε_{ijklm}	614.25	69.37	768	0.79
4	δ_{ijkl}	184.8	20.98	192	0.96
3	γ_{ijk}	64.54	7.29	48	1.34
2	β_{ij}	15.27	1.73	12	1.27
1	α_i	5.58	0.63	3	1.86
0	Total	885.45	100.00	1023	—

Source: Moellering and Tobler, 1972, p. 44.
†See Figure 12.6B.
Notes: TSS = total sum of squares, df = degrees of freedom.

To reinforce Moellering and Tobler's analysis, the formulae given in equations (12.10) can be extended to a five-level hierarchy to obtain

$$\hat{\sigma}_\varepsilon^2 = 0.79, \hat{\sigma}_\delta^2 = 0.043, \hat{\sigma}_\gamma^2 = 0.024, \hat{\sigma}_\beta^2 = -0.001, \hat{\sigma}_\alpha^2 = 0.0023.$$

The preponderance of variance at the ε level supports Moellering and Tobler's conclusions. The negative value for $\hat{\sigma}_\beta$ is due to sampling variation. This can be handled by setting $\hat{\sigma}_\beta^2 = 0$ and pooling the α and β levels to yield, from Table 12.2, $SS_{(\alpha+\beta)} = 20.85$ with $15df$, which implies $MS_{(\alpha+\beta)} = 1.39$ and $\hat{\sigma}_{(\alpha+\beta)}^2 = 0.001$. Working with MS_ε, MS_δ, MS_γ and $MS_{(\alpha+\beta)}$, application of the appropriate versions of equations (12.11) gives

$$H_0: \sigma_{(\alpha+\beta)}^2 = \sigma_\gamma^2 = \sigma_\delta^2 = 0; \quad F = 1.76$$

$$H_0: \sigma_\gamma^2 = \sigma_\delta^2 = 0; \quad F = 1.70$$

$$H_0: \sigma_\delta^2 = 0; \quad F = 1.22.$$

On the basis of these results, $H_0: \sigma_\gamma^2 = \sigma_\delta^2 = 0$ is just rejected at the $\alpha = 0.05$ significance level because of the extra degrees of freedom (Appendix Table A4). We conclude that the γ and δ levels show slight components of variance, but that the bulk of the variability is concentrated at the ε level.

12.3.3 *Extensions of the model*

An important extension of (12.5) is described in Cliff and Ord (1972) and in Cliff *et al.* (1975, Chapter 10). As we have noted in Figure 11.1 geographers are interested in space–time modelling, and a question which Figure 11.1 raises is 'which of the components shown (the spatial, or "simultaneous effects" component; the time component; or the space–time interaction or covariance component) is the most important?' It may be shown that, if x_{it} is the observation for the ith 'county' in the tth time period on the random variable, X, then

$$x_{it} = \mu + \alpha_i + \beta_t + \gamma_{it} + \varepsilon_{it}, \quad \begin{aligned} i &= 1, 2, ..., n, \\ t &= 1, 2, ..., T, \end{aligned} \tag{12.12}$$

may be used to examine this question. Here n is the number of counties, T is the number of time periods, μ is the overall mean, α_i is the effect of the ith region, β_t is the effect of the tth time period, and γ_{it} is the interaction space–time effect [confounded with the random disturbance, ε_{it} when only one observation is available for each (i, t) pair].

As with the spatial scale model, (12.5), one of the advantages of (12.12) is that it not only enables the researcher to determine which component is the most important in accounting for variability in the data, but it also decomposes the space–time variation into *independent* components. Each component can thus be modelled separately in further analysis. This is of great importance in forecasting models (see Section 16.6), where frequently there are more parameters than data, which prevents simultaneous estimation.

12.4 Fourier and Spectral Analysis

To illustrate the principles involved in spectral analysis, let us consider the time series of monthly unemployment rates for Weston-super-Mare

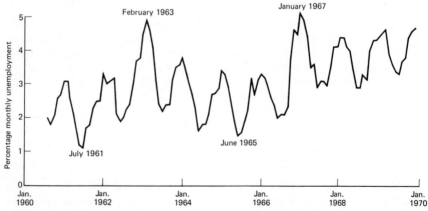

Figure 12.7   Percentage unemployment by month for Weston-super-Mare, August 1960–December 1969.

(England), 1960–69, shown in Figure 12.7. The time series is discrete, and displays a clear cyclical behaviour. Since Weston-super-Mare has a strong tourist trade, employment in the town is markedly seasonal, with high unemployment in winter, and low unemployment in summer. If we can assume that the time series is stationary in the wide sense (definition 10.1, Section 10.4.2), then it would not be unreasonable to try to model the series as a sum of harmonic terms. In particular, we might consider (Granger, 1969, p. 3) the linear cyclical model

$$Y_t = \sum_{j=1}^{m} a_j \cos(\omega_j \theta + \varphi_j) + \varepsilon_t. \tag{12.13}$$

In this model, Y_t would represent the percentage of unemployment at time t, while the $\{\varepsilon_t\}$ are random disturbances of the usual form. In order to define the terms in the remainder of the model, we need to consider the form of a cosine curve in more detail.

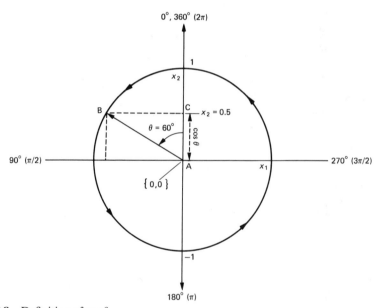

Figure 12.8　Definition of $\cos\theta$.

12.4.1　*The cosine curve*

Suppose we have an $\{X_1, X_2\}$ cartesian co-ordinate system as shown in Figure 12.8, and that a circle of unit radius centred upon the origin $\{0,0\}$ has been drawn. If the cosine of the angle, θ, is now defined in the usual way as

$$\cos\theta = AC/AB, \tag{12.14}$$

a plot of $\cos\theta$ against θ produces Figure 12.9. The equation of the curve is

$$X_2 = \cos\theta, \quad 0 \leqslant \theta \leqslant 2\pi. \tag{12.15}$$

In Figure 12.9, the *wavelength* (*period* or *cycle*), *w*, is the distance between similar points on the curve, such as peak to peak or trough to trough. The *amplitude*, *a*, is half the vertical height from peak to trough on the curve. We also note that the curve repeats itself in the *basic interval* of 2π. That is, the curve has a period of 2π.

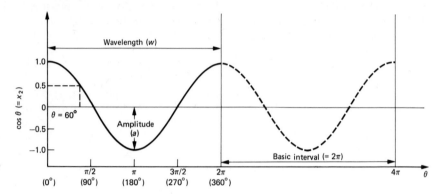

Figure 12.9   The cosine curve. Plot of $\cos\theta$ against θ.

Figure 12.9 shows one particular cosine curve. It is not difficult to imagine, however, that we could generate a whole series of cosine curves, each with its own wavelength and amplitude. We denote the wavelength of the typical curve, *j*, by w_j, and the amplitude by a_j. The number of waves in the basic interval, 2π, is referred to as the *angular frequency*, ω_j, where

$$\omega_j = 2\pi/w_j, \tag{12.16}$$

implying

$$w_j = 2\pi/\omega_j. \tag{12.17}$$

Sometimes in time series analysis, the wavelength is expressed as the number of

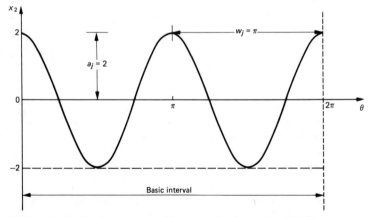

Figure 12.10   Cosine curve used in example of equation (12.18).

cycles per unit division of the basic interval. This *cyclical frequency* is $1/w_j$. We may thus write our general cosine curve as

$$X_2 = a_j \cos(\omega_j \theta). \tag{12.18}$$

Example: Consider the curve shown in Figure 12.10. Let us use (12.18) to determine X_2 at the position $\theta = \pi$. The wavelength of the curve is π, and so, from (12.16), $\omega_j = 2$, as it clearly is. Substituting into (12.18), we have

$$X_2 = 2\cos(2.\pi) = 2\cos 360° = 2.$$

The curve given in equation (12.18) starts with its crest at zero, but it may start elsewhere if $\omega_j \theta$ is modified by the addition of a factor, φ_j, known as the *phase shift*, $0 \leqslant \varphi_j \leqslant 2\pi$. Thus

$$X_2 = a_j \cos(\omega_j \theta + \varphi_j), \quad 0 \leqslant \theta, \varphi \leqslant 2\pi. \tag{12.19}$$

The phase shift is the distance of the crest from the origin, regardless of the frequency of the wave being considered. See Figure 12.11.

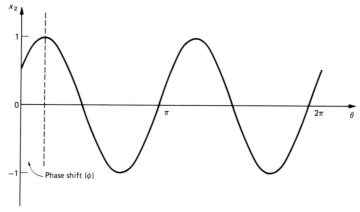

Figure 12.11 Definition of phase shift.

We have shown how any given cosine curve, j, as defined in (12.19), may be characterized in terms of its amplitude, frequency, and phase shift. Comparison of the linear cyclical model, (12.13), with (12.19) shows, since we have used the same notation in both equations, that (12.13) consists of the sum of m cosine waves (that is, purely cyclical components) with amplitudes, a_j, frequencies, ω_j, and phase shifts, φ_j, together with random disturbances. The sum of periodic functions of the type given in (12.13) is known as a Fourier series, and such series form the basis of spectral analysis. From Kendall (1973, p. 95), the typical Fourier series may be written as

$$f(x) = \sum_{j=0}^{\infty} a_j \cos(\omega_j \theta + \varphi_j) \tag{12.20}$$

$$= \sum_{j=1}^{\infty} b_j \cos(\omega_j \theta) + \sum_{j=1}^{\infty} c_j \sin(\omega_j \theta) + \tfrac{1}{2} b_0. \tag{12.21}$$

One of the important features of a Fourier series is that, while obviously simple cyclical patterns such as the unemployment series of Figure 12.7 will be fitted by such a model, many functions can in fact be approximated by a sum of harmonic terms. Thus Figure 12.12 shows how the sum of two simple waves illustrated in the lower part of the diagram can produce a complicated curve. In general, it will be clear from Figures 12.9, 12.10 and equation (12.20) that for a function expanded in a Fourier series, the successive terms will have periods $2\pi, 2\pi/2, 2\pi/3, \ldots$, angular frequencies 1, 2, 3, ..., and cyclical frequencies $1/2\pi$, $2/2\pi, 3/2\pi, \ldots$ (Kendall, 1973, p. 96).

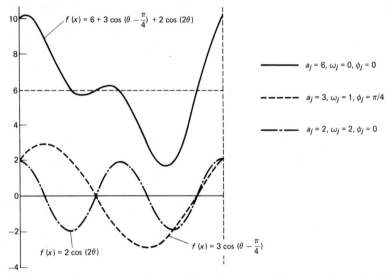

Figure 12.12   Definition of a complicated curve as the sum of two simple waves (adapted from Rayner, 1971, p. 18, Figure 2.5.1).

Having described what a Fourier series is, we are now in a position to outline how spectral analysis proceeds. In the analysis of a single time series of the sort shown in Figure 12.7, Fourier series are fitted to the data using ordinary least squares, and estimates of the unknown parameters, a_j and φ_j, the amplitudes and phase angles, are obtained for each wave (as discussed immediately above, the frequencies are known). Thus a given data set is decomposed into a series of simple waves, each of which goes some way towards describing the form of the compound curve. The analysis is the reverse of the procedure used to construct Figure 12.12; the model breaks down the total variance in the original data into harmonics of different frequencies, each of which accounts for some proportion of the total variance. It is thus another scale components model and may be compared with the nested analysis of variance model of Section 12.3.

The question of how much of the total variance may be attributed to waves of various frequencies is usually resolved by constructing a diagram of the *power spectrum*. The power spectrum is effectively a plot of the percentage of

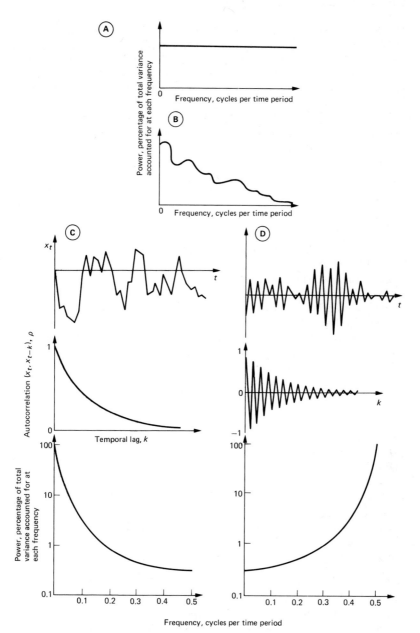

Figure 12.13 Schematic power spectra for a purely random process (**A**), a cyclical process (**B**), and discrete first order autoregressive processes (**C** and **D**). In **C**, the three diagrams show, working from top to bottom, (i) a time series realization with autocorrelation parameter, $\rho = 0.9$, (ii) its autocorrelation function and (iii) its power spectrum. In **D**, the diagrams provide the same information for a series negatively autocorrelated by the amount $\rho = -0.9$. Diagrams **C** and **D** are adapted from Jenkins and Watts, 1968, pp. 219–20.

the total variance accounted for (i.e. the power) against frequency, ω_j (Rayner, 1971, Section 3.4). It can be shown that some commonly occurring time series produce very characteristic power spectra. Figure 12.13 shows schematically the power spectra for purely random, purely cyclical, and purely autoregressive time series. Consider the purely random time series first. Intuitively, we would expect a cosine wave of one frequency to be no better than a cosine wave of any other frequency in accounting for the variability in such a series, and the resulting theoretical power spectrum will therefore be horizontal. In a cyclical series, however, we would expect the cosine wave with a frequency which corresponds most closely with the main period in the original data to account for the largest proportion of the variability in the series. Thus, for example, for the unemployment data shown in Figure 12.7, a wave with a periodicity of 12 months would provide a very good fit. We would also get reasonable fits from waves with periodicities of 3, 4, and 6 months, since some of the peaks of these waves (say every 4th, 3rd and 2nd peak respectively) correspond closely with the 12-month period in the unemployment data. Thus the power spectrum for a cyclical series typically has a declining (damped) wave form itself. The highest peak in the spectrum corresponds with the basic periodicity, or *fundamental wavelength*, in the data (12 months in the example we are discussing); the other peaks correspond to waves with frequencies which are *harmonics* of the fundamental wavelength. Note that in interpreting the power spectrum, low frequencies indicate waves with long periods, while high frequencies represent waves with short periods.

We now consider an autoregressive time series, which may be represented by the model,

$$Y_t = \sum_{j=1}^{m} \rho_j Y_{t-j} + \varepsilon_t, \tag{12.22}$$

so that Y_t is a linear sum of earlier Y values plus a random disturbance. A first-order process would simply be

$$Y_t = \rho Y_{t-1} + \varepsilon_t.$$

If ρ is large and positive (positive autocorrelation), we are arguing that adjacent values in the series are very similar. The series will thus vary smoothly through time. Smooth variations will be fitted most closely by waves of low frequencies (that is, waves with a long period and which therefore also vary smoothly).

Conversely, if ρ is large and negative (negative autocorrelation), the series will alternate rapidly (that is, be very 'spikey'), and these short oscillations will be fitted most closely by waves of very short wavelengths (which are also spikey). Positive autoregressive processes therefore tend to be characterized by concentration of power at low frequencies; negative autoregressive processes typically have concentration of power at high frequencies. These features are evident in Figure 12.13c and D.

Finally, we note that real world time-series are frequently a mixture of cyclical, autoregressive, and random components. These produce very complicated power spectra, and their interpretation is not always easy. 'It is seen then, that the spectrum will suggest the type of model that might be fitted to the data; a very flat spectrum would suggest a white noise (purely random), a smooth spectrum would suggest an [positive] autoregressive model but any sharp spikes would indicate the possible presence of purely cyclical components' (Granger, 1969, p. 8).

12.4.2 *The spectrum of US40*

As a practical demonstration of the methods discussed so far, and of their limitations, we review papers by Tobler (1969a) and Rayner and Golledge (1973) on the spacing of settlements along US Route 40 from Baltimore to San Francisco. In the first of these papers, Tobler recorded the 1960 population of each town within one mile of the highway, and the distance of that town (to the nearest mile) from central Baltimore. The highway is clearly a linear transect in space and, provided we are prepared to regard the settlement process along the highway as a sequential development from east to west, it may be treated like a univariate time series. The requirement of sequential development is made to ensure unilateral directional dependence among the settlements, as in time series observations [cf. the discussion of equations (10.6) to (10.7)]. This assumption is probably not that unrealistic for the problem in hand.

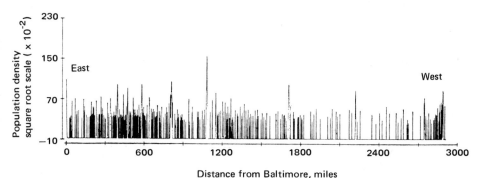

Figure 12.14   Population density versus distance from Baltimore along Highway 40 yielded by the cosine model. Source: Tobler, 1969a, p. 48.

A further assumption of spectral analysis is that the data points are equally spaced along the transect. This requirement is usually met in the time series case—most data are collected at regular intervals (weekly, monthly, quarterly, etc.), but it is a requirement that is rarely satisfied by spatially located data. This was so in Tobler's study, and he obtained an estimated population density at regular (one mile) intervals along the highway by applying four different models to smooth out irregularities in the observed data. The models used were

(1) a 'cylindrical' town, which assumed a uniform distribution of population in all urban areas;

(2) a 'conical' town, which assumed a uniform decline in population density from the centre of each town;

(3) a 'parabolic' town, with parabolic decline in population density from the

centre of each town, but with zero population at the centre, and zero decline at the edge;

(4) a 'cosinusoidal' town, with density slope of zero at the centre and the edge.

These models are formally defined in Section 6.2.1. The population densities yielded by the cosine model, against distance from Baltimore, are shown in Figure 12.14.

The power spectra obtained from an analysis of the population densities produced by each of the four models were very similar; that for the cosine model is illustrated in Figure 12.15. The results are similar for each model, and 'the over-all shape of the spectrum suggests an autoregressive model for the processes involved in creating a distribution of towns along US 40' (Tobler, 1969a, p. 51). The spectra may be compared with the theoretical spectrum for an autoregressive process shown in Figure 12.13. Tobler attributed this autoregressive structure to the fact that central place competition (discussed in Section 5.2) tends to produce spatial organization in town sizes.

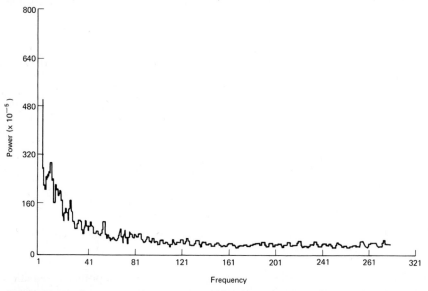

Figure 12.15   Spectral density for Highway 40 data shown in Figure 12.14. Source: Tobler, 1969a, p. 50.

However, it is clear that any massaging of a data set prior to analysis must have some effect upon the results. Thus, Rayner and Golledge (1973), in a re-examination of Tobler's data, suggested that the shape of the spectrum given in Figure 12.15 is largely a function of the population-smoothing model used. When unsmoothed population data are used, the observed spectrum is consistent with a random generating process for settlement spacing. See Figure 12.16. The confidence bands around the average value for the variance show the probability limits for the estimates if the data are random. This finding links back to Curry's (1964) notion that there is likely to be a strong random component in settlement size and spacing (i.e. the random spatial economy of Section 4.2.1).

As we noted in Section 10.4.3, the estimation of the power spectrum is based upon the assumption that the data are stationary in time and space. If this assumption is not met, the spectrum is often distorted at low frequencies. For example, if the data possess a linear trend, they are non-stationary within the terms of definition 10.1. It is fairly clear that a simple linear trend will be approximated by waves with a very, very long period. That is, the power spectrum will look like that from a first order positive autoregressive process. In particular, the spectrum will be of the form, $y = 1/x^2$ (Kendall, 1973, p. 99). In any practical example, it may be difficult to decide whether spectra of the form, $y = 1/x^2$, are the result of non-stationary data or of a genuine autoregressive process. This sort of problem forms the background to comments by Cliff and Ord (1975b), who have noted that Tobler's original results may have been partly influenced by non-stationarities in the data, since there is a greater degree of settlement on the seaboards of the USA than elsewhere.

12.4.3 *Two-dimensional (spatial) spectral analysis*

So far, we have concentrated upon the spectral analysis of a single univariate time series, or of spatial transects which can be treated in the same manner.

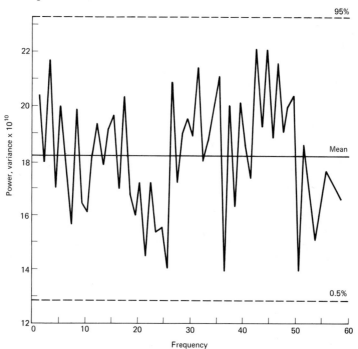

Figure 12.16 Power spectrum of unsmoothed US 40 population data. Source: Rayner and Golledge, 1973, p. 345.

Usually, however, spatial data are two dimensional, and the methods described can be extended to that situation. Rayner is one of the few geographers to have written on two-dimensional spectral analysis, and the following account and examples are based upon work that he has either authored or co-authored.

The analysis proceeds by fitting a double Fourier series to the values of a variate, Y, which have been collected at regular intervals on an $\{X_1, X_2\}$ cartesian co-ordinate system. The set of values in this *data domain* may be denoted, $\{y(x_1, x_2)\}$. The double series replaces the single series used in the time series case [equation (12.21)]. That is, a double summation is used to handle terms in the X_1 and X_2 directions of the cartesian grid, compared with the single summation for the unidimensional time series case. The Fourier surface obtained may be viewed as equivalent to the trend surface described in Section 12.2, except that the surface has been modelled with harmonic terms (sines and cosines) instead of polynomials.

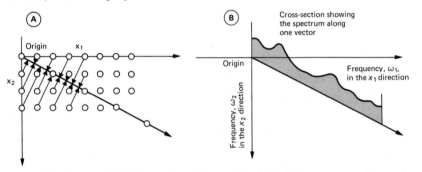

Figure 12.17   Graphical illustration of the way in which data are arranged to produce the estimates along one vector in the two dimensional spectrum. **A** Projection of data in the data domain onto a line of specific orientation; **B** Two-dimensional spectrum. Source: Rayner and Golledge, 1972, p. 351.

The next step in the two-dimensional case is to calculate a power spectral surface (the *frequency domain*) to replace the graphs of Figures 12.13, 12.15 and 12.16 used in the one-dimensional situation. The interpretation of the spectral surface has been outlined in Rayner (1971, Chapter 9) and in Rayner and Golledge (1972, pp. 350–51) as follows. Consider the data domain shown in Figure 12.17A. Imagine that a straight line transect has been drawn through the origin of the cartesian grid, and that all the two-dimensional data have been mapped on to the transect line in the manner shown by the arrows. Rayner and Golledge argue that a cross-section taken through the spectral surface, in the same position and orientation as the line transect in the data domain, may be interpreted as a one-dimensional power spectrum of all the data mapped on to the transect in the manner described above (Figure 12.17B). Alternatively, Rayner and Golledge indicate that a cross-section through the spectral surface may be viewed as the result of fitting to the raw data, orthogonally to the orientation of the cross-section, sets of parallel waves of varying frequencies. All waves of a specific frequency will produce a single point on the cross-section. See Figures 12.18A and B. Thus high power at a particular point on a cross-section implies a good fit of waves of that frequency at 90° to the cross-section (that is, a periodicity in the data domain at 90° to the cross-section in the frequency domain).

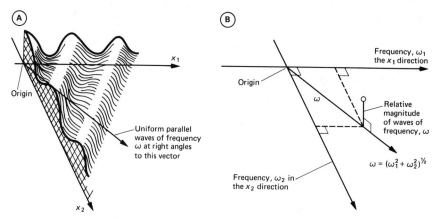

Figure 12.18   Production of a single estimate in the frequency domain from parallel sinusoidal waves of constant spacing in the data domain. **A** Data domain; **B** Spectrum (frequency domain). Source: Rayner and Golledge, 1972, p. 351.

It is evident that orientation is the crucial feature of this kind of analysis. The method tells us something about the variability in the pattern of variate values in different directions across a map.

To illustrate the above ideas, we examine the population distribution in a 120×120 square mile portion of North Dakota. The location of settlements is shown in Figure 12.19, and the spectrum of population in Figure 12.20A. The construction of diagrams like Figure 12.20A is considered in Rayner (1971, Chapter 9). The variance explained (power) has been estimated for bands of adjacent frequencies, and each band or block in Figure 12.20A has been labelled by its central frequency $[r_1, r_2]$. The origin appears in the middle of the r_1 axis. See Figure 12.20B and C for a further illustration of the relationships between orientation of patterns in the data domain and the corresponding power spectral surfaces (cf. the discussion of Figure 12.18).

In the spectrum of Figure 12.20A, the ridges of high explained variance show north–south trends, confirming the east–west arrangement of the settlement pattern shown in Figure 12.19. The breaks in the ridges in the frequency domain are suggestive of several broken lines of settlement in the data domain, rather than a few continuous lines (Rayner and Golledge, 1972). From those authors, the frequency in cycles per unit of distance is given by

$$f_1 = \frac{r_1}{2M_1 \Delta X_1}, \tag{12.23}$$

and

$$f_2 = \frac{r_2}{2M_2 \Delta X_2}, \tag{12.24}$$

where $M_i = \max r_i$ and ΔX_i is the interval of measurement for distance in the data domain (1 mile in the example). The spacing between settlements shown in Figure 12.19 is about 6–8 miles in an east–west direction, and equation (12.24) yields this sort of figure and its harmonics.

***

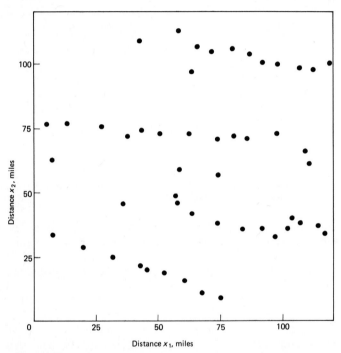

Figure 12.19   Location of settlements in the sample region of North Dakota. Source: Rayner and Golledge, 1972, p. 363.

There is some overlap between the methods discussed so far in this chapter and the techniques for point pattern analysis considered in Chapter 13, in that Bartlett (1963, 1964) and Rayner (1971) have shown how spectral methods may be applied to point patterns. An *event array* is constructed by specifying the location of each settlement in the array as a one; all other data points appear as zeros. The spectrum of the event array for the Dakota data appears in Figure 12.21, and is similar to Figure 12.20A.

Finally, in this sub-section, we note that sometimes the two-dimensional spectrum reveals no particular directional bias in the patterns formed by observations in the data domain. One might then consider variance explained against frequency, irrespective of orientation, by averaging around the semicircles of constant frequency as shown in Figure 12.22. If this is done for Figure 12.21, we obtain Figure 12.23, which brings out again the main periodicity at about 6–8 miles.

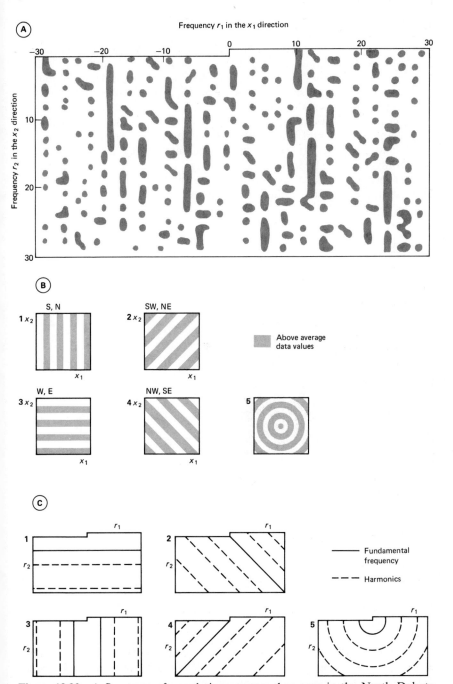

Figure 12.20 **A** Spectrum of populations greater than zero in the North Dakota sample region. Source: Rayner and Golledge, 1972, p. 364. **B** Sample data-domain patterns and their corresponding power spectra (**C**).

12.4.4 *Estimation problems*

Our discussion of the spectral approach has been deliberately slanted to give an intuitive feel for the way in which the methods work and the kinds of problems to which they may be applied. We have not considered estimation problems in any formal sense because the mathematics required frequently go beyond the background assumed in this book. The interested reader will find rigorous accounts in Granger and Hatanaka (1964), Fishman (1968), Rayner (1971), and Jenkins and Watts (1968). In addition, the last named give flow charts and computer algorithms for the techniques they describe, while the commonly-available BMD computer package (Dixon, 1964) includes spectral analysis programs. However, in order to use spectral analysis correctly, some important practical points must be mentioned.

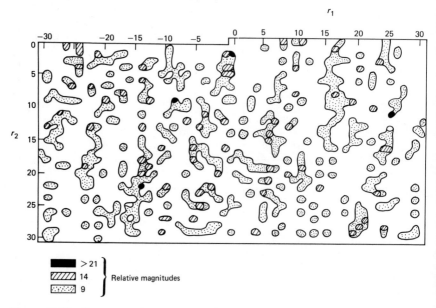

Figure 12.21   Spectrum of event array of North Dakota data. Source: Rayner and Golledge, 1972, p. 365.

It has been commonly assumed (Granger and Hughes, 1968, p. 83) that the length of each time series required before spectral methods can be used is between 100 and 200 terms, and in the spatial case, probably between 300 and 400. The object of papers by Granger and Hughes (1968) and by Neave (1972) was to look at the effect upon the results obtained when series of length 30–100 are analysed. Series of this size commonly occur in geography. Their conclusions, which were reached after an examination of the results of spectral analyses of data generated by purely random (white noise) and first-order autoregressive processes, may be summarized as follows:

(1) The power spectral estimates at low frequencies are likely to be seriously biased downwards (that is, the percentage of variance explained will be

underestimated) if the data are analysed in deviation (i.e. $z_i = x_i - \bar{x}$) rather than raw form. 'The results for the power spectrum indicate that gross features of the spectral shape, such as a large peak, may be found with short series, but that any more subtle features, particularly near zero frequency, may not be found' (Granger and Hughes, p. 98). Neave is even stronger, 'estimation of the spectrum [under any circumstances] at low frequencies is well-nigh impossible with short series' (p. 402).

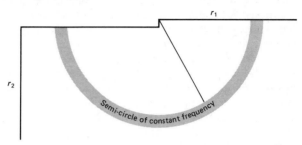

Figure 12.22 Construction of average variance explained for a given frequency, irrespective of orientation.

(2) Spectral analysis obviously will not pick up periodicities in the data which are less than the length of the interval between observations. In general, if t is the length of the interval, then periods of less than $2t$ or angular frequencies higher than π/t will not be detected. This limiting value is called the *Nyquist frequency* (Kendall, 1973, p. 97).

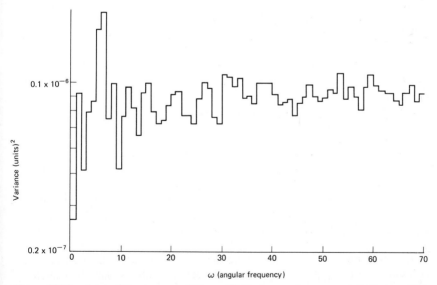

Figure 12.23 Averaged spectrum of Figure 12.21. Source: Rayner and Golledge, 1972, p. 365.

12.5 Space–Time Spectral Analysis

12.5.1 *Principles of the method*

Like the autocorrelation measures, spectral techniques can also be used to explore the patterns in space–time data sets. Granger (1969) has outlined a methodology by which this may be done. Suppose that we have n spatial locations, and that a time series of observations is available for each of the locations. We use $X_{i(t)}$ to denote the time series for the ith location. Granger has suggested that *cross-spectral* analysis may be employed to make comparisons between pairs of regional series. The proposed method does not permit simultaneous examination of the interrelationships between all the spatially located time series. However, Granger's idea has one very important advantage. Spectral analysis, as described in Section 12.4.2, assumes temporal stationarity, while the two-dimensional spectral approach outlined in Section 12.4.3 assumes spatial stationarity. The multi-directional dependence among spatially located observations, as opposed to the unidirectional dependence among time series observations $[X_t = f(X_{t-k})]$, means that temporal stationarity is usually much easier to achieve than is spatial stationarity. See Section 10.3. As Granger (1969, p. 27) has commented, his method of analysis means that, for a time–space data set, we need only to suppose that the process generating the data is time-stationary, and not that it is also spatially stationary. Indeed, as we shall see, the method really aims to identify non-stationarities between regions.

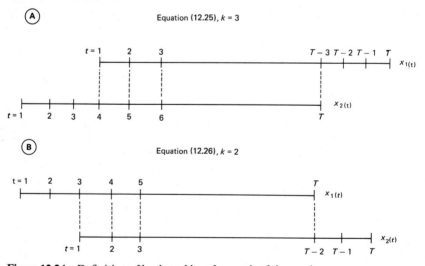

Figure 12.24   Definition of leads and lags for a pair of time series.

Suppose that $n = 2$, and that therefore our two T element time series may be denoted by $X_{1(t)}$ and $X_{2(t)}$. Cross-spectral analyses usually begins by computing the cross-covariance between the two series. This is done in order to establish whether the two series are moving together (in phase), or whether one series leads or lags the other. Following Kendall and Buckland (1960, p. 155), we say that an event occurring at time $t+k$ $(k > 0)$ *lags behind* an event occurring at time t; the extent of the lag is k. Conversely, an event occurring k time units before an event at t [that is, at $(t-k)$, $k > 0$], is said to *lead*, or to *lag negatively*, the event at t. The lag is of order $-k$. The cross covariance at lag k between a pair of series may be estimated by

$$r^{(k)}_{X_{1(t)}, X_{2(t)}} = \frac{1}{T-k} \sum_{t=1}^{T-k} (x_{1(t)} - \bar{x}_1)(x_{2(t+k)} - \bar{x}_2),$$

$$k = 0, 1, 2, ..., m, \quad (12.25)$$

when the lag is positive, and by

$$r^{(-k)}_{X_{1(t)}, X_{2(t)}} = \frac{1}{T-k} \sum_{t=1}^{T-k} (x_{1(t+k)} - \bar{x}_1)(x_{2(t)} - \bar{x}_2),$$

$$k = 0, 1, 2, ..., m, \quad (12.26)$$

when the lag is negative.
In (12.25)

$$\bar{x}_1 = \frac{1}{T-k} \sum_{1}^{T-k} x_{1(t)}, \quad \bar{x}_2 = \frac{1}{T-k} \sum_{1}^{T-k} x_{2(t+k)},$$

while in (12.26),

$$\bar{x}_1 = \frac{1}{T-k} \sum_{1}^{T-k} x_{1(t+k)}, \quad \bar{x}_2 = \frac{1}{T-k} \sum_{1}^{T-k} x_{2(t)}.$$

In addition, m is the maximum lag or *truncation point* up to which the equations are to be solved. Looked at graphically (Figure 12.24), equation (12.25) may be viewed as computing the cross-covariance between the overlapping parts of the two series when series two has been slid k time intervals to the *left* of series one. Conversely, in equation (12.26), we compute the cross-covariance between the overlapping parts of the two series when series two has been slid k time intervals to the *right* of series one. Figure 12.24 also makes clear the definition of lead and lag. Thus in Figure 12.24A, suppose that the same event happened at $t = 1$ in both series. With reference to some fixed starting point, by the time the event occurred in series one, it would already have happened three time periods earlier in series two. Series one lags behind series two. Conversely, in Figure 12.24B, the event at $t = 1$ in series one occurred two time intervals earlier than the corresponding event in series two, and so series one leads series two. The purpose of comparing two time series in this way is to establish 'the intensity of the relationship between two series for various leads or lags' (Kendall, 1973, p. 131). For example, if one had several regional economic time series, this sort of analysis could be used to establish whether one regional series consistently led all other regions. This might imply that such a region could be used as an economic lead indicator of behaviour in other areas. We also note that, although we have defined the cross-*covariance* between a pair of series, sometimes the cross-*correlation* is calculated by scaling the covariances of the series by the appropriate variances.

In cross-spectral analysis, the relationship between any pair of series is commonly further summarized by three quantities which are computed from the sample cross-spectrum [the sample cross-spectrum is the Fourier transformation of the sample cross-covariance function (see Jenkins and Watts, 1968, Chapter 8)]. The three measures are (Granger and Hughes, 1968):

(1) *Coherence* (coherency spectrum). Let $f_{X_{1(t)}}$ denote the power spectrum of the time series, $X_{1(t)}$, $f_{X_{2(t)}}$ the power spectrum of the time series, $X_{2(t)}$, and $f_{X_{1(t)}X_{2(t)}}$ the cross-spectrum between the two series. Then the coherence at the angular frequency, ω, is defined as

$$C(\omega) = \frac{|f_{X_{1(t)}X_{2(t)}}(\omega)|^2}{f_{X_{1(t)}}(\omega)f_{X_{2(t)}}(\omega)}. \tag{12.27}$$

In words, the coherence is the square of the correlation coefficient between the two series at the frequency, ω. Note the similarity of form between equation (12.27) and the coefficient of determination used in multiple regression analysis. A plot of coherence against frequency for a pair of series yields a *coherence diagram* (Granger, 1969). The diagram shows the strength of the relationship (0 = no relation, 1 = perfect correlation) between the two series at corresponding frequencies. As an example, the reader is referred back to Table 10.4, which was constructed by averaging over the coherences for all ω.

(2) *Phase angle* (phase spectrum). The phase angle at a frequency, ω, is defined as the difference between the phase shifts of the two series at that frequency. A *phase diagram* may be constructed as a plot of the phase angle against frequency. Granger (1969) has indicated that the diagram may be interpreted in terms of the time lag of a given frequency in one series over the same frequency in the other series. It is important to reiterate that there is a phase angle for each frequency, and that a single measure of lag based on the phase angles would have to be defined as some sort of average, which might be very misleading.

(3) *Gain*. The gain at the frequency, ω, is defined as

$$R(\omega) = \left\{ \frac{f_{X_{1(t)}}(\omega)C(\omega)}{f_{X_{2(t)}}(\omega)} \right\}^{\frac{1}{2}}. \tag{12.28}$$

Kendall (1973, p. 131) and Granger and Hughes (1968, p. 84) interpret gain as the regression coefficient of the series $X_{1(t)}$ on the series $X_{2(t)}$ at the frequency, ω (cf. the formula for the regression coefficient in regression analysis).

A full discussion of all three measures appears in Granger and Hatanaka (1964). In summary, they are all ways of measuring the degree of interaction between regional time series, and they can therefore be used to determine how regions mesh together in terms of their temporal behaviour.

12.5.2 *Regional examples*

As an illustrative example of cross-spectral analysis, we consider a paper by Bassett and Haggett (1971). These authors examined the regional time series of unemployment rates for eight closely adjacent employment exchange areas in the Southwest of England. The locations of the area are shown in Figure 12.25. The data were collected at monthly intervals from July 1960 to December

1969. Therefore $T = 114$ and $n = 8$. The data for one of the areas, Weston-super-Mare are plotted in Figure 12.7. Economically, Bristol is the regional centre in the Southwest, and it is of interest to see how far unemployment rates in other areas react to changes in unemployment levels in Bristol.

****

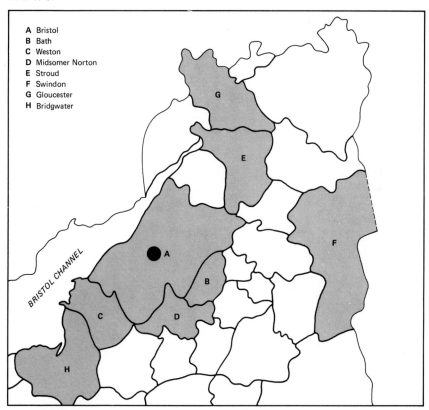

A Bristol
B Bath
C Weston
D Midsomer Norton
E Stroud
F Swindon
G Gloucester
H Bridgwater

BRISTOL CHANNEL

Figure 12.25   The locations of the eight exchange areas in the Bristol region. Source: Bassett and Haggett, 1971, p. 400.

Like the representative series shown in Figure 12.7, most of the data Bassett and Haggett analysed were not trend free. Recall from the discussion in Section 12.4.2 that trend is a form of non-stationarity. The authors therefore de-trended the data using simple linear regression techniques, and the cross-spectral analysis was based upon the de-trended series. An alternative method of de-trending the data would have been to use a moving average scheme (Kendall, 1973, Chapter 3). However, the trouble with moving averages is that such polynomials frequently remove as trend some of the long wavelength cycles in a series; one of the aims of the Bassett and Haggett study was to examine cyclical patterns in the data.

Cross-correlations were computed at monthly intervals between all pairs of

Table 12.3 Largest cross correlations and corresponding leads and lags†(in months) between unemployment series.*

	Bath	Weston	Midsomer Norton	Stroud	Swindon	Gloucester	Bridgwater
Bristol	(0.97)(0, +1)	(0.86)(0)	(0.88)(+2, +3)	(0.91)(+1)	(0.54)(+6)	(0.85)(−1, −2, −3)	(0.83)(+2, +3)
Bath		(0.92)(0)	(0.91)(+2, +3)	(0.92)(+1, +2)	(0.51)(+4, +5)	(0.89)(−1)	(0.88)(+2)
Weston			(0.92)(+2, +3)	(0.86)(+1, +2)	(0.41)(+2, +3)	(0.94)(0)	(0.92)(+1, +2)
Midsomer Norton				(0.87)(−1)	(0.49)(+1)	(0.83)(−1, −2, −3)	(0.87)(−1, −2)
Stroud					(0.21)(+5, +6)	(0.93)(−3)	(0.86)(−1)
Swindon						(0.25)(−6)	(0.68)(−2)
Gloucester							(0.81)(+2, +3)

* Bristol region, 1960—69.
† Following the convention of equations (12.25) and (12.26), a + indicates that the row region lags behind the column region, while a − indicates that the row region leads the column region. Several values for lead or lag indicate that the correlation coefficient did not vary significantly over those values of k.
Source: Bassett and Haggett, 1971, p. 404.

series up to a truncation point of six months. The maximum value of the correlation coefficient and the lag at which it occurred are recorded in Table 12.3. The results suggested (Bassett and Haggett, 1971, p. 402) that the contiguous areas of Bristol, Weston-super-Mare and Bath are roughly in phase. The more distant areas of Stroud, Midsomer Norton and Bridgwater tended to lead Bristol by 1–3 months, while Gloucester lagged Bristol. The low correlations between Swindon and other series, and the significant lead of Swindon over other areas, caused Bassett and Haggett to believe that the Swindon area 'stands outside the general pattern of changes within the Bristol region.'

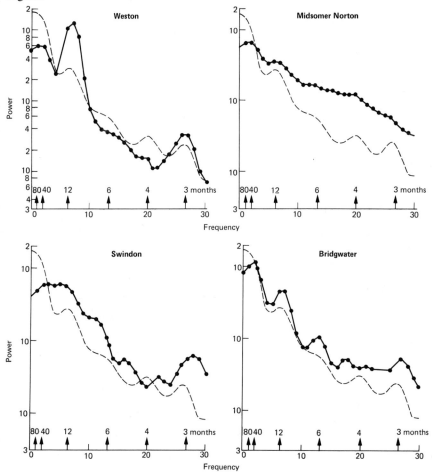

Figure 12.26   Estimated power spectra for four of the Bristol region series. The log of the spectral estimate, or power, has been plotted on the vertical axis. On the horizontal axis, the angular frequency, ω_j, corresponding to the jth datum point is given by $\omega_j = j\pi/40$. The unit time interval is taken as one month. The Bristol spectrum is shown as a broken line on the plots. Vertical arrows denote seasonal harmonics. Source: Bassett and Haggett, 1971, pp. 406–7.

The power spectra for four of the series appear in Figure 12.26. Comparison with the theoretical spectra shown in Figure 12.13 suggests that each may be interpreted as a mixture of autoregressive and cyclical components. Certainly, the twelve-month seasonal fluctuation in unemployment, and its harmonics, is readily picked out except for Swindon. There is also some evidence for a 40-month cycle in the less industrialized areas of Weston-super-Mare, Bridgwater, and Midsomer Norton.

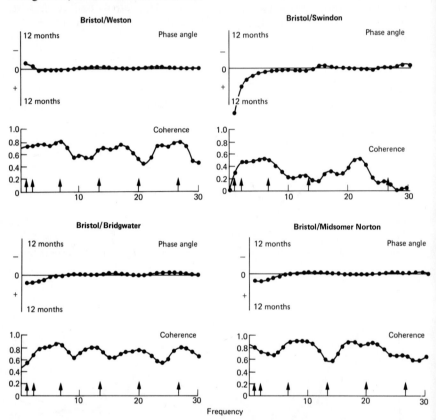

Figure 12.27   Phase angles and coherences at various frequencies between Bristol and other series. The frequencies and seasonal harmonics correspond with those in Figure 12.26. Following the convention used in equations (12.25) and (12.26), Bristol is the base or reference series, and so, for the phase angles, + implies Bristol lags behind the other series, while − implies Bristol leads. Source: Bassett and Haggett, 1971, pp. 408–9.

In order to explore further the relationship between Bristol and the other areas, the authors computed the coherences and phase angles between the Bristol series and each of the other series at various angular frequencies. The results for the same four series as Figure 12.26 are plotted in Figure 12.27. The phase diagrams for Bristol/Swindon, Bristol/Bridgwater and Bristol/Midsomer Norton show that each series led Bristol at all frequencies up to the seasonal frequency. In the case of Bristol/Weston, the phase diagram shows that the series lagged Bristol at the two lowest frequencies, but led at higher frequencies. By averaging the phase angles over the first four frequencies they obtained values consistent with Table 12.3. Bristol, Bath and Weston-super-Mare were roughly in phase. The Bristol/Swindon phase diagram was sufficiently different from the rest as again to imply that Swindon may, economically, lie outside the Bristol region. In summary, the bulk of the evidence implies that the maxim, 'when Bristol sneezes, the rest of region catches cold', is an inadequate explanation of unemployment patterns in the area. Further work using these data is reported in Cliff, Haggett, Ord, Bassett and Davies (1975, Chapters 7 and 10). See also Hepple (1975) for a similar analysis of unemployment patterns in Northeast England, 1961–66, and of bankruptcies by county in nineteenth-century England as a reflection of interregional trade cycles.

12.5.3 *Estimation problems*

In addition to the problems discussed in Section 12.4.4 for the univariate time series case, the following points should be noted in cross-spectral analysis of short time series (Granger and Hughes, 1968; Neave, 1972):

(1) The coherences are biased towards $\frac{1}{2}$, and the confidence bands around the estimates are so wide as to be of little value. Gain, which is related to coherence [see equations (12.27) and (12.28)], is therefore also affected.

(2) The phase diagram is relatively unaltered.

(3) So-called 'pre-whitening' of the data can be very valuable in cross-spectral analysis. It may reduce the bias in the estimates and give more accurate approximations for the confidence bands. Granger and Hughes describe pre-whitening as (p. 98) 'applying a linear transformation, such as first differencing (cf. Section 10.3.2), to the data before analysis begins in an attempt to produce a flatter spectrum than had the original data.'

(4) There are no precise rules for fixing a value for the truncation point (number of lags), m. If a small value of m is chosen, the variance of the power spectral estimates will be reduced, but bias will be increased. If m is large, the reverse occurs. As a rough rule of thumb, Granger and Hatanaka (1964) suggest $m \leqslant \frac{1}{3}T$. See also Jenkins and Watts (1968, Chapter 7).

12.6 Conclusions

In this chapter, we have looked at, with examples, three methods for decomposing spatial and space–time data into their scale components of variation. Trend surface analysis can be used to separate out regional, local and specific effects in spatially located data in which the variability is assumed to be continuous from one spatial scale to another. Conversely, in the Model II Analysis of Variance, which can be applied to both spatial and time–space data, the total variability is assumed to be generated as the sum of independent variation from each scale level. Spectral analysis also provides a way of isolating the components of variability in spatial and temporal data, and, in addition, of assessing how the components of several different regional time series are interrelated.

13 **Point Patterns**

13.1 Introduction

Consider a map which shows the locations of phenomena by a series of points. Typical examples are provided by a distribution map of the cities of the United States, or of the adopters of an innovation in a study area. A basic question which may be asked is the following: what kind of spatial *pattern* is formed by the objects? Are the cities of the United States, for example, clustered in the eastern half of the country or regularly spaced? Following Rogers (1969a, p. 47) we define *pattern* as a 'characteristic of spatial arrangement which describes the spacing of a set of objects with respect to one another.'

The analysis of spatial point patterns has been important in geography for a number of years because 'pattern is the geometrical expression of location theory' (Rogers, 1969a, p. 47). As a result, a whole series of methods for point pattern analysis have been employed by geographers, although the mathematical theory of most of the techniques has been developed largely by ecologists and statisticians. (See the review by Pielou, 1969.) Two basic classes of techniques may be recognized, namely those based on *area* methods (such as quadrat count and polygon analysis), and those based on *distance* methods (such as nearest neighbour analysis). In this chapter, we consider techniques in both classes. We deal with area based approaches in Sections 13.2–13.5, and with distance approaches in Section 13.6.

13.2 Quadrat Count Analysis, I: Probability Distributions

Consider a map exhaustively divided by a regular lattice of square cells into small sub-areas or quadrats. A frequency distribution of the number of quadrats with $x = 0, 1, 2, ...$ objects of a specified kind within them can then be constructed, and it is this frequency distribution which forms the basis of quadrat count analysis. Some 'feel' for the relationship between particular point patterns and their corresponding frequency distributions may be given

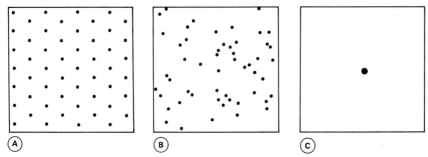

Figure 13.1 **A** Perfectly regular, **B** random, and **C** perfectly clustered spatial point patterns ($n = 52$). Source: Rogers, 1969a, p. 51.

by comparing Figures 13.1–13.2, and Table 13.1. The first figure shows how $n = 52$ points may be located in a study area so as to form (A) perfectly regular, (B) random[1], and (C) perfectly clustered point patterns. If the study area is partitioned up with a 10×10 regular lattice (i.e. $N = 100$ cells), as in Figure 13.2, the frequency distributions of the number of quadrats with $x = 0, 1, 2, ...$ points in them thus obtained are given in the first four rows and columns of Table 13.1.

Table 13.1   Fitting the Poisson distribution to different spatial point patterns.*

Number of points per quadrat	Observed frequencies of quadrats			Expected frequency with Poisson model
	Perfectly regular	Random	Perfectly clustered	
0	48	59	99	59.45
1	52	32	0	30.92
2		7	0	8.04
3+		2	1	1.59
$N =$	100	100	100	100.00
X^2	26.21	0.60	64.96	
$\chi^2_{(1)}, \alpha = 0.05$	3.84	3.84	3.84	

*$n = 52$ points; $N = 100$ quadrats.
Source: Rogers, 1969a, p. 53.

[1] By 'random' we mean that each and every location in the study area has an equal and independent chance of receiving a point, and that each point is assigned independently of every other point. This is a restricted use of the term, although it is widely used in ecology (cf. Pielou, 1969). The definition implies that the points will be uniformly distributed in the plane.

Once the observed frequency distribution has been constructed, the method proceeds by comparing this distribution with the theoretical distribution produced by some postulated spatial point process. The set of theoretical distributions generally used by geographers for this purpose is the family of Poisson models (Harvey, 1968b), and we now examine some of the members of this family.

13.2.1 *The simple Poisson benchmark*

Suppose that we postulate a spatial point process in which each quadrat in Figure 13.2 has an *equal* and *independent* chance of receiving a point. A *realization* (that is, a map) from such a process will produce a purely random spatial pattern of points such as that shown in Figure 13.2B, and the probability, $P(X = x)$, of finding x points in a specific quadrat is given by the formula,

$$P(X = x) = e^{-\lambda}\frac{\lambda^x}{x!}, \quad x = 0, 1, 2, ..., \tag{13.1}$$

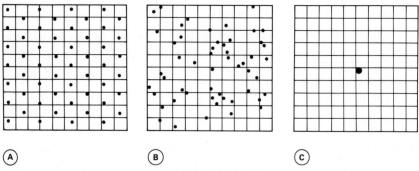

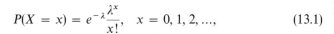

Figure 13.2 System of quadrats for **A** perfectly regular, **B** random, and **C** perfectly clustered spatial point patterns ($n = 52$). Source: Rogers, 1969a, p. 51.

the Poisson probability function. Note that the assumptions of equality and independence imply that the simple Poisson process is strictly stationary and strictly isotropic within the terms of definitions 10.3 and 10.4. The unknown parameter, λ, in equation (13.1) is the arithmetic mean, i.e. the average number of objects per quadrat.

In Table 13.1, the *expected* number of quadrats with $x = 0, 1, 2$ points in them, under the Poisson law, is determined in the following way. The mean, λ, is estimated from the data by the observed average number of objects per quadrat. With the 52 points and 100 quadrats of Figures 13.1 and 13.2, this yields the estimated mean of $\hat{\lambda} = 0.52$. Substitution of $\hat{\lambda}$ into equation (13.1) with, successively, $x = 0, 1, 2$, yields $P(X = 0) = 0.5945$, $P(X = 1) = 0.3092$, and $P(X = 2) = 0.0804$. The end category, $P(X = 3+)$, is obtained as $1.0 - [P(X = 0) + P(X = 1) + P(X = 2)] = 0.0159$. The expectations are given by $N\{P(X = x)\}, x = 0, 1, 2, 3+$.

Goodness of fit. We may evaluate the goodness-of-fit between the observed and expected frequency distributions using an X^2 goodness-of-fit test, remembering, where necessary, to combine classes in the contingency table so that none of the expected counts is less than three. The calculated X^2 value is referred to tables of the chi-square distribution with $R - 2$ degrees of freedom, where R is the number of classes used in calculating X^2 (see Appendix Table A3). One degree of freedom is lost in carrying out the X^2 test, *while an additional degree of freedom is lost for every parameter of the expected distribution which has to be estimated from the data* (in this case, one, for $\hat{\lambda}$). In Table 13.1, as we would expect, such a test leads us to accept the null hypothesis of no significant difference between the observed and expected counts for Figure 13.1B at the $\alpha = 0.05$ significance level, but to reject the null hypothesis for Figures 13.1A and 13.1C.

Interpretation of the Poisson process. One of the reasons why the Poisson process forms an important benchmark against which to compare observed point patterns is that there is some empirical evidence to suggest that aggregate human behaviour patterns can be adequately described by random process models as, for example, in Sections 4.2.1 and 4.3.3. It is also a central, if debatable, proposition in the systems literature (Chorley and Kennedy, 1971, p. 203) that some aspects of the second law of thermodynamics may apply to human activity. This law implies that molecular systems in the physical world tend in the long run towards a state of maximum entropy, in which the energy for change among the particles in the system has been dissipated and the particles are randomly located (cf. Sections 2.5 and 4.3.3). Measuring the degree of randomness in a realization of a process may thus provide a guide as to the degree of organization in a system. Since we are only drawing a loose analogy with a very strict physical law, this interpretation should not be pushed too far. For our purposes, we may simply note that comparison of an observed spatial point pattern with the expected outcome for a Poisson process (at the same density of points per unit area) does provide us with a measure of the amount and kind of order present in that pattern.

This idea can be explored further by recognizing that in a Poisson distribution, the mean and variance are equal. Therefore, in a purely random pattern, the ratio, Di = variance/mean, is unity. A ratio of greater than unity occurs when the point pattern is more clustered than random, while a ratio of less than unity is indicative of a more regular than random pattern. From Bartko, Greenhouse and Patlak (1968), we may test formally for significant departure of the variance/mean ratio from unity as follows. Given a sample of size n from a Poisson process, $(n - 1) Di$ is approximately distributed as $\chi^2_{(n-1)}$, provided n is not too small. As noted above, the expected value of the ratio, $E(Di)$, is 1. The statistic,

$$d = [2(n-1)Di]^{\frac{1}{2}} - (2n-1)^{\frac{1}{2}}, \qquad (13.2)$$

will therefore be approximately normally distributed with zero mean and unit variance for moderate and large n. Cliff and Ord (1973, p. 68) have applied this statistic to Matui's counts of houses in the Tonami Plain, Japan, shown in

Figures 13.3 and 12.6. They concluded that a simple Poisson model was not an adequate description of the data. See Section 13.4.

13.2.2 *Generalized Poisson processes in space*

Matui's data are but one example of the many point patterns which display degrees of order which cannot be approximated by a simple Poisson process. These complicated mixtures of random, uniform and clustered components can often be modelled using the so-called *generalized* and *compound* Poisson distributions, which we consider in this and the next sub-sections. Patil and Joshi (1968) and Ord (1972a) give full accounts of the theory involved.

We can illustrate the properties of each distribution by considering the settlement of a newly occupied territory (Cliff and Ord, 1973, pp. 58–9). Let us assume that the first settlers choose their locations at random, and that later settlers choose their locations near to the early settlements (cf. Section 4.2). Thus we can think of this process as showing *true contagion*, and a point map of such a process would exhibit clustering of houses. An example of a model for this kind of contagious process is the *negative binomial* distribution. This distribution assumes an initial Poisson pattern of points with further points assumed to cluster around the original points according to a logarithmic series growth law. We are thus thinking in settlement terms of an initial random distribution of village nuclei in the study area, being generalized with the passage of time by the accretion of new houses around the original nuclei according to a logarithmic growth law. In the notation of Gurland (1957), we write

$$\text{negative binomial} \sim \text{Poisson} \vee \text{logarithmic.} \qquad (13.3)$$

In this notation, $\sim$, means 'is given by'. The name before the $\vee$ (here Poisson) is the probability law describing the locations in the plane of the initial centres of points, and it is equivalent to the distribution of the number of clusters per quadrat. The name after the $\vee$ (logarithmic) is called the *generalizing distribution*; it defines the probability law describing the growth of 'offspring' around the initial point locations, and it therefore gives the distribution of the number of individuals per cluster (i.e. the cluster size). The generalized models

> envisage a random (Poisson) distribution of . . . clusters, each cluster containing one or more objects, the number [of objects] within each cluster following the generalizer distribution. In so far as the existence of a cluster means that an object is 'more likely' to have similar objects nearby, we may say that these processes represent *true contagion* (Ord, 1972a, p. 124).

13.2.3 *Compound Poisson processes in space*

An alternative way of viewing the colonization process is to assume that each settler chooses his site independently, but that some sites are more attractive than others. That is, the density parameter, λ, in the simple Poisson model of equation (13.1) is not a constant, but instead, it is a function of location. A *compounding distribution* is used to specify how the parameter λ varies over space. The compound Poisson models are thus sometimes known by the

(A) *****

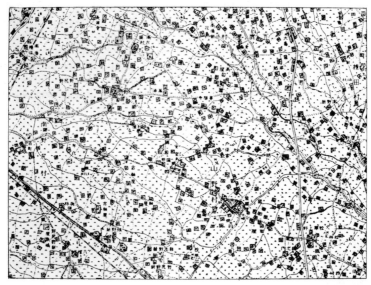

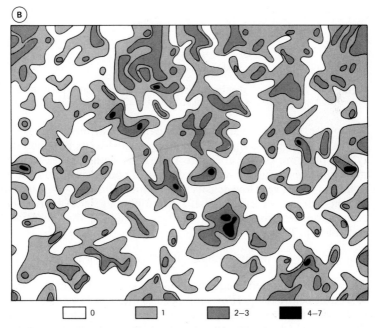

| | 0 | | 1 | | 2–3 | | 4–7 |

Figure 13.3 **A** A section of topographic map (1:20,000 Military Land Survey) showing the western part of Hukuno town. **B** Map showing the density of houses per 100 m² for the area shown in (**A**). Source: Cliff and Ord, 1973, p. 67.

alternative names of *heterogeneity* or *apparent contagion* models, in that the settlement of each quadrat in a study area may be viewed as a separate realization of a Poisson process, each with its own particular density parameter (λ). Areas with a high density parameter will thus appear *visually* as 'clusters', compared with areas with a low density parameter, even though the pattern in each quadrat may be regarded as an outcome of a simple Poisson process. The visual appearance arises because of the variability in the density parameter, λ, from quadrat to quadrat. The simple Poisson model of equation (13.1) is, in effect, a compound Poisson with λ constant from quadrat to quadrat.

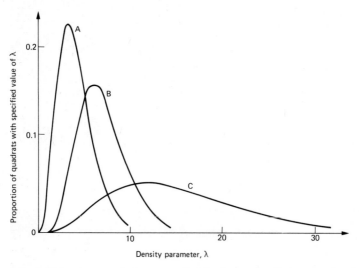

Figure 13.4   Some typical gamma distribution curves. In interpreting the vertical axis, note that the proportions have been scaled so that the area under each curve is one.

Suppose, however, that λ follows a gamma distribution ($\equiv \frac{1}{2}\chi^2$). The shape of this curve depends upon the values assigned to its parameters, and some typical plots are shown in Figure 13.4. Thus, with curve A, we would expect most quadrats to have a very low density of houses; in contrast, C yields a few quadrats with a very low density of settlement, but also some quadrats with a very high density of settlement. If λ does follow a gamma distribution, then the compound Poisson model resulting is again the negative binomial distribution. That is,

$$\text{negative binomial} \sim \text{Poisson} \wedge \text{gamma.} \tag{13.4}$$

The notation adopted in equation (13.4) is standard for compound processes. The name before the $\wedge$ (Poisson) specifies the basic law governing the spacing of individuals within each quadrat, while the second name (after $\wedge$) specifies the way in which the density at which the Poisson process is operating, varies from quadrat to quadrat.

For the compound models, geographical concepts such as the region imply that λ, in addition to being described by a specific law, is also likely to vary slowly or smoothly over space; that is, there will be positive spatial autocorrelation between quadrats (on λ). (See Chapter 11.) Conversely, there should be no spatial autocorrelation between quadrats in the generalized Poisson models since each quadrat is assumed to be an independent realization of the specified stochastic process.

Rogers (1965) has fitted the negative binomial to quadrat counts of the numbers of different kinds of stores (e.g. antique, ladies' clothing, and furniture) in Stockholm. The satisfactory fits obtained were interpreted as indicating that retailers of the same consumer goods cluster together as a response to the needs of comparison shopping. However, the location of shops in an area is also a response to the areal areal distribution of purchasing power. ?
Since purchasing power is unevenly distributed over a city, Rogers suggests that it could equally well be argued that the location of stores is Poissonian, but that the average number of stores per quadrat fluctuates according to the variations in purchasing power across the city. If this distribution of purchasing power follows the gamma law, we would be arguing for a compound process to generate the negative binomial.

Table 13.2   Compound and generalized Poisson distributions.

Name of distribution (plus references)	Compound or generalized form (P = Poisson)
Negative binomial (Pascal) (Fisher, 1941; Feller, 1943; Quenouille, 1949b)	$P \vee$ logarithmic $P \wedge$ gamma
Pólya–Aeppli (Pólya, 1931)	$P \vee$ geometric Pascal $\underset{k}{\wedge}$ Poisson
Neyman Type A (two parameter) (Neyman, 1939; Feller, 1943)	$P \vee P$ $P \wedge P$
Thomas (Thomas, 1949)	$P \vee P$ (one 'parent' plus random number of offspring)
Poisson–binomial (McGuire *et al.*, 1957, Sprott, 1958)	$P \vee$ binomial Binomial $\wedge P$
Poisson–Pascal (Katti and Gurland, 1961; Shumway and Gurland, 1960)	$P \vee$ Pascal Pascal $\wedge P$
Short (Cresswell and Froggart, 1963; Kemp, 1967)	$P \vee$ (Poisson with zeros added)

Source: Ord, 1972a, p. 126.
Notes: In the case of the Pólya–Aeppli distribution, the notation ' $\underset{k}{\wedge}$ ' means that the compounding is done on the negative binomial parameter, k, defined in Table 13.3.

13.2.4 Model comparisons

We may now summarize the distinction between the generalized and compound Poisson processes. The former are used to model true contagious growth. They postulate a random distribution of initial nuclei, and subsequent growth of clusters around the nuclei according to some generalizing distribution. Conversely, the compound process arises when the spatial point pattern is essentially Poissonian (random), but the density of the pattern is different from quadrat to quadrat. The way in which density varies is specified by the compounding distribution (e.g. the gamma distribution).

To illustrate the spatial implications of generalized and compound processes, we have considered in equations (13.3) and (13.4) just two ways of either generalizing or compounding a Poisson distribution. Many different generalizers and compounders exist, and some of the possibilities of geographical interest are summarized in Table 13.2. The notation of Sections 13.2.2 and 13.2.3 has been used. Table 13.2 and the discussion in Sections 13.2.2–13.2.4 raise the issue of selection between models, to which we now turn.

13.3 Quadrat Count Analysis, II: Selection Criteria

Our treatment in this section is divided into three parts. We consider first the geographical significance of the various distributions, since this, in itself, may suggest which models are appropriate in different circumstances. We then show how a model may be selected simply on the basis of the shape of the frequency distribution of quadrat counts, and finally we describe how to fit the various models to an observed frequency distribution.

13.3.1 *Geographical significance of different distributions*

(a) *Generalized models.* The generalized models listed in Table 13.2 are important whenever we are dealing with geographically contagious growth processes. In addition to the illustrations already given, spatially contagious growth is a feature of all diffusion processes dominated by the neighbourhood effect (Section 7.2.1). Apart from innovation diffusion, many diseases also spread contagiously. Examples are provided by the measles epidemics considered in Section 11.5, foot-and-mouth epizootics (Tinline, 1972) and fowl pest disease (Martin and Oeppen, 1975). The rapid space-filling implied by geometric or logarithmic growth of initial cluster centres suggests that two distributions, the Pólya–Aeppli and the (generalized) negative binomial, may be particularly valuable for processes which are in the initial and middle sections of the logistic curve shown in Figure 7.5. For example, Hägerstrand (1965b) has noted for his diffusion models, that, 'in the first stages, the number of adopters forms a geometrical progression, each generation $[g_i]$ having twice the preceding number of adopters $(g_i = 2^i)$. From g_5 and onwards [as competition occurs] it more and more often happens that tellings become directed to individuals who are already adopters ...' Thus, if the initial adopters of an innovation in a study area are randomly located, the number of adopters per quadrat in later time periods may frequently be described by the Pólya–Aeppli.

   Polya–Aeppli model: An assumption of the Pólya–Aeppli model is that the parent individuals (initial adopters) all appear in the study area at the *start* of the diffusion process (Anscombe, 1950). This implies that the geometric growth over time in the total number of adopters takes place as a result of the conversion of potential adopters by initial acceptors with whom the potential adopters come into contact. The contacts are thus assumed to take place within a *closed* population of potential adopters and carriers of the innovation. Commonly, however, this picture will be complicated by the migration of individuals into and out of the study area, and by existing adopters ceasing to pass on information about the innovation (through loss of interest, for example).[2] In these circumstances, the negative binomial may be more appropriate.

Negative binomial model: Anscombe (1950) has suggested that if the following assumptions can be sustained for a diffusion process, this model will produce a good fit:

(1) the initiators of the innovation (carriers of the disease) arrive in the study area uniformly through time;

(2) there is a constant 'birth probability' from individual to individual in the rate at which potential adopters accept from the initiators;

(3) there is a constant 'death probability' from adopter to adopter describing the chance that a given adopter will cease to pass on information.

See Getis (1974) for a further discussion of the use of the Pólya and negative binomial models in a diffusion context.

Short model: This model is obtained when cluster growth is described by a Poisson distribution with 'added zeros'. Pielou (1969, pp. 88–9) describes how, spatially, this might arise. If a study area has been divided into quadrats so that, say, the settlement pattern can be analysed, it may happen that some of the quadrats are uninhabitable (for example, marsh or mountainous land), while the other quadrats are habitable units among which the individuals are dispersed at random. Then the variate, the number of objects per quadrat, will have a variance greater than its mean, and the distribution will be Poisson with added zeros; that is, the vacant quadrats will be a mixture of those that cannot be inhabited (the added zeros) and those which, although they are habitable, are empty through the chance operation of the stochastic process. Although this is geographically very plausible, the trouble with the Short distribution is that all the methods of estimating the parameters of the model (required at the fitting stage) give estimates with very large standard errors (Kemp, 1967).

(b) *Compound models.* These are important if we are prepared to attach some degree of credibility to Curry's (1964, 1967) notion of the random spatial economy. The models are relevant in any situation where it is suspected that an uneven spatial distribution in some phenomenon related to the one being analysed may modify an essentially Poissonian pattern in the latter. Thus in Rogers's example discussed in Section 13.2.3, it was suggested that an uneven purchasing power surface affected the locations in a city of shops which might otherwise have formed a Poisson pattern. In general, settlement, migration, and interaction of all kinds take place against a physical and economic

---

[2] We note that the Pólya–Aeppli distribution, like the other generalized models, can be modified to handle the 'survival' or otherwise of the parent individuals as transmitters (cf. the Neyman Type A and Thomas's distributions in Table 13.2).

background of varying potential or favourability (such as rich areas as opposed to poor areas, marsh as opposed to dry land, and so on).

Of the models listed in Table 13.2, the first six have been mentioned in the geographical literature. Dacey (1968, 1969a) and Cliff and Ord (1973) have fitted the negative binomial to quadrat counts of settlements in Japan and Puerto Rico. The same model has been applied by Harvey (1966) to Hägerstrand's (1953) maps showing the locations of adopters of pasture improvement grants, (1928–33), and of milking machines (1944), in the Asby district of Sweden. Rogers (1965) has fitted the negative binomial, Neyman Type A and Thomas's double Poisson to point patterns of different types of shops in Stockholm, and he has also outlined the structure of the Poisson binomial distribution in the same article. The Poisson Pascal is considered by that author (1964) as well.

13.3.2 *Comparison of distributions*

Rogers (1974, Section 3.6) has attempted to rank order some of the distributions we have discussed according to the degree of clustering of a point pattern which they can represent. His scale covers point patterns arranged along a continuum which runs from perfectly clustered, through random, to perfectly regular. It may be compared with the scale proposed by Clark and Evans (1954) for nearest neighbour distances (see Section 13.6.1). The ranking is done on the basis of the behaviour of the variance/mean ratio, Di, defined for equation (13.2). The scale may be shown schematically in the following way (Rogers, 1974, p. 29).

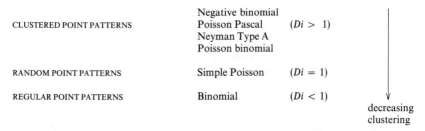

The scheme must be used with caution, however; as we shall see in Figure 13.6, many distributions are embedded in a more general family (for example, the Poisson Pascal covers the region from the Neyman Type A to beyond the negative binomial), and distributions may approach each other as limiting forms.

Anscombe (1950) has also tried experimentally to quantify the differences between some of the distributions. He calculated the percentage of the total number of quadrats in an area which would have $x = 0, 1, 2, \ldots$ objects in them for each of the following distributions: (a) the Neyman Type A, (b) the Pólya–Aeppli, (c) the negative binomial, and (d) Thomas's double Poisson. Anscombe concluded that, if a large proportion of the quadrats in an area are occupied, there is little to choose between the various distributions. Conversely, if the proportion is small, great differences can occur. Figure 13.5

shows the expected percentage frequencies of quadrats with 0, 1, ... objects in them that would arise if the observed data had sample means, m'_1, and variances, m_2, as follows: $m'_1 = 20$, $m_2 = 220$ (Figure 13.5A); $m'_1 = 6$, $m_2 = 24$ (Figure 13.5B). These diagrams show that the Neyman Type A and the closely related Thomas's distributions are multi-modal), and that the modes are located at values of x approximately equal to multiples of m_2. The Pólya–Aeppli always has one or two modes, while the negative binomial always has one. Anscombe therefore suggests that unless the observational data display clear evidence of multi-modality, one should be reluctant to use the Neyman and Thomas models.

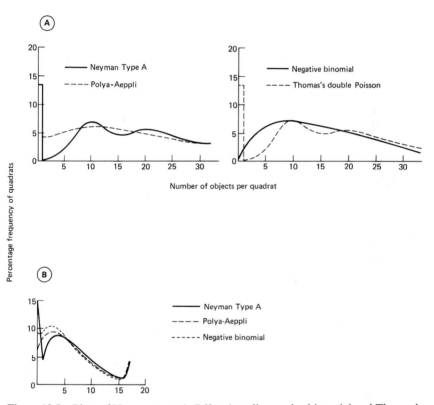

Figure 13.5 Plots of Neyman type A, Pólya Aeppli, negative binomial and Thomas's distributions. Based on tables given in Anscombe, 1950, pp. 364–5.

13.3.3 *Statistical choice of models*

When faced with a particular data set, geographical theory may give neither *a priori* indication as to which of the distributions listed in Table 13.2 should be fitted, nor suggest whether the data have been generated by a generalized or compound process. In these circumstances, Ord (1972a, Section 6.9) has outlined two possible strategies:

Table 13.3   Probability functions for var

Distribution	Probability function	Moments
Simple Poisson	$P(X = x) = e^{-\lambda}\dfrac{\lambda^x}{x!}, x = 0, 1, 2, ...$	$\mu_1' = \lambda$
Negative binomial	$P(X = x) = \dbinom{x+k-1}{k-1}p^k q^x, x = 0, 1, 2, ...$	$\mu_1' = kq/p$
		$\mu_2 = kq/p^2$
Pólya–Aeppli	$P(x = 0) = e^{-\lambda}$ $P(X = x) = e^{-\lambda}\theta^x \displaystyle\sum_{j=1}^{x}\dbinom{x-1}{j-1}\dfrac{1}{j!}\left\{\dfrac{\lambda(1-\theta)}{\theta}\right\}^j, x = 1, 2, ...$	$\mu_1' = \dfrac{\lambda}{1-\theta}$ $\mu_2 = \dfrac{\lambda(1+\theta)}{(1-\theta)^2}$
Neyman Type A	$P(X = x) = \dfrac{\lambda_2^x}{x!}e^{-\lambda_1}\displaystyle\sum_{j=0}^{\infty}\dfrac{j^x}{j!}(\lambda_1 e^{-\lambda_2})^j, x = 0, 1, 2, ...$	$\mu_1' = \lambda_1\lambda_2$ $\mu_2 = \lambda_1\lambda_2(1+\lambda_2)$
Thomas's double Poisson	$P(X = 0) = e^{-\lambda_1}$ $P(X = x) = e^{-\lambda_1}\displaystyle\sum_{j=1}^{x}\dfrac{\lambda_1^j(j\lambda_2)^{x-j}}{j!\,(x-j)!}e^{-j\lambda_2}, x = 1, 2, ...$	$\mu_1' = \lambda_1(\lambda_2+1)$ $\mu_2 = \mu_1'(\lambda_2+1)+$
Poisson binomial	$P(X = x) = e^{-\lambda}\displaystyle\sum_{j=0}^{\infty}\dbinom{nj}{x}p^x q^{nj-x}\dfrac{\lambda^j}{j!}, x = 0, 1, 2, ...$	$\mu_1' = n\lambda p$ $\mu_2 = \mu_1'(np+q)$
Short	$P(X = 0) = \exp[\lambda(e^{-\theta}-1)-\varphi]$ $(x+1)P(X = x+1) = \varphi P(X = x)+\lambda\theta e^{-\theta}\displaystyle\sum_{i=0}^{x} P(X = x-i)\dfrac{\theta^i}{i!}, x = 1, 2, ...$	$\mu_1' = \varphi+\lambda\theta$ $\mu_2 = \varphi+\lambda\theta(1+\theta$ $\mu_3 = \varphi+\lambda\theta(1+3$

Notes   [a] Source Ord (1972a, Appendix B). See also Patil and Joshi (1968).
   [b] Pielou (1969, p. 94) has suggested that k is a measure of spatial clumping in the point p
   low degrees of spatial clumping.
   [c] n_0 = frequency of quadrats with $x = 0$; n_1 = frequency of quadrats with $x = 1$.
   three frequencies, n_0, n_1, and $N - n_0 - n_1$.

wn eters	Interpretation of parameters	Estimators	Tables[a]
	mean number of objects per quadrat	$\hat{\lambda} = m'_1$	G.E.C. Defense Systems Dept. (1962)
	proportional to no. of quadrats occupied	$\hat{p} = m'_1/m_2$	Williamson and Bretherton (1963)
	'propagation' or diffusion rate (Harvey, 1968); inversely proportional to size of cluster[b].	$\hat{k} = m'_1 \hat{p}/(1-\hat{p})$ $\hat{q} = (1-\hat{p})$	
	mean number of clusters per quadrat	$\hat{\lambda} = m'_1(1-\hat{\theta})$	Sherbrooke (1968)
	$1/(1-\theta) =$ mean number of objects per cluster	$\hat{\theta} = \left(\dfrac{m_2}{m'_1} - 1\right)\Big/\left(1 + \dfrac{m_2}{m'_1}\right)$	
	mean number of clusters per quadrat	$\hat{\lambda}_1 = m'_1/\hat{\lambda}_2$	—
	mean number of objects per cluster	$\hat{\lambda}_2 = (m_2 - m'_1)/m'_1$	
	mean number of clusters per quadrat	$\hat{\lambda}_1 = \ln N - \ln n_0$ (footnote c)	—
	mean number of objects per cluster	$\hat{\lambda}_2 = \ln\left(\dfrac{\hat{\lambda}_1 n_0}{n_1}\right)$	
	mean number of clusters per quadrat	$\hat{\lambda} = \dfrac{(n-1)(m'_1)^2}{n(m_2 - m'_1)}$	—
	mean number of objects per cluster	$\hat{p} = \dfrac{m_2 - m'_1}{(n-1)m'_1}$	—
		$\hat{q} = (1-\hat{p})$	
	mean number of clusters per quadrat	$\hat{\lambda} = (m_2 - m'_1)/\hat{\theta}^2$	
	mean number of objects per cluster	$\hat{\theta} = \left[\dfrac{m_3 - m_2}{m_2 - m'_1}\right] - 2$	—
	proportion of land uninhabitable	$\varphi = m'_1 - \hat{\lambda}\hat{\theta}$	

alues are consistent with pronounced clumping, while high k values are indicative of

mators given for the Thomas distribution are the restricted ML estimators based on the

(1) fit several alternative models to the data and select the one which is the 'best fit' as judged by, say, the X^2 test;

(2) pre-screen the data in some way and select a model on that basis.

As Ord notes, both approaches raise difficulties. The utility of (1) is limited by the fact that we may be testing different models for goodness-of-fit using different degrees of freedom. Also, the X^2 test itself may not be strictly valid, as we shall see below, if the models are not fitted in particular ways. When approach (2) is used, this 'prior look at the data' costs us, approximately, one degree of freedom (Ord, 1972a, p. 132).

The second, pre-screening approach, works for the class of generalized Poisson distributions. We use μ'_1, μ_2 and μ_3 to denote the first, and second and third central moments respectively of the theoretical distributions. The ratios,

$$I = \mu_2/\mu'_1,$$
(13.5)

and

$$S = \mu_3/\mu_2$$
(13.6)

are defined as in Section 9.7.2. Ord has shown (see Figure 13.6) that these ratios take on distinct values for each distribution. The selection procedure consists of evaluating the sample moments, m'_1, m_2 and m_3 (corresponding to μ'_1, μ_2 and μ_3 respectively) from the data, and plotting the sample I, S values on the chart. The appropriate distribution can then be identified.

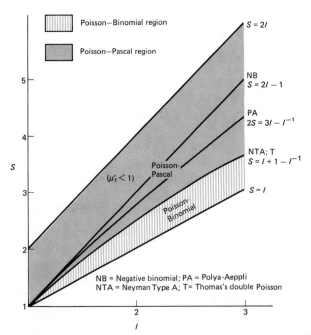

Figure 13.6 The I, S chart for the contagious discrete distributions. NB = negative binomial; PA = Pólya-Aeppli; NTA = Neyman Type A; T = Thomas's double Poisson. Source: Ord, 1972a, p. 134.

13.3.4 *Fitting of models*

Several methods are available for fitting a given model to the data. These are described in Ord (1972a, pp. 135–47) and Rogers (1974, Chapter 4). The simplest approach, employed here, is the so-called *method of moments*. We first describe the steps involved and then comment upon the method. The fitting procedure is illustrated with a regional example in the next section (13.4).

The method of moments has already been used in Section 13.2.1 to fit the simple Poisson to the data in Table 13.1, namely:

Step 1. Specify the probability function, $P(X = x)$, for the particular distribution [cf. equation (13.1)].

Step 2. Obtain expressions for the first two or three moments (μ'_1, μ_2, and possibly μ_3) of the specified distribution. These moments will be expressed in terms of the unknown parameters of the distribution.

Step 3. Calculate m'_1, m_2 and m_3 from the sample data.

Step 4. Substitute these numerical values for the quantities, μ'_1, μ_2 and μ_3, in the equations obtained at step 2.

Step 5. Solve the resulting simultaneous equations to obtain estimates of the unknown parameters.

Step 6. Substitute the parameter estimates into the probability function defined in step 1 to obtain values for $P(X = x)$, the probability that any given quadrat will contain $x = 0, 1, 2, \ldots$ objects.

Step 7. Determine the expected number of quadrats with $x = 0, 1, 2, \ldots$ objects in them by multiplying the corresponding step 6 probabilities by N, the total number of quadrats.

In Table 13.3 we give, for the various distributions which we have discussed in some detail in this chapter, their probability functions, theoretical moments, expressions for the unknown parameters in terms of the sample moments, and the physical interpretation of the parameters. For some of the distributions listed, tables of $P(X = x)$, $x = 0, 1, 2, \ldots$ exist for various parameter values. Ord (1972a, Appendix B) provides a comprehensive list of such tables, and we have reproduced in the table some of the principal sources.

As a fitting procedure, the method of moments is statistically *inefficient*; that is, it yields larger standard errors for the estimates of the parameters of a given distribution, compared with a fully efficient procedure such as maximum likelihood which lies beyond the mathematical scope of this book. This has implications for the X^2 test used to evaluate the goodness-of-fit between observed and expected counts as in Table 13.1. Strictly speaking, this test is only valid, and a known full degree of freedom lost for each parameter of the model estimated from the data, if fully efficient estimation procedures such as maximum likelihood are used (Chernoff and Lehmann, 1954). If inefficient estimators are employed, we cannot be certain of the degrees of freedom associated with the test (Ord, 1972a, p. 144). However, if the test is carried out as though fully efficient estimators have been used, the X^2 value may be used as a *guide*. It is also worth noting that in the case of the simple Poisson the maximum likelihood and moment estimators are identical.

13.4 Quadrat Counts: Regional Example

13.4.1 *Initial results*

To illustrate the fitting of the distributions listed in Table 13.3, we collapsed Matui's (1932) map of counts of isolated houses in Hukuno Town, Japan (shown in Figures 12.6 and 13.3) into the frequency array given in the first two columns of Table 13.4. The first three moments of the sample data are $m'_1 = 0.759167$, $m_2 = 0.889499$, and $m_3 = 1.565798$, yielding $I = 1.17$ and $S = 1.76$ [equations (13.5) and (13.6)]. Use of these I, S values with Figure 13.5 places the distribution in the Poisson–Pascal region. The expected frequency counts for the various theoretical distributions are shown in Table 13.4, along with the results of the X^2 test and degrees of freedom with (a) class values 4 and $5+$ *combined* and (b) class values 4 and $5+$ treated *separately*. The estimates for the various parameters appear in Table 13.5. The X^2 values in Table 13.4 show how different groupings of the end classes for the test can produce quite marked differences in the assessment of the goodness-of-fit of a distribution. The changes are most dramatic in the case of the Poisson and Neyman Type A models. There is also a doubling of the X^2 value for the Thomas distribution if classes 4 and $5+$ are treated separately. In this small example, the Thomas distribution is treated charitably since the observed and expected values coincide in two of the six classes because of the fitting procedure. The results also show the importance of getting close correspondence to the tail classes (low frequencies) in choosing a particular distribution. On balance, the Short

Table 13.4 Discrete distributions based upon the Poisson series fitted to Matui's data.†

Number of houses per quadrat	Observed number of quadrats	Expected number of quadrats						
		Poisson	Negative binomial	Polya–Aeppli	Neyman Type A	Thomas††	Poisson binomial	Short
0	584	561.7	595.5	596.4	597.4	584.0	599.5	577.9
1	398	426.4	385.9	384.0	381.6	398.0	377.0	416.1
2	168	161.9	153.3	154.2	157.4	157.6	157.6	151.3
3	35	41.0	48.1	49.4	48.7	46.4	49.4	38.7
4	9	7.8	13.1	12.8	13.1	11.2	12.9	9.4
5+	6	1.3	4.2	3.2	1.8	2.8	3.6	6.5
		Classes 4, 5+ combined						
X^2 value		7.71	5.88	6.26*	5.57	3.56	6.59*	3.10
Degrees of freedom		3	2	2	2	2	2	1
		Classes 4, 5+ analysed separately						
X^2 value		21.06*	7.63	9.78*	16.65*	7.58	9.23*	3.10
Degrees of freedom		4	3	3	3	3	3	2

† Tonami plain, Japan.
†† It is a property of the fitting procedure that, in the case of Thomas's distribution, the observed and expected frequencies are identical in the first two classes. See Thomas (1949).
*Significant at $\alpha = 0.05$ level.

and negative binomial models appear to provide the best fits, a result which is not out of line with calculated I, S values. Finally, we note that the variance/mean test defined in equation (13.2) gives $Di = 1.17$ and $d = 4.03$, confirming the (slight) areal inhomogeneity in the density of houses in Figure 13.3 implied by the fits of the negative binomial and Short models.

Table 13.5   Parameter estimates used to fit models in Table 13.4.

Poisson	Negative binomial	Pólya– Aeppli	Neyman Type A	Thomas	Poisson binomial	Short
$\hat{\lambda} = 0.76$	$\hat{p} = 0.85$ $\hat{k} = 4.42$	$\hat{\lambda} = 0.70$ $\hat{\theta} = 0.08$	$\hat{\lambda}_1 = 4.42$ $\hat{\lambda}_2 = 0.17$	$\hat{\lambda}_1 = 0.72$ $\hat{\lambda}_2 = 0.06$	$\hat{\lambda} = 2.21$ $\hat{p} = 0.17$	$\hat{\lambda} = 0.01$ $\hat{\theta} = 3.19$ $\hat{\varphi} = 0.72$

Notes

(1) To obtain the parameter estimates for the Poisson binomial, we set $n = 2$. See McGuire, Brindley and Bancroft (1957).

(2) In fitting the negative binomial, note that k is non-integer. Thus, in solving the expression for $P(X = x)$ in Table 13.3 we defined $r!$, for the arbitrary real number r, as

$$\Gamma (r+1) = r! = r\Gamma(r-1).$$

Here, $\Gamma (r) = \int_0^\infty x^{r-1}e^{-x}dx$, the gamma function tabled in Appendix Table A5.

13.4.2 Scale changes and equifinality

It is evident from Table 13.2 that quite different spatial processes can produce the same final probability distribution. That is, different processes are *equifinal*. Thus, although in Section 13.4.1, we were able to say that the negative binomial is a good description of the location of houses in Hukuno Town, we are still unable to be sure of the *generating process* producing the pattern of locations. As the discussion in Sections 13.2.2 and 13.2.3 showed, on geographical grounds we could argue for settlement patterns being produced either by the generalized or the compound models of the negative binomial. We would like some way of deciding which process was in fact responsible for the observed spatial pattern of houses. Although there is no certain way of doing this, some progress can be made. Since most of the research on this topic has been done in connection with the negative binomial model, we outline the principles with special reference to that distribution, and illustrate them by application to the Hukuno Town data.

Ord (1972a, Section 7.8) has shown for time series that the compound and generalized forms of the negative binomial can be distinguished by looking at the way in which the parameters of the model vary with changes in the length of the time interval used to collect the data. Cliff and Ord (1973, pp. 59–68) have extended this procedure to the spatial case. Suppose that the study area has been partitioned into quadrats of a certain size (cf. Ord's 'length of time interval'), and that a 'good fit' of the negative binomial to the frequency array of objects in the quadrats has been obtained. Denote the parameters of the model by p and k as in Table 13.3, and assume that the estimated values of these parameters for the lattice are α and β respectively. Suppose now that the same study area is subdivided into quadrats of a different size by combining s

adjacent quadrats in the first lattice to create each new quadrat in the second lattice. We summarize in Table 13.6 for both the compound and generalized versions of the negative binomial model the way in which the estimated parameter values vary with changes in quadrat size. In this table, $a = \alpha/(1 - \alpha)$. 'Thus by calculating estimates for p and k for different sized lattices, we can see which of the models [generalized or compound] appears to be nearer the truth' (Cliff and Ord, 1973, p. 60). We would stress that the proposed method of discrimination is only approximate since it assumes that the quadrats combined to form larger quadrats have the same value of λ initially in the compound model. Other accounts which examine the way in which the parameters of the negative binomial alter with changes in quadrat size are those of Getis (1967) and Dacey (1968).

Table 13.6   Changes in parameter values with changing quadrat size for the compound and generalized negative binomial models.

Model	Parameter	Parameter values	
		Lattice 1	Lattice 2
Compound	p	$\dfrac{a}{a+1}$	$\dfrac{a}{a+s}$
	k	β	β
Generalized	p	α	α
	k	β	$s\beta$

To apply this approach to the Hukuno Town data, Cliff and Ord (1973, Chapter 3) constructed eight further lattices from the reference lattice (lattice 1) by combining adjacent quadrats in various ways as shown in Figure 13.7. The negative binomial was fitted by maximum likelihood to each lattice, and Figure 13.8 shows the estimates for k and p obtained. Also illustrated are the 'expected' values according to the generalized and compound processes. These quantities were calculated as described above, taking lattice 1 as the reference lattice. While it is clear that the data are not a simple outcome of either the generalized or the compound processes, it is also evident that the values of k and p for the compound model are closer to, and 'track' along better with, the estimated values, than do the k and p values for the generalized model.

13.4.3 *Evidence of spatial autocorrelation*

Supporting evidence can be obtained by testing for spatial autocorrelation between quadrats. Recall from the discussion following equation (13.4) that independence betwen quadrats is suggestive of the generalized process, whereas positive spatial autocorrelation between quadrats is suggestive of the compound model. Cliff and Ord (1973, Chapter 3) tested for spatial

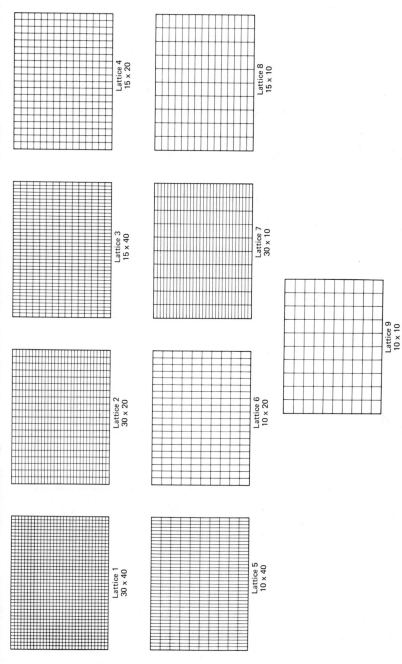

Figure 13.7 Reference (lattice 1) and derived lattices used with Matui's data to investigate the effect of scale changes upon the parameter values of the negative binomial distribution.

autocorrelation between quadrats in all lattices shown in Figure 13.7. The coefficient, I, defined in equations (11.7), (11.18) and (11.20), was employed. Two forms of **W** were tried: (a) $w_{ij} = 1$ if quadrats i and j had a common vertex or edge, and $w_{ij} = 0$ otherwise (the queen's case, by analogy with chess); (b) $w_{ij} = 1$ if quadrats i and j had a common edge, and $w_{ij} = 0$ otherwise (the rook's case). They detected significant positive spatial autocorrelation between quadrats at the $\alpha = 0.05$ significance level for all lattices and weighting systems used except the queen's case for lattices 8 and 9. These results again point to the compound model as being more plausible than the generalized version for these data. Bissell (1972a, b; 1973) has extended this type of analysis by investigating the use of the negative binomial model with irregular quadrat systems (for example, counties), in contrast to the regular lattices studied in this chapter.

13.4.4 *Other problems and emerging approaches*

Another problem with the quadrat method is that, while density information about the point pattern is retained, information on the locations of the quadrats with respect to each other is lost when the map is collapsed into a frequency distribution. Quite different maps can produce very similar frequency distributions of counts.

A further difficulty is the choice of quadrat size for the analysis. It is evident from Figure 13.8 that different quadrat sizes yield different parameter

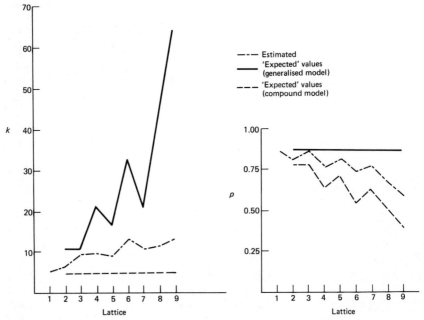

Figure 13.8 Parameter values for the negative binomial distribution applied to Matui's data. Lattices 1–9 are as defined in Figure 13.7.

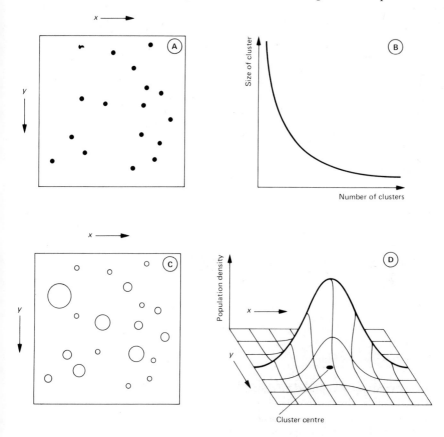

Figure 13.9 Components in the centre-satellite model. **A** Poisson location of the individual cluster centres. **B** Logarithmic curve describing the size distribution of centres. **C** One spatial realization of the size-number relations shown in (**B**). **D** Variations in the density of objects within a single cluster, with the density at increasing distances from the cluster centre based upon the normal probability law.

estimates. This is not surprising since we are, in effect, dealing each time with a different county system. Once again, we come up against the scale dependence of many statistical models discussed in Section 10.6.1. In general, the balance of the literature on this topic (Skellam, 1958; Pielou, 1957; Harvey, 1968b) seems to suggest that quadrat size should be chosen in such a way that (a) quadrats are not small enough for quadrat boundaries to cut through any spatial clusters in the data, and (b) quadrats are not so large that they contain several clusters. One attempt to overcome the quadrat size problem is by the development of a *centre–satellite model*, which explicitly incorporates the spatial spread of clusters (Neyman and Scott, 1952, 1958, 1972; Warren, 1962; Matérn, 1972a; Cliff and Ord, 1975b). The model is made up of the following components:

(1) an initial (Poisson) pattern of cluster centres;

(2) a cluster size distribution such as the logarithmic with independence between clusters usually assumed;

(3) a location law to describe the position of each individual within a cluster with respect to the cluster centre. Individuals are usually assumed to locate independently of each other. The isotropic bivariate normal distribution is commonly used in this context. See Figure 13.9.

The complexity of the model means that analytical solutions are available for only a few special cases, but the structure of the components outlined above means that simulation models can be constructed (cf. that of Morrill described in Section 4.2.3).

Despite the range of Poisson-based distributions considered in this chapter, many others exist. Dacey's (1964, 1966a, b) papers provide outstanding examples of the kinds of modifications that can be made, while a summary listing appears in McConnell (1966). One class of models which has not been considered in detail in the geographical literature comprises the doubly stochastic Poisson processes of Matérn (1960, 1971), Bartlett (1963) and Grandell (1972). In these models, the Poisson process is described by λ, which is itself generated by a stochastic process. Thus with quadrat data, the Poisson process might give the number of settlements in each area, while the underlying mechanism generating λ could describe the amount of land available for settlement.

13.5 Polygon Techniques

An alternative area-based method to quadrat counts for point pattern analysis is to describe the pattern using *Thiessen polygons*. These are also known as *Dirichlet regions* and *Voronoi polygons* (Matérn, 1972a, b). The construction of a net of such polygons for a point pattern is illustrated in Figure 13.10:

   (A) lines are drawn from each point to each adjacent point;

   (B) each of these inter-point lines is bisected to give the midpoint of the line;

   (C) from each midpoint, a boundary line is drawn at right-angles to the

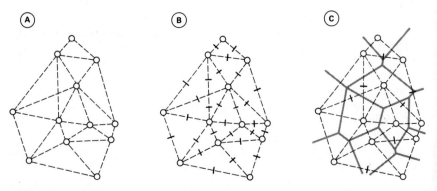

Figure 13.10 Stages in the construction of Thiessen polygons using the inter-point lines method. Adopted from Kopec, 1963, p. 25.

original inter-point line to create a series of *convex* polygons, such that the area within each polygon is nearer to the enclosed point than it is to any other point. Such polygons have been used in the central place literature (e.g. Bogue, 1950, p. 17 and Dacey, 1965) to define the spheres of influence of urban centres. In this case, the procedure depends critically upon the assumption that each centre dominates all the area that lies geometrically nearest to it (cf. Section 2.7).

The construction of Thiessen polygons by this method is a time consuming procedure and there is usually some inprecision over the choice of inter-point lines employed in drawing the boundaries around a given centre. This is illustrated in Figure 13.10B, where some of the inter-point lines have not been used. Kopec (1963) has suggested an alternative method of delineation shown in Figure 13.11. Consider two adjacent points which are a distance, *d*, apart. Draw circles of radius *d* centred on each of the points. The side of the polygon (between the two points) is located by drawing a line through the points of intersection of the circles. In Figure 13.11, the polygons of Figure 13.10 are reconstructed using this method. Kopec's method eliminates the need to draw inter-point lines and thus reduces the risk of error arising from inappropriate choice of them in the delineation of the polygons. Rhynsburger (1973)

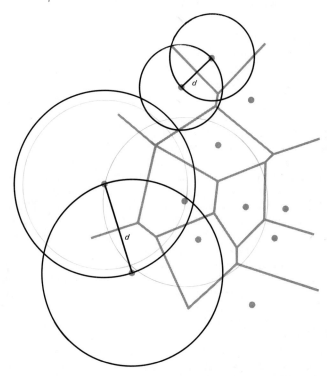

Figure 13.11 The construction of Thiessen polygons using the intersecting circles method.

describes a computer program which unambiguously constructs Thiessen polygons. Whatever the construction method used, a point pattern is required for a more extensive region than the actual study area, in order properly to close off the polygons at the edge of the study area.

Unlike quadrat count methods, a polygon net does preserve information on the relative locations of points in the pattern. However, given a system of polygons for an observed point pattern, in order to proceed statistically we need (a) a set of descriptive parameters for the polygons, and (b) knowledge of the values of these parameters for some theoretical point patterns to afford a basis for further development. As we have seen, in the case of quadrat counts, we have an extensive range of theoretical spatial point processes upon which we can draw for our bases of comparison. Similar sorts of results for Thiessen polygons are almost non-existent. Thus the use of polygon methods, rather than quadrat counts, to retain spatial information carries with it penalties which far outweigh this advantage.

The theoretical work that exists has focussed almost entirely upon the derivation of the expectations of various parameters for the system of Thiessen polygons obtained when the point pattern is an outcome of a simple Poisson process in the plane (Matérn, 1972a, b; Boots, 1973). As before, we denote the density of the process per unit area by λ. The parameters and their expectations, as summarized from the above authors, are:

parameter	*expectation*
number of sides (corners)	6
cell perimeter	$4/\sqrt{\lambda}$
length of a side	$\frac{2}{3}\sqrt{\lambda}$
area	$1/\lambda$

In addition, μ_2 (area) $= 0.28018/\lambda^2$. However, the sampling distributions of these statistics are not known in a usable form, and so there is no basis for an analytical test of significance unless we appeal to normal theory via a limit theorem. One way out of the impasse would be to extend the Monte Carlo experiment suggested by Boots (1973). Several realizations (m, say) of a Poisson process at density λ might be generated. The various parameters could then be evaluated for each pattern and the sampling distributions constructed empirically. But m would have to be substantially larger than the five used by Boots. This kind of approach might also be used to generate the sampling distributions for the parameters for other theoretical spatial point processes. The proposed method is simply an application of Hope's (1968) procedure for hypothesis testing described in Cliff and Ord (1973, Chapter 4) and considered already in Section 10.3.3. Given Rhynsburger's (1973) computer program, the method should be fairly straightforward computationally.

Parallel work in ecology (Pielou, 1969, Chapter 12; Matérn, 1972b) has concentrated on the so-called *L*- and *S*- mosaics. The *L*-mosaic is a two-colour choropleth map produced by the random colouring (either black or white) of cells created when a study area is partitioned by a system of random lines. The

S-mosaic is created by random colouring of the Thiessen polygons defined by an outcome of a spatial Poisson point process.

13.6 Distance Based Methods

A large number of distance-based measures of dispersion in point patterns have been proposed in the literature, and the principal ones have been summarized in Holgate (1965, 1972), Ord (1972b) and Cliff and Ord (1975b). M. F. Dacey of Northwestern University has worked more than any other geographer with the various techniques, and has been largely responsible for introducing the methods (chiefly from ecology) into the discipline. Dacey's early work using distance measures (e.g. Dacey, 1962, discussed in Section 4.2.1) was founded upon a classic paper by Clark and Evans (1954), whose arguments we now follow.

13.6.1 *Basic first nearest neighbour techniques*

Clark and Evans wished to determine the extent to which an observed spatial point pattern departed from (Poissonian) randomness, and they proposed a measure based upon *nearest neighbour distances*. Let the distance between individual i and individual j be d_{ij}. If $d_i^{min} = \min_{j \neq i} d_{ij}$, and $d_i^{min} = d_{ik}$, then we say that individual k is the (first) *nearest neighbour* of i. Clark and Evans proposed the statistic,

$$\bar{d}_0 = \frac{1}{n} \sum_{i=1}^{n} d_i^{min}, \tag{13.7}$$

the mean distance between nearest neighbours, as a measure of spacing among the points in a study area. In geographical applications, the summation is usually taken over all n points in the study area, although, as we shall see, there are problems with this procedure. Clark and Evans showed that, for a Poisson process in the plane with density parameter, λ, the expected mean distance between nearest neighbours, $\bar{d}_E$, is

$$\bar{d}_E = 1/2\lambda^{\frac{1}{2}}. \tag{13.8}$$

They then suggested that the ratio,

$$D_1 = \bar{d}_0/\bar{d}_E, \tag{13.9}$$

provides a measure of the degree of randomness in a pattern.[3] In particular, $D_1 = 1$ in a perfectly random pattern, $D_1 = 0$ (implying $\bar{d}_0 = 0$) in a perfectly clustered pattern, and $D_1 = 2.15$ in a maximally spaced, perfectly regular pattern, when the points will be located at the vertices of a hexagonal grid. D_1 is thus defined on the interval $[0, 2.15]$, and 'in any given distribution, the mean observed distance to nearest neighbour is $[D_1]$ times as great as would be

---

[3] In most geographical applications, λ, the mean number of points per unit area, is known, which permits the construction of tests of randomness based directly upon nearest neighbour distances. If λ is not known, see Persson (1971) and Holgate (1965, 1972) for ways of estimating λ and tests of randomness based on $\hat{\lambda}$.

expected in a random distribution of the same density. Thus a $[D_1]$ value of 0.5 would indicate that nearest neighbours are, on the average, half as far apart as expected under conditions of randomness' (Clark and Evans, 1954, p. 25).

Ord (1972b, p. 16) has noted that the exact sampling distribution of the test statistic (13.7) cannot be derived in a form which is easy to use. However, Clark and Evans have assumed, via the Cental Limit Theorem, that the quantity, $\bar{d}_0$, is approximately normally distributed when n is very large with mean $\bar{d}_E$, as given in equation (13.8) and standard deviation, $\sigma_{\bar{d}} = 0.26136/\sqrt{\lambda n}$ [variance $= (4 - \pi)/4n\pi\lambda$]. This suggests that an approximate test of statistically significant departure from randomness in a point pattern is to treat the quantity,

$$z = \frac{\bar{d}_0 - \bar{d}_E}{\sigma_{\bar{d}}}, \tag{13.10}$$

as a standard normal deviate.

A very similar measure to (13.7) has been proposed by Skellam (1952) and Moore (1954), namely

$$D_2 = \pi\lambda \sum_{i=1}^{n} (d_i^{\min})^2/n. \tag{13.11}$$

A more certain test of significance exists for this statistic than for the Clark and Evans measure, since under the null hypothesis of randomness in the point pattern, $2D_2$ is distributed as χ^2 with $2n$ degrees of freedom. $D_2 = 0$ when perfect clustering of points exists, $D_2 = 1$ for a random point pattern, and $D_2 = 3.63$ for a maximally spaced pattern. See Dacey (1975) for a detailed discussion of the distribution theory of (13.7) and (13.11) as a function of n, and recommendations as to which statistic to use for different values of n. Dacey also considers other statistics related to (13.11) which use the F-distribution as the basis of a test of significance.

13.6.2 *Independence assumption*

As Hsu and Mason (1974) and Cliff and Ord (1975b) have noted, the tests of significance suggested for both the Clark and Evans, and Skellam and Moore statistics depend critically upon the assumption that the n nearest-neighbour distances are independent observations. If this assumption cannot be sustained, the tests of significance are no longer valid (see the discussion of the Cental Limit Theorem in Section 8.3.1).

> This proviso is not to be taken lightly, since if k is the nearest neighbour for i, we know that $d_k^{\min} \leqslant d_{ik}$. *That is, we cannot include all the individuals in the study area in the sample* (Cliff and Ord, 1975b, Section 4.1).

Since nearest neighbour analysis must not be based upon all points in the study area, by implication a sample of points should be used instead. Ways of doing this are either (a) to measure the nearest-neighbour distances for all points inside randomly selected small quadrats within the study area, or (b) to analyse nearest-neighbour distances for successive points on randomly located line transects.

13.6.3 *Boundary problems*

A related issue is raised by the treatment of points whose nearest neighbours lie outside the boundary of the study area. Again boundary effects render invalid the tests of significance proposed. As discussed in Section 10.2.1, one way out of the difficulty is to map the study area on to a torus. This is not that unreasonable since the Poisson process against which we are comparing our observed point pattern is strictly stationary and isotropic (see Section 10.4.3). Finally we note that both the independence and boundary problems discussed above apply as well to the methods considered in the remainder of this chapter.

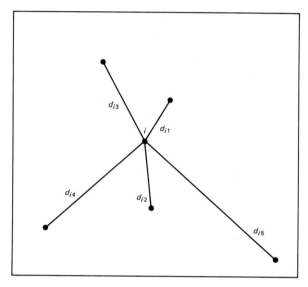

Figure 13.12 Order neighbour distances for the point *i*.

13.6.4 *Extensions of basic nearest-neighbour methods*

Dacey (1963) and Holgate (1965) have defined the *order neighbour distances* from the reference point *i* to the *R* nearest objects to *i* as

$$d_{i1} \leqslant d_{i2} \leqslant d_{i3} \leqslant \dots \leqslant d_{iR};$$

that is, d_{ik} represents the distance from *i* to its *k*th nearest neighbour, $k = 1, 2, \dots R$ (see Figure 13.12). We may test whether the distances to *k*th nearest neighbours depart significantly from random expectation using equation (13.11) as our test statistic since Dacey, Skellam and Moore have independently shown that $2D_2$ is distributed under the null hypothesis as χ^2 with $(2kn)$ degrees of freedom for distances to the *k*th nearest neighbour.

Another extension of the basic nearest-neighbour idea is the so-called *sectoral* or *regional* nearest neighbour method (Clark and Evans, 1954; Dacey and Tung, 1962). A circle divided into *k* equal sized sectors, as shown in Figure

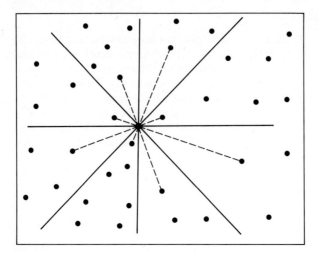

Figure 13.13   The sectoral nearest neighbour method for the typical reference point, *i*, with $k = 8$. The pecked lines link the reference point to its nearest neighbour in each sector.

13.13, is placed over each sampled reference point. $k = 6$ is a common choice. The distances between the reference point and its first nearest neighbour in each sector are measured. Then either D_1 [equation (13.9)] or D_2 [equation (13.11)] is evaluated with $n = mk$, where *m* is the number of reference points used. Dacey and Tung have also worked with *k* regional nearest-neighbour means as follows. The distance from each reference point, *i*, to the first nearest-neighbour in each sector is measured. These *k* measurements are labelled d_{ik}, such that

$$d_{i1} \leqslant d_{i2} \leqslant \dots \leqslant d_{ik},$$

and the *k* regional or sectoral means are defined as

$$\bar{d}_{ik} = \sum_i d_{ik}/n, \quad k = 1, 2, \dots \tag{13.12}$$

or

$$\bar{d}_{ik} = \sum_i d_{ik}^2/n, \quad k = 1, 2, \dots \tag{13.13}$$

13.6.5 *Reflexive nearest neighbour methods*

In a pattern which is an outcome of a Poisson point process in the plane, Pielou (1969, pp. 121–22) has noted that there will be a large number of points for which $d_i^{\min} = d_k^{\min} = d_{ik}$ (that is, *i* is the first nearest-neighbour of *k*, and vice versa). Specifically, the proportion of such reflexive pairs will be 0.6215. An excessively high proportion of reciprocal pairs would imply that 'individuals tended to occur as isolated [evenly spaced] couples' (Pielou, 1969,

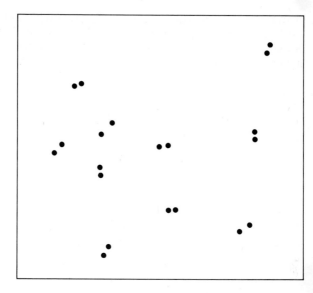

Figure 13.14　A point pattern in which pairs of points are reflexive nearest neighbours.

p. 122), as in Figure 13.14. Clark (1956) recognized this same fact when he showed that, for points randomly located on a line, the proportion of points which are first order reflexive nearest-neighbours is 2/3. Clark has suggested that values in excess of this proportion indicate some uniformity in the pattern, while values less than this proportion are symptomatic of grouping. Dacey (1969b) has provided general formulae to compute $\pi_k(r)$, the proportion of reflexive rth order nearest-neighbours in k-dimensional space. These results form the basis of reflexive nearest neighbour analysis. Dacey (1960) has illustrated the technique with an examination of the spacing of river towns in excess of 20,000 population along the central Mississippi valley. See Figure 13.15, where directed arrows are drawn from each point to its rth nearest neighbour. In Figure 13.15, there are five reflexive pairs of first nearest neighbours, three of second and two of third. Dacey's (1969b) results, and these data, enable Table 13.7 to be prepared. This table suggests a more grouped

Table 13.7　Reflexive nearest-neighbour analysis.*

Reflexive points:	Number	Observed proportion	Expected proportion	Description of pattern
Nearest-neighbour order:				
First	10	0.588	0.667	Grouped
Second	6	0.353	0.370	Slightly grouped
Third	4	0.235	0.272	Slightly grouped

*River towns in the central Mississippi valley.

than random spacing of towns along the river, which apparently contradicts a qualitative assessment of the spacing made by Burghardt (1959, p. 322)[4]. Burghardt argued that the towns 'reveal an interesting uniformity of spacing along the rivers [in the central lowlands of the USA].'

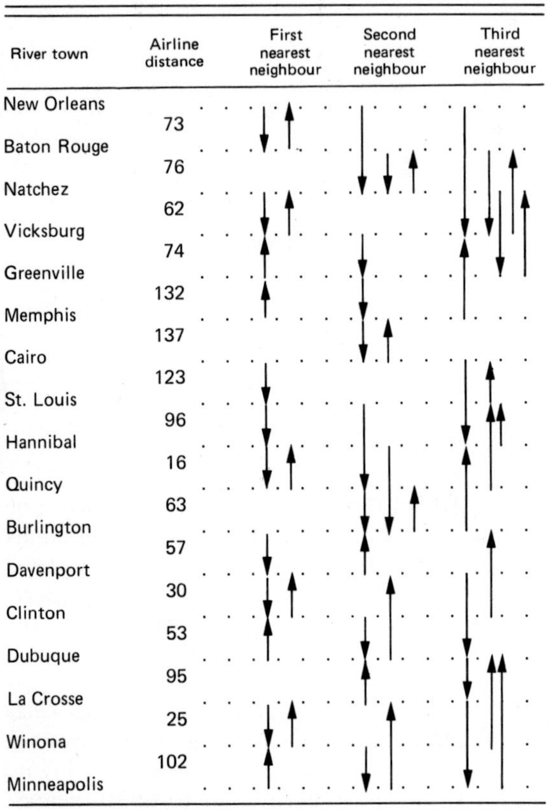

River town	Airline distance	First nearest neighbour	Second nearest neighbour	Third nearest neighbour
New Orleans	73			
Baton Rouge	76			
Natchez	62			
Vicksburg	74			
Greenville	132			
Memphis	137			
Cairo	123			
St. Louis	96			
Hannibal	16			
Quincy	63			
Burlington	57			
Davenport	30			
Clinton	53			
Dubuque	95			
La Crosse	25			
Winona	102			
Minneapolis				

Figure 13.15 Spacing of river towns in excess of 20,000 population in the central Mississippi valley. Source: Dacey, 1960, p. 60.

However, a comment by Porter (1960) demonstrates that reflexive nearest-neighbour analysis can produce some seemingly odd results. Figure 13.16 shows the spacing of towns along two hypothetical rivers. On the river Doring, the towns are uniformly spaced, while on the river Anyder, they occur in uniformly spaced couples. The results of the analysis for the river Anyder illustrate well how examination of higher order neighbours can detect the 'isolated couples' referred to (above) by Pielou; first order reflexive neighbours describe the pattern within couplets, while higher order neighbours describe

---

[4] An alternative way of examining the spacing of river towns would be to apply directly to the airline distances the 'broken stick', or random partitions of a uniform interval, model described in Cliff, Haggett, Ord, Bassett and Davies (1975, Chapter 3).

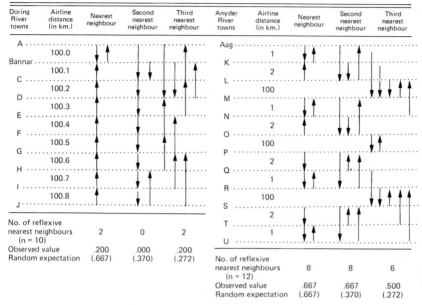

Figure 13.16 Reflexive nearest neighbour analysis of town-spacing along two hypothetical rivers, the Doring and the Anyder. Source: Porter, 1960, p. 299.

the spacing of the couplets. In the case of the river Doring, however, the technique seems to break down. Clark's guidelines for the interpretation of the observed values of the test statistic imply a clustered pattern for what are constructed as almost exactly uniformed spaced *individual* points. Possibly, however, it is the guidelines, rather than the technique, which are in error. As Pielou (1969, p. 122) states, 'how we might interpret observed departures from expectation [in the proportion of reflexive pairs] is not clear except for the obvious conclusion that an excessively high proportion of reciprocal pairs would support the hypothesis (if it were being tested) that individuals tended to occur as isolated couples.' More work is clearly needed on this topic to determine if isolated *individual* points as well as clustered patterns, generally produce values of the test statistic which are less than expectation.

13.6.6 *Choice of tests*

In a sense, the various distance-based measures that we have described lie between the quadrat count and Thiessen polygon approaches in terms of the insight they give into the processes which may have produced a particular spatial point pattern. Quadrat methods permit us to examine the applicability of a whole range of theoretical point processes to a given observed point pattern. The distance-based measures are slightly less sophisticated, in that they permit no finer assessment than is possible with the clustered → random → uniform scale. At the present time, Thiessen polygon methods enable us to determine only the randomness or otherwise of a point pattern. However, as we would anticipate, the more about our data we expect a statistical method to tell us, the more demanding of our data and skill in analysis the technique will be; and, in our choice of approach, we must trade off what we want to achieve against what the data will stand.

For quadrat methods, we have already outlined in Section 13.3 some ways of selecting a particular theoretical distribution with which to compare our observed spatial point pattern. What guidelines can be suggested which will enable us to pick, from the range of distance-based measures described, the most appropriate statistic for a given problem? No full study has been made which assesses the relative power of the various tests against selected alternative hypotheses to randomness. Dacey and Tung (1962, p. 86) have made some comparison between the order neighbour and sectoral (regional) methods, and they reached the following conclusions:

(1) 'The order method evidently has a lower power efficiency than the regional method for detecting the presence of randomness in a pattern.'

(2) 'The regional method is particularly suited for pattern interpretation when a tendency towards even spacing of points is suspected.'

(3) 'The regional method has less efficiency than the order method when the locations are biased towards grouping or clustering.'

13.7 Conclusions

In this chapter, we have shown how quadrat, polygon, and distance methods may be used to describe the spatial pattern formed by a set of points located in a study area. Of the three approaches, quadrat count analysis is likely to be the most suggestive of the kinds of processes generating the point pattern. We have illustrated how various discrete probability distributions may be fitted to an observed frequency array of quadrat counts, and we have given some criteria for selecting an appropriate model. Some of the problems raised by the quadrat method, such as choice of quadrat size, equifinality, and evaluation of the goodness-of-fit of a model, have been considered. For Thiessen polygons, we have described two ways in which the polygons can be constructed. Our overriding criticism of this approach is the lack of distribution theory for the summary parameters of the set of polygons for any spatial patterns other than that produced by a simple Poisson process. In contrast, while the various distance-based tests are not as suggestive of process as quadrat methods, they have been developed in such a way that we can make some (quite limited) assessment of the relative strengths of random, clustered, and uniform components in producing a spatial point pattern (cf. Mead, 1974). The application of distance methods poses less problems than does the use of quadrat counts, but they provide less information. Thus, for example, whereas nearest-neighbour tests might tell us whether a particular point pattern is more clustered than random, we would use quadrat methods to try to infer the structure of the process producing that clustered pattern. Nevertheless, if it is desired solely to test whether or not a point pattern is random, Holgate (1972) has indicated that order distances are preferable to quadrat counts on power grounds. However, it should be clear from this chapter that despite the large volume of geographical literature in which methods of locational analysis have been used, we still have very little 'feel' for what kinds of patterns in spatial data produce what sorts of results when analysed; this comment applies to most of our techniques, and not just to point pattern methods.

Our coverage of point pattern methods has not been exhaustive. Other distance-based methods are described in Holgate (1965) and in Cliff and Ord (1975b). Alternative summary measures are the mean centre and variance of a spatial pattern (Bachi, 1963; Neft, 1966). A further interesting approach is that of Medvedkov (1967), who uses entropy measures to decompose point patterns into random and uniform components.

Part Three:

Regional Applications

If everything occurred at the same time there would be no development. If everything existed in the same place there could be no particularity. Only space makes possible the particular, which then unfolds in time . . . to let this space-conditioned particularity grow without letting the whole run wild—that is political art. (AUGUST LÖSCH, The economics of location, 1939, p. 508).

14 Region Building

14.1 Introduction

Although regions are traditionally a central theme in geographical writing, geographers have always been curiously reticent about the ways in which regions can be built up. This reticence is particularly unfortunate in that it is in precisely this field that human geographers have much to offer, both to other social sciences and to government and business. Already geographers have worked on improving the regional structure of both hospitals (Godlund, 1961), schools (Yeates, 1963), and social administration areas (Massam, 1975), as well as the more widely known cases of local government boundaries. This chapter sets out to bring together the explicit techniques that have been used in regional delimitation and in grouping.

14.2 The Regional Concept

14.2.1 *Types of regions*

Regions have a central, indeed almost theological, status in geography. As Harvey (1969, p. 125) observes, the region was 'sometimes accorded the status of a "theoretical entity" rather like an atom or neutron which could not be precisely observed but whose existence could be inferred from its effects. The areal differentiation of the earth's surface could thus be "explained" with reference to this theoretical object which governed human spatial organization.' Despite heavy criticism, typified by Kimble's essay on the 'Inadequacy of the regional concept' (in Stamp and Wooldridge, 1951, pp. 151–74) and some stout defence (e.g. Minshull, 1967), regions continue to

450

remain one of the most logical and satisfactory ways of organizing geographical information. Modern monographs like Brookfield and Hart's *Melanesia* (1971) continue to join the regional 'classics' of the past— Demangeon on Picardy, Sauer on the Ozarks, Bowman on the Andes.

It is not our purpose to pursue the somewhat mystical interpretation of the term 'region', except to note that debate within academic geography rumbles on. The more prosaic view adopted here is that regions perform much the same role as a class in any science, and that regionalization may be approached as a special form of classification. This view has been argued by Bunge (1962, pp. 14–26) and Grigg (1965), who disagree with conventional schemes for treating regions as if they present unique problems in classification, insisting that they are merely the areal aspects of a classification problem common to all sciences. To emphasize this point, we may tabulate a number of terms common in the geographical literature and range them against their general classification counterparts. A 'single-feature' region may be reduced to classification using a 'single category'; 'regional boundary' to 'class interval'; 'homogeneous region' to 'class with low areal variance'. Bunge argues that, rather than depreciating regional geography, this approach places geography alongside those natural sciences many of which either went through a *taxonomic* phase at some time in their evolution (e.g. chemistry) or have a strong continuing interest in this phase (e.g. botany). Conventions in geographical works, such as ignoring either the oceans or the land areas of the world in most non-climatic regional systems, may be seen as parallels to conventions in natural science. In biology, for example, the plant and animal 'kingdoms' are commonly regarded as separate even though they do jointly form part of total biology.

Three main types of region are usually recognized in geography: uniform, nodal, and planning regions (see Figure 14.1 and Table 14.1).

Table 14.1   Categories of region.

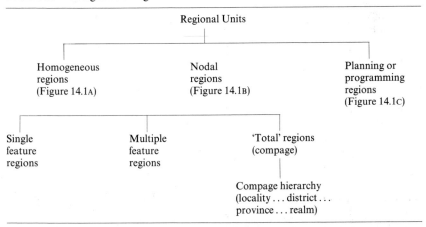

(a) *Uniform regions* may be defined as contiguous areas within which, conditional upon the purpose for which the regional system is being defined, place-to-place variations may be regarded as trivial. More formally, a set of

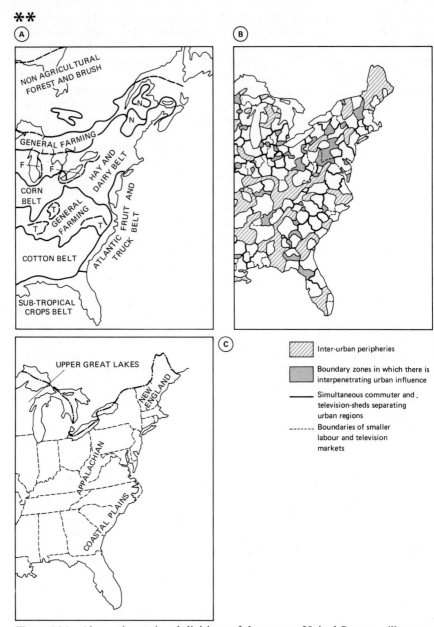

Figure 14.1 Alternative regional divisions of the eastern United States to illustrate homogenous, nodal, and planning regions respectively. **A** Agricultural regions. (F = Fruit region of the Great Lakes Shore, N = Nonagricultural lands within the General Farming Belt, T = Sections of the southern General Farming Belt specializing in tobacco.) **B** Commuting areas around larger cities. **C** Planning regions set up under the Area Redevelopment Act of 1961 and modified by the Appalachian Regional Development Act of 1965. Source: Paterson, 1975, pp. 66, 130, 132.

uniform regions may be defined as that arrangement of regional boundaries for which

$$\frac{\text{External (between region) variation}}{\text{Internal (within region) variation}} = \text{maximum} \qquad (14.1)$$

(cf. analysis of variance). Characteristically, uniform regions are non-overlapping and completely exhaust the space available (i.e. no county in the study area being regionalized is not assigned to a region). Uniform regions are sometimes termed homogeneous or formal regions (Figure 14.1A).

(b) *Nodal regions* may be defined as areas (contiguous or non-contiguous) within which:

$$\frac{\text{Internal (within region) bonds}}{\text{External (between region) bonds}} = \text{maximum.} \qquad (14.2)$$

Note that nodal regions are defined in terms of bonds or links between *pairs* of places. Unlike uniform regions, nodal regions may be overlapping and interpenetrating. Nodal regions are sometimes termed functional regions (Figure 14.1B).

(c) *Planning regions* may be defined as areas, contiguous or non-contiguous, delimited on an *ad hoc* basis for purposes of administration or organization. Planning regions may be overlapping or non-overlapping; they may exhaust the complete study area, or be confined to any part of that area. An objective in the design of planning regions is to maximize overlap between the needs of administration and 'naturally occurring' uniform or nodal regions (Figure 14.1C).

14.2.2 *Scale in regional hierarchies*

That scale problems have long troubled geographers is rather plainly shown in the attempts made to define regions in scale terms. With uniform regions (Table 14.1), the system applied by Fennemann (1916) to the landform divisions of the United States, with its recognition of major divisions, provinces, and sections, was scale-based and had a major effect on human geography (Table 14.2). Unstead (1933), in an interesting paper on 'systems of regions', put forward the scheme which filled in at the smaller levels the system Fennemann had begun at the larger scale.

Linton (1948) integrated both preceding systems in a seven-stage scheme which ran through the whole range from the smallest unit, the site, to the largest, the continent. More recently Whittlesey (in James, Jones, and Wright, 1954, pp. 47–51) presented a 'hierarchy for compages', with details of the appropriate map scales for study and presentation, and followed this with a model study on Southern Rhodesia to illustrate his method (Whittlesey, 1956). In the decades since the Whittlesey scheme was put into operation, and the call was made to '. . . fill this lacuna in geographic thinking' (in James *et al.*, 1954, p. 47) there has not been any rush to adopt it. Of the few significant papers published in this field, only one, that by Bird (1956), subjected Whittlesey's scheme to field testing. Bird's two-scale comparison of the western peninsulas of Brittany and Cornwall suggested that, while a general (or small-scale) approach showed the two areas to be similar, the intensive (or large-scale) study showed that the two peninsulas were quite dissimilar in most details. Bird's deft illustration of the fundamental and very common geographical problem of the scale dependence of analysis passed scarcely without comment.

Table 14.2   Comparative scales and terminology of regional hierarchies.

Approximate size (ml.^{2})	Fennemann, 1916	Unstead, 1933	Linton, 1949	Whittlesey, 1954	Map scales for analysis*
10^0			Site		
10		Stow	Stow	Locality	1/10,000
10^2	District		Tract		
		Tract		District	1/50,000
10^3	Section		Section		
		Sub-region		Province	1/1,000,000
10^4	Province		Province		
		Minor region			
10^5	Major division		Major division	Realm	1/5,000,000
10^6		Major region	Continent		

Source: Haggett. In Chorley and Haggett, 1965a.
*Whittlesey, 1954.

The second major move in the period since Whittlesey's papers came from Philbrick (1957), who published a very full scheme based on the concept of a sevenfold hierarchy of functions. Corresponding to each function is a nodal point with its functional region. Here scale is introduced through the geometric concept of *nesting*, with each order of the hierarchy fitting within the next highest order. Philbrick illustrated the hypothetical case where each central place of a given order is defined to include four central places of the next lower order. This gives a succession, for a seventh-order region, of four sixth-order places, 16 fifth-order places, and so on, down to the final level of 4,096 first-order places. His application of this scheme to the eastern United States, with New York and Chicago in the roles of seventh- and sixth-order centres respectively, was only partly successful, but the attempt to introduce a scale component into a system of nodal regions has given an important lead.

14.2.3 *Partitioning vs grouping procedures*

Classification is a procedure by which we impose some sort of order on geographical reality. The logical rules by which classification proceeds may be illustrated by set theory. The Venn diagrams in Figure 14.2 consist of a *universal set*, U, composed of a set of six countries (shown for the purposes of this discussion by x_1, x_2, ..., x_6). Each country forms an element in the universal set.

We can proceed to classify the countries in U in either of two ways: by logical division or else by grouping.

(i) *Logical division* or 'classification from above' proceeds by dividing the universal set according to a particular property. In order to follow this method, we must have prior information on the property being used as an indicator, and thus this approach is sometimes called a deductive one. In Figure 14.2B, we partition the set by criterion A, say a European location, so as to give a set A, together with its complement A' (non-European locations).

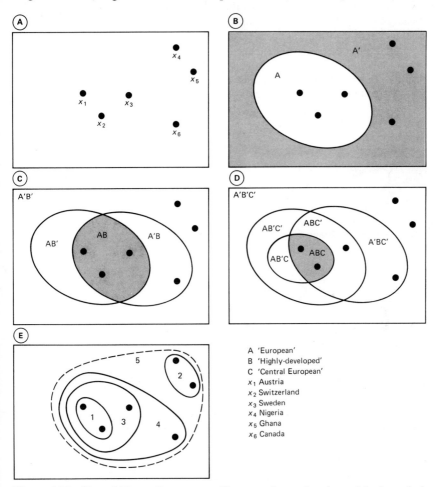

Figure 14.2 Use of Venn diagrams to illustrate the regional partitioning of six countries by (a) logical division [**B** to **D**] and (b) grouping [**E**].

Note that the two classes A and A' are non-overlapping, and completely exhaust the space available. We can go on to add further classificatory criteria. These may be independent of the first (like criterion B, 'highly-developed countries' shown in Figure 14.2c) or directly related to the first in a hierarchic manner (like criterion *C*, 'Central European' countries, shown in Figure 14.2D). Each new criterion breaks down the universal set into cross-partitions (e.g. Central European, highly developed countries, set {*ABC*}). Observe, however, that some of these partitions may be empty. This is because we can find no elements to put in it (e.g. Central European non-highly developed countries, {*AB′C*}).

(ii) *Grouping* or 'classification from below' proceeds by grouping the individual elements, x_1, x_2, ..., x_n according to certain criteria of similarity. Thus, we might join x_1 and x_2 so that the union, $x_1 \cup x_2$, forms a set, 1. If a measure of similarity is average income *per caput*, then Austria and Switzerland might be linked in this way. Likewise, two African countries, x_4 and x_5, might be linked to form set 2, and so on. 'The sets so formed may then be united to form super-sets, and the procedure can continue until the last union of sets yields the universal set' (Harvey, 1969, p. 330). Figure 14.2E shows this progressive grouping process.

✳✳

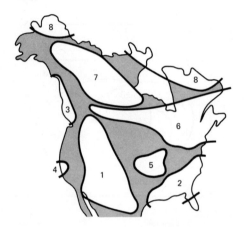

Figure 14.3   Core areas (unshaded) for the division of North America into eight climatic regions. The borderline (shaded) areas were subsequently assigned to the regional cores using discriminant analysis. Source: Casetti, 1964, p. 71.

In practice, the sharp division between the two main procedures, partitioning and grouping, may not be maintained. For example, we may be able to partition only part of our universe by logical division; remaining elements may then be assigned to these cores by a grouping process. Casetti (1964), in a study of North American climate, used a two-stage procedure. First, 70 stations (elements) x_1, x_2, ..., x_{70} which comprised the universal set were logically divided on the basis of Koppen's climatic classification into eight regions (sets A_1, A_2, ..., A_8). Second, discriminant analysis was used to check on this initial classification relative to their climatic similarities and differences, and elements were regrouped on this basis (Figure 14.3). Such an iterative approach, alternating the two main procedures of division and grouping, is likely to offer a useful compromise strategy in region building.

14.2.4 *Probabilistic aspects of boundary overlap*

So far in our discussion, we have assumed that regions can be partitioned or grouped in an unambiguous fashion. In practice, the contrary situation is more likely. Sinnhuber (1954) has illustrated the remarkable range of definitions that have been given to what is variously designated Central Europe, Mitteleuropa, or Europe Central. Sixteen human geographies, ranging from that of Schjerning in 1914, to Gottmann in 1951, show a great variety in their regional definitions. Figure 14.4A shows these boundaries. Surprisingly, areas included within the term Middle Europe extend outside the limits of the map, and Sinnhuber ruefully observes that the Iberian peninsula is the only part of Europe not included by at least one author. Conversely, the area which all the authors agree belongs to Central Europe is remarkably small—no more than Austria and Bohemia–Moravia. This core area is shaded in Figure 14.4A.

✱✱

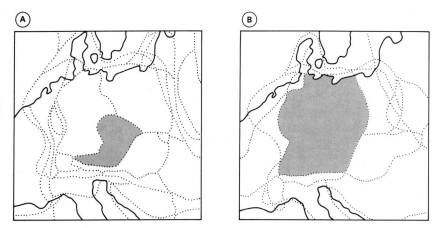

Figure 14.4 Alternative definitions of Mitteleuropa in terms of human (**A**) and physical (**B**) criteria. Areas of common overlap shaded. Source: Sinnhuber, 1954, pp. 19, 24.

That this core is not itself an adequate solution is shown by the companion map (Figure 14.4B) based on six concepts of Middle Europe as given by geographers writing over a comparable time period (1887 to 1937), but using physical criteria. This map shows a large core area with much less variation in the alternative definitions; one which includes within it the Austria–Bohemia–Moravia core area of the previous analysis. In set theory terms, the area included with all definitional boundaries represents the union (∪) of all sets; conversely, the core area represents the intersection of all the sets (∩).

Operations with regional sets can be extended to embrace probability concepts. Consider the set of maps of regions within a city shown in Figure 14.5. Each of three criteria (*A*, *B*, *C*) for defining areas of social need are shown, together with the set combinations: clearly the intersection $A \cap B \cap C$

represents the region of greatest concern. As Table 14.3 shows this critical ABC region makes up about 17 per cent of the city by area. Does this share indicate a high concentration of social need, or might we have expected this degree of overlap (i.e. spatial concentration) on purely random grounds?

Table 14.3   Evaluation of a regional partition ($A \cap B \cap C$) in terms of observed and expected areas.

| Regional criterion | Observed areas | | Expected areas | | |
	Individual maps*	Combined map†	Proportion	Number of city blocks	Observed ÷ expected
A	36	16	.288	17.3	.93
B	24	5	.128	7.7	.65
C	12	1	.048	2.9	.35
AB	—	9	.192	11.5	.78
AC	—	1	.072	4.3	.24
BC	—	0	.032	1.9	—
ABC	—	10	.048	2.9	3.48
Not covered	—	18	.192	11.5	1.56
Total	—	601	1.000	60.0	—

*Figure 14.5A, B, C.   †Figure 14.5D.

To answer this question, we need to look again at the first three maps in Figure 14.5. Criterion A applies to 36 of the sixty city blocks. If we assume each city block has an equal and independent chance of being marked A, then we can express this as a probability, $P(A) = 36/60 = 0.60$. By a similar argument, the probabilities for the other two indicators are $P(B) = 0.40$ and $P(C) = 0.20$. If there were no implied association between the three criteria (i.e. each map was independent of the others), the chances of combining the independent events within the city could be resolved by probability theory. We have

$$E[A] = P(A) - [\{P(A).P(B) + P(A).P(C)\} - P(A).P(B).P(C)]$$
$$E[B] = P(B) - [\{P(A).P(B) + P(B).P(C)\} - P(A).P(B).P(C)]$$
$$E[C] = P(C) - [\{P(A).P(C) + P(B).P(C)\} - P(A).P(B).P(C)]$$

$$E[AB] = P(A)P(B) - P(A).P(B).P(C)$$
$$E[AC] = P(A)P(C) - P(A).P(B).P(C)$$
$$E[BC] = P(B)P(C) - P(A).P(B).P(C)$$

$$E[ABC] = P(A).P(B).P(C),$$

(14.3)

where $E[A]$ is the expectation of the event A, and so on. Thus, the expectation of encountering an AB class within the city could be estimated from (14.3) as $(0.6 \times 0.4) - (0.6 \times 0.4 \times 0.2) = 0.192$ (see Table 14.3). In other words, we should expect between eleven and twelve of the city blocks to be coded AB under a random hypothesis, rather than the nine blocks actually observed in Figure 14.5D. Inspection of the ratio between observed and expected shares in the last column of Table 14.3 shows that the high deprivation region, ABC, represents a spatial concentration more than three times greater than would be expected to occur under the random hypothesis.

We can standardize this concentration ratio by taking into consideration the maximum regional overlap that could possibly be obtained with the three criteria. As Figure 14.5F shows, the best results obtainable is where the three sets are nested and the intersection *ABC* covers twelve city blocks, i.e. *ABC* is spatially coincident with the area covered by the smallest set (*C*). Using this information, we can define a concentration index (C.I.) as

$$\text{C.I.} = \frac{R - E[R]}{\max(R) - E[R]},\qquad(14.4)$$

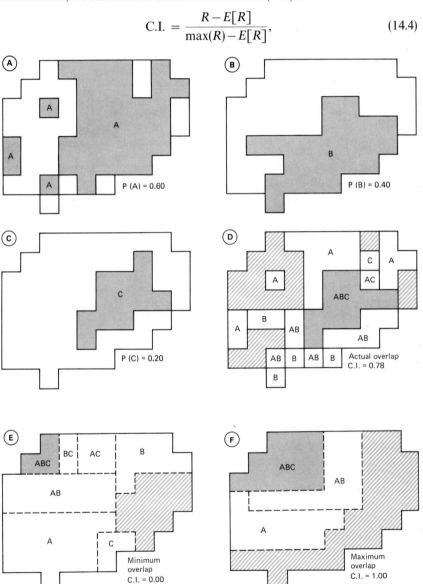

Figure 14.5 Regional partitions in a probabilistic framework.

where R is the actually observed area of the regional core (i.e. the ten blocks in Figure 14.5D), and $E[R]$ is the expected area of the regional core (i.e. 2.9 blocks, from Table 14.3). For the distribution shown in Figure 14.5D, the value of C.I. $= (10-2.9)/(12-2.9) = 0.78$. Positive values of C.I. in the range $0 < \text{C.I.} \leqslant 1$ indicate the degree to which the observed regional overlap is better (greater) than that expected under random intersection of the areal indicators used to define it. Negative values of C.I. would be generated by sets with even less overlap than that expected under the random hypothesis, but these are unlikely to be of interest in a regionalization study. Note that the index need not be confined to the area of overlap (i.e. city blocks), but could be weighted by the population of each block.

14.3 Regions as Combinatorial Problems

Where a small number of counties have to be assigned to a fixed number of regions, complete enumeration of all possible allocations of counties to regions may be feasible, and the 'best' grouping for the purpose in hand chosen. Figure 14.6 illustrates such a complete enumeration for a four-county problem. Cliff and Haggett (1970) show that the number of alternative combinations rises explosively with n, the number of counties, so that this approach is not feasible in most practical situations. In such cases, heuristic methods may be necessary which allow (a) isolation of suitable groups of counties to act as 'cores' around which others might be aggregated, and (b)

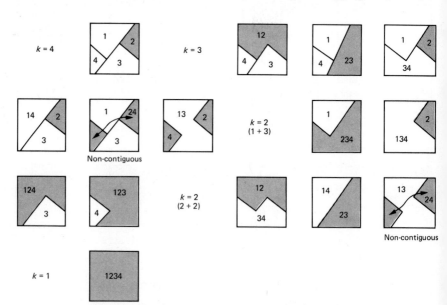

Figure 14.6 All possible regional divisions for a hypothetical four county case. The number of regions is indicated by k. Note that two of the partitions yield non-contiguous areas and may be considered classes rather than regions *sensu strictu*.

exploration of the likely compromises that may need to be made in order to attain certain desired mosaic patterns.

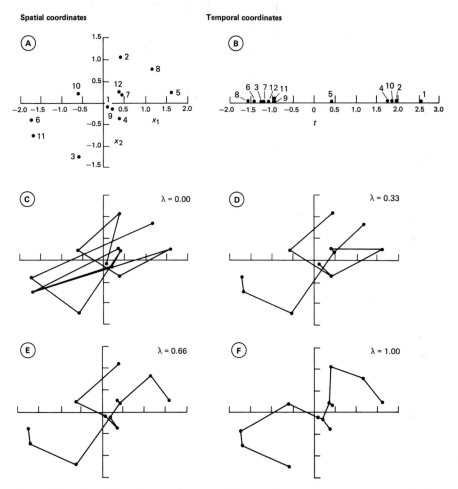

Figure 14.7 Spatial and temporal co-ordinates of twelve centres and minimal spanning trees for various values of λ. Source: Cliff *et al.*, 1975, p. 24.

To illustrate this point, we draw upon an example given in Cliff, Haggett, Ord, Bassett and Davies (1975, Section 2.5) in the remainder of this section. Cliff *et al.* assigned random co-ordinates in the spatial (X_1, X_2) and time (T) dimensions to 12 county centroids. To make direct comparison possible, the random co-ordinates were standardized to zero means and unit standard deviations. Figure 14.7A shows the locations of the 12 centres in the two-dimensional space, and Figure 14.7B their locations in the one-dimensional (T) space. In terms of a real world problem, the spatial co-ordinates (X_1, X_2) of the county centroids would represent the locations on a map of the counties to be grouped, while the time locations might be defined by, say, the date at which each county exceeded a particular population density threshold. Let the distance metric d_{ij}, represent the separation between counties i and j in space, and t_{ij} their separation in time. The objective of a purely *geographical* grouping procedure would be to minimize the distance between counties comprising a group in terms of the $\{d_{ij}\}$ values, while the objective of a purely *temporal* grouping procedure would be to minimize the distances between counties comprising a group in terms of the $\{t_{ij}\}$ values.

Using the standardized locational scores shown in Figures 14.7A and B, matrices of inter-county distances can be calculated and a *minimal spanning tree* (MST) constructed. The MST is formed by an iterative procedure. Initially, each county centre is linked to its first-order nearest neighbour in terms of the d_{ij} or t_{ij} metric. Then each sub-graph so formed is linked to its first-order nearest sub-graph. This procedure is terminated when all the n counties in the matrix are linked in a single graph. The graph is composed of $n-1$ links and has a tree-like form. Figure 14.7F shows the MST for the spatial $\{d_{ij}\}$ matrix. It should be compared with the MST for the temporal $\{t_{ij}\}$ matrix shown in Figure 14.7C.

Table 14.4   Values for the $n-1$ link trees mapped in Figure 14.7.

	Mean link length in standard scores*	
	MST	MST*
Spatial matrix (d_{ij})	-1.042	1.352
Temporal matrix (t_{ij})	-1.013	1.285

* $\bar{d}_{ij} = \bar{t}_{ij} = 0; s(d_{ij}) = s(t_{ij}) = 1$.
Source: Cliff *et al.*, 1975, p. 25.

Using a similar argument, we may construct iteratively the maximal spanning tree, (MST*). This is formed by linking each county to its $(n-1)$th nearest neighbour, that is, to its most distant neighbour. Sub-graphs formed by this process are then linked by joining the most distant sub-graphs until all n counties are linked into a single graph. The lengths of the MST and MST* form the lower and upper bounds for the distribution of all tree graphs (Table 14.4). These extremes are useful in providing a yardstick against which the relative 'efficiency' of any individual tree, of length L, may be judged. Here, the percentage efficiency is defined as

$$\frac{L(\text{MST}^*) - L}{L(\text{MST}^*) - L(\text{MST})} \times 100. \tag{14.5}$$

If we adopt a non-spatial strategy, and minimize the temporal metric (Strategy I in Table 14.5 and Figure 14.7C), then the spatial efficiency is rather low at only 41.4%. If we adopt the opposite approach and minimize the spatial metric (Strategy IV in Table 14.5 and Figure 14.7F), then the temporal efficiency is reduced to only 44.4 per cent.

However, Strategy I and Strategy IV represent extreme or 'pure' strategies. Since both d_{ij} and t_{ij} are measured in a similar triangular matrix with time and space distances recorded in a standardized metric, they can be simply combined. Such a combined distance measure (c_{ij}) can be given as

$$c_{ij} = \lambda d_{ij} + (1 - \lambda)t_{ij} \qquad (14.6)$$

where λ represents a weighting constant with the limits ($0 \leqslant \lambda \leqslant 1$). When $\lambda = 0.00$ we have a purely temporal strategy, and when $\lambda = 1.00$ we have a purely spatial strategy. Mixed strategies with $\lambda = 0.33$ and $\lambda = 0.66$ are shown in Figures 14.7D and E respectively. As Table 14.5 shows, these 'mixed' strategies yield intermediate results with an average efficiency about 20 per cent greater than that of the extremes.

Table 14.5   Relative efficiency of alternative linkage strategies.

Spatial weighting	Spatial efficiency (%)	Temporal efficiency (%)	Averaged efficiency (%)
Strategy I[a]: $\lambda = 0.00$	41.4	100.0	70.7
Strategy II[b]: $\lambda = 0.33$	86.6	96.4	91.5
Strategy III[b]: $\lambda = 0.66$	95.7	88.4	92.3
Strategy IV[c]: $\lambda = 1.00$	100.0	44.4	72.2

[a]'Pure' non-spatial strategy.
[b]'mixed' strategy.
[c]'pure' spatial strategy.
Source: Cliff *et al.*, 1975, p. 26.

Cliff *et al.* (1975) argue that construction of a shortest-spanning tree based on a weighted combination of time and space distances provides two useful insights into the region-building process. First, the study link *persistence* gives some heuristic guides to the selection of nucleii around which counties can be aggregated. We can observe that as the spatial constraints are progressively weakened (compare F, E, and D in Figure 14.7) the pattern of links that forms the minimal spanning tree changes. Indeed, when they are completely relaxed (Figure 14.7C), none of the links in the original 'spatial' solution is part of the temporal solution. Nevertheless, by studying the changing patterns we can

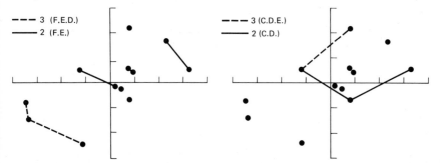

Figure 14.8   **A** Link persistence from $\lambda = 1.00$ (purely spatial strategy) to $\lambda = 0.33$. **B** Link persistence from $\lambda = 0.00$ (purely temporal strategy) to $\lambda = 0.66$. The pecked lines denote persistence for three values of λ, and solid lines persistence for two values of λ. The code letters C–F refer to Figure 14.7. Source: Cliff *et al.*, 1975, p. 26.

isolate those links that show substantial stability in terms of the originating space and time MSTs (see Figure 14.8). The more persistent the links and the more resilient they prove to changes in the λ weighting, the more likely they are to provide stable nucleii for region-building procedures. Special interest would attach to links which formed part of *both* the spatial and temporal MSTs and therefore were invariant over the whole range of λ. No such links were found in the randomly based experiments conducted here, but they are likely to occur occasionally in empirical regionalization problems.

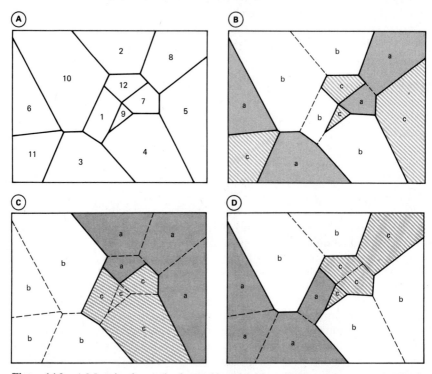

Figure 14.9   **A** Mosaic of counties formed by Dirichlet cells about the centres in Figure 14.7 **A**. **B** Three-region partition (a, b, and c) based on temporal graph [Figure 14.7 **C**]. **C** Similar partition based on spatial graph [Figure 14.7 **F**]. **D** Similar partition based on persistent bonds [Figure 14.8]. The heavy lines denote the regional boundaries in **B**, **C** and **D**. Source: Cliff *et al.*, 1975, p. 28.

Second, the study of MST partitions gives some insights into the kind of regional mosaic that is likely to result from county groupings. Consider the mosaic of county boundaries that is produced by constructing Dirichlet cells around each of the twelve county centres shown in Figure 14.7A. The mosaic is illustrated in Figure 14.9A. Let us assume that we wish to aggregate these twelve counties into three regions (termed *a*, *b*, and *c*), with each region comprising four counties. Regional grouping may be considered analogous to partitioning a graph into sub-graphs. Thus, if we select any one of the MST graphs shown in Figure 14.7, we can partition it into our three groups (*a*, *b*, and *c*) by counting back four counties from each end of the selected graph. (We have taken the ends of the graph to be that pair of nodes which is separated by a shortest path equal in length to the diameter of the graph.) On this basis, Figure 14.7c yields the county mosaic shown in Figure 14.9B, while that of 14.7F yields Figure 14.9c. As we would expect, the regional partition based on the graph with the highest temporal efficiency (Figure 14.9B) is far less satisfactory: both region *a* and region *c* are split rather than contiguous, so that the three regions form eight spatial fragments. By experimenting with variations in the weighting factor (λ), we can construct a series of graphs and mosaics so as to find a regional system which gives an appropriate trade-off between geographical simplicity and temporal order. Figure 14.9D shows one such intermediate solution in which we have attempted to preserve as many as possible of the persistent bonds shown in Figure 14.8. In this case, only one region (*b*) is split and the three-region system forms four spatial fragments.

14.4 Regions as Assignment Problems

We have seen in the previous section how regions may be identified by the demarcation of regional cores around which other units may be agglomerated. This method is of some special value in the study of nodal regions where the centre is well established and the problem is solely one of identifying its limits. More commonly, however, we are faced with unit areas (such as states or counties) whose limits are already fixed, and here our problem is one of *assignment*, i.e. placing these units in a given regional class. This assignment process may be either (i) a simple classification procedure in which like units are grouped regardless of their location or alternatively, (ii) a more complex procedure in which both the location and contiguity of the areas have to be taken into account.

14.4.1 *Association analysis*

One of the simplest kinds of grouping problem is encountered where we begin with a series of spatial units (say, counties or settlements) for each of which we have a set of characteristics which are either present (1) or absent (0). We start with a binary data matrix with locations along the rows and characteristics down the columns. Clearly our region-building problem is to assign locations with similar (1, 0) characteristics into the same regions, and vice versa.

Williams and Lambert (1959–62), two Southampton botanists, first attacked this problem in attempting to develop ecological regions based on the presence or absence of *m* plant species at *n* particular sites. Their approach was first to measure the degree of association between all pairs of species (i.e. between all pairs of columns in the data matrix) using the usual X^2 statistic,

$$X^2 = \sum_{i=1}^{k} \frac{(O_i - E_i)^2}{E_i}, \qquad (14.7)$$

where O_i and E_i refer to the observed and expected frequencies respectively of the ith term in a $k \times k$ contingency table. In the Williams–Lambert case, $k = 4$ (a 2×2 table), since there are only four possible ways in which two species can be compared, *viz.* both species present $(1, 1)$, both absent $(0, 0)$, or one or the other present $(1, 0;$ or $0, 1)$.

The X^2 values between all pairs of species were recorded in an $m \times m$ matrix and the rows summed. Williams and Lambert suggested that the highest row sum (max $\sum X^2$) indicates the plant species which is most efficient in 'splitting'

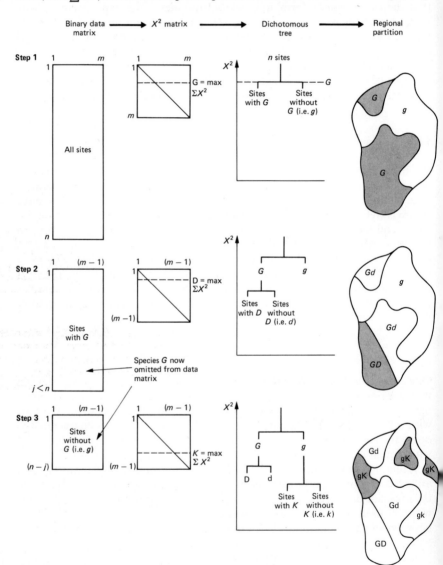

Figure 14.10 Flow diagram of main steps in regional splitting using association analysis.

the sites into two classes (because that species has the highest overall degree of association/dissociation with the other species, and it can therefore be taken as an indicator species). If we label this first indicator species as G, then sites can be separated on the basis of its presence (G) or absence (g) (Figure 14.10). In association analysis, this isolation of an indicator species provides the basis for an initial regional classification. Regional splitting now proceeds independently for each region. As Figure 14.10 shows, region G is split on the basis of species D into GD and Gd; region g on the basis of species K into gK and gk. Splitting into ever-smaller regions is continued until the X^2 values fall below a statistically significant threshold (conventionally the 95 per cent level. See Table A3).[1]

Association analysis is a useful illustration of the process by which the totality of spatial units (e.g. quadrats or counties) form the starting point from which a regional partitioning or splitting scheme proceeds. It has been used in some geographical studies, notably that of Caroe (1968), who analysed the occupational structure of East Anglian towns in the nineteenth century. More frequently, however, regionalization commences with the individual unit and builds upwards, by a step-by-step grouping process, and it is to this approach that we now turn.

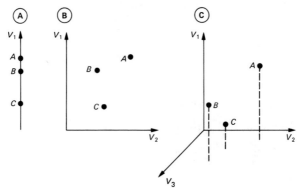

Figure 14.11   Plotting of three values (A, B, and C) in one, two, and three dimensional space.

14.4.2 *Distance grouping in N-dimensional space*

In grouping procedures, we frequently describe things which are similar as 'near' one another. Thus, we may refer to 'children' as a group composed of individuals near to one another in age, or the 'Third World' as a group of countries near to one another in development status. We use 'distance' in a non-geographical sense as distance along an age scale, or along a development scale.

Consider the classification problem posed by the three points, A, B, and C in Figure 14.11. In the simple case of one dimension represented by a single vector, V_1 (Figure 14.11A), A and B are close together. They remain close when

[1] One difficulty with this procedure is that the spatial basis of the data is likely to introduce dependence among the observations, thus breaking an assumption of the X^2 test. See Section 10.2.

a second dimension, vector V_2, is added (Figure 14.11B). When a third dimension is added, V_3, we can see that the position is changed and B is now much nearer to C (Figure 14.11c). Although we cannot show graphically a fourth dimension, vector V_4, there is no mathematical limit to adding this, and further vectors, to give a theoretical multidimensional space, i.e. *N*-dimensional space.

Provided that the vectors are all orthogonal, distance between points in *N*-dimensional space follows from the well-known rule of the 'square of the hypotenuse' (Pythagoras's theorem). It can be briefly written as

$$D_{ij} = \sqrt[2]{\sum_{v=1}^{N} (x_{iv} - x_{jv})^2}. \tag{14.8}$$

Here D_{ij} is the distance (similarity) between points i and j, x_{iv} denotes the score of observation unit (point) i on the vth variate or characteristic, x_v, and the summation is over the number of dimensions ($v = 1, 2, ..., N$) in the space.

Note that, since the relationship (14.8) only holds when the individual vectors are orthogonal, we cannot simply use the original variates describing the data since these are likely to be intercorrelated and thus non-orthogonal. Principal components analysis is usually adopted to change the original non-orthogonal vectors into orthogonal components although, alternatively, a generalized distance measure such as Mahalanobis's d^2 statistic could be used to allow for the intercorrelation among the variates. Most grouping programs proceed, therefore, not on the original observations but on the component scores (e.g. Steiner, 1965).

The object of classification is then simply to place in one group areas which are near together (homogeneous) in *N*-dimensional space and to separate groups which are far apart (heterogeneous) in a similar space field. Berry (1961b) has illustrated this technique with reference to the service industry characteristics of nine census divisions of the United States in 1954 (Figure 14.12A). Here he was concerned with six orthogonal components, and he measured the squared distance between points (D^2) in six-dimensional space. This showed that, of the nine census divisions, New England (*a*) and East North Central (*b*) had most in common (a D^2 value of only 0.69), while East South Central (*h*) . . . the heart of the 'South' . . . and Pacific (*f*) were most dissimilar (with a D^2 value of nearly 35). By placing the two nearest divisions together, the nine units were reduced to eight. Distances between the remaining eight regions were calculated, and the two Great Plains regions (*d* and *e*) added together. By repeating this process, the regions were progressively diminished until finally the whole of the United States formed a single region. These successive stages are shown in the nine maps of Figure 14.12B. We can thus have nine different levels of regional breakdown of the United States, each one efficient at its particular level. Which of these is the most efficient?

Berry (1961b, p. 273) has shown that, in this breakdown process (in which we proceed from many to few regions), we are progressively gaining in generality and progressively losing in definition. Perfect detail is available only with all nine original regions; perfect generality is available only if we regard the whole United States as one unit. This loss of detail can be calibrated using the distance measured previously (within-group D^2) and ranges from zero with all nine divisions to 343.47 with only one region. Figure 14.13 plots this progressive loss of detail by the use of a 'linkage tree', which shows the combination of regions as they were made, step by step, and mapped in Figure 14.12B. We should note in particular that the loss of detail (as measured by the

**

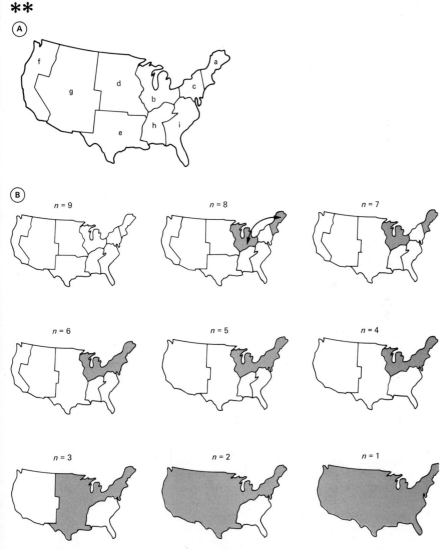

Figure 14.12   Stages in the regional grouping of census divisions in the United States by multivariate analysis. n = number of regions. Source: Berry, 1961b, p. 272.

within-group D^2) is plotted on a logarithmic scale, emphasizing the very small loss of detail in the first five grouping steps. Specifically, only 3.5 per cent of the detail was lost in these steps. This means that we can learn almost as much by regarding the United States as four large regions as we can from nine smaller census districts.

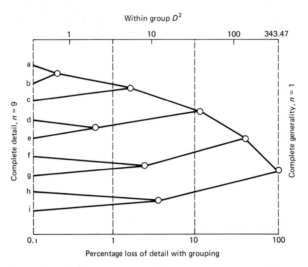

Figure 14.13 Linkage tree of the grouping shown in Figure 14.12 with percentage loss of detail. Symbols refer to the census regions. Source: Berry, 1961b, pp. 272, 273.

The implication of Berry's maps is that, while we must choose the regional breakdown that serves our particular research purposes, we need to be aware of its relative efficiency. If it matters little whether we need two, three, or four service regions in the United States, then the loss of detail suggests it is worth adopting four regions (only 3.5 per cent loss), or three regions (10 per cent loss), rather than two regions (40 per cent loss).

The process of linking one observation or county to another in the manner of Figure 14.12 is less straightforward than it appears there. Cormack (1971) has reviewed the very large number of ways in which 'similarity' or 'nearness' can be measured (see Table 14.6). One of those in commonest use is Ward's (1963) *hierarchical grouping method*, and we describe this here to illustrate the main steps in the process of group formation:

Start with n points, link the closest pair, then calculate their centroid and the average intragroup distance. The next step begins with $n-2$ points plus one centroid; these are treated as $n-1$ points, the closest pair is again linked, and the centroid of that pair is calculated. If the previous centroid is linked, it will have a weight of two when average intragroup distance is calculated this second time. The increment to average intragroup distance by performing this step is calculated. The process is repeated step by step and culminating in a final step where a pair of presumably complex centroids is linked and the single centroid of the n points results (Berry, 1967, p. 238).

Table 14.6 Indices of similarity used in regional grouping.*

1. Euclidean distance $\sum\limits_{v=1}^{N} w_v(x_{iv} - x_{jv})^2$

 Unstandardized: $w_v = 1$
 Standardized by standard deviation, s: $w_v = 1/s_v^2$. Denote by $\varDelta^2$
 Standardized by range: $w_v = 1/\max\limits_{ij}(x_{iv} - x_{jv})^2$

2. City-block metric $\sum\limits_{v=1}^{N} w_v|x_{iv} - x_{jv}|$
 Mean character difference: $w_v = 1/N$

3. Minkowski metrics $\left[\sum\limits_{v=1}^{N} |x_{iv} - x_{jv}|^{1/\lambda} \right]^{\lambda}$

4. Angular separation $\dfrac{\sum\limits_{v=1}^{N} x_{iv} x_{jv}}{\left[\sum\limits_{v=1}^{N} x_{iv}^2 \sum\limits_{v=1}^{N} x_{jv}^2 \right]^{\frac{1}{2}}}$

5. Correlation $p_{ij} = \dfrac{\sum\limits_{v=1}^{N} (x_{iv} - \bar{x}_i)(x_{jv} - \bar{x}_j)}{\left[\sum\limits_{v=1}^{N} (x_{iv} - \bar{x}_i)^2 \sum\limits_{v=1}^{N} (x_{jv} - \bar{x}_j)^2 \right]^{\frac{1}{2}}}$

6. Profile similarity index: $\dfrac{2k_m - \Delta^2}{2k_m + \Delta^2}$, where

 $P(\chi_p^2 < k_m) = 0.5$

7. Coefficient of nearness: $\{\sqrt{(2N)} - \Delta\}/\{\sqrt{(2N)} + \Delta\}$

8. 'Canberra' metric: $\sum\limits_{v=1}^{N} |x_{iv} - x_{jv}|/(x_{iv} + x_{jv})$

9. $\dfrac{2a}{2a + b + c}$

10. $\dfrac{a}{a + b + c}$

11. Simple matching: $\dfrac{a + d}{a + b + c + d}$

*In this table, x_i is the value of the variate X for observation unit i, while $v = 1, 2, \ldots, N$ indexes the number of dimensions in the space. The last three indices relate to binary characters, where a, b, c, and d refer to the number of characters possessed or not possessed in a 2×2 table $\begin{array}{|c|c|} \hline a & b \\ \hline c & d \\ \hline \end{array}$. Source: Cormack, 1971, p. 325.

The grouping procedure may be simply illustrated using a hypothetical matrix of distances for four stations: *A* to *D*. See Table 14.7. Searching the first matrix shows the lowest distance value is 3.00 at the *BC* intersection. Since these are the cells most alike, they are combined into a single region and the distance between the new region and the remaining two stations is computed. The new $(n-1) \times (n-1)$ matrix contains the same distances between *A* and *D*, but new (approximate) distance values from *BC* to *A* and *D* are inserted equivalent to the means of the distance values in the 4×4 matrix. The lowest value in the new matrix is identified and the grouping cycle repeated. Three regions are replaced by two, and two by one in successive cycles. The linkage tree formed by this grouping process is shown in Table 14.7D.

Table 14.7   Stages in the grouping of a 4×4 distance matrix.

(A)

	A	B	C	D
A		6	20	15
B			3	9
C				12
D				

(B)

	BC	A	D
BC		13	10.5
A			15
D			

(C)

	BCD	A
BCD		14
A		

(D)

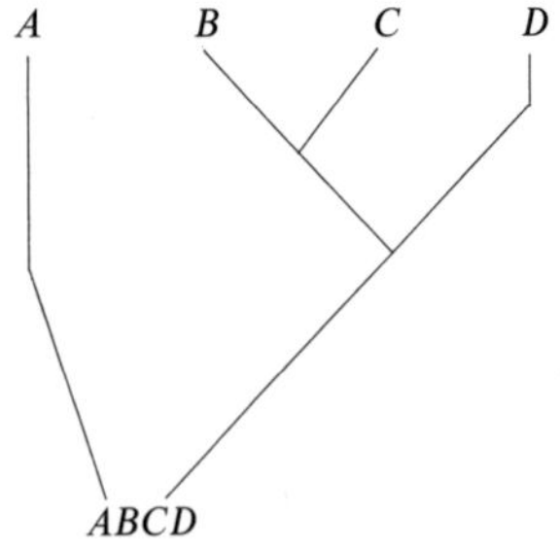

Source: Cox, 1968, pp. 24–5.

14.4.3 *Assignment of boundary cases*

We may argue that the methods outlined above are not specifically geographical, but that they merely classify geographical data. This is the view taken by Hagood and Price (1952, p. 542) when they state, in the course of an agricultural classification of the United States, that '... California cannot be put into the same region as New Jersey because of geographical separation.' In the same way, we find Bunge (1962, p. 16) arguing that it is the implicit inclusion of the category of location that makes for a regional, as opposed to a purely classificatory, approach to the earth's surface. It is, of course, possible to modify grouping procedures so that *both* nearness in taxonomic space *and* spatial contiguity are taken into account. Figure 14.14 compares two

✳✳✳

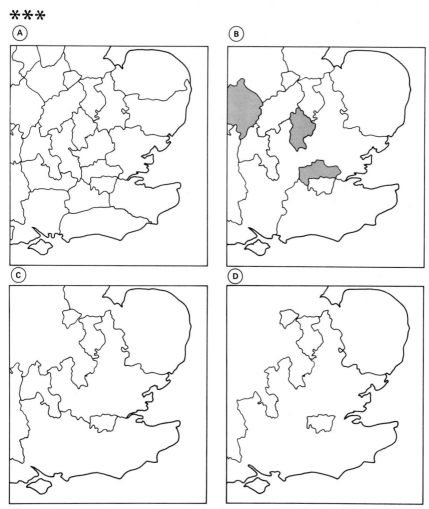

Figure 14.14   Grouping under contiguity constraints. Multifactor regionalization of English counties on the basis of 1961 employment data. **A** South and east England showing counties prior to grouping; i.e. 100 per cent detail. **B** Step 30 in the *non-contiguous* grouping sequence retaining 78 per cent of the original detail. Note that three non-contiguous counties (shaded) are grouped together. **C** Step 30 in the *contiguous* grouping sequence retaining 76 per cent of the original detail. **D** Step 35 in the same *contiguous* grouping sequence with 56 per cent of the original detail retained. Source: Spence, 1968.

groupings of English employment regions using (a) spatially constrained and (b) unconstrained rules. By 'spatially constrained', we imply a linkage procedure which joins two regions if they are (i) near in classification space, in the sense of having similar employment characteristics, and are *simultaneously* (ii) adjacent in geographical space, in the sense of being contiguous to each other.

In seeking to build up contiguous regions we need, then, to carry on a sort of progressive comparison of any unit with its neighbours. In effect, we are asking how nearly does a given area match its neighbours. Thus, in the case of California, we would be concerned to compare that state with its contiguous neighbours, Oregon, Nevada, and Arizona, but not (at least, not in the first rounds of analysis) with Missouri or Oklahoma.

Two of the techniques that have been used with some success in this

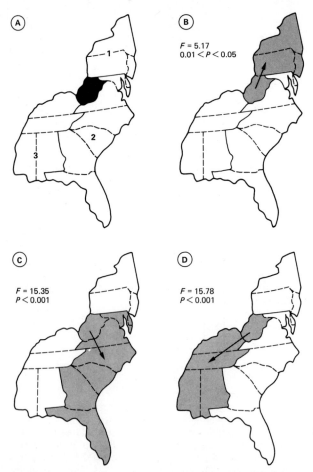

Figure 14.15   Assignment of West Virginia to three alternative regional groups in the southeastern United States with significance levels from variance analysis. Source: Zobler, 1958, p. 146.

comparing process are illustrated here: variance analysis and correlation analysis.

(a) *Variance analysis.* The total variation displayed by a set of observations can be measured by its variance, i.e. the sums of squares of deviations from the arithmetic mean. As noted in Section 12.3, it can, in certain circumstances, be separated into components associated with specific sources of variation.

Zobler (1958) used variance analysis to decide whether, in terms of its industrial population (number of workers in manufacturing and primary industries in 1950), the state of West Virginia should be grouped with one of three state regions: (1) Mid-Atlantic; (2) South Atlantic; (3) East South Central. The state regions are shown in Figure 14.15A, with West Virginia shaded. Inspection of the figures for the states making up the three regions and for West Virginia gives no decisive indication as to which existing region the problem state should be added to, and a more rigorous approach was adopted. Zobler argued that, when regions are being constructed from smaller units, there are two sources of variation. There is variation among the states within a region (*within-region variation*) and variation among the regions (*between-region variation*). Variance analysis was used to measure this variation within and between regions under three conditions, with West Virginia assigned to each of the three regions in turn (Table 14.8). The between-region variance (showing the variation of the regions around the mean of all the regions) was divided by the within-region variance (showing the variation of the states around their respective regional means) to give the variance ratio, F. If the two variances are equal, the value of this ratio is one, and the more F rises above one, the greater the interregional differentials. In broad terms, the variance ratio describes how successful the grouping procedure has been in keeping like states together and keeping unlike states apart.

Table 14.8   Regional assignment using variance analysis.*

Variance ratios:	Between-region variance	Within-region variance	Variance ratios, F
Alternative assignment of West Virginia:			
To Mid-Atlantic region	46.09	8.91	5.17†
To South Atlantic region	71.55	4.66	15.35‡
To East South Central region	72.13	4.57	15.78‡

Source: Zobler, 1958, p. 146.
  *Eastern United States, 1950.
  †Significant at the 95 per cent confidence level.
  ‡Significant at the 99.9 per cent confidence level.

The results in Table 14.8 show that, although West Virginia *could* be assigned to any of the three regions, the optimum allocation was to join it to Alabama, Mississippi, Kentucky, and Tennessee in the East South Central division (Figure 14.15D). Conversely, the worst classification on this analysis would be to place it with New Jersey, New York, and Pennsylvania in the Mid-Atlantic division (Figure 14.15B).

(b) *Correlation and regional 'bonds'*. To illustrate the approach, we consider work by Hagood (1943) and Hagood and Price (1952, pp. 541–7). The problem studied by Hagood was to divide the United States into some six to a dozen contiguous groups of states, with each group of states to be made as homogeneous as possible with respect to some 104 items taken from the 1940 Censuses of Population and Agriculture. These items were equally divided into two major groups, agriculture and population, and these were in turn divided into further sub-groups, 14 in all. These groups varied in size from information on crops (12 items) in the agriculture group, to information on race (5 items) in the population group.

These items were used to draw up 'agriculture-population profiles' of each state. First, all the 104 items were standardized so that the mean value for the (then) 48 states for each item was 50.0 and the standard deviation 10.0. Second, Pearson product moment correlation coefficients (*r*) were calculated between the profiles of adjacent states. The resulting coefficients varied from very high values between like states (e.g. Alabama and Georgia had a coefficient of +0.92) to very low values between unlike states (e.g. Ohio and its southern neighbour, Kentucky, had a coefficient of only +0.01, suggesting that the line between North and South remains strong in the United States). Part of Hagood's map is reproduced in Figure 14.16. Here, for an area of the northern United States, the values of the coefficients have been replaced by lines of varying width. The result shows the scaffolding of 'regional bonds' between the thirteen states; it emphasizes the strong north–south links between Montana and Wyoming, between the two Dakotas, Nebraska and Kansas, and between Minnesota and Iowa. Likewise we see the rather weak links east–west across the grain of the country.

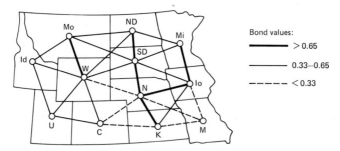

Figure 14.16   Pattern of interstate correlation bonds in the north-central United States. Source: Hagood and Price, 1952, p. 545.

In practice, Hagood used these correlation bonds to supplement a single comparative index, the 'composite agriculture-population index', which she calculated by principal components analysis, in much the same way as Thompson *et al.* (1962) calculated a single index of economic health for New York state. Delineation began with the easily recognizable regional nuclei which formed the centres of homogeneous regions. Once these had been established, the marginal states were allocated to one of these nuclei on the basis of both its composite index and its intercorrelations with its neighbours.

This distinction between 'nuclear' and 'marginal' states is brought out clearly in Table 14.9. This shows that, on average, Alabama is nearly three times more like its adjoining neighbour states than is Missouri. Alabama clearly lies deep within the heart of the South, with strong similarities to its neighbours, while Missouri lies on the border of four of the six major regions recognized by Hagood. As its highest link lay with the state of Illinois, Missouri was finally assigned to a Great Lakes region.

Table 14.9   Coefficients of similarity (r) for agriculture-population profiles.*

State:	Nuclear type (Alabama)	Marginal type (Missouri)
Number of neighbouring states	4	8
Coefficients of similarity:		
Maximum r bond	0.92	0.45
Minimum r bond	0.44	0.08
Mean of all r bonds	0.75	0.29

Source: Hagood and Price, 1952, p. 545.
                    *For Alabama and Missouri, 1950.

We find, then, that correlation bonds do not solve regional problems in the sense of creating homogeneity where none exists. What they appear to do is to help legislate in difficult cases and make the reasons for the choice, however marginal that choice may be, clear to the observer.

14.5 Regions as a Districting Problem

The districting problem may be regarded as a direct extension of the cases considered in Section 14.4. It is treated separately here insofar as it relates to a special set of regional applications (notably the electoral and school districting issues), and it demands the use of linear programming (LP) techniques. Details of the LP algorithms are presented as part of the treatment of optimization methods in Chapter 15 (see especially Sections 15.2 and 15.4.3).

14.5.1 Optimizing school districts

One of the earliest applications of computer solution to a regionalization problem was Yeates's (1963) study of Wisconsin school districts. Figure 14.17A shows the location of schools and existing school district boundaries for a sample quadrat from the study area. Over the whole section studied by Yeates (Grant County, Wisconsin), the problem was to redesign school district boundaries so as to minimize the cost of bussing 2,900 high school children to the thirteen high schools, given certain side constraints on school capacity. To reduce the size of the computational problem, both schools and pupils' homes were assumed to lie in the centre of the square-mile section in which they were located; school boundaries were then redrawn on this simplified basis (Figure

14.17B) by including the whole square-mile section within a school area, if the greater part was in that section. Since 754 sections were occupied by children from the 13 schools, the problem was specified as a 754 × 13 matrix. With these data, optimum boundaries were determined such that (i) total distance bussed to schools was minimized; (ii) each school was filled to its capacity (1961).

****

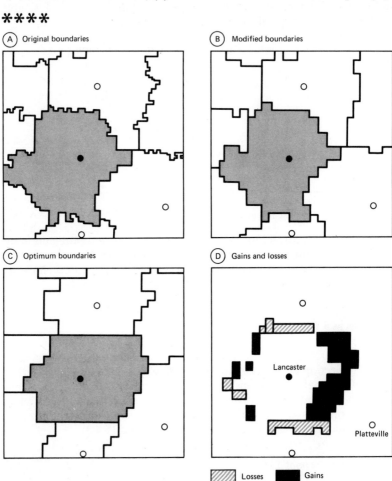

Figure 14.17 Distance-minimization approach to the construction of optimum boundaries in a sample quadrat of Grant County, Wisconsin, United States. **A** Original boundaries; **B** Modified boundaries; **C** Optimum boundaries; **D** Gains and losses. Source: Yeates, 1963, pp. 8, 9.

Subject to a number of restrictions, the problem can be expressed algebraically as:

$$\text{Minimize} \sum_{i=1}^{n} \sum_{j=1}^{m} d_{ij} x_{ij} \qquad (14.9)$$

where d_{ij} is the distance from the ith section to any jth high school, x_{ij} is the number of schoolchildren in the ith section bussed to the jth high school, n is the number of sections and m is the number of high schools. See Sections 15.2 and 15.4.3 for a statement of the problem in terms of the transportation problem. The boundaries resulting from this minimum solution are illustrated in Figure 14.17c. Comparison with the boundaries of the formalized school districts shows that there is considerable change and overlap. The boundaries of Lancaster high school in Figure 14.17D show losses to the north and south (shaded) but large gains (black) from the neighbouring Platteville high school on the east. How important are the changes appearing in Yeates's reallocation? Analysis is made more difficult by two factors (1) the fact that the theoretical boundaries were based on the distribution of children's homes in a single year (1961), while the actual school districts must remain static over a longer time; and (2) the difficulty of comparing the actual ground distance covered along roads by the children with the cross-country (direct) distance used in the theoretical analysis. Table 14.10 gives the results for a sample study of two high schools in the area, Boscobel and Platteville, where a comparison of the distances both by road and cross country suggests savings of the order of 0.4 to 0.3 miles. No firm figures on the transport costs were available, but rough approximations suggested that if the revised boundaries were adopted, then this might have saved (then) some \$3,000 to \$4,000 each year on school transport.

Table 14.10　Distances travelled with alternative district boundaries.*

High school:	Boscobel	Platteville
Actual school districts:		
Mean road distance to school, miles	6.7	6.4
Mean overland distance to school, miles	5.5	5.6
Theoretical school districts:		
Mean overland distance to school, miles	5.1	5.3
Estimated saving on overland distance, miles	0.4	0.3

Source: Yeates, 1963, p. 9.
　　*Grant County, Wisconsin, United States, 1961.

    Recent studies of school districting have paid special attention to the need to maintain 'balance' in schools between pupils of different kinds. Studies to optimize the black/white colour balance in Florida schools (Belford and Ratcliff, 1972) are paralleled by studies in England for comprehensive schools. Langley's (1974) work illustrates the ways in which the notion of a desired social mix and safe routes (i.e. avoiding crossing traffic-heavy roads) can be built into the design of primary school districts in an English town using extensions of the linear programming approach.

14.5.2 Optimizing electoral districts

Electoral districting forms a second major area of region-building applications. Here, the principle is to assemble the sets of enumeration districts into contiguous or compact electoral legislative districts of equal weight (i.e. equal voting population). The generally agreed criteria on which electoral boundaries should be drawn are: (a) *equality* of the voting population; (b) *contiguity*, in the sense that the district should be in one piece and should be compact in terms of ease of communication between various parts of the district; and (c) *homogeneity*, in that it should have common social, political and economic interests. It should be noted that no scheme can ever have complete equality because the balance of population changes as time passes.

The drawing of such equitable political boundaries has become of greater interest since the historic Baker versus Carr decision in the United States Supreme Court in March 1962. In this, the court ruled that 'The apportionment of seats and districting of states must be so arranged that the number of inhabitants per legislator in one district is substantially equal to the number of inhabitants per legislator in any other district in the same state' (Silva, 1965, p. 20). The case was precipitated by a group of voters in Tennessee claiming that their votes were 'debased' by inequities in the State's existing apportionment districting. Tennessee had continued to elect its State legislators on the basis of an apportionment adopted in 1901, even though in the intervening sixty years there had been radical shifts in the distribution of the population from rural areas to cities and suburban areas. The situation in Tennessee was paralleled by situations in other American states, and, altogether, the courts found that 37 of the American states needed some redrawing of electoral boundaries. Reapportionment on the basis of 'one man, one vote' caused relatively few problems; but the equal population rule is not in itself sufficient to guarantee that economic, political and cultural sub-groups are adequately represented in the legislature. Haggett (1975a, pp. 437–40) gives examples of the common practice of 'gerrymandering' electoral districts to gain political advantage for a ruling party.

Since the 1962 court decision, a number of proposals have been advanced for 'non-partisan' redistricting algorithms. These usually consist of computer programs designed to produce sets of regions from preselected bases of voting equality, spatial contiguity, and homogeneity. The general form of such algorithms is shown in Figure 14.18. The major steps are: (1) choose arbitrary or reasonable district centres for the n electoral legislative districts (LDs); (2) compute the matrix of distances between the numeration district (ED) centres and the trial centres, solve the transportation problem (see Sections 15.2 and 15.4.3) and combine areally split electoral districts; (3) compute the new centre of gravity for each legislative district (i.e. the centre of gravity of all the enumeration districts assigned to that legislative district in step (2); (4) if the new centres differ from the trial centres, cycle back to step (2). If not, terminate. Since the solution is obtained by a 'local' rather than a 'global' optimum, some procedures allow recycling to step (1), in which the researcher arbitrarily selects a new set of trial centres.

Operational definitions of 'population equality' and 'contiguity' for electoral districts have been examined at length by Kaiser (1966). Let p_i denote

the population of the ith in a set of n districts, and $P = \sum\limits_{i=1}^{n} p_i$, the total

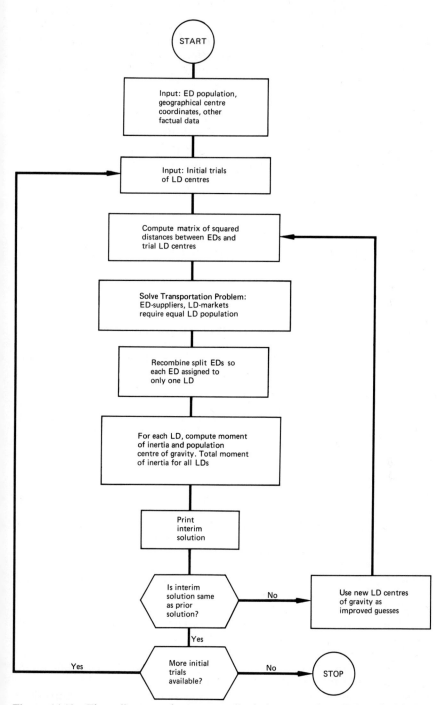

Figure 14.18 Flow diagram of computer districting procedure (LD = legislative district; ED = enumeration district). Source: Hess *et al.*, 1965, p. 1000.

population of the area. We use $r_i = p_i \div (P/n)$ to indicate the population ratio of district i. Under the ideal situation of perfect population equality among all the districts, $r_i = 1$, $i = 1, 2, ..., n$, implying each $p_i = P/n$. In practice, as a measure of population equality, Kaiser defines the measure

$$b = 1 - \sqrt{1 - g^2}, \tag{14.10}$$

where $g = \sqrt[n]{\prod_i r_i}$. The quantities b and g both attain maximum values of one if and only if $r_i = 1$, $i = 1, 2, ..., n$ (i.e. when we have perfect population equality). In particular, Kaiser has shown $0 \leqslant b \leqslant 1, 0 \leqslant g \leqslant 1$ and $b < g$ for $g < 1$.

As a compactness index, Kaiser has proposed

$$v = \left(\sum_i 2\pi t_i / a_i^2 \right) \Big/ n, \tag{14.11}$$

where a_i is area of the ith electoral district and t_i is the moment of inertia of the area of the district, *viz*:

$$t_i = \int \int (x^2 + y^2) dx \, dy. \tag{14.12}$$

Here, the origin is at the centre of gravity of the area and the integration is over the area. The division by n is to make v comparable regardless of the number of districts. The most compact geometrical shape, in the sense of having the smallest moment of inertia, is a circle, and it can be shown that the moment of inertia of a circle of the same area, a_i, as district i is $a_i^2 / 2\pi$. All that Kaiser is doing in equation (14.11), therefore, is to divide the moment of inertia of the district by that of a circle of the same area to provide a dimensionless measure of compactness as judged by the benchmark of a circle. We note $1 \leqslant v \leqslant \infty$; $v = 1$ when all districts are perfectly compact (circular).

To link together the measures of population equality (b) and of compactness (v), Kaiser used a criterion function f:

$$f = b^w / v, \tag{14.13}$$

where w is a weight, $0 \leqslant w \leqslant \infty$. The choice of w depends on the relative weight we wish to place on population equality as opposed to area compaction. When w is zero the f criterion is concerned only with the latter, and where w is one both criteria are equally weighted. Choosing w very large will force population equality at the expense of geographically unwieldy areas.

Computer procedures for districting which use the twin bases of population equality and compactness have been proposed by Weaver and Hess (1963), Nagel (1965), Kaiser (1966) and Mills (1967). The Weaver and Hess procedure is typical of the group in that it proceeds iteratively from an initial input of population, and gives the population, area, geographical co-ordinates and other factual data about each basic enumeration district. The enumeration districts are the smallest indivisible units into which the population of a state is broken for electoral purposes. Figure 14.19 shows the results of the first three stages of the redistricting of Sussex County, New Jersey, USA. The maps show in sequence the distribution of enumeration districts and trial centres, the initial six districts, and the first and second re-assignments of population to these centres. The second re-assignment showed an improvement of from five to one per cent in the maximum deviation of population from the mean, and a significant improvement in compactness. A similar redistricting of the 12 downstate congressional districts of Illinois, USA, is reported by Kaiser. The weighting function (*w*) was set at 1.00 to give equal weight to compactness

****

Figure 14.19   Stages in the boundary optimization process for Sussex County, USA. The numbers indicate population values. Source: Weaver and Hess, 1963, p. 306.

and population equality, and 200 computer runs were made, each one allocating the 101 counties to 12 randomly selected initial districts. The present boundaries of the congressional districts and the best of the 200 solutions ($f = 0.762$) are shown in Figure 14.20.

Mills (1967) has applied the procedure outlined in Figure 14.18 to assign local polling districts to electoral wards in the urban area of Bristol, England. Although the procedure is heuristic and does not guarantee unique optimal solutions, it does provide a good guide. Mills was able to introduce considerable flexibility into the algorithm by permanently assigning some polling districts to certain wards so as to secure a natural barrier as a ward boundary (e.g. the River Avon in the Bristol case) or to avoid bisecting a uniform housing estate. Table 14.11 shows the convergence properties of a computer run. Iteration 0 refers to the hand calculation used as the starting point of the run. Although compactness and population variation show

***

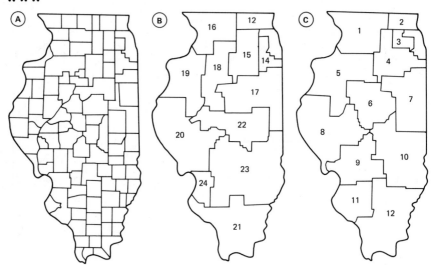

Figure 14.20 Proposed reapportionment of electoral districts in Illinois, central United States. **A** County system. **B** Existing congressional districts. **C** Proposed districts. Source: Kaiser, 1966, pp. 210–2.

convergence, these do not always improve monotonically. Mills's findings also illustrate the point that there may be several solutions to the electoral districting problem, each with almost identical values for equality and compactness but with *different* spatial configurations. Clearly, one of these regional solutions may be advantageous to one particular party, a second

Table 14.11   Convergence properties for a sample of computer runs.*

| | *End of Iteration* | | | | | |
	0	*1*	*2*	*3*	*4*	*5*
Compactness	199	177	162	152	151	151
Population variation	0.176	0.169	0.158	0.148	0.148	0.148
No. of changes	—	34	12	8	6	0

Source: Mills, 1967.

*Data for Bristol C.B., England, 1954.

regional solution may favour another political party. Thus, while the region-building algorithm described above eliminates gerrymandering and reduces the scope for boundary rigging, the final spatial choice is likely to retain a partisan element in favour of one party.

14.5.3 *Other districting applications*

Designers of medical care and other social provision programmes are increasingly using regional optimization methods. In an early study, Morrill (Garrison, *et al.*, 1959, pp. 244–76) analysed the effect of freeway construction on medical care areas for selected regions within the United States. Figure 14.21 shows the medical service areas for a sample region in western Pennsylvania, and Figure 14.21c the estimated shifts in boundaries after highway improvements. The results show that the effects are felt in all interrelated counties, and not just those through which the highway passes; and that highway improvements brought a greater flow in services, but at a lower unit cost. More recent applications are summarized by Massam (1975) and Shannon and Dever (1974).

✳✳✳

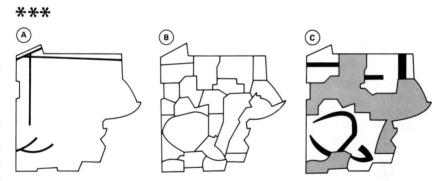

Figure 14.21   Revision of medical care boundaries in western Pennsylvania in response to the building of the new highways shown in **A**. Boundaries of medical care areas before (**B**) and after (**C**) highway construction. Solid shading indicates the areas over which boundaries have shifted while medical care areas wholly unaffected by the new highways are stippled. Source: Morrill, in Garrison *et al.*, 1959, pp. 266–7.

14.6 Nodal Regions and Graphs

Our discussion of region-building methods has so far been conducted mainly in terms of formal or homogeneous regions. To a large degree, procedures developed for these can be extended to include nodal regions. For example, if we substitute *dyads* (i.e. pairs of counties), for single counties, we can follow the taxonomic procedures of Section 14.4.2. Grouping of dyads within component space leads to regional aggregations (in this case *nodal* regions) in just the same way that grouping of counties yielded homogeneous regions. Thus Goddard (1970) was able to develop a nodal regional structure for central London from a principal components analysis of dyadic data on taxi flows. The fullest account of dyadic components analysis is given by Berry (1966, pp. 189–237) as part of a massive study of commodity flows for 63 commodities moving between 36 trade blocks within India. The 1260×63 matrix was reduced to a 12-component orthogonal structure, and a methodology for linking this simplified flow structure to non-flow changes was developed. The combination of regional taxonomies for both locational and dyadic data suggests an important link in interpreting regional networks of both formal and nodal kinds.

Despite this evidence of similarities between the two main types of regions, there remains a set of techniques which have been developed to tackle the special problems of nodal regions. The data input for nodal regionalization consists of dyadic scores measuring flows or links between each county and all other counties in the system under analysis. Typically, such scores measure spatial interaction of some kind, e.g. number of commuters, migrants, commodities, messages, or telephone calls.

14.6.1 *Primary linkage analysis*

The use of graph theory in the interpretation of transport networks has already been encountered (see Sections 3.2.3, 3.3 and 9.7), and we have suggested in Section 14.3 that it can be used to identify core regions through a study of link persistence. In a pioneering paper, Nystuen and Dacey (1961) have shown how the same type of analysis may be extended to the regionalization of flow data. A study of intercity telephone calls led them to argue that '. . . within the myriad relations existing between cities, the network of largest flows will be the ones outlining the skeleton of the urban organization within the entire region' (Nystuen and Dacey, 1961, p. 7).

Since Nystuen and Dacey built up a regional hierarchy using the dominant

Table 14.12   Matrix of flow between pairs of centres.*

To centre:	a	b	c	d	e	f	g	h	i	j	k	l	Class
From centre:													
a	00	**75**	15	20	28	02	03	02	01	20	01	00	Satellite
b	**69**	00	45	50	58	12	20	03	06	35	04	02	Dominant
c	05	**51**	00	12	40	00	06	01	03	15	00	01	Satellite
d	19	**57**	14	00	30	07	06	02	11	18	05	01	Satellite
e	07	40	**48**	26	00	07	10	02	37	39	12	06	Dominant
f	01	06	01	01	10	00	**27**	01	03	04	02	00	Satellite
g	02	16	03	03	13	**31**	00	03	18	08	03	01	Dominant
h	00	04	00	01	03	03	06	00	12	**38**	04	00	Satellite
i	02	28	03	06	43	04	16	12	00	**98**	13	01	Satellite
j	07	40	10	08	40	05	17	34	**98**	00	35	12	Dominant
k	01	08	02	01	18	00	06	05	12	**30**	00	15	Satellite
l	00	02	00	00	07	00	01	00	01	06	**12**	00	Satellite
Total:	113	337	141	128	290	071	118	065	202	311	091	039	
Rank order:	8	1	5	6	3	10	7	11	4	2	9	12	

Source: Nystuen and Dacey, 1961, p. 35.

*Hypothetical data.

outflow from each city, their method has become known as primary linkage analysis. The approach is essentially a simple one. As an illustration, consider Table 14.12 which shows a hypothetical matrix of cities ($a, b ... l$) for which the numbers in the matrix measure the flow (e.g. telephone calls) from one city to another. Thus the flow from city d to city a is 19 units, and that from city k to city i is 12 units, and so on. The relative magnitude or hierarchical *order* of the city is measured by the total incoming flow and is given by the column total, i.e. city b with a total of 337 units is the first city, j the second city, and so on. Hierarchical relations between cities are determined by the largest *outgoing* flow to a higher-order city (*nodal flow*). These are shown in the matrix by heavier type. Thus the largest flow from a is to b (i.e. $a \rightarrow b$).

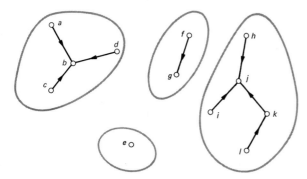

Figure 14.22 Nodal structure of the matrix shown in Table 14.12 in terms of graph theory. Source: Nystuen and Dacey, 1961, p. 35.

Examination of the matrix shows, however, that for four of the cities ($b, e, g,$ and j) the largest flow is to a 'lower-order' city (where order is determined by the column totals). These cities form the *terminal points* of the graph. Beginning with these four terminal points (Figure 14.22) the other eight cities can be plotted with vectors linking them directly or indirectly to the terminals according to the nodal flow from each city. The resulting hierarchical structure describes the nodal structure of the region in terms of four distinct clusters (*sub-graphs*) of varying sizes.

Washington State was used by Nystuen and Dacey (1961, pp. 38–42) to illustrate the application of this matrix method to a specific region. Using 40 cities in and adjacent to the state, a 40×40 matrix was set up with flow data for long-distance telephone traffic. Certain cities north of Seattle were omitted because of lack of data. Analysis of the matrix in terms of graph theory showed: (1) a large regional hierarchy centred on Seattle, with nested hierarchies around Yakima and Spokane; (ii) a separate system centred on Portland; and (iii) two small independent systems centred on Pasco and Moses Lake (Figure 14.23). The findings accord reasonably well with other empirical evidence on the regional organization of the state, but point up the unexpected independence of the two small interior systems.

Even with this fairly elementary application, the utility of graph theory is readily apparent. It allows decisions to be made on the relative strength of regional 'bonds' and, given appropriate empirical data, is likely to be useful in both administrative and business applications of region-building. Published examples of its use range from identifying nodal regions within the Solent region in southern England using shopping-behaviour data (Davis and Robinson, 1968) to a nationwide study of telephone traffic in South Africa (Board, Davies, and Fair, 1970). In an ongoing study of telephone traffic in Australia, Holmes (1973) has used primary linkage analysis to structure the relationship between some 700 urban centres.

***

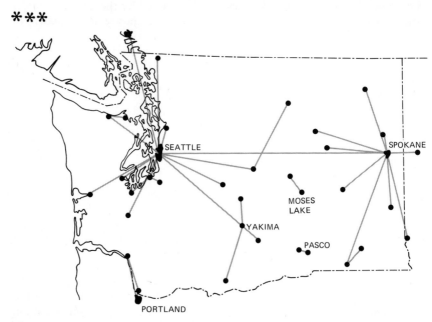

Figure 14.23   Nodal structure of the state of Washington, northwestern United States, based on graph theory analysis of flows between cities. Source: Nystuen and Dacey, 1961, p. 39.

14.6.2 *Multiple linkage analysis*

Nystuen and Dacey urged caution in interpreting the primary link as evidence of urban dominance. It is clear that an outflow representing, say, ten per cent of all flows should be regarded as of quite different importance to one of 90 per cent. In a study of Queensland telephone traffic, Holmes (1973) found a strong inverse relationship between hierarchical order and traffic dispersion. Small hamlets directed, on average, a much larger percentage of their outgoing traffic to the leading destination (48 per cent), compared to villages (33 per cent) and small towns (21 per cent). Evidence of this kind suggests the need for supplementary information; the information provided by a single dominant link needs to be combined with that from other subdominant links. If, however, we wish to use more than one link from each town or county, then a criterion is needed to separate the 'significant' from the 'insignificant' flows.

Holmes and Haggett (1975) have proposed a criterion for determining the number of significant flows, using an extension of the Weaver method described in Section 9.4.2. They rank all the k outflows from a centre by volume from the largest (w_1) to the smallest (w_k). A set of k cycles of expected flows $\{\hat{w}_i\}$ is then generated in the following way.

$$\text{1st cycle:} \quad \hat{w}_1 = \sum_{i=1}^{k} w_i$$

$$\hat{w}_2 = \hat{w}_3 = ... = \hat{w}_k = 0$$

$$\text{2nd cycle:} \quad \hat{w}_1 = \hat{w}_2 = \tfrac{1}{2} \sum_{i=1}^{k} w_i \tag{14.14}$$

$$\hat{w}_3 = \hat{w}_4 = ... \hat{w}_k = 0$$

$$\text{jth cycle:} \quad \hat{w}_1 = \hat{w}_2 = ... \hat{w}_j = \frac{1}{j} \sum_{i=1}^{k} w_i$$

$$\hat{w}_{j+1} = \hat{w}_{j+2} = ... \hat{w}_k = 0.$$

The goodness of fit between the set of observed flows $\{w\}$ and each of the sets of expected flows $\{\hat{w}\}$ is measured by the coefficient of determination (r^2). As Figure 14.24 shows, the trajectory of r^2 values varies depending on the particular pattern of outflows. In the first case, the maximum $(r^2 = 0.866)$

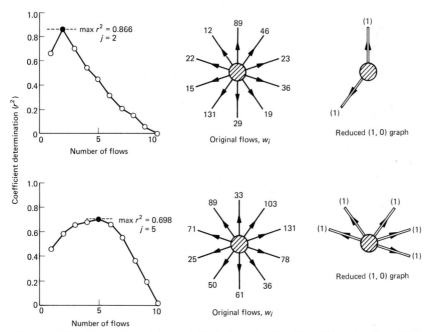

Figure 14.24   Illustration of the variable-link method for identifying significant links in a set of flows. Source: Holmes and Haggett, 1975.

occurs at the second cycle; in the second (max. $r^2 = 0.698$) at the fifth. Significant flows were identified as those up to and including the highest r^2 value.

Regional application of this variable link method has been made by Holmes and Haggett to migration flow data in New York State and in France. Their findings suggest that the additional information enriches the structural relations only baldly outlined by the analysis of primary links. A number of parallel approaches to multiple link analysis have been put forward, notably that of transaction flow analysis (Brams, 1966; Soja, 1968) and graph hierarchization analysis (Rouget, 1972). Each provides a basis for identifying significant or salient links by comparing an observed flow with that which might be expected under some appropriate null hypothesis. There remains considerable latitude over the ways in which salient links are used to group areas into nodal regions. Some of the most interesting work in this area continues to come from France (e.g. Ponsard, 1969), where the tradition of work in graph theory associated with Berge remains strong.

14.7 Conclusions

Region-building is one of the commonest applied problems encountered in locational analysis. For both the private and public sectors, efficient regional divisions provide one of the ways of reducing the cost of spatial interaction (whether measured in terms of pupils' journey to school, patient flows to hospitals, or efficient marketing movements for a company). Despite the advances that have been made in regionalization methods, this chapter has shown that familiar problems remain. Regional divisions represent a compromise between spatial contiguity on the one hand and grouping counties with like characteristics on the other (see Section 14.3). The number of possible regional divisions or combinations in any study area is usually very large indeed. Thus, any proposed scheme is less likely to be a single sharply-peaked optimum, than one of a set of rather similar near-optimal solutions. Grigg's (1965; and in Chorley and Haggett, 1967) studies of the regional concept in the light of numerical taxonomy have cleared up much of the mysticism which previously surrounded the term 'region'. Its elusiveness is now seen to lie in the inherent variability of the earth's surface which is being cast into regions, and the multitude of purposes for which different regional schemes can be drawn.

15 Allocating

15.1 Introduction

Suppose we have a study area in which there are located n suppliers of a good and m markets or demand points for that good. We assume that transport links exist between the suppliers and the markets. A basic geographical question which may be asked about such a system is this: 'What is the optimal pattern of trade in the good?' where the 'optimal pattern' is defined as that spatial configuration of flows of the commodity from suppliers to markets which minimizes the total transport costs over the entire system. Scott (1971a) has referred to problems of this genre as *spatial allocation problems*. Classical papers on spatial allocation problems, which are cited in Scott, are those of Henderson (1955a, b; 1958) who analysed the pattern of coal production and distribution in the USA, Land (1957) who considered coking coal movements over the British railway system, and Morrill and Garrison (1960) who examined the regional stability of trade in wheat and flour in the USA. Related work is that of Samuelson (1952) on spatial price equilibrium.

Although we have defined the system to be studied in terms of commodity flows, the same sort of question arises in the provision of social services. For example, the n 'suppliers' might be school districts within a city, and the 'markets' might be schools. The problem would then be to design an optimal pattern of 'bussing' of children to schools (see Section 14.5.1). Alternatively, one might think of hospitals ($\equiv$ markets) to be supplied by patients drawn from various catchment areas, and try to design a least-cost allocation of patients to hospitals (see Section 14.5.3; Garrison, Berry, Marble, Nystuen and Morrill, 1959; Gould and Leinbach, 1966). Similar sorts of problems arise in urban planning in, for example, the design of traffic-flow systems to facilitate journey-to-work trips from residential suburbs ($\equiv$ suppliers) to city centres ($\equiv$ markets).

All the allocation problems mentioned above are transportation problems of one sort or another, and there exists a wide variety of *linear programming models* which can be used to analyse such problems. It is the purpose of this chapter to outline the properties of some of these models. The most commonly used of the models is the *transportation problem* which, with adaptations, can be employed to examine all the case studies mentioned above. We therefore deal with this model at some length in Sections 15.2 and 15.3. Among the topics considered are the way in which the analysis of patterns of trade with linear programming models can give insights into the structure of location rents in the trading system, and solution algorithms. Extensions of the model are considered in Section 15.4.

Such has been the interest in linear programming techniques that much research has gone into more advanced adaptations of the basic methods. Thus there exists a literature on topics such as integer, geometric and dynamic programming, and the relationships of linear programming models to entropy maximizing models and game theory. Some of these topics are considered in Section 15.5.

15.2 The Transportation Problem

We have noted that the goal of the spatial allocation model is to define, for a given commodity, that pattern of flows from suppliers to markets which will minimize the total transport costs over the system. Such a pattern of shipments is called the optimal configuration, and the model is therefore normative ('as things ought to be') rather than a model of reality. The differences between the normative and real world shipment patterns therefore provide us with a measure of the level of economic efficiency reached by the system under study. In that the model is normative, it is best applied only to those economic systems in which it is reasonable to expect that something approaching optimality (as defined) might be achieved. Scott (1971a, p. 1) has noted that the economic systems which are most appropriately analysed with the model 'correspond on the one hand to a system of complete centralization of decision-making, and on the other to complete decentralization of decision-making [where perfect competition exists]. ... It is in the nature of such systems to attempt to seek out cost minimizing solutions.'

15.2.1 *Formal model structure—the primal problem*

We use i to denote the typical supplier in the economic system, and j to denote the typical market. Let x_{ij} represent the volume of the given commodity shipped from supplier i to market j at the per unit transport cost, c_{ij}. The good is assumed to be homgeneous across all suppliers. Then the cost of the shipment from i to j will be $c_{ij}x_{ij}$, and the total transport costs over the entire set of n suppliers and m markets will be $\sum_{i=1}^{n} \sum_{j=1}^{m} c_{ij}x_{ij}$. Let S_i indicate the total volume of the good that the ith supplier is capable of supplying (his supply capacity), and D_j denote the demand of the jth market. The $\{S_i\}$ and $\{D_j\}$ are assumed to be perfectly inelastic (invariant) to cost and price changes. The linear program for the transportation problem may then be written as

$$\text{Minimize } Z = \sum_{i=1}^{n} \sum_{j=1}^{m} c_{ij} x_{ij}, \tag{15.1}$$

subject to

$$\sum_{j=1}^{m} x_{ij} \leqslant S_i, \quad i = 1, 2, ..., n, \tag{15.2}$$

$$\sum_{i=1}^{n} x_{ij} \geqslant D_j, \quad j = 1, 2, ..., m, \tag{15.3}$$

and

$$x_{ij} \geqslant 0, \quad i = 1, 2, ..., n; j = 1, 2, ..., m. \tag{15.4}$$

The set of equations (15.1)–(15.4) together make up the linear program. It comprises an *objective function* [equation (15.1)] which is to be minimized subject to a *constraint set* [inequalities (15.2)–(15.3)]. Constraint 15.2 states that the total shipments from the typical supplier i to all j markets must not exceed the supply capacity of that supplier. Constraint (15.3) ensures that the sum of the shipments from all i suppliers into the jth market at least satisfies the demands of the jth market. Inequality (15.4) is a *side condition* which prevents a solution to the program which has negative shipments. (15.1)–(15.4) are linear in their relationships; hence the program is a linear one.

The relations (15.1)–(15.4) also constitute what is known as the *primal* part of the linear program. For every primal problem, there exists a *dual*, whose structure we need to explore before we can show how the primal may be solved for any real-world problem.

15.2.2 *The dual equations*

The dual equations are as follows:

Objective function.

$$\text{Maximize } Z' = \sum_{j=1}^{m} D_j v_j - \sum_{i=1}^{n} S_i u_i, \tag{15.5}$$

subject to

$$v_j - u_i \leqslant c_{ij}, \quad i = 1, 2, ..., n; j = 1, 2, ..., m, \tag{15.6}$$

and side conditions (generally, though not essential)

$$v_j, u_i \geqslant 0, \quad i = 1, 2, ..., n; j = 1, 2, ..., m. \tag{15.7}$$

There is a formal relationship between the primal and the dual of every linear program. A comparison of equations (15.1)–(15.4) with (15.5)–(15.7) will make clear the links. (See Dorfman, Samuelson and Solow, 1958, p. 40, for details.)

(1) If the primal is a resource allocation problem, we shall see that the dual is a valuation problem.

(2) If the primal is a minimization problem, the dual will be a maximization problem, and vice versa.

(3) The dual objective function has one variable (v_j, u_i) for each primal constraint.

(4) The dual has as many constraints as there are variables (x_{ij}) in the primal.

(5) The coefficients (c_{ij}) of the primal objective function are the constants in the dual constraints; the constants (S_i, D_j) in the primal constraints become the coefficients of the dual objective function variables.

(6) The sense of the inequalities in the dual constraints is the reverse of the sense of the inequalities in the primal constraints; however, the inequalities in the side conditions of both the primal and the dual usually have the same sense. The primal constraints given in (15.2)–(15.3) cause a slight difficulty in view of this set of relationships, and commonly (15.2) is multiplied through by -1 to outflank the problem.

15.2.3 *Interpretation of the dual*

The interpretation of the dual has been considered in a classic paper by Stevens (1961). In the economics literature, the $\{u_i\}$ and $\{v_j\}$ are called shadow prices on supply capacity at i and demand at market j respectively; that is 'u_i is the value of the commodity FOB at source i, and v_j is its value delivered at consumer j' (Stevens, 1961, p. 17). The dual objective function therefore seeks to maximize, for the system as a whole, the gain in the value of the commodity as a result of marketing that good. At the same time, the dual constraints (15.6) express the requirement that the gain in the value of the commodity between supplier i and market j cannot exceed the transport costs, c_{ij}, between i and j; this is the condition for a spatial price equilibrium.

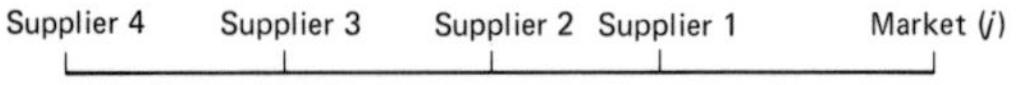

Supplier 4   Supplier 3   Supplier 2   Supplier 1   Market (j)

Figure 15.1   Relative spatial locations of suppliers and market.

As Stevens (1961) has shown, however, the $\{u_i\}$ and the $\{v_j\}$ do have a clear spatial interpretation. Following Stevens (1961), consider a system composed of four suppliers with inelastic supply capacities, $S_1, ..., S_4$, and a single market with an inelastic demand D_1. Suppose that the relative spatial locations of the suppliers and the market are as shown in Figure 15.1. The commodity being studied is assumed to be homogeneous, and the per unit cost of production of the good at each supplier is taken to be the same. In price terms, therefore, there will be a common base price, p, for all suppliers composed of production costs plus normal profits. Turning to Figure 15.2, let market forces now act upon the system shown in Figure 15.1. No-one is allowed to earn excess profits, and the transport costs $\{c_{ij}\}$ are taken to be solely an increasing function of distance between each of the i suppliers and the market. Supplier one will enter the market first, since he is the closest of the four suppliers to j, and he can therefore sell the commodity at the cheapest price in the market; he can supply S_1 units of the good at the delivered price $DP_1 = p+c_{11}$. Since the total demand of the market is not met by supplier one, the market will then turn to the next cheapest supplier, two, who can supply S_2 units of the good at DP_2. Supplier three will then enter the market. Since his supply capacity can more than meet the outstanding demand of the market, supplier three will, although he delivers at price DP_3, have some slack (unused) capacity, and he will be the marginal supplier. Supplier four will be unable to enter the market. DP_3 will be the *equilibrium market price* of the commodity. In that DP_3 is a measure of the value of the good delivered at the market, $DP_3 = v_1$ (that is, the $\{v_j\}$ represent the equilibrium market prices at each of the j markets). In any solution of the transportation problem, all the constraint inequalities are replaced by strict equalities, and we can rewrite the dual constraint (15.6) as

$$v_j - u_i = c_{ij}$$

or

$$u_i = v_j - c_{ij}. \tag{15.8}$$

See Figure 15.2. The spatial interpretation of the $\{u_i\}$ is that they are location rents. That is, if the restriction on the earning of excess profits is removed, they represent the excess profits that an entrepreneur can earn by virtue of his superior location alone. Thus suppliers one and two could let their prices drift up to DP_3 without fear of competition from suppliers three and four, simply because they have a location closer to the market than those other suppliers.

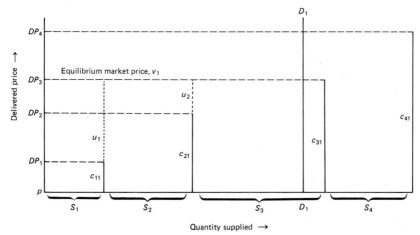

Figure 15.2   Demand and supply relationships for a transportation problem with four suppliers and one market. Adapted from Stevens, 1961, p. 18.

Theoretically, the marginal supplier, three, has zero location rent. However, Scott (1971a) has argued that in a system in which the earning of excess profits is permitted, there will be a tendency for the equilibrium market price to move up to marginally below DP_4, since it is not until $v_1 = DP_4$ that supplier four can enter the system. In Figure 15.2, then, suppliers one–three may, in practice, have their location rents increased by the amount $u_3 = DP_4 - c_{31}$.

**Location rents
Quartiles**

Lowest

Highest

Figure 15.3 Location rents for supply areas of iron ore in the UK based upon transport costs by road and rail. Note that the Jurassic limestone belt of the East Midlands, the country's most important internal ore supply region, has the most unfavourable location rents. Source: Chisholm and O'Sullivan, 1973, p. 84.

To provide a spatial interpretation for the $\{v_j\}$, Stevens assumed that, in Figure 15.2, a unit of supply capacity was established at the market, j. The market clearly has the highest location rent of all. A supplier at the market would incur no transport costs in supplying that market, and so from (15.8), $u_i = v_j$. That is, the v_j are 'a direct measure of the location rent per unit on marginal warehouse capacity established at the market' (Stevens, 1961, p. 20).

The reader is referred to Stevens's paper for details of the way in which the analysis can be extended to construct location rent surfaces and transport gradient lines for multiple supply and demand locations. Chisholm and O'Sullivan (1973) have used the dual of the transportation problem to identify areas of high and low location rents in the British Isles for a wide range of commodities marketed by road and rail between 78 origin and destination zones. (See Figure 15.3.) The idea of location rents also ties into Perroux's (1970) growth pole theory. We can think of poor location-rent areas as being in need of some growth stimulus; or alternatively of high location-rent areas as favouring economic growth.

15.3 The Transportation Algorithm

A general purpose procedure for the solution of linear programs in the *simplex algorithm* described, for example, in Dorfman, Samuelson and Solow (1958, p. 67–93). However, in the case of the transportation problem, a specialization of the simplex algorithm, known as the *stepping stone* method (Charnes and Cooper, 1954) can be used. It is described in Haggett and Chorley (1969, pp. 204–10) and in Scott (1971a, pp. 5–14), and we now summarize the procedure. Consider the hypothetical example shown in Figure 15.4. Diagram A shows the locations in a market system of three coal mines ($M_1 - M_3$) and four cities ($C_1 - C_4$) linked by a simple railway network. The supply capacity, S_i, of each of the mines, the demand of each city, D_j, in, say, thousands of tons, and a pattern of per unit transport costs between each mine and each city are shown in Table 15.1A. The transport costs are directly proportional to the distances between mines and cities. We now wish to find the pattern of coal production for the system which represents the solution to equations (15.1)–(15.4).

The solution algorithm starts by first defining an initial feasible solution; that is, any configuration of flows which satisfies equations (15.1)–(15.4). The cost of that pattern of shipments is determined. The algorithm then proceeds in a systematic, iterative fashion to adjust the initial configuration of flows until the least-cost pattern is found.

15.3.1 *Initial feasible solution*

The initial feasible solution is found by the *northwest corner rule*. We start in the northwest corner of Table 15.1A and allocate as much as possible of M_1's production to C_1, subject to satisfying the constraints (15.2) and (15.3). All of M_1's production (four units) is therefore assigned to C_1 (see Table 15.1B). However, this still leaves C_1 three units of coal short in terms of its total demand. We therefore turn next to M_2 who, with fifteen units production capacity, can more than meet that outstanding demand. Three units of coal are therefore assigned from M_2 to C_1. C_1's demand is now met. We next consider C_2. C_2 must receive *in toto* six units of coal, all of which can be supplied by M_2 without infringing M_2's capacity constraint. C_2 has thus been dealt with, and we can now consider C_3. C_3 has a demand for ten units of coal. Even after supplying C_1 and C_2, M_2 has six units of capacity left, and we therefore assign these six units to C_3. This still leaves C_3 with four units of demand to be met, which now must come from M_3. Finally, the remaining part of M_3's capacity (five units) is allocated to C_4. C_4 has a demand of five units, since $\sum_i S_i = \sum_j D_j$.

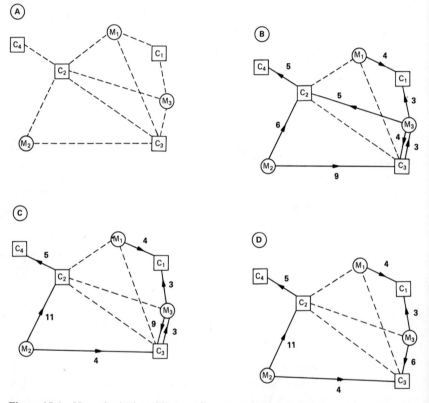

Figure 15.4   Hypothetical problem to allocate coal produced at three mines, M_1–M_3, to four city markets, C_1–C_4. **A** Relative locations of cities and mines and structure of railway network. **B** Pattern of shipments for initial feasible solution. **C** Pattern of shipments after first iteration. **D** Optimal pattern of shipments. Note that any shipments to C_4 have to pass through C_2 because of the structure of the railway network; other shipments through intervening cities or mines may also occur. Source: Haggett and Chorley, 1969, p. 205.

The total cost of this program of shipments is, from equation (15.1) and Tables 15.1A and B, $Z = (2 \times 4) + (3 \times 10) + (6 \times 6) + (9 \times 6) + (3 \times 4) + (20 \times 5) = 240$. The pattern of shipments is mapped in Figure 15.3B.

15.3.2 *The iterative algorithm*

The procedure for improving upon this initial feasible solution has the following steps.

Step 1. Since $\sum_i S_i = \sum_j D_j$ for our system, we can replace the inequalities in the primal and dual constraints by strict equalities. The dual constraint (15.6) thus becomes

$$v_j - u_i = c_{ij} \tag{15.9}$$

or

$$u_i = v_j - c_{ij} \tag{15.10}$$

or

$$v_j = c_{ij} + u_i. \tag{15.11}$$

Working with the relationships (15.9)–(15.11), the first step is to compute the location rents for all suppliers and markets for which $x_{ij} > 0$ (it is evident from Section 15.2.3 that location rents cannot exist without transport costs being incurred). We know from Figure 15.2 that the location rent of the marginal supplier in any system is zero. By convention, in order to set the solution of equations (15.9)–(15.11) into motion, we assume that the marginal supplier is the first, M_1. Then we have

$$v_1 = c_{11} + u_1 = 2 + 0 \tag{15.11 bis}$$
$$u_2 = v_1 - c_{21} = 2 - 10 \tag{15.10 bis}$$
$$v_2 = c_{22} + u_2 = 6 - 8 \tag{15.11 bis}$$
$$v_3 = c_{23} + u_2 = 9 - 8 \tag{15.11 bis}$$
$$u_3 = v_3 - c_{33} = 1 - 3 \tag{15.10 bis}$$
$$v_4 = c_{34} + u_3 = 20 - 2. \tag{15.10 bis}$$

See Table 15.1c.

Step 2. The $\{u_i\}$ and $\{v_j\}$ are used to compute *opportunity costs* $\{o_{ij}\}$ for every cell in which x_{ij} is not greater than zero. The opportunity costs are defined as

$$o_{ij} = v_j - u_i. \tag{15.12}$$

See Table 15.1c. We next calculate the quantities, $\{o_{ij} - c_{ij}\}$, and enter these figures in the main body of Table 15.1d. The rationale for these operations has been summarized by Scott (1971a, p. 18) as follows:

[Because of the definition of the shadow prices, v_j and u_i] the opportunity cost o_{ij} is a measure of what seller i apparently would lose by not selling at the market j. Whenever the condition $o_{ij} - c_{ij} > 0$ is found, then, there is always some positive advantage to increasing shipments from i to j. By contrast whenever the condition $o_{ij} - c_{ij} \leqslant 0$ is found then there is no advantage whatever in making a shipment from i to j [because transport costs would be at least as great as the financial gain that could be made by selling at the market].

Table 15.1 Steps in the transportation algorithm for the coal marketing problem of Figure 15.4.

A The per unit transport costs (c_{ij}) appear in the body of the table. Note that $\sum S_i = \sum D_j = 28$

From \ To	C_1	C_2	C_3	C_4	Supply capacities S_i
M_1	2	4	7	5	4
M_2	10	6	9	8	15
M_3	1	11	3	20	9
Demands D_j	7	6	10	5	Totals 28

B Flows (x_{ij}) comprising an initial feasible solution. $Z = 240$

From \ To	C_1	C_2	C_3	C_4	Supply capacities S_i
M_1	4				4
M_2	3	6	6		15
M_3			4	5	9
Demands D_j	7	6	10	5	Totals 28

C Shadow prices; opportunity costs (o_{ij}) in table body

u_i	v_j	2	−2	1	18
	From \ To	C_1	C_2	C_3	C_4
0	M_1		−2	1	18
−8	M_2				26
−2	M_3	4	0		

D $o_{ij} - c_{ij}$

From \ To	C_1	C_2	C_3	C_4
M_1		−6	−6	13
M_2				⑱
M_3	3	−11		

E Shipments (x_{ij}) from initial feasible solution and $+s$ and $-s$ giving general pattern of shipment increases and decreases

From \ To	C_1	C_2	C_3	C_4
M_1	4			
M_2	3	6	6−	+
M_3			4+	5−

F Flows (x_{ij}) comprising the first iteration solution. $Z = 150$

From \ To	C_1	C_2	C_3	C_4	Supply capacities S_i
M_1	4				4
M_2	3	6	1	5	15
M_3			9		9
Demands D_j	7	6	10	5	Totals 28

G Flows (x_{ij}) comprising the optimal solution.
   $Z = 141$

From \ To	C_1	C_2	C_3	C_4	Supply capacities S_i
M_1	4				4
M_2		6	4	5	15
M_3	3		6		9
Demands D_j	7	6	10	5	Totals 28

Note: $Z = \sum_i \sum_j c_{ij} x_{ij}$

Table 15.1 – *Cont.*

Scott's quotation is now applied to Table 15.1D. If $o_{ij} - c_{ij} \leqslant 0$ for all cells with opportunity costs, the pattern of shipments is optimal and no improvement can be made. Conversely, if cells exist in which $o_{ij} - c_{ij} > 0$, the cell which has the biggest $(o_{ij} - c_{ij})$ has the most to gain from having a positive shipment. This cell (the ringed cell in Table 15.1D) is called the pivot cell, and it is the cell about which we shall make our systematic improvements.

Step 3. We have to assign some positive shipment to the ringed cell. In so doing, we must make compensating adjustments in the other cells if the primal constraints are not to be broken. The adjustments are made in two stages, namely: first, by setting up a general pattern of shipment increases (+) and decreases (−); and second, by assigning numerical values to the increases and decreases.

In determining the general pattern of shipment increases and decreases, the first stage is to assign a + sign (indicating a shipment increase) to the pivot cell. A positive shipment in cell [2, 4] implies that we must decrease one of the existing shipments from supplier 2 if the supply capacity constraint, S_2, is not to be broken. Let us reduce the shipment in cell [2, 3], and indicate this fact by inserting a − sign in the cell. As a result of this change, we must increase one of the existing shipments into market 3 if the primal constraint (15.3) is to be met with respect to D_3. Cell [3, 3] is the only candidate, and so we must insert a + sign in it. Finally, cell [3, 4] must have its shipment level reduced to ensure that the supply capacity constraint, S_3, is maintained.

The method of assigning +'s and −'s described above is always the same; starting from the pivot cell, we move orthogonally from row to column to row to column, and so on, over cells with positive shipments in them, and assign an alternating pattern of −'s and +'s. The assignment procedure finishes whenever a − sign is located in the same column as the pivot cell. The configuration of +'s and −'s *must* form a closed circuit. The pattern of +'s and −'s indicates a general pattern of shipment increases (+cells) and decreases (−cells) which will (1) reduce the overall cost of the program and (2) because of the compensating nature of the +'s and −'s, still ensure that the primal constraints are met.

Once this general pattern of increases and decreases has been mapped out, the final stage of the improvement procedure can be carried out, namely the replacement of the circuit of $+$'s and $-$'s by actual values. We wish to assign as large a shipment as possible to the pivot cell. Bearing in mind that whatever we add to that cell has to be taken away from the cells with a $-$ sign in them [in order to maintain constraint (15.2)], the size of the shipment added to the pivot cell can only be as large as the *smallest* shipment in the set of cells containing $-$ signs, if the primal side condition that all $x_{ij} \geqslant 0$ is to be maintained. From Table 15.1E, this value is five. We therefore produce our revised pattern of shipments by adding five to or subtracting five from each cell with a $+$ or a $-$ in it. Five is added if the cell contains a $+$; five is subtracted if the cell contains a $-$. This completes the first iteration of the algorithm. The revised allocation pattern appears in Table 15.1F. The cost of the new program is $Z = 150$, as compared with $Z = 240$ for the initial feasible solution. See Figure 15.4c.

The iterative nature of the algorithm means that we now repeat exactly steps 1–3 above. The second iteration solution, which is also the optimal pattern of shipment, appears in Table 15.1G and is mapped in Figure 15.4D.

15.3.3 *Degeneracy*

Examination of Tables 15.1B, F and G shows that, at all stages in the search for an optimal pattern of shipments, there were six non-zero flows. In fact, it can

Table 15.2   Procedure for overcoming the degeneracy problem.

A

From \ To	1	2	3
1	4	3	
2	2−		6+
3	+		2−

B

From \ To	1	2	3
1	4−	3	+
2			8
3	2+		0−

C

From \ To	1	2	3
1	4	3−	0+
2		+	8−
3	2		

D

From \ To	1	2	3
1	4		3
2		3	5
3	2		

Flows (x_{ij}) from supplier i to market j shown in bold type.
Source: Scott, 1971a, p. 13.

be shown that, in any solution of the transportation problem for a system of n suppliers and m markets, the number of non-zero flows, N say, will be less than or equal to $(n+m-1)$. The model thus gives a very parsimonious description of a trading system. Usually $N = n+m-1$. If $N < n+m-1$, this is known as a *degeneracy*. In the solution algorithm 'degeneracy as defined above leads to apparent program breakdown so that it appears impossible either to compute a full set of shadow prices or, often, to make any systematic improvements in the program structure' (Scott, 1971a, p. 12).

The treatment of degeneracy has been discussed by Scott (1971a, pp. 12–3), and we now summarize his account. In Table 15.2A, a non-degenerate solution for a hypothetical trading system is shown, together with the pattern of +'s and −'s required for program improvement. Cell $[3, 1]$ is the pivot cell. At this stage, there are $n+m-1 = 5$ non-zero flows. Replacement of the +'s and −'s by actual values results in the pattern of flows shown in Table 15.2B, which is degenerate. The degeneracy is overcome by selecting any blank cell (called by Scott the θ cell) and treating it as if it contained a positive shipment. As the algorithm proceeds, the θ cell has shadow prices computed for it in the usual way. At the program readjustment, stage, if the θ cell receives a + sign, then the cell is simply assigned a value equal to the value being added to or subtracted from the other + and − cells, and the degeneracy is overcome. However, if the θ cell receives a − sign, we cannot proceed, since subtraction of a value from the cell would break the primal side condition that $x_{ij} \geqslant 0$. In that case, the θ cell returns to being a blank cell and the pivot cell becomes the θ cell.

To illustrate these points, we return to the degenerate solution shown in Table 15.2B. The pivot cell is $[1, 3]$, while the θ cell designated by Scott and a possible pattern of +'s and −'s for program improvement are also shown. The θ cell has received a − sign. Therefore, in Table 15.2C, the θ cell has reverted to being a blank cell again, and the pivot cell has become the θ cell. The set of +'s and −'s in Table 15.2C has resulted in a + appearing in the θ cell, leading to the revised, non-degenerate, pattern of shipments shown in Table 15.2D.

15.3.4 *Slack variables*

In many trading systems, it is common for slack production capacity to exist; that is, for $\sum_i S_i > \sum_j D_j$. This kind of situation is handled in the transportation problem in the following way. Consider again the coal marketing example given in Table 15.1. Suppose that the supply capacities of $M_1 - M_3$ are increased to 6, 18 and 10 units of coal respectively. The revised problem written in table form appears in Table 15.3A. In Table 15.3A, we have introduced a dummy market, C_5, to handle the slack capacity. The cells in this column will attract purely fictitious shipments from each supplier equal to the total unused capacity of that supplier. The per unit transport cost attached to every cell in the slack column is zero because we assume that it costs nothing to ship nothing. The demand, D_j, of the slack column is equal to $\sum_i S_i - \sum_j D_j$, the amount by which total supply exceeds total demand. D_5 is, therefore, the total slack capacity in the system. With the introduction of the dummy demand column, $\sum_{j=1}^{5} D_j = \sum_{i=1}^{3} S_i$, as in Table 15.1A. The problem is solved in exactly the same way as the ordinary transportation problem. The initial feasible solution is shown in Table 15.3B, and the optimal pattern of shipments,

Table 15.3   The transportation problem for the coal marketing problem of Figure 15.4.

A $\{S_i\}$, $\{D_j\}$; per unit transport costs (c_{ij}) in body of table

To From	C_1	C_2	C_3	C_4	C_5	S_i
M_1	2	4	7	5	0	6
M_2	10	6	9	8	0	18
M_3	1	11	3	20	0	10
D_j	7	6	10	5	6	Totals 34

B   Flows (x_{ij}) comprising initial feasible solution

To From	C_1	C_2	C_3	C_4	C_5	S_i
M_1	6					6
M_2	1	6	10	1		18
M_3				4	6	10
D_j	7	6	10	5	6	Totals 34

$$Z = 236$$

C   Flows (x_{ij}) comprising optimal pattern of shipments

To From	C_1	C_2	C_3	C_4	C_5	S_i
M_1	6					6
M_2		6	1	5	6	18
M_3	1		9			10
D_j	7	6	10	5	6	Totals 34

$$Z = 125$$

reached after four iterations (one of which was degenerate) is shown in Table 15.3c. The value of the objective function (15.1) for this pattern is $Z = 125$ (compared with $Z = 141$ for the original problem with no slack capacity), and the set of flows is mapped in Figure 15.5.

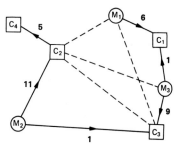

Figure 15.5 Optimal pattern of shipments for the coal marketing problem with slack capacity.

Comparison of Tables 15.1G and 15.3c shows that M_2 is at the economic margin for this system of production, in that M_2 is the mine whose full production potential is not required. Clearly, the ability of the transportation model to indicate which are the marginal producers in any economic system is of considerable interest from a planning point of view.

15.4 Extensions of the Transportation Problem

15.4.1 *The Beckmann–Marschak and the trans-shipment problems*

The economic system considered in the transportation problem is very simple and comprises solely suppliers and markets linked by a transport network. A much more realistic system might involve a production process and have the components shown in Figure 15.6, namely:

(1) A set of n production points which supply some commodity (say iron ore) to various transformation centres (say steel mills). The per unit production

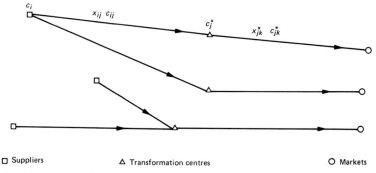

□ Suppliers   △ Transformation centres   ○ Markets

Figure 15.6 A hypothetical system of suppliers, markets and transformation centres for the Beckmann–Marschak problem.

cost of the ith supplier is denoted by c_i, while the per unit cost of shipment of the commodity from supplier i to transformation centre j is denoted by c_{ij}. The volume of the commodity shipped is denoted by x_{ij}.

(2) At the jth transformation centre, the commodity is processed (into steel) at a per unit transformation cost, c_j^*. There are t transformation centres.

(3) x_{jk}^* units of the finished commodity are then shipped from the jth transformation centre to the kth market at a per unit transport cost, c_{jk}^*. There are m markets.

As Scott (1971a, pp. 26–8) has noted, this statement of the Beckmann–Marschak (1955) problem differs from the transportation problem in that it involves an input–output process and a two commodity (the raw and processed materials) spatial allocation process. In addition, it is argued (see, for example, Woodward, 1971) that transport costs are now, in contrast to the past, a relatively unimportant element in the total cost of a production process, compared with other factors of production such as labour and rates. The introduction of the $\{c_i\}$ indicates how to enter into a model more complicated production cost functions than that used in the simple transportation problem.

The linear program for the Beckmann–Marschak problem is written as

Minimize
$$Z = \sum_{i=1}^{n} \sum_{j=1}^{t} (c_i + c_{ij})x_{ij} + \sum_{i=1}^{n} \sum_{j=1}^{t} c_j^* x_{ij}$$

$$+ \sum_{j=1}^{t} \sum_{k=1}^{m} c_{jk}^* x_{jk}^*, \tag{15.13}$$

subject to

$$(1) \sum_{j=1}^{t} x_{ij} \leqslant S_i, \quad i = 1, 2, ..., n, \tag{15.14}$$

$$(2) \sum_{j=1}^{t} x_{jk}^* \geqslant D_k, \quad k = 1, 2, ..., m, \tag{15.15}$$

$$(3) \, a_j \sum_{i=1}^{n} x_{ij} - \sum_{k=1}^{m} x_{jk}^* = 0, \quad j = 1, 2, ..., t, \tag{15.16}$$

and

$$(4) \sum_{i=1}^{n} x_{ij} \leqslant K_j, \quad j = 1, 2, ..., t. \tag{15.17}$$

The side conditions, $x_{ij} \geqslant 0$ and $x_{jk}^* \geqslant 0$ are also imposed. In equations (15.13)–(15.17), we make the following notational definitions in addition to those already given earlier in this section; S_i and D_k are used as in the transportation problem; a_j is an input–output coefficient (cf. input–output analysis) indicating how much of the finished commodity is produced, per unit of input of the raw material, at the jth transformation centre, and K_j is the total transformation capacity (in terms of raw material input) at j.

The terms in the objective function of the model give (from left to right) the costs over the system of (1) producing the raw material and shipping it to the transformation centres; (2) transforming the raw material into a finished product at the transformation centres; and (3) shipping the finished commodity from the transformation centres to the markets. Relations (15.14) and (15.15) are supply and demand constraints as in the transportation problem. Relation (15.15) is a *conservation condition* (Scott, 1971a) which ensures that the quantity of the finished good leaving the jth transformation centre cannot exceed the volume of that good which the factory can produce. Constraint (15.17) prevents the stockpiling of the raw commodity at the transformation centres.

The Beckmann–Marschak model thus examines the pattern of production, manufacture and trade in a single commodity for a system of n suppliers, t transformation centres and m markets. Its extension to multi-commodity systems provides the basis of the general inter-regional equilibrium models discussed in, for example, Isard (1960, pp. 467–92), Moses (1960), and Hurter and Moses (1964). In addition, we note that the *trans-shipment problem* (Orden, 1956) is also related to the Beckmann–Marschak model. In the trans-shipment problem, the transformation centres of the Beckmann–Marschak model are simply trans-shipment points between suppliers and markets at which no processing of the raw commodity occurs. Thus, the objective function of the trans-shipment problem is obtained from equation (15.13) by deleting the middle term,

$$\sum_{i=1}^{n} \sum_{j=1}^{t} c_j^* x_{ij},$$

while the constraints are given by relations (15.14)–(15.16), with $a_j = 1$ in (15.16). Constraint (15.17) disappears.

The best geographical application of the models discussed in this section is that of Casetti (1966) who studied the coal industry of Quebec and Southern Ontario. The industry is based around the Great Lakes–St Lawrence Seaway. Casetti formulated the problem as a cost minimization pattern of shipments over the seaway which ensured that all steel mills were adequately supplied with coal and iron ore and that all finished steel was taken to the markets. Casetti's model included input–output coefficients governing the transformation of coal and iron ore into steel.

15.4.2 Network problems

A series of network problems closely related to the transportation problem are considered in Scott (1971a, b). We focus in particular upon those discussed in Scott (1971a). The simplest of these is the so-called *capacitated transportation problem*. This is just the transportation problem given in equations (15.1)–(15.4), but with the additional constraint that

$$x_{ij} \leqslant C_{ij}, \quad i = 1, 2, ..., n; j = 1, 2, ..., m, \tag{15.18}$$

where C_{ij} is the carrying capacity of the transport link between supplier i and market j. Thus a minimum cost shipment program is obtained which recognizes that the carrying capacity of no transport link may be exceeded. See Gauthier (1968) for an application of the model.

In many networks, for example urban road systems, the carrying capacity of the road to move, say, commuters to and from home and place of work is a very real and binding constraint. The urban planner may then be faced with investment decisions on highway improvements to relieve such capacity constraints. Suppose first that the total costs of the proposed improvements have to fall within a fixed budget, B (Scott, 1971a, p. 30). An investment programme which will produce the maximum reduction in system operating costs is given by taking equations (15.1)–(15.3) of the transportation problem and adding the further constraints,

$$x_{ij} - y_{ij} \leqslant C_{ij} \tag{15.19}$$
$$\text{or} \quad x_{ij} \leqslant C_{ij} + y_{ij}$$

and

$$\sum_{i=1}^{n} \sum_{j=1}^{m} b_{ij} y_{ij} \leqslant B, \tag{15.20}$$

and the side conditions, $x_{ij}, y_{ij} \geqslant 0$, $i = 1, 2, ..., n; j = 1, 2, ..., m$. In these equations, previously used notation is retained. In addition, y_{ij} is a solution variable giving the increase in carrying capacity made to the road between i and j, and b_{ij} is the per unit cost of increasing capacity on that road. The solution to the model therefore gives the total capacity of the road between i and j as $C_{ij} + y_{ij}$ (existing + new capacity). Constraint (15.19) prevents the flow, x_{ij}, from exceeding this capacity, and constraint (15.20) ensures that the total amount spent on adding new capacity is less than the total available budget, B.

If there is no overall budget constraint, Scott (1971a) has argued that new investment should be made in such a way that operating and capital costs are jointly minimized. An appropriate model is the following.

Minimize

$$Z = \sum_{i=1}^{n} \sum_{j=1}^{m} c_{ij} x_{ij} + \sum_{i=1}^{n} \sum_{j=1}^{m} b_{ij} y_{ij}, \tag{15.21}$$

subject to

$$\sum_{j=1}^{m} x_{ij} \leqslant S_i, \tag{15.22}$$

$$\sum_{i=1}^{n} x_{ij} \geqslant D_j, \tag{15.23}$$

$$x_{ij} - y_{ij} \leqslant C_{ij}, \quad \text{or} \quad x_{ij} \leqslant C_{ij} + y_{ij} \tag{15.24}$$

and

$$x_{ij} - y_{ij} \geqslant 0, \quad i = 1, 2, ..., n; j = 1, 2, ..., m.$$

In the objective function, the first term gives the operating costs, and the second investment costs. See Quandt (1960) and Ridley (1969) for a further consideration of models for the investment of capital on highway improvements.

15.4.3 *Region building*

As we have seen in Chapter 14, a traditional geographical problem is how to delimit regions of one sort or another. If we can regard the problem as one of aggregating sub-areas into larger areal units, then evidently this is a problem in classification. As discussed in Section 14.4.3, the distinctive feature of regional, as opposed to aspatial, classification is that it is usual to permit the grouping together only of sub-areas which are physically contiguous, so that compact, non-fragmented regions are produced. We have suggested in Section 14.5 how the problem may be approached using the transportation problem. Thus, Yeates (1963) was concerned with the delimitation of school zones in Wisconsin, while other work discussed in that section described ways of drawing electoral boundaries by assigning, say, polling districts within a city to wards in a non-partisan fashion. The steps of an appropriate algorithm are given in Mills (1967) as:

(1) Choose arbitrary ward centres.

(2) Solve the transportation problem. In the model, the $i = 1, 2, ..., n$ 'suppliers' are the polling districts, while the $j = 1, 2, ..., m$ 'markets' are the ward centres. In the objective function, [equation (15.1)], the $\{c_{ij}\}$ are the squared distances from the geographical centres of each polling district to the ward centres, while the variate, X, describes the number of voters in each polling district (assumed located at each district geographical centre). The use of squared distances as transport 'costs' effectively ensures that a compact assignment of polling district voting populations to wards will occur.

The objective function is minimized subject to the constraints

$$\sum_{i=1}^{n} x_{ij} = P \quad j = 1, 2, ..., m, \tag{15.25}$$

$$\sum_{j=1}^{m} x_{ij} \leqslant p_i \quad i = 1, 2, ..., n, \tag{15.26}$$

and $x_{ij} \geqslant 0$. Here, x_{ij} is the number of voters in polling district i assigned to ward j. P is the total number of voters allowed in each ward; it is usually very important in electoral problems to set P equal in each ward. Finally, p_i denotes the number of voters in polling district i. Constraint (15.25) thus ensures that the assignment of districts to wards produces wards with equal numbers of voters, while constraint (15.26) prevents the assignment of voters from each district to the various wards exceeding the number of voters present in that district. The model generally splits some districts between wards. If these splits are regarded as undesirable, adjustments are made by hand.

(3) Find the new geographical centre of each ward as the centre of gravity of the districts assigned to the ward in step (2).

(4) If any of the new centres differs from the old, recycle to step (2); otherwise the algorithm is terminated.

Although we have illustrated the use of the transportation problem in region building with reference to a very specific example, it should be evident that the model can be extended to cover a wide range of regionalization problems to which only non-quantitative approaches have so far been applied.

15.5 Further Programming Models*

15.5.1 *The Herbert–Stevens residential site selection model*

Geographers, planners and economists have long been interested in urban land use models and, in particular, in the operation of the urban housing market. As a result, a distinguished line of models based upon the classic economic theory of perfect competition, profit maximization, and so on, has been developed. See, for example, Alonso (1960, 1964); Herbert and Stevens (1960); Ingram, Kain and Ginn (1973); Lowry (1964); Senior and Wilson (1974) and several papers by Harris cited therein. Although dissatisfaction with this approach is voiced (Harvey, 1973), it remains an important research area. Of the models mentioned, we examine here the linear programming model of Herbert and Stevens. The primal is used to allocate household groups to housing areas within a city; the dual ties into the literature on welfare economics by giving insights into the levels of subsidy required to permit financially deprived households to buy homes. In addition, Senior and Wilson (1974) have shown how the model may be derived using maximum-entropy methods, thus linking the material discussed in this section back to that considered in Section 2.5.

The primal problem. Suppose that the housing stock in an urban area can be classified into types, such that each type is relatively homogeneous with respect to the kind of houses it comprises. Thus one type might be composed of large detached single-family dwellings, another flats, and so on. Let there be $k = 1, 2, ..., n$ house types. In addition, we assume that the urban area can be exhaustively partitioned into $i = 1, 2, ..., l$ sub-areas. We suppose that there are N households to be located in homes within the urban area, where the N households are classifiable into $j = 1, 2, ..., m$ distinctive household groups, such as young single people, married couples with children, etc. All households in a given household group are taken to have similar budgets to allocate to the purchase of a house and to have similar requirements and tastes for different kinds of houses. Let B_{jk} denote the annual size of the budget that a household in group j would be prepared to spend on a type k house. B_{jk} will therefore reflect the household's preference for different types of houses. Thus for a married couple with children, B_{jk} might be large for a single-family dwelling, but zero, say, for a flat. Let c_{jk}^i denote the annual cost of a type k house in sub-area i to a household in group j.

The objective function of the model is written as

$$\text{Maximize} \quad Z = \sum_{i=1}^{l} \sum_{j=1}^{m} \sum_{k=1}^{n} x_{jk}^i (B_{jk} - c_{jk}^i), \qquad (15.27)$$

where x_{jk}^i represents the number of households in group j located by the model in type k houses in area i. Senior and Wilson (1974, p. 211) interpret $(B_{jk} - c_{jk}^i)$ as the bid rent for houses in different locations. The objective function therefore locates all the households in the study area in such a way as to maximize their total savings, or bid rents, while at the same time matching the households as closely as possible (as judged by their $\{B_{jk}\}$) to the types of houses they require. The constraints are

$$\sum_{j=1}^{m} \sum_{k=1}^{n} s_k^i x_{jk}^i \leq L^i, \quad i = 1, 2, ..., l, \tag{15.28}$$

$$\sum_{i=1}^{l} \sum_{k=1}^{n} -x_{jk}^i \leq -N_j, \quad j = 1, 2, ..., m, \tag{15.29}$$

and all $x_{jk}^i \geq 0$. In constraint (15.28), we have followed Senior and Wilson (1974, p. 211) and have used s_k^i to represent the amount of land occupied by a type k house in sub-area i. L^i is the total residential land available in sub-area i, and so the constraint ensures that the land occupied by households in area i does not exceed the amount available. In constraint (15.29), N_j denotes the number of households in household group j, and this constraint therefore ensures that all households are located.

The dual. The dual of the model is written as

$$\text{Minimize} \quad Z' = \sum_{i=1}^{l} r^i L^i - \sum_{j=1}^{m} v_j N_j \tag{15.30}$$

subject to

$$s_k^i r^i - v_j \geq B_{jk} - c_{jk}^i, \quad i = 1, 2, ..., l; j = 1, 2, ..., m; k = 1, 2, ..., n; \tag{15.31}$$

and all $r^i \geq 0$. There are no restrictions on the $\{v_j\}$. Here r^i is the annual cost (rent) per unit of land in area i and v_j is the annual financial subsidy per household for all households in group j. In the objective function (15.30), the first summation gives the total rents paid, and so 'maximization of bid rents in the primal problem is seen to be equivalent to the minimization of actual rents paid in the dual' (Senior and Wilson, 1974, p. 212). Once again, therefore, we see that the model is locating households, subject to the constraint set, as cheaply as possible in the urban area. The second summation in (15.30) arises because constraint (15.29) in the primal requires that all households must be located somewhere. The $\{B_{jk}\}$ of some household groups may be insufficient to permit this, and they will qualify for a positive financial subsidy, v_j, in the dual. This subsidy increases the amount that such households can afford for housing up to the minimum level required to locate them. From a social welfare point of view, identification of groups needing such financial support is an important product of the model. A negative v_j indicates a cash surplus in the bid rent of the household group concerned. See Herbert and Stevens (1960) and Senior and Wilson (1974) for a full discussion of the properties of the $\{v_j\}$. The constraints (15.31) prevent the unit rent in each area from falling below the unit rent paying ability of any household that might locate on the site.

Entropy approaches. In their discussion of the Herbert–Stevens model, Senior and Wilson (1973, 1974) argue that in practice the operation of the urban housing market will result in a sub-optimal, rather than an optimal, allocation of households to houses. Such a sub-optimal allocation can be obtained using entropy maximizing methods. Taking the Herbert–Stevens model, the entropy function, E, may be defined as [cf. equation (4.5) and (4.6)]

$$E = -\sum_{i=1}^{l} \sum_{j=1}^{m} \sum_{k=1}^{n} \log x_{jk}^i!, \tag{15.32}$$

which is related to the probability that the distribution $\{x_{jk}^i\}$ occurs. Senior and Wilson indicate that Shannon's definition of entropy,

$$-\sum_{i=1}^{l} \sum_{j=1}^{m} \sum_{k=1}^{n} x_{jk}^i \log x_{jk}^i,$$ could also have been used. Maximization of either of these entropy functions subject to any known constraints will yield the most probable distribution of the households among the housing stock of the urban area (cf. the gravity model of Section 2.5). The constraints imposed are

$$\sum_{j=1}^{m} \sum_{k=1}^{n} s_k^i x_{jk}^i = L^i \tag{15.33}$$

and

$$\sum_{i=1}^{l} \sum_{j=1}^{m} x_{jk}^i = N_j \tag{15.34}$$

as in the linear programming model [equations (15.28) and (15.29)]. Senior and Wilson state that while a sub-optimal allocation of households to the sub-areas is expected in the entropy model, some kind of maximizing behaviour should still be built in. They therefore impose the objective function of the programming model as a constraint, namely,

$$Z = \sum_{i=1}^{l} \sum_{j=1}^{m} \sum_{k=1}^{n} x_{jk}^i (B_{jk} - c_{jk}^i), \tag{15.35}$$

except that Z is to take a value less than in the programming model.

Maximization of (15.32) subject to (15.33)–(15.35) yields

$$x_{jk}^i = e^{-\lambda^{i(1)} s_k^i} e^{\lambda_j^{(2)}} e^{\mu(B_{jk} - c_{jk}^i)} \tag{15.36}$$

where $\lambda^{i(1)}$ is the Lagrangian multiplier associated with constraint (15.33), $\lambda_j^{(2)}$ that with constraint (15.34), and μ that with constraint (15.35). See Senior and Wilson (1974) for further details, the derivation of the dual, and a discussion of the conditions under which the solution of the entropy maximizing model approaches that of the linear programming model. Cliff (1965) provides an empirical application of the Herbert–Stevens model to the city of Evanston, Illinois.

15.2.2 Game theory

The use of game theory in geography is reviewed by Gould (1963, 1965) and in Abler, Adams and Gould (1972, pp. 478–89). Game theory provides a framework for determining an optimal strategy for behaviour in situations of risk and uncertainty. As an example, Abler, Adams and Gould consider the case of pioneer farmers making decisions about which crops to grow in almost total ignorance of the environment. 'In such a context, the environment, or nature, will be considered as a vindictive, [loss] minimizing player in a game played by men against her' (Abler, Adams and Gould, 1972, p. 478). We have already briefly considered such games in Section 6.5.1; our approach is more formal here.

Figure 15.7 Alternative locational strategies for the siting of nine lobster pots between two different marine environments. Hypothetical pays-off for the 'storm' situation are shown (see Table 15.4). Adapted from Abler, Adams and Gould, 1972, p. 481.

The simplest kind of game is illustrated by the example given in Figure 15.7, which is based upon Abler, Adams and Gould (1972, p. 479). Suppose there exists a village from which lobster fishing is carried out. If the lobster pots are placed in the lagoon, there is little danger of them being lost in storms, compared with placement in the open sea, but the lobsters are of an inferior quality and fetch less money when sold. The game to be played is summarized in Table 15.4. The marginal text records (1) the locational strategies available to the fishermen for placement of their lobster pots and (2) the environmental responses. The elements, $\{a_{ij}\}$, in the body of the table, or *pay-off matrix*, **A**, are the expected pays-off (say in money terms representing the value of the lobsters caught) to Player 1 by Player 2; thus a_{ij} is the pay-off to Player 1 by Player 2 if Player 1 plays the strategy associated with row i and Player 2 plays the strategy associated with column j of the matrix. One can imagine a similar pay-

Table 15.4 The payoff matrix for the lobster fishermen playing against the environment.

			Player 2 (*the environment*)		
			Strategy I Storm	Strategy II No storm	
	Strategy I	All pots in lagoon	17.3	11.5	
Player 1 (the fishermen)	Strategy II	Some pots in lagoon, some outside	5.2	17.0	$= \mathbf{A} \equiv \{a_{ij}\}$
	Strategy III	All pots outside lagoon	−4.4	20.6	

Source: Abler, Adams and Gould, 1972, p. 482.

off matrix, A^* say, showing the expected pays-off to Player 2 by Player 1. If $A^* = -A$, then the game is called a *zero sum* game, and because there are only two players, it is a *two person* game. Note that a_{31} is negative because the fishermen lose the value of their pots in that case. In this game, Player 1 (the fishermen) is a maximizing player (that is, he wishes to find the placement strategy for his lobster pots which will yield to him the largest possible pay-off in the A matrix), while Player 2 (the environment) is a minimizing player who wishes to minimize his losses. The ideas of minimizing, maximizing and optimal strategies form the basis of linear programming, and Dorfman, Samuelson and Solow (1958, pp. 446–64) and Rogers (1971, pp. 323–40) have shown how two person zero sum games may be formulated in linear programming terms.

The fishermen have $m = 3$ strategies. They can select either just one strategy (a pure strategy) or choose some mixture of the m strategies. Since the former is a special case of the latter, we assume that the fishermen wish to find the best set of probabilities $\{p_i\}$ with which each of the $i = 1, 2, ..., m$ strategies should be selected; that is the fishermen wish to find the mixture of strategies which will maximize their expected pay-off. Evidently, $\sum\limits_{i=1}^{m} p_i = 1$ and $p_i \geqslant 0$.

Suppose the fishermen know their optimal mixed strategy. We can then calculate the expected loss of the environment to the fishermen for each of its $1, 2, ..., j, ..., n$ pure strategies. Thus if the environment plays strategy I, its loss will be

$$E_1 = p_1 a_{11} + p_2 a_{21} + p_3 a_{31} = p_1(17.3) + p_2(5.2) + p_3(-4.4).$$

In general, if Player 2 plays strategy j, his expected loss will be

$$E_j = p_1 a_{1j} + p_2 a_{2j} + ... + p_m a_{mj}, \quad j = 1, 2, ..., n.$$

Since Player 2 will seek to minimize his losses, we can define the value, V (assumed $\geqslant 0$) of the game to Player 1 as the minimum of Player 2's possible losses when he plays any pure strategy against Player 1's optimal mixed strategy. Thus

$$V = \min(E_1, ..., E_n) = \min\left(\sum_{i=1}^{m} p_i a_{i1}, ..., \sum_{i=1}^{m} p_i a_{in}\right),$$

where Player 1 has solved the problem of finding $p_1, ..., p_m$ so as to maximize the above minimum value. Using this definition of the value of a game, Dorfman, Samuelson and Solow (1958, p. 448) write down the inequalities for each pure strategy of Player 2, given the optimal mixed strategy of Player 1, as

$$\left. \begin{array}{l} z_1 = p_1 a_{11} + p_2 a_{21} + ... + p_m a_{m1} - V \geqslant 0 \\ \quad\vdots \qquad\qquad \vdots \qquad\qquad\qquad \vdots \\ z_n = p_1 a_{1n} + p_2 a_{2n} + ... + p_m a_{mn} - V \geqslant 0 \end{array} \right\} \tag{15.37}$$

$$p_1 \quad + p_2 \quad + ... + p_m \qquad = 1 \tag{15.38}$$

$$p_i \geqslant 0, \quad i = 1, 2, ..., m, \tag{15.39}$$

the constraint set of a linear program. Player 1 has the maximization problem of choosing the $\{p_i\}$ so as to maximize V, that is,

$$\text{Maximize} \quad Z = 0p_1 + \ldots + 0p_m + 1p_{m+1},$$

where $V \equiv p_{m+1}$, while recognizing that the constraints (15.37)–(15.39) hold. Since the constraint inequalities of a linear program maximization problem should be of the form '$\leqslant$' rather than '$\geqslant$' [see, for example, equations (15.28)–(15.29)], Dorfman, Samuelson and Solow multiply the constraints though by (-1) to give the linear programme in its final form as

$$\text{Maximize} \quad Z = 0p_1 + 0p_2 + \ldots + 0p_m + 1p_{m+1}$$

subject to

$$-p_1 a_{11} - \ldots - p_m a_{m1} + p_{m+1}1 \leqslant 0$$
$$\vdots \qquad \vdots \qquad \vdots$$
$$-p_1 a_{1n} - \ldots - p_m a_{mn} + p_{m+1}1 \leqslant 0$$
$$p_1 + p_2 \ldots + p_m + p_{m+1}0 \leqslant 1,$$

and all $p_i \geqslant 0$.

Player 2, of course, wishes to minimize V, and so we could write down the dual of Player 1's problem to obtain an appropriate minimization problem for Player 2 (the primal/dual relationship of linear programming discussed in Section 15.2.3).

Thus, having written the game theory model as a linear program, we can solve for the unknown $\{p_i\}$ using standard linear programming methods.[1]

15.5.3 *Other programming models*

Throughout this chapter, we have considered only *linear* programming. Frequently, however, variables may not be linearly related, and methods such as geometric programming exist to handle variables which are related in non-linear ways. In addition, in many problems, it may be realistic to permit only integer values for the solution variables (integer programming). We also note that the models we have considered are restricted in that they examine the behaviour of an economic system at only one point in time. If we wish to examine the dynamics of change, then dynamic programming is a possible technique. Space prevents coverage of these important extensions of the basic models, and the reader is referred to Intriligator (1971) and to Scott (1971b) for a consideration of these methods.

15.6 Conclusions

In this chapter we have considered a series of linear programming models of various aspects of trading and social systems. We have focussed in particular upon the transportation problem and its extensions. We have shown how to write down and solve the primal problem which identifies the optimal spatial

---

[1] Other methods of solution for the two person zero sum game are available which are preferable from a computational viewpoint.

pattern of production and trade in a commodity. The dual variables of the model can be interpreted as location rents, and the relationship of these rents to regional development policy has been briefly discussed. Another common planning problem is that of deciding where to invest money on highway improvements which are designed to relieve binding capacity constraints on roads. Developments of the transportation problem which isolate appropriate optimal investment programs have been outlined. In the final part of the chapter, we have shown how linear programming techniques can be used in region building and in modelling the allocation of households to houses in an urban area. We have also explored the relationship of linear programming methods to entropy maximizing and game theoretic models.

16 Forecasting

16.1 Introduction

Man has always been curious to know what the future holds. Only recently, however, have geographers become interested in formal methods of forecasting. Thus, as late as 1970, Curry was able to write: 'However unlikely it may seem, this statement [paper] appears to be the first discussion of the forecasting of future maps in the geographical literature.' The geographer's interest in forecasting has been stimulated in part by the requirements for, and the attempts of planners to make, regional forecasts as a basis for policy and investment decisions. Indeed, Hägerstrand (1971) has argued that the current concern with forecasting in the academic world at large is a response to the urgent problems facing society at the moment, and that 'the opinion is spreading that if mankind shall have a future at all, we need to be able not only to forecast coming events but consciously and purposely to invent this very future.' In addition, from a theoretical point of view, it might be argued that the ability to forecast accurately should represent an ultimate goal of geographical research, in that this ability ought to imply a fairly clear understanding of the processes which produce spatial patterns.

In this chapter, we look at some of the forecasting models available to the geographer. The methods to be described are suitable for *short* and *medium* term forecasting only. Following Kendall (1973, p. 115), we note that the meaning of these terms depends upon the problem in hand:

> In meteorology, for example, 'short-term' may mean only two or three days ahead, and 'medium' refer to the next few months; whereas in economics, 'short-term' means a few months, perhaps as much as a year, 'medium' usually refers to the next five years, and everything after that is 'long-term'.

Since most of the variables handled by the location analyst are also of interest to the economist, we shall use Kendall's definition of 'short' and 'medium' term, and assume that the models to be described are really best suited for forecasting, at the most, 5–10 years ahead.

A second rule of thumb commonly used to determine how far ahead one may reasonably hope to forecast is that the forecasting model should be calibrated using two time periods of historic data for every one year ahead one wishes to forecast (Christ, 1966). This guideline arises from the assumption inherent in the structure of the models, that the past holds the key to the future. The models all depend to some degree upon identifying the basic patterns of behaviour that have existed in the past in the data set being analysed, and then using this structural information to provide a forecast.

Forecasting usually implies a time dimension, and the human geographer has been particularly interested in regional forecasting; that is predicting, say, levels of population, unemployment, or the incidence of a particular disease, at the regional level. We are thus thinking in terms of a space–time process or, in Curry's description, forecasting future maps. Sometimes, however, we may wish to make a purely spatial forecast. Interpolation of missing values on a map (the 'missing data' problem of the historical geographer) is the most commonly occurring form of purely spatial forecast. However, as Cliff and Ord (1975b, Section 6) have noted, a time–space process may appear as a purely spatial process because either

(1) the process has converged to an equilibrium state, and observations are available only for this equilibrium state; or

(2) the data are available only for a single time period.

Despite the growing interest in spatial and time–space forecasting, the literature on model-building aspects is still scant. This is in marked contrast to the wealth of literature on single region time series forecasting (e.g. Box and Jenkins, 1970; Kendall, 1973). Some basic references on spatial and time–space methods are given in Curry (1970) and Cliff, Haggett, Ord, Bassett and Davies (1975, Chapter 10). So far, the bulk of the literature has focussed upon ways of adapting time series methods to the time–space and spatial situations, and the layout of this chapter follows that format. Most of the chapter (Sections 16.2–16.5) is devoted to a consideration of time–space methods, while purely spatial forecasting techniques are considered briefly in Section 16.6. Much of the material discussed is based upon the accounts in Cliff and Ord (1975b) and Cliff et al. (1975, Chapter 10). The treatment is formal, and more general accounts appear in Haggett (1973, 1975d, Chapter 21).

16.2 The Basic Space–Time Autoregressive model (STAR)[1]

16.2.1 *The model*

Suppose that our data matrix has n counties and T time periods as in Figure 11.1. Denote the variate of interest by Y, and let the value of Y in area i at time t

[1] This short-hand notation follows that of Box and Jenkins (1970, Chapter 3).

****

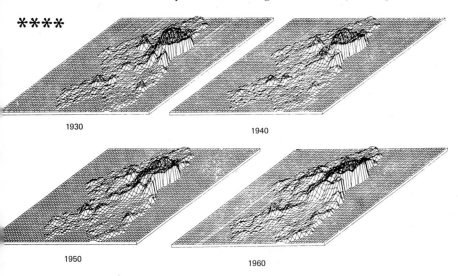

1930

1940

1950

1960

Figure 16.1 Distribution of population in a portion of the Detroit region, 1930, 1940, 1950 and 1960 (non-linear vertical scale). Note the similar levels of population in contiguous sub-areas which is suggestive of an autoregressive structure for the operator. Source: Tobler, 1969, p. 248.

be y_{it}. Ignoring the simultaneous effects shown in Figure 11.1, we might postulate the representative model,

$$y_t = \mathbf{B} \cdot y_{t-1} + \varepsilon_t , \quad t = 1, 2, ..., T, \qquad (16.1)$$
$$(n \times 1) \quad (n \times n) (n \times 1) \quad (n \times 1)$$

to handle the remaining features of Figure 11.1 Here, $\mathbf{B}$ is a matrix of parameters, and we assume that $\varepsilon_t \sim N(\mathbf{O}, \sigma^2 \mathbf{I})$; that is, the errors are taken to be normally distributed with zero means and variance–covariance matrix $\sigma^2 \mathbf{I}$. The model expresses the dependence of values of Y in the typical county i at time t upon values of that variate in other counties in the previous time period. The model is thus first order autoregressive in time, and of order n in space. This is made clear by rewriting equation (16.1) as

$$E(Y_{it} | \text{past history}) = a y_{i,t-1} + \sum_j w_{ij} y_{j,t-1}, \qquad (16.2)$$

where $E(Y_{it} | \text{past history})$ is the expected value of Y_{it} conditional upon its past history. In this model, the first term on the right-hand side is the purely temporal autoregressive component of Figure 11.1, while the second term defines the lagged in time spatial covariances. The $\{w_{ij}\}$ are known structural weights as used in equation (10.6).

We may suspect that the time–space process is not just autoregressive, but that variation in Y is also a function of k concomitant (exogenous) regressor variables. Two cases are of interest. First, a given regressor variable may take on the *same* value in each sub-area of the study region. For example, suppose that we wished to forecast levels of unemployment in each of the n employment districts of Southwest England. We might propose that unemployment is partly a function of a national economic variable such as the level of the *Financial Times* Ordinary Share Index, or GNP (that is, some national economic lead indicator) in addition to local effects. Such a global variable would have the same value at time t in each of the n employment districts. A possible model is (Cliff and Ord, 1975b),

$$\mathbf{y}_t \quad = \quad \mathbf{B} \quad . \ \mathbf{y}_{t-1} + \quad \mathbf{C} \quad . \ \mathbf{x}_{t-1} + \quad \boldsymbol{\varepsilon}_t \quad , \quad t = 1, 2, ..., T. \ (16.3)$$
$$(n \times 1) \quad (n \times n) \ (n \times 1) \quad (n \times k) \ (k \times 1) \quad (n \times 1)$$

Here, $\mathbf{x}_t$ is a vector of the values of the global variables, $X_1, X_2, ..., X_k$, at time t, and $\mathbf{C}$ is a matrix of parameters. The elements in the ith row of $\mathbf{C}$ tell us something about the relative importance of each of the global variables in sub-area i.

The second case of interest occurs when the k exogenous variables can take on different values in each of the n sub-areas in each time period, so that we have an $(n \times k)$ matrix, $\mathbf{X}_{t-1}$, instead of the $(k \times 1)$ vector $\mathbf{x}_{t-1}$. Then, following Cliff and Ord (1971, Section 5.2), we may specify the model,

$$\mathbf{y}_t \quad = \quad \mathbf{B} \quad . \ \mathbf{y}_{t-1} + \mathbf{X}_{t-1} \ . \quad \mathbf{c} \quad + \quad \boldsymbol{\varepsilon}_t \quad , \quad t = 1, 2, ..., T. \ (16.4)$$
$$(n \times 1) \quad (n \times n) \ (n \times 1) \quad (n \times k) \ (k \times 1) \quad (n \times 1)$$

Using Box and Jenkins's shorthand notation, equations of the form of (16.3) and (16.4) may be referred to as STARR models (*s*pace–*t*ime *a*uto*r*egressive models with additional *r*egression components).

Model (16.4) can be rewritten in a form to which standard econometric simultaneous equation methods may be applied (Huang, 1970, Chapter 10; Johnston, 1972, Chapters 12 and 13) namely:

$$\mathbf{A} \quad \mathbf{y}_t \quad = \quad \mathbf{B} \quad . \ y_{t-1} + \mathbf{X}_{t-1} \ . \quad \mathbf{c} \quad + \quad \boldsymbol{\varepsilon}_t \quad , \quad t = 1, 2, ..., T,$$
$$(n \times n)(n \times 1) \quad (n \times n) \ (n \times 1) \quad (n \times k) \ (k \times 1) \quad (n \times 1)$$

which yields   (16.4*)

$$\mathbf{y}_t \quad = \quad \mathbf{A}^{-1} \begin{bmatrix} \ \mathbf{B} & . \ \mathbf{y}_{t-1} + \mathbf{X}_{t-1} \ . & \mathbf{c} & + & \boldsymbol{\varepsilon}_t \ \end{bmatrix} \ t = 1, 2, ..., T.$$
$$(n \times 1) \quad (n \times n) \ (n \times n) \ (n \times 1) \quad (n \times k) \ (k \times 1) \quad (n \times 1)$$

Here, $\mathbf{A}$ is a matrix of pre-determined (or estimated) structural weights expressing the simultaneous effects among areas (cf. Figure 11.1). However, it is evident that, in order to use any of the models described for forecasting, the terms on the right-hand sides of the equations must be lagged in time vis-a-vis the terms on the left-hand sides. It is therefore difficult to see how the information provided by the simultaneous effects (purely spatial autoregressive component) of Figure 11.1 can be used in any practical time–space forecasting model. While such terms form the basis of some purely spatial, as opposed to time–space, forecasting models (see Section 16.6), we do not consider them further here.

One way of calibrating the models considered so far is, using ordinary least squares, to estimate the parameters *en bloc* over the T time periods (Cliff and

Ord, 1975b, Section 6.4). Note, however, that stationarity is assumed to permit estimation of the models (Section 10.4). Since this assumption is commonly violated by a temporal trend in the mean, we may need to adopt the counter measures discussed in Section 10.3.3. The simplest of these is to use variables for change, that is, the differences,

$$\nabla y_{it} = y_{it} - y_{i,t-1},\qquad(16.5)$$

rather than the original variables.

16.2.2 *Regional applications*

Tobler (1967, 1969b, 1970) has used STAR models to estimate the linear spatial transfer function (linear operator) which best transforms a map at time t into that at $t+1$. Tobler assumed that data had been collected at regular spatial intervals. We can regard such data as a geographical matrix or map. Let $Z_{pq}(t)$ denote the random variable on the map in cell (p, q) at time t. Then we may formulate the linear operator as

$$E\{Z_{pq}(t+1)\} = a + \sum_{j=-k}^{k} \sum_{i=-k}^{k} b_{ij} z_{p+i,q+j}(t),\qquad(16.6)$$

where a $(2k+1) \times (2k+1)$ operator is postulated. The ordinary least squares estimators of the coefficients in (16.6) are unbiassed, conditional upon the observed values for the earlier time period being given. Tobler (1969b) employed this model to examine the temporal change (1960–66) in business land use in Winston–Salem, and inter-censal population changes (1930–60) in Detroit. In the former case, a 3×3 operator was estimated, and in the latter, a 5×5 operator. See Figure 16.1. Similar work giving population projections to the year 2001 for townships in Ontario is described in Curry and Bannister (1974).

Another study of considerable interest is that of Tinline (1971), who applied the same model to Hägerstrand's Swedish data considered in Section 7.2. Recall that these data give the annual numbers and locations of farmers who accepted a subsidy granted from 1928 onwards by the Swedish government to encourage farmers of small units to convert woodland on their farms into pasture. In addition to least squares, Tinline also fitted (16.6) using the minimum absolute deviations (MAD) criterion, minimize $\sum |e_i|$. The 5×5 MAD operator obtained by Tinline which best transformed the 1930 pattern of adopters of the subsidy into the 1931 pattern is shown below. These weights may be compared with Hägerstrand's mean information field (MIF) given in Section 7.2.2. As discussed in Cliff and Ord (1973, p. 86),

0.35	0.72	0.79	0.68	0.00
0.20	0.09	0.00	0.00	0.21
0.33	0.00	1.02	0.00	0.00
0.00	0.00	0.00	0.00	0.17
0.00	0.58	1.59	0.00	0.00

there is a tendency for the coefficients in the border cells of the operator to be higher than the values in the inner cells (exclusive of the central weight). The operator is described by Tinline as 'doughnut-shaped, with an outer ring of higher values, and an inner ring of lower values.' This may be contrasted with the rapid but smooth decay of probabilities postulated by Hägerstrand in his MIF. Recall from Section 7.6.2 the evidence which implied that, compared with the real world, Hägerstrand's MIF led to overconcentration of new adopters in areas of original adopters, and to underestimation of numbers of new adopters in areas more distant from the belt of original adopters. It is interesting that the spatial pattern of weights in Tinline's operator also points to this conclusion, although Mollison (1975) is less convinced.

16.3 Integrated Space–Time Models

16.3.1 *Space–time integrated moving average model (STIMA)*

Consider again the unemployment example outlined immediately above equation (16.3). Although levels of unemployment generally display a clear time–space autoregressive structure (Cliff *et al.*, 1975, Section 10.7), many unforeseen factors may also influence the future unemployment rate. Thus, the chance closure of isolated factories in a study region is difficult to anticipate, but such closures may produce 'shocks' to the system which can persist over several time periods and affect those areas from which the factories drew their labour force; that is, there will be multiplier effects. Similarly, the opening of new plant is difficult to foresee, particularly as government policy changes. We may handle these sorts of occurrences by viewing the changes in Y as a function of a series of shocks to the system which arrive randomly in time and space. This yields the representative space–time integrated random shocks, or moving average, model (STIMA) as

$$\nabla y_{it} = \varepsilon_{it} + b\varepsilon_{i,t-1} + c \sum_j w_{ij} \varepsilon_{j,t-1}, \qquad (16.7)$$

where b and c are parameters, and the epsilons are random shocks with zero means, constant variance, and zero correlations. The word, 'integrated', has been proposed by Box and Jenkins to indicate the possibility of repeated application of the difference operator, ∇, to eliminate trend, seasonal components, and so on. Equation (16.7) can be extended to cover more than one time lag.

A basic problem with (16.7) is estimating the model because the epsilons are unknown. Box and Jenkins (1970, Chapter 7) give a non-linear least squares estimation procedure which can be employed. Alternatively, Durbin (1959) has shown that the model may be approximated by an autoregressive scheme of very high order, which can be fitted by ordinary least squares.

16.3.2 *Exponential smoothing models*

A moving average scheme which has been widely discussed in the time series literature is the so-called *exponential smoothing* model (Kendall, 1973, Chapter 9). Suppose that we have available a time series for a single region, and that y_t,

y_{t-1} ... denote the terms of the series. In making a forecast we may often want to give more weight to observations occurring in the recent past, as opposed to observations taken a long time ago (possibly because older observations are less accurate or reliable); that is, we may feel that temporally distant observations should be *discounted* (in the sense of carrying less weight, and not in the sense of being ignored) compared with more recent observations. The exponentially weighted moving average,

$$\tilde{y}_t = \sum_{k=0}^{m} (1-\gamma)^k y_{t-k} \Big/ \sum_{k=0}^{m} (1-\gamma)^k, \qquad (16.8)$$

is a model which achieves this purpose. Here γ is a weighting constant, $0 \leqslant \gamma \leqslant 1$, and m is the maximum temporal lag. This scheme discounts observations exponentially with temporal distance from t. The moving average is readily updated as new observations arrive, since it can be shown that

$$\tilde{y}_t = \gamma y_t + (1-\gamma)\tilde{y}_{t-1}. \qquad (16.9)$$

To use this model for forecasting, we simply take the latest available moving average as our forecast value; thus $\tilde{y}_t$ is the one step ahead forecast, made at time t, of y_{t+1}. Following Kendall (1973, pp. 118–19), let the error made at $t-1$ in forecasting y_t be e_t (that is, $e_t = y_t - \tilde{y}_{t-1}$). Result (16.9) then implies that the one step ahead forecast of y_{t+1} made at time t, namely $\tilde{y}_t$, may also be written as

$$\tilde{y}_t = \tilde{y}_{t-1} + \gamma e_t; \qquad (16.10)$$

that is, the forecast, made at time t, of y_{t+1} is simply the forecast made of y_t at time $t-1$, increased by γ times the error made in that forecast.

Equation (16.9) is related in the following way to the general STIMA model given in equation (16.7). Rewriting (16.7) for a single region time series as

$$\nabla y_{t+1} = \varepsilon_{t+1} - b\varepsilon_t, \qquad (16.11)$$

we have, from (16.5),

$$y_{t+1} = y_t + \varepsilon_{t+1} - b\varepsilon_t, \qquad (16.12)$$

which may be re-expressed as

$$\tilde{y}_t = y_t + \tilde{\varepsilon}_{t+1} - b\tilde{\varepsilon}_t \qquad (16.13)$$

in terms of forecast values. At time t, $\tilde{\varepsilon}_{t+1} = 0$ and $\tilde{\varepsilon}_t = y_t - \tilde{y}_{t-1}$. Substitution of these results into equation (16.13) yields

$$\tilde{y}_t = (1-b)y_t + b\tilde{y}_{t-1}, \qquad (16.14)$$

which is the same as equation (16.9) with $(1-b) \equiv \gamma$. Thus the exponential smoothing model is exactly the forecast equation for a first order integrated moving average process. The model is usually treated separately, however, because, as we shall see, γ is generally selected by a direct search procedure, rather than properly estimated.

The great virtue of the exponential smoothing model from a forecasting point of view is its simplicity, and, once γ is obtained, its ease of updating. The model is also the most straight forward of the so-called adaptive forecasting methods. Kendall (1973, p. 119) comments as follows:

> The precise meaning of 'adaptive' is not clear. In a sense every method of forecasting is adaptive if it brings into account any observations made since the last forecast. Nor is [γ] 'adapted' [updated] except perhaps occasionally. The general understanding of the term seems to be that 'adaptive' forecasting allows the updating of forecasts with a minimum of delay and arithmetical nuisance.

All the models considered in this chapter are therefore adaptive within the broader definition given by Kendall, although they cannot be updated as rapidly as can the exponential smoothing model.

16.3.3 *Spatial extensions of the exponential smoothing model*

Cliff *et al.* (1975, Section 10.2.2) have considered the addition of a spatial dimension to the time series exponential smoothing model. To do this, the authors defined $\bar{y}_{i-s}$ as the arithmetic mean of the observations which were the sth spatial nearest neighbours of i. Equation (16.8) was reformulated to give the spatial weighted moving average,

$$\check{y}_i = \sum_{s=0}^{l} (1-\varphi)^s \bar{y}_{i-s} / \sum_{s=0}^{l} (1-\varphi)^s, \tag{16.15}$$

where l is the maximum spatial lag. Note that in this equation, we are reducing the spatial information to a one-dimensional series by computing $\bar{y}_{i-s}$. The next stage was to combine equations (16.8) and (16.15) as

$$\check{\tilde{y}}_{it} = \sum_{k=0}^{m} \{(1-\gamma)^k\} \check{y}_{i,t-k} / \sum_{k=0}^{m} (1-\gamma)^k. \tag{16.16}$$

For large m, this reduces to

$$\check{\tilde{y}}_{it} = \gamma \check{y}_{it} + (1-\gamma)\check{\tilde{y}}_{i,t-1}, \tag{16.17}$$

where $\tilde{\ }$ and $\check{\ }$ denote averaging over time and space respectively. The term, $\check{y}_{it}$, the spatial average for location i at time t, is given by equation (16.15). Thus, for the typical area, i, spatial averaging is carried out for each value of t using equation (16.15) with a given value of φ, and these spatial averages are then smoothed over time. The forecast for the ith area is simply the latest available value of $\check{\tilde{y}}_{it}$. Equation (16.16) reduces to (16.8) when $\varphi = 1$ and to (16.15) when $\gamma = 1$.

The parameter(s) of the exponential smoothing model can be estimated analytically by finding those parameter values which satisfy the least squares criterion for the quantities, $\{y_t - \check{\tilde{y}}_t\}$. See Kendall (1973, p. 119) for details. Commonly, however, since there are only one or two parameters to be estimated, different combinations of parameters are simply substituted into the model, and a direct search is carried out to find empirically the parameter values which minimize the errors. This technique was employed by Cliff *et al.*

(1975, Section 10.2.4), where model (16.17) was used to forecast the incidence of measles outbreaks in 27 areas of Cornwall, England.

Extensions of the exponential smoothing model exist. Holt (1957) and Winters (1960) have formulated a three parameter model (the Holt–Winters model) which will handle seasonal elements in a time series, while Harrison (1965) has proposed a similar model in which harmonic terms are used to represent the seasonal elements. See also Chisholm and Whitaker (1971, p. 26).

16.3.4 *The space–time autoregressive integrated moving average model with additional regression terms (STARIMAR)*

Clearly, many different effects underlie most time–space data sets, and we might wish to combine the features of the models discussed in Sections 16.2 and 16.3 into a general STARIMAR model as follows (Cliff *et al.*, 1975, Section 10.3.3):

$$\nabla y_{it} = \alpha_1 + \alpha_2 x_{i,t-1} + \beta \nabla y_{i,t-1} + \gamma \sum_j w_{ij} \nabla y_{j,t-1} + u_{it}, \tag{16.18}$$

STARR   MA

additional regression term | pure temporal auto-regressive terms | lagged in time spatial covariances

where

$$u_{it} = \varepsilon_{it} + b\varepsilon_{i,t-1} + c \sum_j w_{ij} \varepsilon_{j,t-1} \tag{16.19}$$

MA

is the random component. In this model, the quantities, $\alpha_1, \alpha_2, \beta, \gamma, b$ and c are parameters. The estimation of the model is involved, and the reader is referred to Box and Jenkins (1970, Chapter 7) for details of the method and a computational algorithm. An alternative procedure, using a recursive ordinary least squares method, is described in Martin (1975). Martin's approach is much simpler than that of Box and Jenkins, and yields approximately the same results.

16.4 Model Identification*

16.4.1 *The identification problem*

Suppose that we wish to fit one of the models described in the previous sections to an actual data set. Two questions can be posed immediately which together summarize the so-called *model identification* or *specification* problem. The questions are:

(1) Which model should be selected? We have a choice of four basic forms— STAR, STARR, MA, and STARIMAR.

(2) Having chosen a particular form of model, what orders of temporal and spatial lags should be included in the model? Applying Tukey's (1962)

principle of parsimony, we want as few parameters as possible to estimate, consistent with an adequate representation of the time–space process.

If geographical theory on the data set in hand is strong enough to provide, *a priori*, answers to both these questions, well and good. If not, we must pre-screen the data in some way in order to reach an appropriate decision. Consequently, we now outline a method of model identification.

Box and Jenkins (1970, Chapter 6), when faced with the identification of time series forecasting models, approached the problem via temporal autocorrelation and partial autocorrelation analysis. Their work consisted of identifying the characteristic forms of correlograms (cf. Section 11.5) for temporal autoregressive, moving average, and mixed autoregressive/moving average processes. In an important paper, Martin and Oeppen (1975) have extended the Box–Jenkins methodology to the time–space situation. Their analysis is based upon the principles outlined and applied in Section 11.5 except that temporal and spatial interactions are looked at simultaneously, rather than separately as in those sections. The remainder of this section summarizes their findings. An alternative procedure for model identification is described in Bennett (1975a).

16.4.2 *The Martin–Oeppen procedure*

Recalling the notation of equation (11.33), Martin and Oeppen define the spatial lag operator, L, as, in our notation,

$$L^0 y_{it} = y_{it} \tag{16.20}$$

and

$$L^s y_{it} = \sum_j w_{ij} y_{j,t}, \quad s > 0, \tag{16.21}$$

where s denotes the spatial lag which is s steps away from area i, and the summation is over the j areas at spatial lag s from i. They then rewrite the various models considered in Sections 16.2–16.4 in lag operator form, namely:

(1) STAR

$$y_{it} = \sum_{s=0}^{l} \sum_{k=1}^{m} a_{sk} L^s y_{i,t-k} + \varepsilon_{it}. \tag{16.22}$$

As before, k denotes temporal lag k from t, while l and m denote the maximum number (order) of spatial and temporal lags respectively over which the summations are to be made.

(2) STMA

$$y_{it} = - \sum_{s=0}^{l} \sum_{k=1}^{p} c_{sk} L^s \varepsilon_{i,t-k} + \varepsilon_{it}. \tag{16.23}$$

(3) STARMA

$$y_{it} = \sum_{s=0}^{l} \sum_{k=1}^{m} a_{sk} L^s y_{i,t-k} - \sum_{s=0}^{l} \sum_{k=1}^{p} c_{sk} L^s \varepsilon_{i,t-k} + \varepsilon_{it}. \tag{16.24}$$

Let Y_1 and Y_2 be two time–space variables. Denote the value of Y_1 (or Y_2) in county i at time t by y_{1it} (or y_{2it}). Martin and Oeppen propose, as an estimator of the correlation between the spatially and temporally lagged terms, $L^g y_{1,t-j}$ and $L^s y_{2,t-k}$ (an estimator of the autocorrelation if Y_1 and Y_2 are the same variable), the quantity,

$$r_{gjsk} = \frac{\sum_{i=1}^{n} \sum_{t=v+1}^{T} L^g z_{1i,t-j} L^s z_{2i,t-k}}{\left[\sum_{i=1}^{n} \sum_{t=1}^{T} (L^g z_{1i,t})^2\right]^{\frac{1}{2}} \left[\sum_{i=1}^{n} \sum_{t=1}^{T} (L^s z_{2i,t})^2\right]^{\frac{1}{2}}} \qquad (16.25)$$

where $v = \max(j, k)$. In this equation, we have for the typical variable, a, say,

$$L^s z_{ai,t-k} = L^s(y_{ai,t-k} - \bar{y}_a) = L^s y_{ai,t-k} - \bar{y}_a, \qquad (16.26)$$

where

$$\bar{y}_a = \frac{1}{nT} \sum_{i=1}^{n} \sum_{t=1}^{T} y_{ait}. \qquad (16.27)$$

If we define the variables, $\tilde{z}_{1gj} = L^g z_{1i,t-j}$ and $\tilde{z}_{2sk} = L^s z_{2i,t-k}$, then equation (16.25) may be rewritten as

$$r_{gjsk} = \frac{\sum_{i=1}^{n} \sum_{t=v+1}^{T} \tilde{z}_{1gj} \tilde{z}_{2sk}}{\left[\sum_{i=1}^{n} \sum_{t=1}^{T} \tilde{z}_{1g}^2\right]^{\frac{1}{2}} \left[\sum_{i=1}^{n} \sum_{t=1}^{T} \tilde{z}_{2s}^2\right]^{\frac{1}{2}}}, \qquad (16.28)$$

$$= \mathrm{corr}(\tilde{z}_{1gj}, \tilde{z}_{2sk}), \qquad (16.29)$$

in the same sense as a conventional product moment correlation coefficient (Martin and Oeppen, 1975). In other words, the quantities (16.25), (16.28) and (16.29) are ordinary product moment correlation coefficients between the (lagged) variables, $\tilde{z}_{1gj}$ and $\tilde{z}_{2sk}$. The structure of equation (16.25) may be compared with that of equation (11.39). When $g = j = 0$ and $Y_1 = Y_2$, the equations are basically the same, except the summations now extend over time and space, rather than solely over space as in (11.39). The solution of (16.25) for $g = j = 0$ and $Y_1 = Y_2$ yields the time–space (auto)correlogram, as opposed to the purely spatial (auto)correlogram produced by (11.39); that is, we obtain the autocorrelations between county values of the variate at t and values of the variate at different temporal and spatial lags (i.e. between the $\{z_{it}\}$ and the $\{L^s z_{i,t-k}\}$).

Identification of an appropriate forecasting model requires not only computation of the time–space correlogram, but also of the time–space partial correlogram. The partials tell us the degree of correlation between the variate values in the counties at, say, time t (the $\{z_{it}\}$) and the variate values in those counties which are k temporal and s spatial lags away (the $\{L^s z_{i,t-k}\}$), *with the effect of all other spatially and temporally lagged variates held constant*. Just as the computation of the purely *spatial* partial autocorrelations in Section 11.5.2 required the calculation of the intercorrelations among the spatially lagged

Table 16.1   Matrix of autocorrelations among the spatia**l**

		$k=0$	$k=1$				$k=2$			
		$s=0$	$s=0$	$s=1$	$s=2 \ldots$	$s=l$	$s=0$	$s=1$	$s=2 \ldots$	$s=l$
$j=0$ $g=0$		r_{0000} (1.0)	r_{0001}	r_{0011}	$r_{0021} \cdots$	r_{00l1}				
$j=1$	$g=0$	r_{0100}	r_{0101} (1.0)	r_{0111}	$r_{0121} \cdots$	r_{01l1}				
	$g=1$	r_{1100}	r_{1101}	r_{1111} (1.0)	$r_{1121} \cdots$	r_{11l1}				
	$g=2$	r_{2100}	r_{2101}	r_{2111}	$r_{2121} \cdots$ (1.0)	r_{21l1}				
	$\cdot$	$\cdot$	$\cdot$	$\cdot$	$\cdot$ $\cdot$	$\cdot$				
	$g=l$	r_{l100}	r_{l101}	r_{l111}	$r_{l121} \cdots$	r_{l1l1} (1.0)				
$j=2$	$g=0$									
	$g=1$									
	$g=2$									
	$g=l.$									
$j=m$	$g=0$	r_{0m00}								
	$g=1$	r_{1m00}								
	$g=2$	r_{2m00}								
	$\cdot$	$\cdot$								
	$g=l$	r_{lm00}	r_{lm01}	r_{lm11}	$r_{lm21} \cdots$	r_{lml1}				

...orally lagged variates, $\tilde{z}_{gj}$ and $\tilde{z}_{sk}$.

	$k = m$			
	$s = 0$	$s = 1$	$s = 2$ ...	$s = l$
	r_{000m}	r_{001m}	r_{002m} ...	r_{00lm}
		r_{011m}		
		r_{111m}		
		r_{211m}		
		r_{l11m}		
	r_{lm0m}	r_{lm1m}	r_{lm2m} ...	r_{lmlm}

In this table, the subscripts g and s refer to typical spatial lags, and j and k to typical temporal lags. For example, $r_{2111}(\equiv r_{gjsk})$ is the sample autocorrelation between (i) variate values two spatial lags and one temporal lag away from a reference zone and (ii) those values which are one spatial and one temporal lag away from the reference zone. See Figure 16.2. Source: Martin and Oeppen, 1975, p. 103.

variates, so Martin and Oeppenz proceed to evaluate the matrix of time–space intercorrelations between the variables, $\tilde{z}_{gj}$ and $\tilde{z}_{sk}$, as a basis for obtaining the time–space partial autocorrelations. Equation (16.25) is repeatedly solved over the range of values of the subscripts g, j, s and k, to build up the matrix of intercorrelations shown in Table 16.1 and Figure 16.2. The marginal information corresponds with the subscripts attached to r in equation (16.25). The first row and column of the matrix give the time–space correlogram, while the remainder of the matrix gives the intercorrelations between *all* pairs of lagged in time and space variables, $\tilde{z}_{gj}$ and $\tilde{z}_{sk}$. It is evident from Table 16.1 that there is a clear block structure to the matrix. Thus, excluding the first row and column, the block of terms in the top left-hand corner of the matrix gives the intercorrelations between the variate values, $\{L^g z_{i,t-1}\}$ and $\{L^s z_{i,t-1}\}$. The matrix is symmetric about the leading diagonal, and, as usual, all the leading diagonal terms are unity.

Note from Table 16.1 and Figure 16.2B that, in addition to the sorts of bonds illustrated in Figure 16.2A, which imply the dependence of future maps on those of the past, terms like those illustrated in the first column of diagrams of Figure 16.2B also appear in the matrix of Table 16.1. These represent an apparent paradox, i.e. the dependency of past maps on the future. These terms arise because the correlation coefficient (which is acausal) is being used to summarize relationships which apparently have a clear causal structure running from the past to the future. Although this may appear to be a serious deficiency in Martin and Oeppen's method, the idea of the reversibility of time has been exploited by geographers to justify running diffusion models backwards through time to estimate past patterns, such as unknown sources of innovations. See Chapter 7. In the time series literature, the same problem arises and it is assumed away by requiring that the process to be identified is weakly stationary (definition 10.1, Section 10.4.2), so that the covariance between points depends only upon their *relative*, not *absolute*, locations in time. If the assumption of weak stationarity is applied to a time–space process, then Table 16.1 may be modified as follows:

(1) calculate the autocorrelations (a) in row 1 and column 1 of the matrix, and (b) the blocks of terms in rows $j = 1$ and columns $k = 1, 2, \ldots, m$;

(2) fill in the remaining part of the upper triangle of the matrix by repeating *each* block of terms defined in (1b) down the diagonal of the matrix upon which it lies.

(3) complete the lower triangle of the matrix by symmetry.

Given a correlation matrix of the form,

$$
\mathbf{R} =
\begin{bmatrix}
1 & \rho_{12} \rho_{13} & \cdots & \rho_{1p} \\
  & 1 \rho_{23} & \cdots & \rho_{2p} \\
  & & \cdot & \cdot \\
  & & & \cdot \\
  & & & \cdot \\
  & & & 1
\end{bmatrix}
$$

[2] In the remainder of this section, we take $Y_1 = Y_2$, so that (16.25), (16.28) and (16.29) are measures of autocorrelation. This means that the lagged variables, $\tilde{z}_{1gj}$ and $\tilde{z}_{2sk}$, can be redefined with the simpler subscripting, $\tilde{z}_{gj}$ and $\tilde{z}_{sk}$.

Kendall and Stuart (1967, Section 27.5) define the partial correlation between two variates, x_d and x_g, with the effects of the other $(p-2)$ variates held constant, as

$$\rho_{dg.12...(d-1),(d+1)...(g-1),(g+1)...p} = \frac{-c_{dg}}{(c_{dd}c_{gg})^{\frac{1}{2}}}. \tag{16.30}$$

Here, c_{dg} is the co-factor of ρ_{dg} in $|\mathbf{R}|$, the determinant of $\mathbf{R}$ (Johnston, 1972, pp. 78–85).

To apply this result to the present problem, set the matrix in Table 16.1 equivalent to $\mathbf{R}$. Martin and Oeppen define the partial correlation between the $\{z_{it}\}$ and the $\{L^s z_{i,t-k}\}$ as ψ_{00sk}, where

$$\psi_{00sk} = \frac{-c_{00sk}}{(c_{0000}c_{sksk})^{\frac{1}{2}}}. \tag{16.31}$$

Here, c_{00sk} is the co-factor of the correlation between the $\{z_{it}\}$ and $L^s z_{i,t-k}$ in

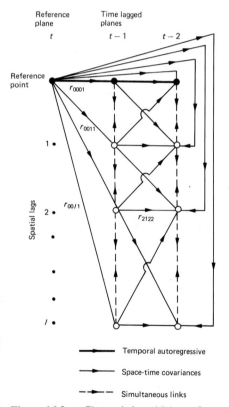

Temporal autoregressive

Space-time covariances

Simultaneous links

Figure 16.2A Channels by which a reference point at t depends upon events at other points on earlier maps (cf. Figure 11.1). The strength of each of these bonds is summarized by a correlation coefficient in Table 16.1, in which representative blocks of the matrix are illustrated.

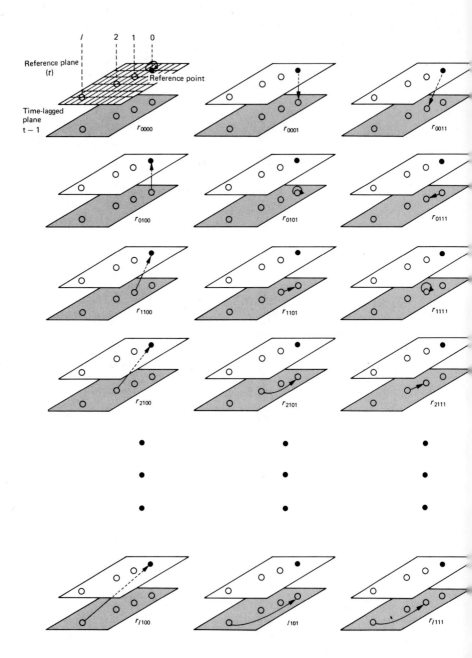

Figure 16.2B Plot of correlation bonds for all terms

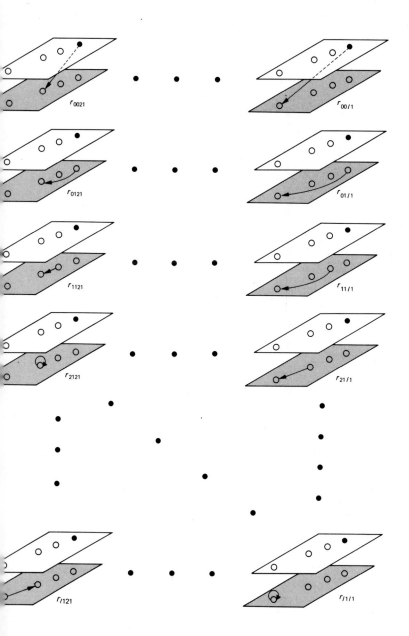

left-hand block of the matrix given in Table 16.1.

$|\mathbf{R}|$. This correlation is the term r_{00sk} in Table 16.1. The other quantities in (16.31) are similarly defined. The subscripting of c is consistent with the subscripting of r in equation (16.25).

Martin and Oeppen summarize the characteristics of the time–space autocorrelations and partial autocorrelations for the various forecasting models as follows:

(1) For a STAR (l, m) process of order l in space and m in time, the autocorrelations should decay approximately exponentially in time and space, while the partials should cut off (that is, be apprximately zero) after lag l in space and m in time.

(2) For a STMA (g, p) process of order g in space and p in time, the autocorrelations cut off after lag g in space and p in time, while the partials decay approximately exponentially in time and space.

(3) STARMA (l, m, g, p) processes display autocorrelations and partials which tail off as a mixture of exponential curves and damped sine waves. The autocorrelations exhibit this tailing off after the first $g-l$ and $p-m$ lags in space and time respectively, and the partials after the first $l-g$ lags in space and $m-p$ in time.

To illustrate these features Martin and Oeppen artificially constructed time–space data sets which conformed to the following first order processes:

(1) STAR process

$$y_{it} = 0.60 y_{i,t-1} + 0.24 L^1 y_{i,t-1} + \varepsilon_{it}.$$

(2) STMA process

$$y_{it} = \varepsilon_{it} - 0.50 \varepsilon_{i,t-1} - 0.25 L^1 \varepsilon_{i,t-1}.$$

(3) STARMA process

$$y_{it} = 0.60 y_{i,t-1} + 0.23 L^1 y_{i,t-1} + \varepsilon_{it} - 0.30 \varepsilon_{i,t-1} - 0.15 L^1 \varepsilon_{i,t-1}.$$

The features of the time–space autocorrelations and partial autocorrelations they obtained from application of the analysis described are given in Figure 16.3. Inspection of these results bears out the verbal description given above.

16.5 Parameter Variation over Time and Space

16.5.1 *Model modification*

Frequently, the time–space system being studied will contain very distinct temporal and areal 'regions'. That is, the structural interrelationships between sub-areas will vary from point to point and from time period to time period. The only really satisfactory way of forecasting for this kind of system is to allow the parameters of the model to vary from one temporal and areal 'region' to another, as well as from one variable to another. Cliff and Ord (1971, 1972) have outlined some models which may be used in this sort of situation. Suppose that we have $i = 1, 2, ..., n$ areas and $t = 1, 2, ..., T$ time periods. Cliff and Ord (1971) considered the model,

$$y_{it} = \beta_{1i,t} + \beta_{2i,t} x_{i,t} + \varepsilon_{it}, \quad i = 1, 2, ..., n; t = 1, 2, ..., T \quad (16.32)$$

where the $\{\beta_{1i,t}\}$ and the $\{\beta_{2i,t}\}$ are parameters, and the $\{\varepsilon_{it}\}$ are random disturbances. Again, the model is only explicative, and autoregressive and/or moving average components could be included.

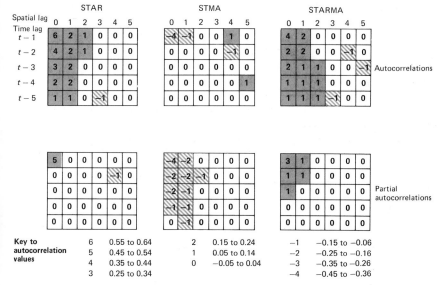

Figure 16.3 Space-time autocorrelations and partial autocorrelations for first order STAR, STMA and STARMA processes (based on Martin and Oeppen, 1975, pp. 107–8).

The usual regression model assumes that $\beta_{jit} = \beta_j$ for all i and $t, j = 1, 2$; i.e. the parameters are fixed over time and space, but differ from variable to variable. This model can be extended in three main ways (Cliff *et al.*, 1975, Section 10.5), namely:

(1) Let $\beta_{jit} = \beta_{jt}$ for all i (that is, assume that the parameters of the model are fixed across space in each time period, but that the parameters can vary from time period to time period). This yields the set of equations (Cliff and Ord, 1971, Section 3.2 and 3.5),

$$\begin{array}{cccc} \mathbf{y}_t & = & \mathbf{X}_t \cdot \boldsymbol{\beta}_t & + & \boldsymbol{\varepsilon}_t \\ (n \times 1) & & (n \times k)(k \times 1) & & (n \times 1) \end{array} \quad , \quad t = 1, 2, ..., T, \qquad (16.33)$$

for k regressor variables, or

$$\begin{pmatrix} \mathbf{y}_1 \\ \mathbf{y}_2 \\ \vdots \\ \mathbf{y}_T \end{pmatrix} = \begin{pmatrix} \mathbf{X}_1 & & \mathbf{0} \\ & \mathbf{X}_2 & \\ \mathbf{0} & & \mathbf{X}_T \end{pmatrix} \begin{pmatrix} \boldsymbol{\beta}_1 \\ \boldsymbol{\beta}_2 \\ \vdots \\ \boldsymbol{\beta}_T \end{pmatrix} + \begin{pmatrix} \boldsymbol{\varepsilon}_1 \\ \boldsymbol{\varepsilon}_2 \\ \vdots \\ \boldsymbol{\varepsilon}_T \end{pmatrix}. \qquad (16.34)$$

Model (16.34) is estimated *separately* for each time period, and the pattern of change over time in the parameter values obtained is studied. In particular, if ordinary least squares may properly be used, a test of $H_0: \beta_{jt} = \beta_j, t = 1, 2, ...,$ T, for the $j = 1, 2, ..., k$ regressor variables against $H_1: \beta_{jt} \neq \beta_j, t = 1, 2, ..., T$, is to evaluate the quantity $F = T(n-k)Q_3/k(T-1)Q_2$ as an F ratio with $k(T-1)$, $T(n-k)$ degrees of freedom. Here, $Q_3 = \sum_{t=1}^{T} (\hat{\beta}_t - \hat{\beta})'\mathbf{X}_t'\mathbf{X}_t(\hat{\beta}_t - \hat{\beta}) = \sum_{t=1}^{T} \mathbf{y}_t'\mathbf{X}_t(\hat{\beta}_t - \hat{\beta})$ and $Q_2 = \sum_{t=1}^{T} (\mathbf{y}_t - \mathbf{X}_t\hat{\beta}_t)'(\mathbf{y}_t - \mathbf{X}_t\hat{\beta}_t)$. In these equations, $\hat{\beta}_t = (\mathbf{X}_t'\mathbf{X}_t)^{-1}\mathbf{X}_t'\mathbf{y}_t$ and $\hat{\beta} = \left(\sum_{t=1}^{T} \mathbf{X}_t'\mathbf{X}_t\right)^{-1}\left(\sum_{t=1}^{T} \mathbf{X}_t'\mathbf{y}_t\right)$. $\hat{\beta}$ is a combined estimator (a kind of weighted average) over the T time periods, and we are using the F ratio to test whether the *individual* $\hat{\beta}_t, t = 1, 2, ..., T$, vary significantly from this 'average' value.

(2) Put $\beta_{jit} = \beta_{ji}$ (that is, fix the parameters through time for a given county, but allow the parameters to vary from county to county. The set of equations,

$$\begin{array}{cccc} \mathbf{y}_i = & \mathbf{X}_i & . \quad \beta_i & + \quad \varepsilon_i, \quad i = 1, 2, ..., n, \\ (T \times 1) & (T \times k) & (k \times 1) & (T \times 1) \end{array} \tag{16.35}$$

or

$$\begin{pmatrix} \mathbf{y}_1 \\ \mathbf{y}_2 \\ \vdots \\ \mathbf{y}_n \end{pmatrix} = \begin{pmatrix} \mathbf{X}_1 & & \\ & \mathbf{X}_2 & \mathbf{0} \\ & \mathbf{0} & \\ & & \mathbf{X}_n \end{pmatrix} \begin{pmatrix} \beta_1 \\ \beta_2 \\ \vdots \\ \beta_n \end{pmatrix} + \begin{pmatrix} \varepsilon_1 \\ \varepsilon_2 \\ \vdots \\ \varepsilon_n \end{pmatrix}, \tag{16.36}$$

are obtained. Estimate (16.35) separately for each county, and study the pattern of parameter changes over space. The F test described in (1) above may be used to test for significant parameter variation over space. The quantities, i and t, and n and T are simply interchanged throughout.

(3) To allow for parameter variations in both time and space, Cliff *et al.* (1975, Section 10.5) considered the decomposition,

$$\beta_{jit} = \beta_{j00} + \beta_{j0t} = \beta_{ji0}, \tag{16.37}$$

where the zero subscripts indicate no variation with respect to that dimension. This decomposition yields the model,

$$y_{it} = \sum_j \beta_{j00}x_{jit} + \sum_j \beta_{j0t}x_{jit} + \sum_j \beta_{ji0}x_{jit} + \varepsilon_{it}, \tag{16.38}$$

or

$$\mathbf{y}_t = \mathbf{X}_t'(\beta + \beta_{0t}) + \begin{pmatrix} \mathbf{x}_{1t}' & \beta_{10} \\ \vdots & \vdots \\ \mathbf{x}_{it}' & \beta_{i0} \\ \vdots & \vdots \\ \mathbf{x}_{nt}' & \beta_{n0} \end{pmatrix} + \varepsilon^{it}, \quad t = 1, 2, ..., T. \tag{16.39}$$

The lack of orthogonality between the components in the decomposition means that simple expressions for the sums of squares attributable to each component are not available. The analysis will proceed using regression methods as described in Kendall and Stuart (1966, Chapter 35).

The basic object of the various schemes outlined above is to identify in which dimension(s) (time, or space, or both) significant structural variations in the parameters of the forecasting model lie. These variations can then be modelled in order to provide estimates of the parameters in future time periods, and so furnish a basis for forecasting. Thus Cliff and Ord (1971, pp. 56–7) suggested that some exogenous variables, $\{Z_r\}$, say, might underlie fluctuations in the parameters, and they proposed the model for the parameters,

$$\beta_{jt} = \beta_j + \beta_{j0t} = \sum_r \gamma_r z_{jtr}, \tag{16.40}$$

where they assumed that only changes over time in the parameters had been detected. They show that the unknown parameters $\{\gamma_r\}$ can be estimated by Aitken's generalized least squares from the equations

$$\hat{\beta}_{jt} = \sum_r \gamma_r z_{jtr} + e_{jt}, \tag{16.41}$$

where e_{jt} is an error term whose properties are determined by the original formulation of the model.

16.5.2 Regional applications of modified models

As an example, we describe the work of Cliff and Ord (1971) who took data giving the *per caput* level of car ownership in each of the 26 counties of Eire, 1953–63. The simple STAR model,

$$y_{it} = a_t y_{i,t-1} + \varepsilon_{it}, \quad t = 1, 2, \ldots, T; i = 1, 2, \ldots, n, \tag{16.42}$$

may be fitted by ordinary least squares (OLS) to the data for each year, where the estimated value of a_t is given by

$$\hat{a}_t = \frac{\sum_i y_{it} y_{i,t-1}}{\sum_i (y_{i,t-1})^2}. \tag{16.43}$$

An approximate F-test of the hypothesis, $H_0: a_t = a$ against $H_1: a_t$ not all equal, was carried out to establish that the parameters of the model did vary significantly from one time period to another. Since levels of car sales tend, in Western nations, to reflect the general economic prosperity of a country, the model

$$\hat{a}_t = \alpha_0 + \alpha_1 \hat{a}_{t-1} + \alpha_2 I_{t-2}, \quad t = 1, 2, \ldots, T, \tag{16.44}$$

may be used to account for variations in the parameters $\{\hat{a}_t\}$; here I_t denotes the excess of imports (CIF) over exports (FOB). Fitting the model using generalized least squares yields the equation,

$$\hat{a}_t = 0.93955 + 0.234576\hat{a}_{t-1} - 0.154605 I_{t-2}, \tag{16.45}$$

enabling forecasts of the future values of the $\{\hat{a}_t\}$ to be made. These are then substituted into (16.42) to produce predictions of the levels of car ownership.

Recall from Section 12.3.3 that the Model II Analysis of Variance may be used to decompose the variation in a time–space variable into orthogonal time effects (τ say), space effects (σ say), and time–space interaction effects (θ say), using the model

$$E(Y_{it}) = \mu + \sigma_i + \tau_t + \theta_{it}, \quad i = 1, 2, ..., n; \ t = 1, 2, ..., T. \quad (16.46)$$

Here μ is the overall mean. Alternatively, treatment of equation (16.46) under the Model I Analysis of Variance provides a further way of allowing parameter variation in forecasting. Following Cliff and Ord (1972), the estimates of the unknown quantities in (16.46) are, for the Model I Analysis of Variance,

$$\hat{\sigma}_i = \bar{y}_{t0} - \bar{y}_{00}$$

$$\hat{\tau}_t = \bar{y}_{0t} - \bar{y}_{00} \quad (16.47)$$

and

$$\hat{\theta}_{it} = y_{it} - \bar{y}_{t0} - \bar{y}_{0t} + \bar{y}_{00},$$

where

$$T\bar{y}_{t0} = \sum_{t=1}^{T} y_{it}, \ n\bar{y}_{0t} = \sum_{i=1}^{n} y_{it}$$

and

$$nT\bar{y}_{00} = \sum_{i=1}^{n} \sum_{t=1}^{T} y_{it}.$$

The important feature of the quantities $\{\hat{\sigma}_i\}$, $\{\hat{\tau}_t\}$ and $\{\hat{\theta}_{it}\}$ is that regression equations may be used to model the variability of each set of parameters separately, and the equations may be estimated by ordinary least squares.

To illustrate the use of this model in forecasting, Cliff and Ord (1972) examined data giving the percentage of students who elected to stay on at school for at least one year beyond the statutory minimum school leaving age of (then) 15 years. The data were collected for the standard regions of the UK (excluding Northern Ireland), 1964–68. Denote the variate values by y_{it}. Since y_{it} has the natural range, (0–100), the transformation,

$$y_{it}^* = \log_e[y_{it}/(100.0 - y_{it})], \quad (16.48)$$

was applied (Wrigley, 1973). The $\{\sigma_i\}$, $\{\tau_t\}$ and $\{\theta_{it}\}$ were estimated. Models of the form

$$\hat{\sigma}_i = \sum_r \gamma_r x_{ri} + e_i, \quad (16.49)$$

$$\hat{\tau}_t = \sum_r \gamma_r' xx_{rt} + e_t, \quad (16.50)$$

and

$$\hat{\theta}_{it} = \sum_r \gamma_r'' z_{rit}' + e_{it} \quad (16.51)$$

may be fitted by OLS to the parameters [cf. equation (16.41)]. In these equations, the $\{x_{ri}\}$, $\{xx_{rt}\}$ and $\{z_{rit}'\}$ are (not necessarily different) regressor variables, and the $\{\gamma_r\}$, $\{\gamma_r'\}$ and $\{\gamma_r''\}$ are to be estimated. In addition, the $\{x_{ri}\}$ and $\{xx_{rt}\}$ must be adjusted to have zero means across space and time respectively, while z_{rit}' is given by the transformation,

$$z_{rit}' = z_{rit} - \bar{z}_{r0t} - \bar{z}_{ri0} + \bar{z}_{r00} \tag{16.52}$$

where z is the original regressor variable (see Cliff *et al.*, 1975, Section 10.6).

In the school leaver example, Cliff and Ord fitted the linear time trend,

$$\hat{\tau}_t = \gamma'(t - \bar{t}), \tag{16.53}$$

to the $\{\hat{\tau}_t\}$, while the model

$$\hat{\theta}_{it} = \gamma_i''(t - \bar{t}), \tag{16.54}$$

was fitted to each region, i, to look for different trends between regions. The authors were unable to find a significant regression with which to model the $\{\hat{\sigma}_i\}$. Forecasts of the percentage of students staying on past 15 years of age in each of the standard regions in 1969 and 1970 were made from the model

$$y_{it}^* = \hat{\alpha}_i + \hat{\tau}_t + \hat{\theta}_{it}, \tag{16.55}$$

where $\hat{\tau}_t = \hat{\gamma}'(t - \bar{t})$ and $\hat{\theta}_{it} = \hat{\gamma}_i''(t - \bar{t})$. A simpler procedure for modelling changes in τ would have been to have used an adaptive form such as $\tau_t = \alpha + \beta\tau_{t-1}$.

16.6 Purely Spatial Forecasting*

If the data set is purely cross-sectional, forecasting is equivalent to interpolation. A common way of estimating the missing observations in a spatial data matrix is by trend surface analysis (see Section 12.2), while the spatial weighted moving average of equation (16.15) could also be used. Curry (1971) has extended this simple sort of spatial moving average to produce cascaded moving averages (cf. Section 12.3). Finally, we have already considered in Section 11.4.2 a purely spatial autoregressive (SAR) model which can be used for interpolation purposes.

Cliff and Ord (1975b, Section 6.3.1) have combined these basic approaches into a general spatial autoregressive, moving average model with additional regression components (SARMAR) with the equation,

$$\mathbf{y} = \underset{\substack{| \\ \text{autoregressive} \\ \text{component}}}{\rho\mathbf{W}\mathbf{y}} + \underset{\substack{| \\ \text{additional} \\ \text{regression} \\ \text{component}}}{\mathbf{X}\boldsymbol{\beta}} + \boldsymbol{\varepsilon} + \underset{\substack{| \\ \text{moving average} \\ \text{component}}}{\gamma\mathbf{A}\boldsymbol{\varepsilon},} \tag{16.56}$$

where $\mathbf{y}$ is a vector of observations corresponding to the n areas or locations, $\mathbf{W}$ and $\mathbf{A}$ represent matrices of known structural weights, and $\mathbf{X}$ is a matrix of known regressor variables; ρ, $\boldsymbol{\beta}$ and γ are unknown parameters. Note that the temporal subscripting has been dropped in equation (16.56), but in all other respects this purely spatial or cross-sectional model is structurally equivalent to the time–space model of equation (16.18).

When $\gamma = 0$, model (16.56) reduces to an autoregressive form. Recall from Section (11.4.2) that this model should not be estimated by OLS since these estimators are inconsistent. From Ord (1975) and Cliff and Ord (1975b, Section 6.3.1), if ε is $N(0, \sigma^2 \mathbf{I})$, the ML estimators are

$$\hat{\boldsymbol{\beta}} = (\mathbf{X}'\mathbf{X})^{-1}\mathbf{X}'\hat{\mathbf{z}}, \tag{16.57}$$

$$\hat{\sigma}^2 = \hat{\mathbf{z}}'\mathbf{M}\mathbf{z}/n, \tag{16.58}$$

and that value of ρ, $\hat{\rho}$ say, which minimizes

$$\hat{\sigma}^n |\mathbf{I} - \rho\mathbf{W}|^{-1}, \tag{16.59}$$

where $\hat{\mathbf{z}} = (\mathbf{I} - \hat{\rho}\mathbf{W})\mathbf{y}$ and $\mathbf{M} = \mathbf{I} - \mathbf{X}(\mathbf{X}'\mathbf{X})^{-1}\mathbf{X}'$. The moving average model is obtained from (16.56) by putting $\boldsymbol{\beta} = \rho = 0$. This model has some intuitive appeal since it can be generated by the averaging of local effects, the $\{\varepsilon_j\}$. Full details of computational schemes which yield the ML estimators for spatial moving average and mixed autoregressive moving average models are given in Ord (1975). A summary account appears in the appendix to Cliff and Ord (1975b).

16.7 Conclusions

In this chapter we have considered ways of adapting some time series forecasting models to the time–space and purely spatial (interpolation) forecasting situations. The models proposed contain autoregressive, moving average and multivariate regression components. The identification and estimation of these models has been discussed. Frequently the time–space system is so varied that we need to allow the parameters of the models to vary over time and/or space if we are adequately to capture the main structural features of the system under analysis. Ways of admitting of such variation have been outlined. For a lengthy application of the sorts of methods described in this chapter, see Bennett (1975b, c, d, e). Bennett attempts to identify the space–time autocorrelation structure among sub-areas in the Northwest region of England for unemployment and employment levels, population and migration patterns, and industrial movement. Models of the sub-area values of these variates are proposed and fitted; the models contain autoregressive components, space–time dependencies and exogenous variables. Dynamic parameter variation is allowed using Kalman filters.

A question of some interest is the following: over time, do the space–time models discussed in Sections 16.2–16.5 converge in some sense to the purely spatial models of Section 16.6; that is, do the space–time models approach some sort of spatial equilibrium. The answer to this question is in general, no; mathematical details are given in Besag (1974), Ord (1974) and Cliff and Ord (1975b, Section 6.1). The models thus stand in contrast to the entropy and linear programming methods of Section 2.5 and Chapter 15, where notions of equilibrium are important.

Postscript

Unfinished buildings are sometimes left with a blank, windowless wall from which another wing may be built at some future stage. As we complete the second edition of this book, we are conscious that our own building task is unfinished. So far as regional applications are concerned, there are two major areas where locational analysis in human geography interfaces with other buildings, themselves only partly complete.

One such interface is towards planning at the urban and regional level. Despite some disappointment with the performance of many of the 'big' planning models developed in the 1960s, the scope for integrating geographical concepts into Lowry-type models remains considerable. Wilson (1974) has produced the first really substantive work on the ways in which demographic, economic, transport, and spatial distribution components can begin to build into comprehensive regional planning models. Work at Leeds, at the Martin Centre at Cambridge, and at the Batelle Institute show some of the directions in which this type of work may lead. Renewed interest in environmental issues has underlined the urban bias in much human geography of the last two decades. Questions raised by the locational organization of the rural land wild landscapes, are coming to the fore and we would expect to see many of the models developed in this book being used and extended in this context. Already the evaluation of recreational pressures and forecasting of future demands for non-urban land play a significant part in the application of spatial interaction models.

A second area of application lies in cross-cultural studies. We noted in our opening chapter the bias towards the contemporary Western world in this volume. As more research findings from non-Western societies become available, we would hope to see a progressive widening of the substantive findings on which this book is based. Nor need such widening be simply in the spatial domain. Increasingly, colleagues in archaeology and prehistory are using locational concepts in the study of early spatial organization. Rich areas of cooperation between these students of the past and human geographers are now opening up to parallel those which have long existed with physical geography in the study of early environments. In the longer run, we would hope to see fields that have been separately labelled as 'historical geography' integrated more closely into a broader and less current time-bound human geography.

So far, we have limited our comments to extending the kinds of macrogeographic work reported here to other, natural areas of application. But, as our preface indicates, some of the most important and interesting work in human geography is going on in the better specification of behavioural assumptions and in such areas of microgeography as space–time budgets, cognitive mapping, in decision-making theory, all areas unreported in this book. If we retain our architectural analogy, then this work might be regarded as occupying another separate building at the present time. If the experience of economics is any guide, the task of linking the micro and macro models will prove difficult. We would hope to explore further in any revised volume how far corridors may be opened between the two buildings.

Appendix

Appendix

1 Glossary of notation

A large amount of notation has been used in this book. In this glossary, we have attempted to summarize and define the main terms which we have used in a consistent way throughout the book. The usual statistical/mathematical conventions have been employed wherever possible, such as Greek letters for population quantities, Roman letters for their sample equivalents, upper case Roman letters for variates, and lower case Roman letters for variate values.

Mathematical Symbols

Δ, ∇	difference operators
$\sum_{(2)}$	$\displaystyle\sum_{\substack{i=1 \\ i \neq j}}^{n} \sum_{j=1}^{n}$
$\sum_{(3)}$	$\displaystyle\sum_{\substack{i=1 \\ i \neq j \neq k}}^{n} \sum_{j=1}^{n} \sum_{k=1}^{n}$
$\rightarrow$	approaches, goes to
$\hat{}$	denotes the estimated value of some parameter
$\check{}$	throughout Chapter 16, denotes *spatial* averaging of a set of variate values
$\tilde{}$	throughout Chapter 16, denotes *temporal* averaging of a set of variate values
$\bar{}$	the mean of some set of variate values
$\cup$	the union of two sets
$\cap$	the intersection of two sets

Notation and important definitions

A, a	area of a sub-region.
α	the size of a test; probability of a Type I error; the probability of a rejecting H_0 when it is true.

b_1	the sample coefficients of skewness, m_3^2/m_2^3. m_j is the jth central moment about the sample mean.
b_2	the sample coefficient of kurtosis, m_4/m_2^2. m_j is the jth central moment about the sample mean.
$\{\beta\}, \{b\}$	the parameters of a regression model.
$\{\hat{\beta}\}, \{\hat{b}\}$	ordinary least squares estimators of the regression coefficients, $\{\beta\}$ or $\{b\}$, respectively.
β_{ij}	regression coefficient for the term $x_1^i x_2^j$ in trend surface analysis.
BB	the weighted number of black–black links in a two colour (black and white) choropleth map. Defined in equation (11.5).
BLUE estimators	the best linear unbiased estimators of the parameters of a model.
BW	the weighted number of black–white links in a two colour (black and white) choropleth map. Defined in equation (11.6).
c	the spatial autocorrelation test statistic defined in equation (11.8).
c_{ij}	(per unit) movement cost between locations i and j.
$C(\omega)$	the coherence between two time series at the frequency ω defined in equation (12.27).
γ	usually a weighting constant, $0 \leqslant \gamma \leqslant 1$.
γ_2	the ratio, κ_4/κ_2^2, proposed as a measure of kurtosis. Is equal to zero for a normal distribution. κ_i is the ith cumulant.
Γ	the gamma function.
$\text{corr}(x_1, x_2)$	the sample correlation between the observations x_{1i}, $x_{2i}, i = 1, 2, ..., n$, on the random variables X_1, X_2.
d_0	mean distance between first nearest neighbours in nearest neighbour analysis.
d_{ij}	generally, euclidean distance between two points i and j.
D	generalized measure of 'distance' or similarity between two points in N-space defined in equation (14.8).
D_1	nearest neighbour statistic defined in equation (13.9).
D_2	nearest neighbour statistic defined in equation (13.11).
D_j	size (mass) of destination centre j in Chapter 2; the demand for a good by centre j in Chapter 15.
Di	the index of dispersion given by m_2/m_1'.
e_i	the ith calculated or sample residual in a regression model.
ε_i	the ith population random disturbance term.
$E(\ )$	expectation operator.
$F, F\text{-test}$	a widely employed test in analysis of variance based upon the ratio of two independent estimators of variance. The test statistic follows the F distribution developed by Fisher and Snedecor.

$f(X)$	some function, f, of X.
$f_1(\mathbf{r}, t + dt)$	the expected number of adopters of an innovation at time $t + dt$ in the small element of area, $d\mathbf{r}$.
G	coefficient of association defined in equation (9.3).
$g_{(r)}$	the observed share size on a variable of the rth largest region in a study area; $g_{(1)}$ is the observed share size of the smallest region.
GROs	General Register Office areas which form the reporting units for epidemiological data in England and Wales.
H	'cost' function to be minimized in locating points of production in Weberian and von Thünen analysis.
H_0	the null hypothesis or hypothesis of no significant difference.
H_1	the alternative hypothesis or research hypothesis accepted when H_0 is rejected.
I	the spatial autocorrelation test statistic defined in equation (11.7).
I_t	the number of adopters (infectives) in a population at time t in chain binomial models.
$IN(\mu, \sigma^2)$	independently normally distributed with mean μ and variance σ^2.
I-S index	used to clasify discrete frequency distributions in Sections 9.7.2 and 13.3.3.
$j \in J$	the set of j counties contiguous to county i.
κ_i	the ith cumulant of a frequency distribution. Defined in terms of the moments of a frequency distribution.
kurtosis	a term used to describe the extent to which a unimodal frequency distribution is 'peaked'.
L^g	spatial (or temporal) lag operator for the typical spatial lag g. For $g = 0$, the reduced form, L, is usually used.
L- and S-mosaics	the pattern of sub-areas formed when a study area is randomly split into sub-units or regions.
Likelihood ratio test	A test of a hypothesis, H_0, against an alternative, H_1, based on the ratio of two likelihood functions, one derived from each of H_0 and H_1.
m_j, m_j'	sample moments corresponding to the population moments μ_j, μ_j' respectively.
μ_j	the jth moment of a variate about the mean, μ; jth central moment.
μ_j'	the jth moment of a variate about the origin; jth crude moment.
μ, μ_1'	the expected, mean or average value; the first moment of a variate.
MAD	minimum absolute derivations criterion (cf. OLS).
MIF	mean information field in Hägerstrand models.
ML estimator	maximum likelihood estimator.
MS	mean square (as in analysis of variance).
MST	minimal spanning tree.

MST*	maximal spanning tree.
N, n	the total number of objects or items being studied.
n_1, n_2	the number of black and white counties respectively in a black and white (two colour) choropleth map.
$n^{(j)}$	$n(n-1) \ldots (n-j+1)$.
$\binom{n}{k}$	the binomial coefficient; $n!/\{k!(n-k)!\}$.
N	as a subscript, the normality assumption defined in Section 11.3.2.
$N(\mu, \sigma^2)$	normally distributed with mean, μ, and variance, σ^2.
O_i	size (e.g. population mass) of origin centre i.
o_{ij}	opportunity cost of shipping a good from supplier i to market j.
OLS estimator	ordinary least squares estimator.
P	(without subscript) *total* population of a country.
P_i, p_i	population of or at location i.
$P(A)$	the probability of the typical event, A, occurring.
Power of a test	$1-P$ (Type II error), the probability of rejecting H_0 when H_1 is true (cf. α).
r, r_{12}	the sample correlation between the observations $x_{1i}, x_{2i}, i = 1, 2, ..., n$, on the random variables, X_1 and X_2.
$r_{12.3}$	the sample partial correlation between the observations $x_{1i}, x_{2i}, i = 1, 2, ..., n$, on the random variables X_1 and X_2 after allowing for the effect of X_3.
r_{gjsk}	the sample correlation between (1) variate values at spatial lag g and temporal lag j from a reference zone and (2) those values at spatial lag s and temporal lag k from the reference zone.
$\mathbf{R}$	a matrix of correlation coefficients.
R	as a subscript, the randomization assumption defined in Section 11.3.2.
$R(\omega)$	the gain between two time series at the frequency ω defined in equation (12.28).
$\rho_{12}\ \rho_{12.3}$	the population analogues of r_{12} and $r_{12.3}$ respectively.
ρ	generally the autocorrelation parameter in spatial and temporal autocorrelation schemes.
s	the sample standard deviation.
s^2	the sample variance, second central moment of the $\{x_i\}$.
σ^2	the variance of X, second moment of X.
$s(i, j)$	the shortest path between two nodes, i and j, in a network.
$\mathbf{S}$	shortest path matrix.
S_1	$= \frac{1}{2}\sum_{(2)} (w_{ij}+w_{ji})^2.$
S_2	$= \sum_{i=1}^{n} (w_{i.}+w_{.i})^2.$
S_i	in Chapter 15, the supply capacity of supplier i.

S_t	the number of susceptibles (potential adopters) in a population at time t in chain binomial models.
$S_{(1)}, S_{(2)}, S_{(3)}, S_{(4)}$	shape indices defined in equations (9.5)–(9.8).
S-I index	used to classify discrete frequency distributions in Section 9.7.2 and 13.3.3.
SS	sum of squares (as in analysis of variance).
STAR	space–time autoregressive model.
STARIMAR	space–time autoregressive integrated moving average model with additional regression components.
STARMA	space–time autoregressive moving average model.
STARR	space–time autoregressive model with additional regression components.
STIMA	space–time integrated moving average model.
STMA	space–time moving average model.
t	as a subscript, generally denotes the typical time period in the time series being analysed.
T	generally, the total number of time periods being studied.
t-test	a statistical test based upon Student's t distribution used to examine hypotheses about sample means.
T_{ij}	movement level (e.g. trips, migration) between two centres i and j.
torus	the three dimensional shape which results when the edges of a plane are joined together so that all end points (boundaries) are eliminated and the surface is continuous. The resulting object resembles a doughnut.
Type I error	the error committed if, as a result of a statistical test, H_0 is rejected when it is true.
Type II error	the error committed if, as a result of a statistical test, H_0 is not rejected when it is false.
u_i	in Chapter 15, the location rent (shadow price) for supplier i of a good.
V_i	population potential of a centre i.
v_j	in Chapter 15, the location rent (shadow price) for market j on a good.
$\text{var}(X)$	the variance of X, second moment of X.
w_{ij}	pre-determined structural weight attached to the link between i and j (assumed to be non-negative).
$w_{.i}$	$\displaystyle\sum_{j=1}^{n} w_{ji}$.
$w_{i.}$	$\displaystyle\sum_{j=1}^{n} w_{ij}$.
W	$\sum_{(2)} w_{ij}$, the sum of the non-negative weights, $\{w_{ij}\}$.
$\mathbf{W}$	the weights matrix with typical element, w_{ij}.
$W(\{T_{ij}\})$	number of microstates making up the macrostate trip distribution pattern, $\{T_{ij}\}$; the entropy function.

X, X_i and Y, Y_i	random variables.
x, x_i	particular value taken on by X or X_i.
$\bar{x}$	the average or mean of the set of x values.
X^2	the test statistic, $X^2 = \sum_{i=1}^{k} \dfrac{(O_i - E_i)^2}{E_i}$, which is approximately distributed as χ^2. Here O_i is the observed frequency in the ith cell and E_i is the expected frequency in that cell under H_0.
χ^2	the chi-squared distribution.
$x(s, t)$	the proportion of potential adopters in a population at location s and time t in epidemic models.
$y(s, t)$	the proportion of adopters in a population at location s and time t in epidemic models.
z_i	either $z_i = x_i - \bar{x}$, or the standard score $z_i = (x_i - \bar{x})/s(x)$.
$z(s, t)$	the proportion of adopters in a population at location s and time t who have ceased to pass on information about an innovation.

2 Statistical tables

This small selection of tables covers only the main statistical methods used in the book. They are reproduced with permission from R. A. Fisher and F. Yates, *Statistical tables for biological, agricultural and medical research* (Oliver and Boyd, Edinburgh) and from R. S. Burington *Handbook of mathematical tables and formulas* (McGraw-Hill, New York) where fuller tables may be found. Numbers given beneath each of the tables which follow indicate sections of the book where they may prove helpful.

Table A1   Areas under the normal curve

Fractional parts of the total area (10,000) under the normal curve, corresponding to distances between the mean and ordinates which are z standard deviation units from the mean.

z	.00	.01	.02	.03	.04	.05	.06	.07	.08	.09
0.0	0000	0040	0080	0120	0159	0199	0239	0279	0319	0359
0.1	0398	0438	0478	0517	0557	0596	0636	0675	0714	0753
0.2	0793	0832	0871	0910	0948	0987	1026	1064	1103	1141
0.3	1179	1217	1255	1293	1331	1368	1406	1443	1480	1517
0.4	1554	1591	1628	1664	1700	1736	1772	1808	1844	1879
0.5	1915	1950	1985	2019	2054	2088	2123	2157	2190	2224
0.6	2257	2291	2324	2357	2389	2422	2454	2486	2518	2549
0.7	2580	2612	2642	2673	2704	2734	2764	2794	2823	2852
0.8	2881	2910	2939	2967	2995	3023	3051	3078	3106	3133
0.9	3159	3186	3212	3238	3264	3289	3315	3340	3365	3389
1.0	3413	3438	3461	3485	3508	3531	3554	3577	3599	3621
1.1	3643	3665	3686	3718	3729	3749	3770	3790	3810	3830
1.2	3849	3869	3888	3907	3925	3944	3962	3980	3997	4015
1.3	4032	4049	4066	4083	4099	4115	4131	4147	4162	4177
1.4	4192	4207	4222	4236	4251	4265	4279	4292	4306	4319
1.5	4332	4345	4357	4370	4382	4394	4406	4418	4430	4441
1.6	4452	4463	4474	4485	4495	4505	4515	4525	4535	4545
1.7	4554	4564	4573	4582	4591	4599	4608	4616	4625	4633
1.8	4641	4649	4656	4664	4671	4678	4686	4693	4699	4706
1.9	4713	4719	4726	4732	4738	4744	4750	4758	4762	4767
2.0	4773	4778	4783	4788	4793	4798	4803	4808	4812	4817
2.1	4821	4826	4830	4834	4838	4842	4846	4850	4854	4857
2.2	4861	4865	4868	4871	4875	4878	4881	4884	4887	4890
2.3	4893	4896	4898	4901	4904	4906	4909	4911	4913	4916
2.4	4918	4920	4922	4925	4927	4929	4931	4932	4934	4936
2.5	4938	4940	4941	4943	4945	4946	4948	4949	4951	4952
2.6	4953	4955	4956	4957	4959	4960	4961	4962	4963	4964
2.7	4965	4966	4967	4968	4969	4970	4971	4972	4973	4974
2.8	4974	4975	4976	4977	4977	4978	4979	4980	4980	4981
2.9	4981	4982	4983	4984	4984	4984	4985	4985	4986	4986
3.0	4986.5	4987	4987	4988	4988	4988	4989	4989	4989	4990
3.1	4990.0	4991	4991	4991	4992	4992	4992	4992	4993	4993
3.2	4993.129									
3.3	4995.166									
3.4	4996.631									
3.5	4997.674									
3.6	4998.409									
3.7	4998.922									
3.8	4999.277									
3.9	4999.519									
4.0	4999.683									
4.5	4999.966									
5.0	4999.997133									

See especially Sections 4.5.2, 8.3.1 and 9.5.1 for applications.

Table A2   Student's *t* distribution.

Degrees of freedom (*df*)	Level of significance for one tailed test					
	.10	.05	.025	.01	.005	.0005
	Level of significance for two tailed test					
	.20	.10	.05	.02	.01	.001
1	3.078	6.314	12.706	31.821	63.657	636.619
2	1.886	2.920	4.303	6.965	9.925	31.598
3	1.638	2.353	3.182	4.541	5.841	12.941
4	1.533	2.132	2.776	3.747	4.604	8.610
5	1.476	2.015	2.571	3.365	4.032	6.859
6	1.440	1.943	2.447	3.143	3.707	5.959
7	1.415	1.895	2.365	2.998	3.499	5.405
8	1.397	1.860	2.306	2.896	3.355	5.041
9	1.383	1.833	2.262	2.821	3.250	4.781
10	1.372	1.812	2.228	2.764	3.169	4.587
11	1.363	1.796	2.201	2.718	3.106	4.437
12	1.356	1.782	2.179	2.681	3.055	4.318
13	1.350	1.771	2.160	2.650	3.012	4.221
14	1.345	1.761	2.145	2.624	2.977	4.140
15	1.341	1.753	2.131	2.602	2.947	4.073
16	1.337	1.746	2.120	2.583	2.921	4.015
17	1.333	1.740	2.110	2.567	2.898	3.965
18	1.330	1.734	2.101	2.552	2.878	3.922
19	1.328	1.729	2.093	2.539	2.861	3.883
20	1.325	1.725	2.086	2.528	2.845	3.850
21	1.323	1.721	2.080	2.518	2.831	3.819
22	1.321	1.717	2.074	2.508	2.819	3.792
23	1.319	1.714	2.069	2.500	2.807	3.767
24	1.318	1.711	2.064	2.492	2.797	3.745
25	1.316	1.708	2.060	2.485	2.787	3.725
26	1.315	1.706	2.056	2.479	2.779	3.707
27	1.314	1.703	2.052	2.473	2.771	3.690
28	1.313	1.701	2.048	2.467	2.763	3.674
29	1.311	1.699	2.045	2.462	2.756	3.659
30	1.310	1.697	2.042	2.457	2.750	3.646
40	1.303	1.684	2.021	2.423	2.704	3.551
60	1.296	1.671	2.000	2.390	2.660	3.460
120	1.289	1.658	1.980	2.358	2.617	3.373
∞	1.282	1.645	1.960	2.326	2.576	3.291

See especially Sections 10.2 and 11.6 for applications.

Table A3   Distribution of χ^2.

Probability

df	.99	.98	.95	.90	.80	.70	.50	.30	.20	.10	.05	.02	.01	.001
1	$.0^3157$	$.0^3628$	.00393	.0158	.0642	.148	.455	1.074	1.642	2.706	3.841	5.412	6.635	10.827
2	.0201	.0404	.103	.211	.446	.713	1.386	2.408	3.219	4.605	5.991	7.824	9.210	13.815
3	.115	.185	.352	.584	1.005	1.424	2.366	3.665	4.642	6.251	7.815	9.837	11.341	16.268
4	.297	.429	.711	1.064	1.649	2.195	3.357	4.878	5.989	7.779	9.488	11.668	13.277	18.465
5	.554	.752	1.145	1.610	2.343	3.000	4.351	6.064	7.289	9.236	11.070	13.388	15.086	20.517
6	.872	1.134	1.635	2.204	3.070	3.828	5.348	7.231	8.558	10.645	12.592	15.033	16.812	22.457
7	1.239	1.564	2.167	2.833	3.822	4.671	6.346	8.383	9.803	12.017	14.067	16.622	18.475	24.322
8	1.646	2.032	2.733	3.490	4.594	5.527	7.344	9.524	11.030	13.362	15.507	18.168	20.000	26.125
9	2.088	2.532	3.325	4.168	5.380	6.393	8.343	10.656	12.242	14.684	16.919	19.679	21.666	27.877
10	2.558	3.059	3.940	4.865	6.179	7.267	9.342	11.781	13.442	15.987	18.307	21.161	23.209	29.588
11	3.053	3.609	4.575	5.578	6.989	8.148	10.341	12.899	14.361	17.275	19.675	22.618	24.725	31.264
12	3.571	4.178	5.226	6.304	7.807	9.034	11.340	14.011	15.812	18.549	21.026	24.054	26.217	32.909
13	4.107	4.765	5.892	7.042	8.634	9.926	12.340	15.119	16.985	19.812	22.362	25.472	27.688	34.528
14	4.660	5.368	6.571	7.790	9.467	10.821	13.339	16.222	18.151	21.064	23.685	26.873	29.141	36.123
15	5.229	5.985	7.261	8.547	10.307	11.721	14.339	17.322	19.311	22.307	24.996	28.259	30.578	37.697
16	5.812	6.614	7.962	9.312	11.152	12.624	15.338	18.418	20.465	23.542	26.296	29.633	32.00	39.252
17	6.408	7.255	8.672	10.085	12.002	13.531	16.338	19.511	21.615	24.769	27.587	30.995	33.409	40.790
18	7.015	7.906	9.390	10.865	12.857	14.440	17.338	20.601	22.760	25.989	28.869	32.346	34.805	42.312
19	7.633	8.567	10.117	11.651	13.716	15.352	18.338	21.689	23.900	27.204	30.144	33.687	36.191	43.820
20	8.260	9.237	10.851	12.443	14.578	16.266	19.337	22.775	25.038	28.412	31.410	35.020	37.566	45.315
21	8.897	9.915	11.591	13.240	15.445	17.182	20.337	23.858	26.171	29.615	32.671	36.343	38.932	46.797
22	9.542	10.600	12.338	14.041	16.314	18.101	21.337	24.939	27.301	30.813	33.924	37.659	40.289	48.268
23	10.196	11.293	13.091	14.848	17.187	19.021	22.337	26.018	28.429	32.007	35.172	38.968	41.638	49.728
24	10.856	11.992	13.848	15.659	18.062	19.943	23.337	27.096	29.553	33.196	36.415	40.270	42.930	51.179
25	11.524	12.697	14.611	16.473	18.940	20.867	24.337	28.172	30.675	34.382	37.652	41.566	44.314	52.620
26	12.198	13.409	15.379	17.292	19.820	21.792	25.336	29.246	31.795	35.563	38.885	42.856	45.642	54.052
27	12.879	14.125	16.151	18.114	20.703	22.719	26.336	30.319	32.912	36.741	40.113	44.140	46.963	55.476
28	13.565	14.847	16.928	18.939	21.588	23.647	27.336	31.391	34.027	37.916	41.337	45.419	48.278	56.893
29	14.256	15.574	17.708	19.768	22.475	24.577	28.336	32.461	35.139	39.087	42.557	46.693	49.588	58.302
30	14.953	16.306	18.493	20.599	23.364	25.508	29.336	33.530	36.250	40.256	43.773	47.962	50.892	59.703

For larger values of *df*, the expression $\sqrt{2\chi^3} - \sqrt{2df - 1}$ may be created as a normal deviate with mean zero and unit variance, remembering that the probability for χ^2 corresponds with that of a single tail of the normal curve.

See especially Sections 13.2.1 and 14.4.1 for applications.

Table A4   Distribution of *F*.

$\alpha = .05$

v_2 \ v_1	1	2	3	4	5	6	8	12	24	∞
1	161.4	199.5	215.7	224.6	230.2	234.0	238.9	243.9	249.0	254.3
2	18.51	19.00	19.16	19.25	19.30	19.33	19.37	19.41	19.45	19.50
3	10.13	9.55	9.28	9.12	9.01	8.94	8.84	8.74	8.64	8.53
4	7.71	6.94	6.59	6.39	6.26	6.16	6.04	5.91	5.77	5.63
5	6.61	5.79	5.41	5.19	5.05	4.95	4.82	4.68	4.53	4.36
6	5.99	5.14	4.76	4.53	4.39	4.28	4.15	4.00	3.84	3.67
7	5.59	4.74	4.35	4.12	3.97	3.87	3.73	3.57	3.41	3.23
8	5.32	4.46	4.07	3.84	3.69	3.58	3.44	3.28	3.12	2.93
9	5.12	4.26	3.86	3.63	3.48	3.37	3.23	3.07	2.90	2.71
10	4.96	4.10	3.71	3.48	3.33	3.22	3.07	2.91	2.74	2.54
11	4.84	3.98	3.59	3.36	3.20	3.09	2.95	2.79	2.61	2.40
12	4.75	3.88	3.49	3.26	3.11	3.00	2.85	2.69	2.50	2.30
13	4.67	3.80	3.41	3.18	3.02	2.92	2.77	2.60	2.42	2.21
14	4.60	3.74	3.34	3.11	2.96	2.85	2.70	2.53	2.35	2.13
15	4.54	3.68	3.29	3.06	2.90	2.79	2.64	2.48	2.29	2.07
16	4.49	3.63	3.24	3.01	2.85	2.74	2.59	2.42	2.24	2.01
17	4.45	3.59	3.20	2.96	2.81	2.70	2.55	2.38	2.19	1.96
18	4.41	3.55	3.16	2.93	2.77	2.66	2.51	2.34	2.15	1.92
19	4.38	3.52	3.13	2.90	2.74	2.63	2.48	2.31	2.11	1.88
20	4.35	3.49	3.10	2.87	2.71	2.60	2.45	2.28	2.08	1.84
21	4.32	3.47	3.07	2.84	2.68	2.57	2.42	2.25	2.05	1.81
22	4.30	3.44	3.05	2.82	2.66	2.55	2.40	2.23	2.03	1.78
23	4.28	3.42	3.03	2.80	2.64	2.53	2.38	2.20	2.00	1.76
24	4.26	3.40	3.01	2.78	2.62	2.51	2.36	2.18	1.98	1.73
25	4.24	3.38	2.99	2.76	2.60	2.49	2.34	2.16	1.96	1.71
26	4.22	3.37	2.98	2.74	2.59	2.47	2.32	2.15	1.95	1.69
27	4.21	3.35	2.96	2.73	2.57	2.46	2.30	2.13	1.93	1.67
28	4.20	3.34	2.95	2.71	2.56	2.44	2.29	2.12	1.91	1.65
29	4.18	3.33	2.93	2.70	2.54	2.43	2.28	2.10	1.90	1.64
30	4.17	3.32	2.92	2.69	2.53	2.42	2.27	2.09	1.89	1.62
40	4.08	3.23	2.84	2.61	2.45	2.34	2.18	2.00	1.79	1.51
60	4.00	3.15	2.76	2.52	2.37	2.25	2.10	1.92	1.70	1.39
120	3.92	3.07	2.68	2.45	2.29	2.17	2.02	1.83	1.61	1.25
∞	3.84	2.99	2.60	2.37	2.21	2.09	1.94	1.75	1.52	1.00

Values of v_1 and v_2 represent the degrees of freedom associated with the larger and smaller estimates of variance respectively.

See especially Section 12.3.2 for an application.

Table A5   Gamma function

Values of $\Gamma(r) = \int_0^\infty e^{-x}x^{r-1}dx$; $\Gamma(r+1) = r\Gamma(r) = r!$

r	$\Gamma(r)$	r	$\Gamma(r)$	r	$\Gamma(r)$	r	$\Gamma(r)$
1.00	1.00000	1.25	.90640	1.50	.88623	1.75	.91906
1.01	.99433	1.26	.90440	1.51	.88659	1.76	.92137
1.02	.98884	1.27	.90250	1.52	.88704	1.77	.92376
1.03	.98355	1.28	.90072	1.53	.88757	1.78	.92623
1.04	.97844	1.29	.89904	1.54	.88818	1.79	.92877
1.05	.97350	1.30	.89747	1.55	.88887	1.80	.93138
1.06	.96874	1.31	.89600	1.56	.88964	1.81	.93408
1.07	.96415	1.32	.89464	1.57	.89049	1.82	.93685
1.08	.95973	1.33	.89338	1.58	.89142	1.83	.93969
1.09	.95546	1.34	.89222	1.59	.89243	1.84	.94261
1.10	.95135	1.35	.89115	1.60	.89352	1.85	.94561
1.11	.94739	1.36	.89018	1.61	.89468	1.86	.94869
1.12	.94359	1.37	.88931	1.62	.89592	1.87	.95184
1.13	.93993	1.38	.88854	1.63	.89724	1.88	.95507
1.14	.93642	1.39	.88785	1.64	.89864	1.89	.95838
1.15	.93304	1.40	.88726	1.65	.90012	1.90	.96177
1.16	.92980	1.41	.88676	1.66	.90167	1.91	.96523
1.17	.92670	1.42	.88636	1.67	.90330	1.92	.96878
1.18	.92373	1.43	.88604	1.68	.90500	1.93	.97240
1.19	.92088	1.44	.88580	1.69	.90678	1.94	.97610
1.20	.91817	1.45	.88565	1.70	.90864	1.95	.97988
1.21	.91558	1.46	.88560	1.71	.91057	1.96	.98374
1.22	.91311	1.47	.88563	1.72	.91258	1.97	.98768
1.23	.91075	1.48	.88575	1.73	.91466	1.98	.99171
1.24	.90852	1.49	.88595	1.74	.91683	1.99	.99581
						2.00	1.00000

See especially Table 13.5 for an application.

Table A6   Pseudo-random numbers.

12651	61646	11769	75109	86996	97669	25757	32535	07122	76763
81769	74436	02630	72310	45049	18029	07469	42341	98173	79260
36737	98863	77240	76251	00654	64688	09343	70278	67331	98729
82861	54371	76610	94934	72748	44124	05610	53750	95938	01485
21325	15732	24127	37431	09723	63529	73977	95218	96074	42138

Table A6   Pseudo-random numbers.

74146	47887	62463	23045	41490	07954	22597	60012	98866	90959
90759	64410	54179	66075	61051	75385	51378	08360	95946	95547
55683	98078	02238	91540	21219	17720	87817	41705	95785	12563
79686	17969	76061	83748	55920	83612	41540	86492	06447	60568
70333	00201	86201	69716	78185	62154	77930	67663	29529	75116
14042	53536	07779	04157	41172	36473	42123	43929	50533	33437
59911	08256	06596	48416	69770	68797	56080	14223	59199	30162
62368	62623	62742	14891	39247	52242	98832	69533	91174	57979
57529	97751	54976	48957	74599	08759	78494	52785	68526	64618
15469	90574	78033	66885	13936	42117	71831	22961	94225	31816
18625	23674	53850	32827	81647	80820	00420	63555	74489	80141
74626	68394	88562	70745	23701	45630	65891	58220	35442	60414
11119	16519	27384	90199	79210	76965	99546	30323	31664	22845
41101	17336	48951	53674	17880	45260	08575	49321	36191	17095
32123	91576	84221	78902	82010	30847	62329	63898	23268	74283
26091	68409	69704	82267	14751	13151	93115	01437	56945	89661
67680	79790	48462	59278	44185	29616	76531	19589	83139	28454
15184	19260	14073	07026	25264	08388	27182	22557	61501	67481
58010	45039	57181	10238	36874	28546	37444	80824	63981	39942
56425	53996	86245	32623	78858	08143	60377	42925	42815	11159
82630	84066	13592	60642	17904	99718	63432	88642	37858	25431
14927	40909	23900	48761	44860	92467	31742	87142	03607	32059
23740	22505	07489	85986	74420	21744	97711	36648	35620	97949
32990	97446	07311	63824	07953	85965	87089	11687	92414	67257
05310	24058	91946	78437	34365	82469	12430	84754	19354	72745
21839	39937	27534	88913	49055	19218	47712	67677	51889	70926
08833	42549	93981	94051	28382	83725	72643	74233	97252	17133
58336	11139	47479	00931	91560	95372	97642	33856	54825	55680
62032	91144	75478	47431	52726	30289	42411	91886	51818	78292
45171	30557	53116	04118	58301	24375	65609	85810	18620	49198
91611	62656	60128	35609	63698	78356	50682	22505	01692	36291
55472	63819	86314	49174	93582	73604	78614	78849	23096	72825
18573	09729	74091	53994	10970	86557	65661	41854	26037	53296
60866	02955	90288	82136	83644	94455	06560	78029	98768	71296
45043	55608	82767	60890	74646	79485	13619	98868	40857	19415
17831	09737	79473	75945	28394	79334	70577	38048	03607	06932
40137	03981	07585	18128	11178	32601	27994	05641	22600	86064
77776	31343	14576	97706	16039	47517	43300	59080	80392	63189
69605	44104	40103	95635	05635	81673	68657	09559	23510	95875
19916	52934	26499	09821	87331	80993	61299	36979	73599	35055
02606	58552	07678	56619	65325	30705	99582	53390	46357	13244
65183	73160	87131	35530	47946	09854	18080	02321	05809	04898
10740	98914	44916	11322	89717	88189	30143	52687	19420	60061
98642	89822	71691	51573	83666	61642	46683	33761	47542	23551
60139	25601	93663	25547	02654	94829	48672	28737	84994	13071

See especially Sections 4.2.3, 7.2.2 and 8.3.7 for applications.

References and author index

References and author index

The numbers in brackets after each reference indicate the sections of the book in which the work is cited.

ABBEY, H. 1952: An examination of the Reed–Frost theory of epidemics. *Human Biology, 24*, 201–33. (7.7.6)

ABLER, R., J. S. ADAMS, and P. R. GOULD. 1972: *Spatial organization: the geographer's view of the world.* Englewood Cliffs, N.J. (15.5.2)

ABRAMSON, N. 1963: *Information theory and coding.* New York. (3.4.2)

ACKERMAN, E. A. 1963: Where is the research frontier? *Annals of the Association of American Geographers, 53*, 429–40. (1.2.1)

AITCHISON, J. and J. A. C. BROWN. 1957: *The lognormal distribution.* Cambridge. (4.3.3)

AKERS, S. B. 1960: The use of the Wye-Delta transformation in network simplification. *Operations Research, 8*, 311–23. (3.4.4)

ALEXANDER, J. W. 1944: Freight rates as a geographic factor in Illinois. *Economic Geography, 20*, 25–30. (6.4.3, 8.2.3)
1963: *Economic geography.* New York. (8.2.3)

ALEXANDER, J. W., E. S. BROWN, and R. E. DAHLBERG. 1958: Freight rates; selected aspects of uniform and nodal regions. *Economic Geography, 34*, 1–18. (5.6.1)

ALEXANDERSSON, G. 1956: *The industrial structure of American cities.* Lincoln, Nebr. (5.3.3, 5.4.1, 5.4.4)

ALLEN, G. R. 1954: The 'courbe des populations'—a further analysis. *Oxford Bulletin of Statistics, 16*, 179–89. (4.3.1)

ALONSO, W. 1960: A theory of the urban land market. *Regional Science Association, Papers, 6*, 149–58. (15.5.1)
1964: *Location and land use.* Cambridge, Mass. (6.6.2, 15.5.1)

ALVES, W. R. 1974: Comment on Hudson's 'Diffusion in a central place system'. *Geographical Analysis, 6*, 303–8. (7.4)

AMADEO, D. and R. G. GOLLEDGE. 1975: *An introduction to scientific reasoning in geography.* New York. (1.2.1, 1.4.4)

ANDERSSON, T. 1897: *Den Inre omflyttningen: Norrland.* Mälmo. (2.2.2)

ANSCOMBE, F. J. 1950: Sampling theory of the negative binomial and logarithmic series distributions. *Biometrika, 37*, 358–82. (13.3.1–2)

APPLEBAUM, W. and S. B. COHEN. 1961: The dynamics of store trading areas and market equilibrium. *Annals of the Association of American Geographers, 51*, 73–101. (2.6.2)

AUERBACH, F. 1913: Das Gesetz der Bevölkerungskonzentration. *Petermann's Mitteilungen, 59*, 74–6. (4.3.1)

BACHARACH, M. 1970: *Biproportional matrices and input–output change.* Cambridge. (4.4.2)

BACHI, R. 1963: Standard distance measures and related methods for spatial analysis. *Regional Science Association, Papers and Proceedings,* **10**, 83–132. (9.6.2, 13.7)

BAILEY, N. T. J. 1957: *The mathematical theory of epidemics.* New York. (7.1, 7.7.1, 7.7.3, 7.7.4, 7.7.6)

1967: The simulation of stochastic epidemics in two dimensions. *Fifth Berkeley Symposium on Mathematical Statistics and Probability Proceedings,* **4**, 237–57. (7.7.7)

1975: *The mathematical theory of infectious diseases.* London. (7.7.1, 7.7.3)

BAIN, J. S. 1954: Economics of scale, concentration, and the condition of entry in twenty manufacturing industries. *American Economic Review,* **44**, 15–39. (5.5.1)

BAKER, A. R. H. 1969: Reversal of the rank–size rule: some 19th century rural settlements in France. *Professional Geographer,* **21**, 389–92. (4.3.2)

BANNISTER, G. 1975: Towards a model of impulse transmissions for an urban system. *Boston University,* Mimeographed. (4.6.3)

BARFORD, B. 1938: *Local economic effects of a large-scale industrial undertaking.* Copenhagen. (5.4.2)

BARROWS, H. H. 1923: Geography as human ecology. *Annals of the Association of American Geographers,* **13**, 1–14. (1.2.3)

BARTHOLOMEW, D. J. 1973: *Stochastic models for social processes.* New York. (7.7.1–3, 7.7.5, 7.7.7, 7.8)

BARTHOLOMEW, H. 1955: *Land use in American cities.* Cambridge. (6.2.4)

BARTKO, J. J., S. W. GREEHOUSE and C. S. PATLAK. 1968: On expectations of some functions of Poisson variates. *Biometrics,* **24**, 97–102 (13.2.1)

BARTLETT, M. S. 1957: Measles periodicity and community size. *Journal of the Royal Statistical Society, A,* **120**, 48–70. (11.5.1)

1960: *Stochastic population models in ecology and epidemiology.* London. (7.7.4, 7.8)

1963: The spectral analysis of point processes. *Journal of the Royal Statistical Society, B,* **25**, 264–96. (12.4.3, 13.4.4)

1964: The spectral analysis of two-dimensional point processes. *Biometrika,* **51**, 299–311. (12.4.3)

BASSETT, K. and P. HAGGETT. 1971: Towards short-term forecasting for cyclic behaviour in a regional system of cities. In M. D. I. Chisholm, A. E. Frey and P. Haggett, Editors. *Regional forecasting.* London. 389–413. (4.6.3, 12.5.2)

BASSETT, K. and D. E. HAUSER. 1975: Public policy and spatial structure: housing improvements in Bristol. In R. F. Peel, M. D. I. Chisholm, and P. Haggett, Editors. *Processes in physical and human geography: Bristol essays.* London. 18–66. (9.4.1)

BATTY, M. 1975: *Urban modelling: algorithms, calibrations, predictions.* Cambridge. (5.3.3)

BECKMANN, M. J. 1958: City hierarchies and the distribution of city size. *Economic Development and Cultural Change,* **6**, 243–8. (2.6.2, 5.2.4)

BECKMANN, M. J. and T. MARSCHAK. 1955: An activity analysis approach to location theory. *Kyklos,* **8**, 125–41. (15.4.1)

BEESLEY, M. 1955: The birth and death of industrial establishments: experience in the West Midlands conurbation. *Journal of Industrial Economics,* **4**, 45–61. (5.5.3)

BELFORD, P. C. and H. D. RATCLIFF. 1972: A network flow model for racially balancing schools. *Operations Research,* **20**, 619–28. (14.5.1)

BELL, G. 1962: Change in city size distributions in Israel. *Ekistics,* **13**, 103. (4.4.1)

BENNETT, R. J. 1974: A review of *Spatial Autocorrelation*, by A. D. Cliff and J. K. Ord. *Environment and Planning*, **6**, 241. (11.2.2)

— 1974a: The representation and identification of spacio-temporal systems: an example of population diffusion in north-west England. *Institute of British Geographers, Publications*, **66**, 73–94. (4.6.3, 7.8, 16.4.1)

— 1975b, c, d, e: Dynamic systems modelling of the north-west region.
1. Spacio-temporal representation and identification
2. Estimation of the spatio-temporal policy model
3. Adaptive parameter policy model
4. Adaptive spacio-temporal forecasts
Environment and Planning, **7**, 525–38, 539–66, 617–36, 887–98. (16.7)

BERRY, B. J. L. 1960: An inductive approach to the regionalization of economic development. *University of Chicago, Department of Geography, Research Papers*, **62**, 78–107. (3.5.2, 4.3.4)

— 1961a: City size distributions and economic development. *Economic Development and Cultural Change*, **9**, 573–88. (4.3.4, 4.4.1, 5.5.3)

— 1961b: A method for deriving multifactor uniform regions. *Przeglad Geograficzny*, **33**, 263–82. (14.4.2)

— 1962: Sampling, coding, and storing flood plain data. *United States, Department of Agriculture, Farm Economics Division, Agriculture Handbook*, **237**. (8.3.2–3, 8.3.5)

— 1964: Approaches to regional analysis: a synthesis. *Annals of the Association of American Geographers*, **54**, 2–12. (1.4.1)

— 1966: Essays on commodity flow and the spatial structure of the Indian economy. *University of Chicago, Department of Geography, Research Papers*, **111**. (14.6)

— 1967: Grouping and regionalization: an approach to the problem using multivariate analysis. *Northwestern University, Studies in Geography*, **13**, 219–51. (14.4.2)

— 1972: Hierarchical diffusion—the basis of developmental filtering and spread in a system of growth centres. In N. M. Hansen, Editor, *Growth centres in regional economic development*. New York, 108–38. (7.4)

BERRY, B. J. L., H. G. BARNUM, and R. J. TENNANT. 1962: Retail location and consumer behaviour. *Regional Science Association, Papers and Proceedings*, **9**, 65–106. (5.2.1, 5.2.3, 5.2.5)

BERRY, B. J. L. and W. L. GARRISON. 1958a: Alternate explanations of urban rank–size relationships. *Annals of the Association of American Geographers*, **48**, 83–91. (4.3.4)

— 1958b: Functional bases of the central place hierarchy. *Economic Geography*, **34**, 145–54. (5.2.1)

BERRY, B. J. L. and F. E. HORTON. 1970: *Geographic perspectives on urban systems*. Englewood Cliffs, N.J. (6.6, 6.6.2)

BERRY, B. J. L., R. J. TENNANT, B. J. GARNER, and J. W. SIMMONS. 1963: Commercial structure and commercial blight. *University of Chicago, Department of Geography, Research Papers*, **85**. (6.2.2, 6.6.1)

BERRY, B. J. L. and D. F. MARBLE, Editors. 1968: *Spatial analysis: a reader in statistical geography*. Englewood Cliffs, N.J. (9.5.1)

BERRY, B. J. L. and A. PRED. 1961: Central place studies: a bibliography of theory and applications. *Regional Science Research Institute, Bibliographic Series*, **1**. (5.2.3)

BERTALANFFY, L. von. 1951: An outline of general system theory. *British Journal of the Philosophy of Science*, **1**, 134–65. (1.2.4)

BESAG, J. E. 1974: Spatial interaction and the statistical analysis of lattice systems (with discussion). *Journal of the Royal Statistical Society, B*, **36**, 192–236. (16.7)

BIRD, J. 1956: Scale in regional study: illustrated by brief comparisons between the western peninsulas of England and France. *Geography*, **41**, 25–38. (14.2.2)

BISSELL, A. F. 1972a: A negative binomial model with varying element sizes. *Biometrika*, **59**, 435–41. (13.4.3)

  1972b: Another negative binomial model with varying element sizes. *Biometrika*, **59**, 691–93. (13.4.3)

  1973: Monitoring event rates using varying sample element sizes. *The Statistician*, **22**, 43–58. (13.4.3)

BLEICHER, H. 1892: *Statistische Beschreibung der Stadt Frankfurt am Main und ihrer Bevölkerung*. Frankfurt. (6.2.2)

BLUMENSTOCK, D. I. 1953: The reliability factor in the drawing of isarithms. *Annals of the Association of American Geographers*, **43**, 289–304. (9.3.2)

BOARD, C. 1962: *The Border region: natural environment and land use in the eastern Cape*. Cape Town. (6.2.4)

BOARD, C., R. J. DAVIES, and T. J. D. FAIR. 1970: The structure of the South African space economy. *Regional Studies*, **4**, 367–92. (14.6.1)

BOGUE, D. J. 1950: *The structure of the metropolitan community: a study of dominance and subdomination*. Ann Arbor. (4.2.2, 5.4.2, 6.2.3, 13.5)

BOOTS, B. N. 1973: Some models of the random subdivision of space. *Geografiska Annaler, B*, **55**, 34–48. (13.5)

BOOTS, B. N. and L. F. LAMOUREAUX. 1972: Working notes and bibliography on the study of shape in human geography and planning. *Council of Planning Librarians, Exchange Bibliography*, **346**. (9.6.1)

BORCHERT, J. R. 1961: The twin cities urbanized area: past, present, and future. *Geographical Review*, **51**, 47–70. (3.5.2)

BOULDING, K. E. 1966: *The impact of the social sciences*. New Brunswick, N.J. (1.4.4)

BOWMAN, I. 1931: *The pioneer fringe*. New York. (7.1)

BOWMAN, K. O. 1973: Power of the kurtosis statistic, b_2, in tests of departures from normality. *Biometrika*, **60**, 623–28. (10.5.2)

BOX, G. E. P. 1953: Non-normality and tests on variances. *Biometrika*, **40**, 318–35. (10.5.1)

BOX, G. E. P., and G. M. JENKINS. 1970: *Time series analysis, forecasting and control*. San Francisco. (7.8, 11.5.1–2, 16.1–2, 16.3.1, 16.3.4, 16.4.1)

BRACEY, H. E. 1962: English central villages: identification, distribution and functions. *Lund Studies in Geography, Series B, Human Geography*, **24**, 169–90. (5.2.5)

BRAMS, S. J. 1966: Transactions and flows in the international system. *American Political Science Review*, **60**, 880–98. (14.6.2)

BRILLOUIN, L. 1964: *Scientific uncertainty and information*. New York. (1.2.4)

BROEK, J. O. M. 1932: *The Santa Clara valley, California: a study in landscape changes*. Utrecht. (1.2.4)

BRONOWSKI, J. 1960: *The common sense of science*. London. (1.4.3)

BROOKFIELD, H. C. and D. HART. 1971: *Melanesia*. London. (14.2.1)

BROOKS, C. E. P. and N. CARRUTHERS. 1953: *Handbook of statistical methods in meteorology*. London. (9.3.1)

BROWN, L. A. 1968: *Diffusion processes and location: a conceptual framework and bibliography*. Philadelphia. (7.1, 7.7.5)

BROWN, L. A., and K. R. COX. 1971: Empirical regularities in the diffusion of innovation. *Annals of the Association of American Geographers*, **61**, 551–59. (7.2.1, 7.3–4)

BROWN, L. A. and E. G. MOORE. 1969: Diffusion research in geography: a perspective. *Progress in Geography*, **1**, 119–57. (7.1, 7.6.2)

BRUNHES, J. 1925: *La géographie humaine*. Two volumes. Paris. (1.2.3, 4.2)

BRUSH, J. E. 1953: The hierarchy of central places in southwestern Wisconsin. *Geographical Review*, **43**, 380–402. (4.2.1)

1968: Spatial patterns of population in Indian cities. *Geographical Review*, **58**, 362–391. (6.6.1)

BRUSH, J. E. and H. E. BRACEY. 1955: Rural service centres in southwestern Wisconsin and southern England. *Geographical Review*, **45**, 559–69. (4.5.1)

BRUSH, J. E. and H. L. GAUTHIER. 1968: Service centres and consumer trips. *University of Chicago, Department of Geography, Research Papers*, **113**. (6.6.1)

BUNGE, W. 1962, 1966: Theoretical geography. *Lund Studies in Geography, Series C, General and Mathematical Geography*, **1**. (1.2.2, 2.2.1, 2.4.2, 2.4.4, 3.3.1–2, 5.2.1, 9.8.1, 14.2.1, 14.4.3)

1964: Patterns of location. *Michigan Inter-University Community of Mathematical Geographers, Discussion Papers*, **3**. (6.3.1)

1971: *Fitzgerald—the geography of a revolution*. Detroit. (1.4.5, 6.6.2)

BURGESS, E. W. 1927: The determination of gradients in the growth of the city. *American Sociological Society, Publications*, **21**, 178–84. (6.6.2)

BURGHARDT, A. F. 1959: The location of river towns in the central lowland of the United States. *Annals of the Association of American Geographers*, **49**, 305–323. (13.6.5)

1969: The origin and developments of the road network of the Niagara peninsula, 1770–1851. *Annals of the Association of American Geographers*, **59**, 417–40. (3.5.3)

BURTON, T. 1963a: The quantitative revolution and theoretical geography. *Canadian Geographer*, **7**, 151–62. (1.4.2)

1963b: A restatement of the dispersed city hypothesis. *Annals of the Association of American Geographers*, **53**, 285–9. (5.4.3)

BYLUND, E. 1960: Theoretical considerations regarding the distribution of settlement in inner north Sweden. *Geografiska Annaler*, **42**, 225–31. (4.2.3)

CARELESS, J. S. M. 1954: Frontierism, metropolitanism, and Canadian history. *Canadian Historical Review*, **35**, 1–21. (4.3)

CAROE, L. 1968: A multivariate grouping scheme—association analysis of East Anglian towns. In E. Bowen, H. Carter, and J. A. Taylor, Editors. *Geography at Aberystwyth*. London, 253–69. (14.4.1)

CARTER, H. 1969: *The study of urban geography*. London. (4.4.2)

CASETTI, E. 1964: Classificatory and regional analysis by discriminant iterations. *Office of Naval Research, Geography Branch, Contract 1228(16) Task 189–135, Technical Report*, **12**. (14.2.3)

1966: Optimal location of steel mills serving the Quebec and Southern Ontario steel market. *The Canadian Geographer*, **10**, 27–39. (15.4.1)

1967: Urban population density patterns: an alternative explanation. *Canadian Geographer*, **11**, 96–100. (6.2.2)

1969: Why do diffusion processes conform to logistic trends? *Geographical Analysis*, **1**, 101–105. (7.3)

CASETTI, E. and R. K. SEMPLE. 1969: Concerning the testing of spatial diffusion hypotheses. *Geographical Analysis*, **1**, 154–9. (6.2.1, 7.3)

CHAPIN, F. S., JR., and S. F. WEISS, Editors. 1962: *Urban growth dynamics in a regional cluster of cities.* New York.

CHAPMAN, G. P. 1970: The application of information theory to the analysis of population distributions in space. *Economic Geography*, **46**, 317–31. (4.3.3)

CHAPPELL, J. E. 1975: The ecological dimension: Russian and American views. *Annals of the Association of American Geographers*, **65**, 144–62. (1.2.2)

CHARNES, A. and W. W. COOPER. 1954: The stepping stone method of explaining linear programming calculation in transportation problems. *Management Science*, **1**, 49–69. (15.3)

CHERNOFF, H. and E. L. LEHMANN. 1954: The use of maximum likelihood estimates in χ^2 tests for goodness of fit. *Annals of Mathematical Statistics*, **25**, 579–86. (13.3.4)

CHICAGO AREA TRANSPORTATION STUDY. 1960: *Final report.* Chicago. (2.3.4)

CHISHOLM, M. D. I. 1960: The geography of commuting. *Annals of the Association of American Geographers*, **50**, 187–8, 491–2. (8.4.2, 10.6.1)
1962: *Rural settlement and land use: an essay in location.* London. (2.6.1, 3.3.2, 4.2.3, 5.5.1, 6.2.4, 6.3.2, 6.4.1, 6.5.1–2, 9.3.4)

CHISHOLM, M. D. I. and P. O'SULLIVAN. 1973: *Freight flows and spatial aspects of the British economy.* Cambridge. (2.5.2, 15.2.3)

CHISHOLM, R. K. and G. R. WHITAKER. 1971: *Forecasting methods.* Homewood, Ill. (16.3.3)

CHORLEY, R. J. 1962: Geomorphology and general systems theory. *United States, Geological Survey, Professional Paper*, **500-B**. (1.1, 1.2.4)
1973: Geography as human ecology. Chapter 7. In Chorley, R. J., Editor. *Directions in Geography.* London, 155–69. (1.2.3)

CHORLEY, R. J. and P. HAGGETT, Editors. 1965a: *Frontiers in geographical teaching: the Madingley lectures for 1963.* London. (1.2.3, 1.4.2, 8.2.1, 14.2.1)
1965b: Trend-surface mapping in geographical research. *Institute of British Geographers, Publications*, **37**, 47–67. (12.2.2)
Editors. 1967: *Models in geography: the Madingley lectures for 1965.* London. (1.4.1–2, 3.3.1, 14.7)

CHORLEY, R. J. and B. A. KENNEDY. 1971: *Physical geography—a systems approach.* London. (13.2.1)

CHORLEY, R. J., D. R. STODDART, P. HAGGETT, and H. O. SLAYMAKER. 1966: regional and local components in the areal distribution of surface sand facies in the Breckland, Eastern England. *Journal of Sedimentary Petrology*, **36**, 209–20. (12.3.1–2)

CHOYNOWSKI, M. 1959: Maps based upon probabilities. *Journal of the American Statistical Associations*, **54**, 385–8. (9.5.2)

CHRIST, C. F. 1966: *Econometric models and methods.* New York. (16.1)

CHRISTALLER, W. 1933: *Die zentralen Orte in Süddeutschland: Eine ökonomisch-geographische Untersuchung über die Gesetzmässigkeit der Verbreitung und Entwicklung der Siedlungen mit städtischen Funktionen.* Jena. (2.6.1, 2.7.1, 4.2.1, 4.5.1, 5.2.2–3, 5.2.5)
1966: *Central places in Southern Germany.* Translated by C. W. Baskin. Englewood Cliffs, N.J. (2.7.1)

CLARK, A. H. 1954: Historical geography. In P. E. James, *et al.*, Editors, *American geography: inventory and prospect.* Syracuse. 70–105. (7.1)

CLARK, C. 1940: *Conditions of economic progress.* London. (9.4.1)
1951: Urban population densities. *Journal of the Royal Statistical Society*, A, **114**, 490–6. (6.1, 6.2.2, 6.6.1)

1967: *Population growth and land use*. London. (4.3.1)

CLARK, C., F. WILSON and J. BRADLEY. 1969: Industrial location and economic potential in Western Europe. *Regional Studies*, **3**, 197–212. (2.4.5)

CLARK, P. J. 1956: Grouping in spatial distributions. *Science*, **123**, 373–4. (13.6.5)

CLARK, P. J. and F. C. EVANS. 1954: Distance to nearest neighbour as a measure of spatial relationships in populations. *Ecology*, **35**, 445–53. (13.3.2, 13.6, 13.6.1, 13.6.4)

CLAWSON, M., R. B. HELD, and C. H. STODDARD. 1960: *Land for the future*. Baltimore. (2.6.1, 6.6.1)

CLIFF, A. D. 1965: Residential site selection in urban areas: an application of the Herbert–Stevens model to the city of Evanston, Illinois. *Northwestern University, Dept. of Geography*, M.A. Thesis. (15.5.1)

1968: The neighbourhood effect in the diffusion of innovations. *Institute of British Geographers, Publications*, **44**, 75–84. (7.3)

1970: Computing the spatial correspondence between geographical patterns. *Institute of British Geographers, Publications*, **50**, 143–54. (7.6.1)

CLIFF, A. D. and P. HAGGETT. 1970: On the efficiency of alternate aggregations in region-building problems. *Environment and Planning*, **2**, 285–94. (14.3)

CLIFF, A. D., P. HAGGETT, J. K. ORD, K. BASSETT, and R. B. DAVIES. 1975: *Elements of spatial structure: a quantitative approach*. Cambridge. (4.3.3, 4.6.1, 4.6.3, 7.7.6, 11.5.1–3, 12.2.1–2, 12.3.1, 12.3.3, 12.5.2, 14.3, 16.1, 16.3.1, 16.3.3–4, 16.5.1)

CLIFF, A. D., R. L. MARTIN, and J. K. ORD. 1974: Evaluating the friction of distance parameter in gravity models. *Regional Studies*, **8**, 281–6. (2.4.2, 4.3.3)

CLIFF, A. D., R. L. MARTIN, and J. K. ORD, 1975a: Map pattern and friction of distance parameters: reply to comments by R. J. Johnston, and by L. Curry, D. Griffith, and E. S. Sheppard. *Regional Studies*, **9**, 285–88. (2.4.2)

1975b: A test for spatial autocorrelation in choropleth maps based upon a modified X^2 statistic. *Institute of British Geographers, Publications*, **65**, 109–29. (10.2.3, 10.3.1)

CLIFF, A. D., and J. K. ORD. 1969: The problem of spatial autocorrelation. In A. J. Scott, Editor. *Studies in Regional Science*. London, 25–55. (10.5.2, 11.6)

1971: A regression approach to univariate spatial forecasting. In M. D. I. Chisholm, A. E. Frey, and P. Haggett, Editors. *Regional forecasting*. London. 47–70. (16.2.1, 16.5.1–2)

1972: Regional forecasting with an application to school-leaver patterns in the United Kingdom. In W. P. Adams and F. M. Helleiner, Editors. *International geography*. Montreal, 965–8. (12.3.1, 12.3.3, 16.5.1–2)

1973: *Spatial autocorrelation*. London. (4.2.1, 7.6.1–2, 9.3.3, 10.2.1, 10.3.2–3, 11.2.1, 11.3.1–4, 11.4.1–2, 11.5.2, 12.3.2, 13.2.1–2, 13.3.1, 13.4.2–3, 13.5, 16.2.2)

1975a: The comparison of means when samples consist of spatially autocorrelated observations. *Environment and Planning, A*, **7**, 725–34. (10.2, 10.2.1, 10.3, 10.3.1, 10.3.3, 11.6)

1975b: Model building and the analysis of spatial pattern in human geography. *Journal of the Royal Statistical Society, B*, **37**, 297–348. (7.3–4, 10.2.3, 10.4.2–3, 10.6.2, 12.4.2, 13.4.4, 13.6, 13.6.2, 13.7, 16.1, 16.2.1, 16.6, 16.7)

1975c: The choice of a test for spatial autocorrelation. In J. C. Davis and M. McCullagh, Editors. *Display and analysis of spatial data*. New York. (11.2.1)

1975d: Space–time modelling with an application to regional forecasting.

Institute of British Geographers, Publications, **64**, 119–28. (7.3)

CLIFF, A. D. and B. T. ROBSON. 1976: An application of a random partitioning model to the urban hierarchy of England and Wales, 1801–1966. Forthcoming. (4.4.1)

COATES, B. E., and E. M. RAWSTRON. 1971: *Regional variations in Britain.* London. (10.6)

COCHRAN, W. G. 1953: *Sampling techniques.* New York. (8.3.5)

COCHRAN, W. G., F. MOSTELLER, and J. W. TUKEY. 1954: Principles of sampling. *Journal of the American Statistical Association,* **49**, 13–35. (8.2.2)

COHEN, J. E. 1966: *A model of simple compeition.* Cambridge, Mass. (4.3.3)

COLE, J. P. 1960: Study of major and minor civil divisions in political geography. *Department of Geography, University of Nottingham.* Mimeographed. (9.6.1)

COLEMAN, A. 1969: A geographical model for land use analysis. *Geography,* **54**, 43–55. (6.2.4, 6.5.2)

CONVERSE, P. D. 1930: *Elements of marketing.* Englewood Cliffs, N.J. (2.3.2)

COOLEY, C. H. 1894: The theory of transportation. *American Economic Association, Publications,* **9** (3). (3.2.3)

COPPOCK, J. T. 1955: The relationship of farm and parish boundaries: a study in the use of agricultural statistics. *Geographical Studies,* **2**, 12–26. (8.2.3)

—— 1960: The parish as a geographical-statistical unit. *Tijdschrift voor Economische en Sociale Geografie,* **51**, 317–26. (8.4.2)

CORMACK, R. M. 1971: A review of classification. *Journal of the Royal Statistical Society, A.* **134**, 321–67. (14.4.2)

COTTERILL, C. H. 1950: *Industrial plant location: its application to zinc smelting.* Saint Louis. (5.6.1,5.6.3)

COURT, A. and P. W. PORTER. 1964: The elusive point of minimum travel. *Annals of the Association of American Geographers,* **54**, 400–6. (9.6.2)

COX, K. R. 1968: On the utility and definition of regions in comparative political sociology. *Ohio State University, Department of Geography,* Mimeographed. (14.4.2)

COXETER, H. S. M. 1961: *Introduction to geometry.* New York. (2.7.1, 5.3.1)

CRESSWELL, W. L. and P. FROGGART. 1963: *The causation of bus driver accidents— an epidemiological study.* London. (13.2.4)

CROWE, P. R. 1938: On progress in geography. *Scottish Geographical Magazine,* **54**, 1–19. (2.2.1)

CROXTON, F. E., D. J. COWDEN, and S. KLEIN. 1968: *Applied general statistics.* New York. (8.3.1)

CURRY, L. 1962: The geography of service centres within towns: the elements of an operational approach. *Lund Studies in Geography, B, Human Geography,* **24**, 31–54. (5.4.3)

—— 1964: The random spatial economy: an exploration in settlement theory. *Annals of the Association of American Geographers,* **54**, 138–46. (4.2.1, 4.3.3, 12.4.2, 13.3.1)

—— 1967: Central places in the random spatial economy. *Journal of Regional Science,* 7, 217–38. (4.2.1, 13.3.1)

—— 1970: Univariate spatial forecasting. *Economic Geography,* **46**, 241–58. (16.1)

—— 1971: Applicability of space–time moving average forecasting. In M. D. I. Chisholm, A. E. Frey and P. Haggett, Editors. *Regional Forecasting.* London. 11–24. (4.6.3, 10.3.2, 16.6)

—— 1972: A spatial analysis of gravity flows. *Regional Studies,* **6**, 131–47. (2.4.2, 4.6.3)

CURRY, L., and G. BANNISTER. 1974: Forecasting township populations of Ontario from time–space covariances. In L. S. Bourne, R. D. MacKinnon, J. Siegel and J. W. Simmons, Editors. *Urban futures for central Canada: perspectives on forecasting urban growth and form.* Toronto. 34–59. (16.2.2)

CURRY, L., D. GRIFFITH, and E. S. SHEPPARD. 1975: Those gravity parameters again. *Regional Studies,* **9**, 289–96. (2.4.2)

DACEY, M. F. 1960: The spacing of river towns. *Annals of the Association of American Geographers,* **50**, 59–61. (13.6.5)

1962: Analysis of central place and point patterns by a nearest neighbour method. *Lund Studies in Geography, B, Human Geography,* **24**, 55–75. (4.2.1, 13.6)

1963: Order neighbor statistics for a class of random patterns in multidimensional space. *Annals of the Association of American Geographers,* **53**, 505–15. (2.7.2, 13.6.4)

1964: Modified Poisson probability law for point pattern more regular than random. *Annals of the Association of American Geographers,* **54**, 559–65. (4.2.1, 13.4.4)

1965: The geometry of central place theory. *Geografiska Annaler, B,* **47**, 111–24. (4.2.1, 13.5)

1966a: A compound probability law for a pattern more dispersed than random and with areal inhomogeneity. *Economic Geography,* **42**, 172–79. (4.2.1, 13.4.4)

1966b: A county seat model for the areal pattern of an urban system. *Geographical Review,* **56**, 527–42. (4.2.1, 13.4.4)

1966c: Population of places in a central place hierarchy. *Journal of Regional Science,* **6**, 27–33. (5.2.4)

1968: An empirical study of the areal distribution of houses in Puerto Rico. *Institute of British Geographers, Publications,* **45**, 51–70. (4.2.1, 13.3.1, 13.4.2)

1969a: Similarities in the areal distributions of houses in Japan and Puerto Rico. *Area,* **3**, 35–37. (4.2.1, 13.3.1)

1969b: Proportion of reflexive nth order neighbors in spatial distribution. *Geographical Analysis,* **1**, 385–88. (13.6.5)

1975: Evaluation of the Poisson approximation to measures of the random pattern in the square. *Geographical Analysis,* **7**, 351–67. (13.6.1)

DACEY, M. F. and T. TUNG. 1962: The identification of randomness in point patterns. *Journal of Regional Science,* **4**, 83–96. (2.7.2, 13.6.4, 13.6.6)

D'AGOSTINO, R. and E. S. PEARSON, 1973: Tests for departure from normality. Empirical results for the distributions of b_2 and b_1. *Biometrika,* **60**, 613–22. (10.5.2)

DÅHL, S. 1957: The contacts of Västerås with the rest of Sweden. *Lund Studies in Geography, B, Human Geography,* **13**, 206–43. (2.2.2)

DAVIS, D. H. 1926: Objectives in a geographic field study of a community. *Annals of the Association of American Geographers,* **16**, 102–9. (2.6.2)

DAVIS, J. C. 1973: *Statistics and data analysis in geology.* New York. (12.2.2)

DAVIS, J. C. and M. McCULLAGH. 1975: *Display and analysis of spatial data.* New York. (8.4.2)

DAVIS, W. K. and G. W. S. ROBINSON. 1968: The nodal structure of the Solent region. *Journal of the Town Planning Institute,* **54**, 18–22. (14.6.1)

DICKINSON, G. C. 1963: *Statistical mapping and the presentation of statistics.* London. (8.2.3, 8.4.1)

DICKINSON, R. E. 1964: *City and region: a geographical interpretation.* London. (6.2.4, 6.6.2)

DIXON, W. J. 1964: *Biomedical computer programs.* Los Angeles. (12.4.4)

DORFMAN, R., P. A. SAMUELSON, and R. M. SOLOW. 1958: *Linear programming and economic analysis.* New York. (15.2.2, 15.3, 15.5.2)

DUERR, W. A. 1960: *Fundamentals of forestry economics.* New York. (2.6.1, 5.6.1)

DUNCAN, O. D., R. P. CUZZORT, and B. DUNCAN. 1961: *Statistical geography: problems of analysing areal data.* Glencoe. (10.6.1)

DUNN, E. S. 1954: *The location of agricultural production.* Gainesville. (2.4.1, 6.3, 6.3.1–2)

DURBIN, J. 1959: Efficient estimation of parameters in moving average models. *Biometrika,* **46**, 306–16. (16.3.1)

DURBIN, J. and G. S. WATSON. 1950, 1951, 1971: Testing for serial correlation in least squares regression I, II, III. *Biometrika,* **37**, 409–28; **38**, 159–78; **58**, 1–19. (11.3.1, 11.4.1)

EDMONSON, M. S. 1961: Neolithic diffusion rates. *Current Anthropology,* **2**, 71–102. (7.1)

E.F.T.A. 1973: *National settlement strategies: a framework for regional development.* Geneva. (5.5.2)

EILON, S., C. D. T. WATSON GANDY, and N. CHRISTOFIDES. 1971: *Distribution management: mathematical modelling and practical analysis.* London. (3.4.2, 5.6.1).

ESCHER, M. C. 1960: *The graphic work of M. C. Escher.* New York. (1.4)

FANO, P. 1969: Organization, city size distributions and central places. *Regional Science Association, Papers,* **22**, 29–38. (4.3.3)

FARMER, B. H. 1957: *Pioneer peasant colonization in Ceylon.* London. (4.2.3, 6.5.2, 7.1)

FELLER, W. 1943: On a general class of contagious distributions. *Annals of Mathematical Statistics,* **14**, 389–400. (13.2.4)

FENNEMANN, N. M. 1916: Physiographic divisions of the United States. *Annals of the Association of American Geographers,* **6**, 19–98. (14.2.2)

FISHER, R. A. 1941: The negative binomial distribution. *Annals of Eugenics,* **11**, 182–87. (13.2.4)

FISHER, R. A. and F. YATES. 1957: *Statistical tables for biological, agricultural, and medical research.* Edinburgh. (4.2.3, 9.3.1, 10.5.2)

FISHMAN, G. S. 1968: *Spectral methods in econometrics.* Santa Monica. (12.4.4)

FLORENCE, P. S. 1944: The selection of industries suitable for dispersal into rural areas. *Journal of the Royal Statistical Society,* **107**, 93–116. (5.5.2, 10.6.1)
    1953: *The logic of British and American industry.* London. (5.5.1, 5.5.2, 5.6.3, 6.5.2)

FOLGER, J. 1953: Some aspects of migration in the Tennessee valley. *American Sociological Review,* **18**, 253–60. (2.6.2)

FOLKE, S. 1972: Why a radical geography must be Marxist. *Antipode,* **4**, 13–18. (1.4.5)

FORD, L. R. JR., and D. R. FULKERSON. 1962: *Flows in networks.* Princeton. (3.4.4)

FORER, P. 1974: Changes in the spatial structure of the New Zealand airline network. *Bristol University, Ph.D. Dissertation.* (9.7.2)

FORGOTSON, J. M. 1960: Review and classification of quantitative mapping techniques. *Bulletin of the American Association of Petroleum Geologists,* **44**, 83–100. (9.4.1)

FOUND, W. C. 1971: *A theoretical approach to rural land-use patterns.* London. (6.5.1, 6.5.3)

FOX, J. W. 1956: Land-use survey: general principles and a New Zealand example. *Auckland University College, Bulletin*, **49**. (6.2.4)

FREUND, J. E. 1967: *Modern elementary statistics*. Third edition. Englewood Cliffs, N.J. (10.1)

FRIEDMANN, J. 1972: A general theory of polarized development. In N. M. Hansen, Editor. *Growth centres in regional economic development*. New York. (6.1)

FRIEDRICH, C. J. 1929: *Alfred Weber's theory of the location of industries*. Chicago. (5.5., 5.6.1)

GARRISON, W. L. 1960: Connectivity of the interstate highway system. *Regional Science Association, Papers and Proceedings*, **6**, 121–37. (3.5.1, 9.7.1)

GARRISON, W. L., B. J. L. BERRY, D. F. MARBLE, J. D. NYSTUEN, R. L. MORRILL. 1959: *Studies of highway development and geographic change*. Seattle. (14.5.3, 15.1)

GARRISON, W. L. and D. F. MARBLE. 1962: The structure of transportation networks. *United States Army, Transportation Research Command, Contract 44–177–TC–685, Task 9R98–09–003–01 Technical Report, 62–11*. (9.7.4)

GATTRELL, A. C. 1975: Complexity and redundancy in binary maps. *Pennsylvania State University, Department of Geography*. Mimeographed. (9.3.3)

GAUTHIER, H. L. 1968: Least cost flows in a capacitated network: a Brazilian example. *Northwestern University, Studies in Geography*, **16**, 102–27. (15.4.2)

GEARY, R. C. 1954: The contiguity ratio and statistical mapping. *The Incorporated Statistician*, **5**, 115–45. (11.4.2)

G.E.C. DEFENSE SYSTEMS DEPARTMENT. 1962: *Tables of the individual and cumulative terms of the Poisson distribution*. New York. (13.3.4)

GETIS, A. 1963: The determination of the location of retail activities with the use of a map transformation. *Economic Geography*, **39**, 1–22. (2.7.3)

— 1967: Occupancy theory and map pattern analysis. *Department of Geography, University of Bristol. Seminar Paper Series A*, **1** (13.4.2)

— 1974: Representation of spatial point pattern processes by Polya models. In M. Yeates, Editor. *IGU Commission on Quantitative Geography, Proceedings of the 1972 meeting*. Montreal, 76–100. (13.3.1)

GETIS, A. and B. N. BOOTS. 1971: Spatial behaviour: rats and man. *Professional Geographer*, **23**, 11—14. (6.6.1)

GIBBS, J. P., Editor. 1961: *Urban research methods*. New York. (4.3.1, 4.5.2, 9.6.1)

GILG, A. W. 1973: A study in agricultural disease diffusion. *Institute of British Geographers, Publications*, **59**, 77–97. (7.1)

GINSBURG, N. 1961: *Atlas of economic development*. Chicago. (3.5.2, 8.2.2, 8.4.1, 9.4.3)

GODDARD, J. 1970: Functional regions within the city centre: a study by factor analysis of taxi flows in central London. *Institute of British Geographers, Publications*, **49**, 161–82. (14.6)

— 1973: *Office linkages and location: a study of communications and spatial patterns in central London*. Oxford. (5.5.2)

GODLUND, S. 1956: Bus service in Sweden. *Lund Studies in Geography, B, Human Geography*, **17**, (7.1)

— 1961: Population, regional hospitals, transport facilities and regions: planning the location of regional hospitals in Sweden. *Lund Studies in Geography, B, Human Geography*, **21**. (14.1)

GOLDTHWAIT, J. W. 1927: A town that has gone downhill. *Geographical Review*, **17**, 527–52. (5.4.2)

GOODCHILD, M. F. 1972: The trade area of a displaced regional lattice point. *Geographical Analysis*, **4**, 105–7. (5.2.2)

GOLLEDGE, R. G. and G. RUSHTON. 1972: Multidimensional scaling—review and geographical applications. *Association of American Geographers, Commission on College Geography, Technical Papers*, **10**. (9.8.2)

GOODRICH, C. 1936: *Migration and economic opportunity*. Philadelphia. (2.4.4)

GOTTMANN, J. 1961: *Megalopolis: the urbanized northeastern seaboard of the United States*. New York. (6.3.2, 6.5.1)

GOULD, P. R. 1960: The development of the transportation pattern in Ghana. *Northwestern University, Studies in Geography*, **5**. (3.5.3)

1963: Man against his environment: a game-theoretic framework. *Annals of the Association of American Geographers*, **53**, 290–7. (6.5.1)

1965: Wheat on Kilimanjaro: the perception of choice within game and learning model frameworks. *General Systems*, **10**, 157–66. (15.5.2)

1967: On the geographical interpretation of eigenvalues. *Institute of British Geographers, Publications*, **42**, 53–86. (9.7.4)

1970: Is Statistix Inferens the geographical name for a wild goose? *Economic Geography (Supplement)*, **46**, 439–48. (10.2, 10.3.1, 11.2.1)

1972: Pedagogic review: entropy in urban and regional modelling. *Annals of the Association of American Geographers*, **62**, 689–700. (2.5.1–2)

GOULD, P. R. and T. R. LEINBACH. 1966: An approach to the geographic assignment of hospital services. *Tijdschrift voor Economische en Sociale Geografie*, **57**, 203–6. (15.1)

GOULD, P. R. and R. R. WHITE. 1974: *Mental maps*. Harmondsworth. (2.4.2)

GRANDELL, J. 1972: Statistical inference for doubly stochastic Poisson processes. In P. A. W. Lewis, Editor. *Stochastic point processes*. New York. 90–121. (13.4.4)

GRANGER, C. W. J. 1969: Spatial data and time series analysis. In A. J. Scott, Editor. *Studies in regional science*. London, 1–24. (10.4.1, 10.4.3, 10.6.2, 12.4, 12.4.1, 12.5.1)

GRANGER, C. W. J. and M. HATANAKA. 1964: *Spectral analysis of economic time series*. Princeton. (12.4.4, 12.5.1, 12.5.3)

GRANGER, C. W. J. and A. O. HUGHES. 1968: Spectral analysis of short series—a simulation study. *Journal of the Royal Statistical Society, A*, **131**, 83–99. (12.4.4, 12.5.1, 12.5.3)

GREEN, F. H. W. 1950: Urban hinterlands in England and Wales: an analysis of bus services. *Geographical Journal*, **96**, 64–81. (2.6.2)

GREENHUT, M. L. 1956: *Plant location in theory and practice: the economics of space*. Chapel Hill. (5.6.2)

GREENWOOD, M. 1931: On the statistical measure of infectiousness. *Journal of Hygiene*, **31**, 336–51. (7.7.6)

GREIG-SMITH, P. 1957, 1964: *Quantitative plant ecology*. London. (12.3.1)

GRIGG, D. B. 1965: The logic of regional systems. *Annals of the Association of American Geographers*, **55**, 465–91. (14.2.1, 14.7)

GRILICHES, Z. 1957: Hybrid corn: an exploration in the economics of technological change. *Econometrica*, **25**, 501–22. (7.3)

GROTEWALD, A. 1959: Von Thünen in retrospect. *Economic Geography*, **35**, 346–55. (6.3.2)

GRYTZELL, K. G. 1963: The demarcation of comparable city areas by means of population density. *Lund Studies in Geography, B, Human Geography*, **25**. (8.2.3)

GUELKE, L. 1971: Problems of scientific explanation in geography. *Canadian Geographer*, **15**, 38–53. (1.4.3–4)

GULLEY, J. L. M. 1959: The Turnerian frontier: a study in the migration of ideas. *Tijdschrift voor Economische en Sociale Geografie*, **50**, 65–72, 81–91. (7.1)

GÜLÖKSÜZ, G. 1975: Rank-size distributions for small settlements in Turkey. *Middle East Technical University, Journal of the Faculty of Architecture*, **1**, 145–52. (4.3.2)

GUNAWARDENA, K. A. 1964: Service centres in southern Ceylon. *University of Cambridge, Ph.D. Thesis*. (4.3.2, 5.2.1, 5.2.5)

GURLAND, J. 1957: Sime interrelations among compound and generalized distributions. *Biometrika*, **44**, 265–68. (13.2.2)

HÄGERSTRAND, T. 1952: The propagation of innovation waves. *Lund Studies in Geography, B, Human Geography*, **4**, 3–19. (7.1)

1953: *Innovationsforloppet ur korologisk synpunkt*. Lund. (7.1, 7.8, 13.3.1)

1955: Statistika primäruppgifter, flykartering och data processing maskiner. *Meddelanden Frans Lunds Geografiska Institut*, **344**, 233–55. (9.8.1, 10.5)

1957: Migration and area: survey of a sample of Swedish migration fields and hypothetical considerations on their genesis. *Lund Studies in Geography, B, Human Geography*, **13**, 27–158. (2.3.1, 2.4.2, 2.4.3, 2.6.2, 4.2, 4.2.3)

1965a: Quantitative techniques for analysis of the spread of information and technology. In C. A. Anderson and M. J. Bowman, Editors. *Education and economic development*. Chicago. 244–80. (7.2.1)

1965b: A Monte Carlo approach to diffusion. *European Journal of Sociology*, **6**, 43–67. (13.3.1)

1967: On Monte Carlo simulation of diffusion. *Northwestern University, Studies in Geography*, **13**, 1–32. (7.2.2, 7.4, 7.6.1, 7.7.2)

1971: Regional forecasting and social engineering. In M. D. I. Chisholm, A. E. Frey and P. Haggett, Editors. *Regional forecasting*. London. 1–7. (16.1)

HAGGETT, P. 1961: Multilevel variance analysis of *sobreiro* distribution in the Tagus–Sado basin, central Portugal. Mimeographed. (6.2.1, 10.5.2, 12.3.2)

1963: Regional and local components in land-use sampling: a case study from the Brazilian Triangulo. *Erdkunde*, **17**, 108–14. (8.3.3)

1964: Regional and local components in the distribution of forested areas in southeast Brazil: a multivariate approach. *Geographical Journal*, **130**, 365–80. (8.3.2, 8.4.2, 10.5.2, 12.2.3)

1965: *Locational analysis in human geography*. (First edition) London. (12.2.3)

1972: Contagious processes in a planar graph: an epidemiological application. In N. D. McGlashan, Editor. *Medical Geography*. London. 307–24. (4.6.1, 11.5.1, 11.5.3)

1973: Forecasting alternative spatial, ecological and regional futures: problems and possibilities. In R. J. Chorley, Editor. *Directions in Geography*. London. 219–35. (16.1)

1975a: *Geography: a modern synthesis*. New York. 546–72. (Preface, 1.2.1, 1.2.4, 1.3, 5.2.3, 8.3.4, 8.4.1, 14.5.2, 16.1)

1975b: Simple epidemics in human populations: some geographical aspects of the Hamer–Soper diffusion models. In R. F. Peel, M. D. I. Chisholm, and P. Haggett, Editors. *Processes in physical and human geography: Bristol essays*. London. Chapter 18. (7.7.4)

1976: Measuring instability in the growth of urban systems: a biproportionate index. *Geoforum*. In press. (4.4.2)

HAGGET, P., and K. A. BASSETT. 1970: The use of trend surface parameters in inter-urban comparisons. *Environment and Planning*, **2**, 225–37. (12.2.2)

HAGGETT, P., and C. BOARD. 1964: Rotational and parallel traverses in the rapid integration of geographic areas. *Annals of the Association of American Geographers*, **54**, 406–10. (8.3.3)

HAGGETT, P., and R. J. CHORLEY. 1969: *Network analysis in geography*. London. (3.1, 3.2.2, 3.3.2, 15.3)

HAGGETT, P., R. J. CHORLEY, and D. R. STODDART. 1965: Scale standards in geographical research: a new measure of area magnitude. *Nature*, **205**, 844–7. (1.2.4)

HAGGETT, P., and K. A. GUNÁWARDENA. 1964: Determination of population thresholds for settlement functions by the Reed–Muench method. *Professional Geographer*, **16**, 6–9. (5.2.1)

HAGOOD, M. J. 1943: Statistical methods for delineation of regions applied to data on agriculture and population. *Social Forces*, **21**, 288–97. (14.4.4)

HAGOOD, M. J., and D. O. PRICE. 1952: *Statistics for sociologists*. New York. (14.4.3, 14.4.4)

HAIG, R. M. 1925–6: Towards an understanding of the metropolis. *Quarterly Journal of Economics*, **40**, 427. (5.5.2)

HALL, A. D., and R. E. FAGEN. 1956: Definition of system. *General Systems Yearbook*, **1**, 18–28. (1.2.3)

HALL, P. 1962: *The industries of London since 1861*. London. (8.4.1)
1966: *Von Thünen's isolated state*. Oxford. (6.3.2)

HAMER, W. H. 1906: Epidemic disease in England. *The Lancet*, 733–39. (7.7.4)

HAMMERSLEY, J. M. 1966: First passage percolation. *Journal of the Royal Statistical Society*, **B, 28**, 491–96. (7.7.7)

HAMMERSLEY, J. M., and D. C. HANDSCOMB. 1963 *Monte Carlo methods*. London. (7.7.7)

HAMMERSLEY, J. M., and R. S. WALTERS. 1963: Percolating and fractional branching processes. *Journal of the Society for Industrial and Applied Mathematics*, **11**, 831–39. (7.7.7)

HAMMOND, R., and P. S. McCULLAGH. 1974: *Quantitative techniques in geography*. Oxford. (10.1)

HANNERBERG, D., T. HÄGERSTRAND, and B. ODEVING. 1957: Migration in Sweden: a symposium. *Lund Studies in Geography, B, Human Geography*, **13**. (2.2.1)

HANSON, N. R. 1958: *Patterns of discovery*. Cambridge. (1.1)

HARDY, T. 1886: *The life and death of the mayor of Casterbridge*. London. (5.4.1)

HARMAN, H. 1960: *Modern factor analysis*. Chicago. (9.4.3)

HARRIS, C. D. 1954: The market as a factor in the localization of industry in the United States. *Annals of the Association of American Geographers*, **44**, 315–48. (2.4.2)

HARRIS, C. D., and E. L. ULLMAN. 1945: The nature of cities. *Annals of the American Academy of Political and Social Science*, **242**, 7–17. (6.6.2)

HARRISON, P. J. 1965: Short-term sales forecasting. *Applied Statistics*, **14**, 102–39. (6.3.3)

HART, J. F. 1954: Central tendency in areal distributions. *Economic Geography*, **30**, 48–59. (9.6.2)

HARTSHORNE, R. 1939: *The nature of geography: a critical survey of current thought in the light of the past*. Lancaster. (1.2.2, 1.2.3, 1.2.4, 1.4.3)
1959: *Perspective on the nature of geography*. London. (1.2.1, 8.1)

HARVEY, D. W. 1963: Locational change in the Kentish hop industry and the analysis of land use patterns. *Institute of British Geographers, Publications*, **33**, 123–44. (6.5.2)

1966: Geographical processes and the analysis of point patterns: testing models of diffusion by quadrat sampling. *Institute of British Geographers, Publications*, **40**, 81–95. (13.3.1)

1968a: Pattern, process and the scale problem in geographical research. *Institute of British Geographers, Publications*, **45**, 71–78. (10.6.2)

1968b: Some methodological problems in the use of the Neyman Type A and negative binomial probability distributions for the analysis of spatial point patterns. *Institute of British Geographers, Publications*, **44**, 85–95. (13.2, 13.4.4, 15.4.4)

1969a: *Explanation in geography.* London. (1.2.2, 14.2.1, 14.2.3)

1969b: Conceptual and measurement problems in the cognitive-behavioural approach to location theory. *Northwestern University, Studies in Geography*, **17**, 35–67. (6.5.3)

1972a: Revolutionary and counter revolutionary theory in geography and the problem of ghetto formation. *Antipode*, **4**, 1–13. (1.4.5)

1972b: Society, the city and the space economy of urbanism. *Association of American Geographers, Commission on College Geography, Resource Papers*, **18**. (6.6.2)

1973: *Social justice and the city.* London. (6.6.2, 15.5.1)

HAWLEY, A. H. 1950: *Human ecology.* New York. (1.2.3)

HAYNES, R. M. 1975: Dimensional analysis: some applications in human geography. *Geographical Analysis*, **7**, 51–68. (2.4.3)

HELVIG, M. 1964: Chicago's external truck movements: spatial interactions between the Chicago area and its hinterland. *University of Chicago, Department of Geography, Research Papers*, **90**. (2.2.2, 2.4.3)

HENDERSON, J. M. 1955a: Efficiency and pricing in the coal industry. *Review of Economics and Statistics*, **37**, 50–60. (15.1)

1955b: A short-run model of the coal industry. *Review of Economics and Statistics*, **37**, 224–30. (15.1)

1958: *The efficiency of the coal industry: an application of linear programming.* Cambridge, Mass. (15.1)

HEPPLE, L. W. 1975: Spectral techniques and the study of interregional economic cycles. In R. F. Peel, M. D. I. Chisholm, and P. Haggett, Editors. *Processes in physical and human geography: Bristol essays.* London, 392–408. (4.6.3, 12.5.2)

HERBERT, D. J., and B. H. STEVENS. 1960: A model for the distribution of residential activity in urban areas. *Journal of Regional Science*, **2**, 21–36. (15.5.1)

HERFINDAHL, O. C. 1969: *Natural resources information for economic development.* Baltimore, Md. (8.4.1)

HESS, S. W., J. B. WEAVER, H. J. SIEGFELT, J. N. WHELAN, and P. A. ZITLAU. 1965: Nonpartisan redistricting by computer. *Operations Research*, **13**, 998–1006. (14.5.2)

HIDORE, J. J. 1963: The relations between cash-grain farming and landforms. *Economic Geography*, **39**, 84–9. (6.5.1)

HIGGS, R. 1969: The growth of cities in a Midwestern region 1870–1900. *Journal of Regional Science*, **9**, 369–75. (5.3.2)

HIGHSMITH, R. M., O. H. HEINTZELMAN, J. G. JENSEN, R. D. RUDD, and P. R. TSCHIRLEY. 1961: *Case studies in world geography.* New York. (8.3)

HODDER, B. W. 1966: Some comments on the origins of traditional markets in

Africa south of the Sahara. *Institute of British Geographers, Publications,* **36**, 97–105. (5.3.1)

HODGE, D., and A. GATTRELL. 1975: Spatial constraint and the location of urban public facilities. *Pennsylvania State University.* Mimeographed. (9.3.3)

HOEL, P. G. 1966: *Elementary statistics* (2nd edition). New York. (10.1)

HOLGATE, P. 1965: Some new tests of randomness. *Journal of Ecology,* **53**, 261–66. (13.6, 13.6.1, 13.6.4, 13.7)
— 1972: The use of distance methods for the analysis of spatial distributions of points. In P. A. W. Lewis, Editor. *Stochastic point processes.* New York, 122–35. (13.6, 13.7, 13.6.1)

HOLMES, J. H. 1973: Population concentration and dispersion in Australian states. *Australian Geographical Studies,* **11**, 150–70. (4.3.1)
— 1973: Telephone traffic in the Queensland urban system. *University of Queensland.* Mimeographed. (14.6.1–2)

HOLMES, J. H., and P. HAGGETT. 1975: Graph theory interpretation of flow matrices: a note on maximization procedures for identifying significant links. *University of Queensland.* Mimeographed. (9.4.2, 14.6.2)

HOLT, C. C. 1957: Forecasting seasonals and trends by experimentally weighted moving averages. *Carnegie Institute of Technology, Research Memoirs,* **52**. (16.3.3)

HOOVER, E. M. 1936: The measurement of industrial localization. *Review of Economics and Statistics,* **18**, 162–71. (9.3.4)
— 1948: *The location of economic activity.* New York.

HOPE, A. C. A. 1968: A simplified Monte Carlo significance test procedure. *Journal of the Royal Statistical Society, B,* **30**, 582–98. (7.6.2, 13.5)

HOSKINS, W. G. 1955: *The making of the English landscape.* London. (4.2.3)

HOTELLING, H. 1921: A mathematical theory of migration. *University of Washington, M.A. Thesis.* (2.4.4)

HOUSE, J. W. 1953: Medium sized towns in the urban pattern of two industrial societies: England and Wales—U.S.A. *Planning Outlook,* **3**, 52–79. (4.5.1)

HOWARD, E. 1920: *Territory in bird life.* London. (2.7)

HOWE, G. M. 1963: *National atlas of disease mortality in the United Kingdom.* London. (1.2.2)

HOYT, H. 1939: *The structure and growth of residential neighbourhoods in American cities.* Washington. (6.6.2)

HSU, S. Y., and J. D. MASON. 1974: The nearest-neighbour statistics for testing randomness of point distributions in a bounded two-dimensional space. In M. Yeates, Editor. *Proceedings of the 1972 meeting of the IGU Commission on Quantitative Geography.* Montreal. (13.6.2)

HUANG, D. S. 1970: *Regression and econometric methods.* New York. (16.2.1)

HUDSON, J. C. 1969a: Diffusion in a central place system. *Geographical Analysis,* **1**, 456–58. (7.3–4)
— 1969b: A location theory for rural settlement. *Annals of the Association of American Geographers,* **59**, 365–81. (4.2.3)
— 1972: *Geographical diffusion theory.* Evanston, Ill. (7.4, 7.7.7)

HUFF, D. L. 1960: A topographical model of consumer space preferences. *Regional Science Association, Papers,* **6**, 159–73. (2.4.2)

HUNT, L. G. 1974: Recent spread of heroin use in the United States. *American Journal of Public Health,* **64**, Supplement, 16–23. (4.6.1)

HURST, M. E. ELIOT, Editor. 1974: *Transportation geography: comments and readings.* New York. (3.2.3, 3.5)

HURTER, A. P., and L. N. MOSES. 1964: Regional investment and interregional programming. *Regional Science Association, Papers,* **13**, 105–19. (15.4.1)

ILLICH, I. D. 1974: *Energy and equity*. London. (5.5.2)

INGRAM, G. K., J. F. KAIN, and J. R. GINN. 1972: *The Detroit prototype of the NBER urban simulation model*. New York. (15.5.1)

INTERNATIONAL GEOGRAPHICAL UNION. 1964: *Abstracts of papers, 20th International Geographical Congress*. London. (3.3.2, 4.3)

INTERNATIONAL URBAN RESEARCH. 1959: *The world's metropolitan areas*. Berkeley. (4.3, 8.2.3)

INTRILIGATOR, M. D. 1971: *Mathematical optimization and economic theory*. Englewood Cliffs, N.J. (15.5.3)

ISARD, W. 1956: *Location and space-economy: a general theory relating to industrial location, market areas, land use, trade and urban structure*. New York. (1.2.2, 2.2.2, 2.7.3, 4.2.2, 4.3.1, 5.5, 5.6.1–2, 6.5.2)

ISARD, W., D. F. BRAMHALL, G. A. P. CARROTHERS, J. H. CUMBERLAND, L. N. MOSES, D. O. PRICE, and E. W. SCHOOLER. 1960: *Methods of regional analysis: an introduction to regional science*. New York. (1.3, 2.1, 2.4.1, 2.4.3–4, 5.4.2, 5.4.4, 5.5, 5.5.1, 5.6.3, 15.4.1)

ISARD, W., and S. CZAMANSKI. 1965: Techniques for estimating multiplier effects of major government programs. *Papers of the Peace Research Society*, **3**, 19–45. (5.3.3)

ISARD, W., and R. E. KUENNE. 1953: The impact of steel upon the Greater New York–Philadelphia industrial region: a study in agglomeration projection. *Review of Economics and Statistics*, **35**, 289–301. (5.4.2)

ISARD, W., and E. W. SCHOOLER. 1955: *Location factors in the petrochemical industry*. Washington. (5.5.1)

ISBELL, E. C. 1944: Internal migration in Sweden and intervening opportunities. *American Sociological Review*, **9**, 627–39. (2.6.2)

JAMES, G., A. D. CLIFF, P. HAGGETT, and J. K. ORD. 1970: Some discrete distributions for graphs with applications to regional transport networks. *Geografiska Annaler, B*, **52**, 14–21. (9.7.2)

JAMES, P. E. 1959: *Latin America*. New York. (6.6.2)

JAMES, P. E., C. F. JONES, and J. K. WRIGHT, Editors. 1954: *American geography: inventory and prospect*. Syracuse. (1.2.4, 14.2.2)

JANES, E. T. 1957: Information theory and statistical mechanics. *Physics Review*, **106**, 620–30. (2.5.2)

JEFFERS, J. N. R. 1959: *Experimental design and analysis in forest research*. Stockholm. (10.5.2)

JENKINS, G. M., and D. G. WATTS. 1968: *Spectral analysis and its applications*. San Francisco. (12.4.1, 12.4.4, 12.5.1, 12.5.3)

JENKS, G. F. 1963: Generalization in statistical mapping. *Annals of the Association of American Geographers*, **53**, 15–26. (9.3.1)

JENKS, G. F., and M. R. C. COULSON. 1963: Class intervals for statistical maps. *International Yearbook of Cartography*, **3**, 119–34. (9.3.1)

JEVONS, F. R. 1973: *Science observed*. London. (1.4.1)

JOERG, W. L. G., Editor. 1932: *Pioneer settlement*. New York. (7.1)

JOHNSON, H. B. 1941: The distribution of German pioneer population in Minnesota. *Rural Sociology*, **6**, 16–34. (2.6.2)
 1957: Rational and ecological aspects of the quarter section: an example from Minnesota. *Geographical Review*, **47**, 330–48. (4.2.1)
 1962: A note on Thünen's circles. *Annals of the Association of American Geographers*, **52**, 213–20. (6.3.2)

JOHNSON, W. W. 1892: *The theory of errors and method of least squares*. New York. (9.6.2)

JOHNSTON, J. 1972: *Econometric methods..* (Second edition) New York. (10.2.2, 10.3.1–3, 11.4.2, 12.2.2, 16.2.1, 16.4.2)

JOHNSTON, R. J. 1971: *Urban residential patterns.* London. (6.6.2)
    1973: On frictions of distance and regression coefficients. *Area*, **5**, 187–91. (2.4.2)
    1975: Map pattern and friction of distance parameters: a comment. *Regional Studies*, **9**, 281–83. (2.4.2)

JONASSON, O. 1925: Agricultural regions of Europe. *Economic Geography*, **2**. (6.4.1)

JONES, E. 1964: *Human geography.* London. (4.2., 4.2.2)

JOHNSON, B. L. C. 1958: The distribution of factory population in the West Midlands conurbation. *Institute of British Geographers, Publications*, **25**, 209–223. (8.4.2)

KAIN, J. F. 1962: The journey-to-work as a determinant of residential location. *Regional Science Association, Papers and Proceedings*, **9**, 137–59. (2.2.1)

KAISER, H. F. 1966: An objective method for establishing legislative districts. *Midwest Journal of Political Science*, **10**, 80–96. (14.5.2)

KANSKY, K. J. 1963: Structure of transport networks: relationships between network geometry and regional characteristics. *University of Chicago, Department of Geography, Research Papers*, **84**. (3.4.3, 3.5.1, 9.7.1)

KARIEL, H. G. 1963: Selected factors areally associated with population growth due to net migration. *Annals of the Association of American Geographers*, **53**, 210–23. (2.4.4)

KARLQVIST, A., and L. LUNDQVIST. 1972: A contact model for spatial allocation. *Regional Studies*, **6**, 401–19. (5.5.2)

KATTI, S. K., and J. GURLAND. 1961: The Poisson Pascal distribution. *Biometrics*, **17**, 527–38. (13.2.4)

KEMP, C. D. 1967: On a contagious distribution suggested for accident data. *Biometrics*, **23**, 241–55. (13.3.1, 13.2.4)

KENDALL, D. G. 1957: La propagation d'une épédémie au d'un bruit une population limitée. *Publications de l'Institut de Statistique de l'Université de Paris*, **6**, 307–11. (7.7.3)
    1965: Mathematical models of the spread of infection. In Medical Research Council. *Mathematics and Computer Science in Biology and Medicine.* London. 213–25. (7.7.3)
    1971: Construction of maps from 'odd bits of information'. *Nature*, **231**, 158–9. (9.8.2)

KENDALL, M. G. *Time series.* London. (10.4.3, 11.3.1, 12.4.1–2, 12.4.4, 12.5.1–2, 16.1, 16.3.2–3)

KENDALL, M. G., and W. R. BUCKLAND. 1960: *A dictionary of statistical terms.* Edinburgh. (8.2.2, 12.5.1)

KENDALL, M. G., and P. A. P. MORAN. 1963: *Geometrical probability.* London. (4.3.3)

KENDALL, M. G., and A. STUART. 1966: *The advanced theory of statistics*, **3**. *Analysis of variance and time series.* London. (12.3.1, 16.5.1)
    1967: *The advanced theory of statistics*, **2**. *Inference and relationship.* London. (10.5.1–3, 16.4.2)

KERMACK, W. O., and A. G. McKENDRICK. 1927: Contributions to the mathematical theory of epidemics. *Proceedings of the Royal Society, A*, **115**, 700–21. (7.7.3)

KERSHAW, K. A. 1964: *Quantitative and dynamic ecology.* London. (8.3.3)

KING, L. J. 1961: A multivariate analysis of the spacing of urban settlements in the United States. *Annals of the Association of American Geographers*, **51**, 222–33. (4.5.2, 10.5.2)

1962: A quantitative expression of the pattern of urban settlements in selected areas of the United States. *Tijdschrift voor Economische en Sociale Geografie*, **53**, 1–7. (4.2.1, 5.2.1)

1969a: The analysis of spatial form and its relation to geographic theory. *Annals of the Association of American Geographers*, **59**, 573–95. (1.2.2)

1969b: *Statistical analysis in geography*. Englewood Cliffs, N.J. (Preface, 10.1, 12.2)

KING, L. J., E. CASETTI, and D. JEFFREY. 1969: Economic impulses in a regional system of cities. *Regional Studies*, **3**, 213–18. (4.6.3)

KLAASEN, L. H., D. H. VAN D. TORMAN, and L. M. KOYCK. 1949: *Hoodfliinen van de sociaal-economische anfwikkeling der gemeente Amerstoort van 1900–1970*. Leiden. (5.4.4)

KLEINROCK, L. 1964: *Communications nets—stochastic message flow and delay*. New York. (3.4.4)

KOLARS, J., and H. MALIN. 1970: Population and accessibility—an analysis of Turkish railroads. *Geographical Review*, **60**, 229–46. (3.4.3)

KOLLMORGAN, W. M. 1969: The woodsman's assaults on the domain of the cattle man. *Annals of the Association of American Geographers*, **59**, 215–39. (6.5.2)

KOLLMORGAN, W. M., and G. F. JENKS. 1951: A geographic study of population and settlement changes in Sherman county, Kansas. *Kansas Academy of Sciences, Transactions*, **54**, 449–94. (4.2.1, 6.2.4)

KOPEC, R. J. 1963: An alternative method for the construction of Thiessen polygons. *Professional Geographer*, **15** (5), 24–6. (13.5)

KRUMBEIN, W. C. 1955a: Composite end-members in facies mapping. *Journal of Sedimentary Petrology*, **25**, 115–22. (9.4.1)

1955b: Experimental design in the earth sciences. *Transactions of the American Geophysical Union*, **36**, 1–11. (10.5.2)

1956: Regional and local components in facies maps. *Bulletin of the American Association of Petroleum Geologists*, **40**, 2163–94. (12.2.3, 12.3.1)

1957: Comparison of percentage and ratio data in facies mapping. *Journal of Sedimentary Petrology*, **27**, 293–7. (10.5.2)

1960: The geological 'population' as a framework for analysing numerical data in geology. *Liverpool and Manchester Geological Journal*, **2**, 341–68. (8.2.2, 8.3.2)

KRUMBEIN, W. C., and F. A. GRAYBILL. 1965: *An introduction to statistical models in geology*. New York. (10.1)

KUHN, H. W., and R. E. KUENNE. 1962: An efficient algorithm for the numerical solution of the generalized Weber problem in spatial economics. *Journal of Regional Science*, **4**, 21–33. (5.6.1)

KUHN, T. S. 1962: *The structure of scientific revolutions*. Chicago. (1.4.1)

KULLDORFF, G. 1955: Migration probabilities. *Lund Studies in Geography, Series B, Human Geography*, **14**. (4.2.3, 10.6.1)

LAKATOS, I., and A. MUSGRAVE, Editors. 1970: *Criticism and the growth of knowledge*. Cambridge. (1.4.1)

LALANNE, L. 1863: Essai d'une théorie des réseaux de chemin de fer, fondée sur l'observation des faits et sur les lois primordiales qui président au groupement des populations. *Comptes Rendus Hebdomadaires des Séances de l'Académie des Sciences*, **42**, 206–10. (3.1)

LAND, A. H. 1957: An application of linear programming to the transport of coking coal. *Journal of the Royal Statistical Society, A*, **120**, 308–19. (15.1)

LANGBEIN, W. B., and W. G. HOYT. 1959: *Water facts for the nation's future: uses and benefits of hydrological data problems.* New York. (8.4.1)

LANGLEY, S. C. 1974: Linear programming applications to school collecting districts. *University of Bristol, Department of Geography, B.Sc. Dissertation.* (14.4.3)

LANKFORD, P. M. 1974: Testing simulation models. *Geographical Analysis*, **6**, 295–302. (7.6.2)

LANGTON, J. 1972: Potentialities and problems of adopting a systems approach to the study of change in human geography. *Progress in Geography*, **4**, 125–79. (1.2.2)

LEA, A. C. 1973: Location allocation models. Part I—Review. Part II—An annotated bibliography. *University of Toronto, M.A. Project.* (5.6.1)

LEARMONTH, A. T. A., and M. N. PAL. 1959: A method of plotting two variables on the same map, using isopleths. *Erdkunde*, **13**, 145–50. (9.4)

LEBART, L. 1969: Analise statistique de la contiguité. *Publications de l'Université de Paris*, **18**, 81–112. (10.3.3)

LEE, D. R., and G. T. SALLEE. 1970: A method of measuring shape. *Geographical Review*, **60**, 555–63. (9.6.1)

LEOPOLD, L. B., M. G. WOLMAN, and J. P. MILLER. 1964: *Fluvial processes in geomorphology.* San Francisco. (4.3)

LEVISON, M., R. F. WARD, and J. W. WEBB. 1973: *The settlement of Polynesia: a computer simulation.* Minneapolis. (7.5.2)

LINSKY, A. S. 1965: Some generalizations concerning primate cities. *Annals of the Association of American Geographers*, **55**, 506–13. (4.3.1)

LINTON, D. L. 1949: The delimitation of morphological regions. *Institute of British Geographers, Publications*, **14**, 86–7. (14.2.2)

LÖSCH, A. 1940: *Die räumliche Ordnung der Wirtschaft.* Jena. (2.7.1)
1954: *The economics of location.* New Haven. (1.4.2, 2.2.1, 2.6.2, 2.7.1, 3.2.2, 3.5.3, 4.2.1, 4.5.2, 4.6.2, 5.2.1–2, 5.2.4, 6.3.2, 6.4.1, 6.5.1)

LOWRY, I. S. 1964: *A model of metropolis.* Santa Monica, Calif. (15.5.1)

LUKERMANN, F. 1965: The 'calcul des probabilités' and the Ecole française de Géographie. *Canadian Geographer*, **9**, 128–37. (1.4.3)
1966: Empirical expressions of nodality and hierarchy in a circulation manifold. *East Lakes Geographer*, **2**, 17–44. (4.4.2)

LUTTRELL, W. F. 1962: *Factory location and industrial movement.* London. (5.6.3)

McCARTY, H. H. 1956: Use of certain statistical procedures in geographical analysis. *Annals of the Association of American Geographers*, **46**, 263. (8.4.2)

McCARTY, H. H., J. C. HOOK, and D. S. KNOS. 1956: The measurement of association in industrial geography. *State University of Iowa, Department of Geography, Report*, **1**. (5.5.2, 5.6.1, 8.4.2, 9.3.4, 12.3)

McCASKILL, M., Editor. 1962: *Land and livelihood: geographical essays in honour of George Jobberns.* Christchurch. (5.4.2)

McCLELLAN, D. 1973: A re-examination and re-consideration of the neighbourhood effect in the diffusion of innovations at the micro scale. Unpublished prize winning essay for the Royal Geographical Society. (7.3)

McCONNELL, H. 1966: Quadrat methods in map analysis. *University of Iowa, Department of Geography, Discussion Papers*, **13**. (13.4.4)

McGUIRE, J. U., T. A. BRINDLEY, and T. A. BANCROFT. 1957: The distribution of the European corn-borer larvae in field-corn. *Biometrics*, **13**, 65–78, (and correction) **14**, 432–44. (13.2.4, 13.4.1)

MACH, E. 1942: *The science of mechanics.* La Salle, Ill. (2.2.1)

MACKAY, J. R. 1953: The alternative choice in isopleth interpolation. *Professional Geographer,* **5**, 2–4. (9.3.2)

 1958: The interactance hypothesis and boundaries in Canada. *Canadian Geographer,* **2**, 1–8. (2.6.2)

McKENZIE, R. D. 1933: *The metropolitan community.* New York. (1.2.3, 6.6.1)

MacKINNON, R. D. 1974: Lag regression models of the spatial spread of highway improvements. *Economic Geography,* **50**, 368–74. (7.8)

MacKINNON, R. D., and M. J. HODGSON. 1969: The highway system of southern Ontario and Quebec: some simple network generation models. *University of Toronto, Centre for Urban and Community Studies, Research Report,* **18**. (3.4.3)

MADDEN, C. H. 1958: Some temporal aspects of the growth of cities in the United States. *Economic Development and Cultural Change,* **6**, 143–69. (4.4.2)

MANSFIELD, E. 1961: Technical change and the rate of innovation. *Econometrica,* **29**, 741–66. (7.3)

MARSDEN, B. S. 1970: Urban delimitation on a density basis: Brisbane, 1861–1966. *New Zealand Geographer,* **26**, 151–61. (9.6.1)

MARSH, G. P. 1864: *Man and nature; or physical geography as modified by human action.* New York. (1.2.4)

MARTHE, F. 1878: Begriff, Ziel und Methode der Geographie. *Geographisches Jahrbuch,* **7**, 628. (1.2.2)

MARTIN, R. L. 1974: On autocorrelation, bias and the use of first spatial differences in regression analysis. *Area,* **6**, 185–94. (10.3.2–3)

 1975: Identification and estimation of dynamic space-time forecasting models for geographical data. *Advances in Applied Probability,* **7**, 455–56. (16.3.4)

MARTIN, R. L., and J. E. OEPPEN. 1975: The identification of regional forecasting models using space–time correlation functions. *Institute of British Geographers, Publications,* **66**, 95–118. (13.3.1, 16.4.1–2)

MASSAM, B. H. 1975: *Location and space in social administration.* London. (2.7.2, 9.6.1, 14.1, 14.5.3)

MASSAM, B. H., and A. F. BURGHARDT. 1968: The administrative subdivision of Southern Ontario: an attempt at evaluation. *Canadian Geographer,* **15**, 193–206. (9.6.1)

MASSAM, B. H., and M. F. GOODCHILD. 1971: Temporal trends in the spatial organization of a service agency. *Canadian Geographer,* **15**, 193–206. (9.6.1)

MASSEY, D. B. 1973: The basic-service categorization in planning. *Regional Studies,* **7**, 1–15. (5.3.3)

MATÉRN, B. 1960: Spatial variation: stochastic models and their application to some problems in forest surveys and other sampling investigations. *Meddelanden Fran Statens Skogsforsknings-institut,* **49**, 1–144. (13.4.4)

 1971: Doubly stochastic Poisson processes in the plane. In G. P. Patil, Editor. *Statistical ecology,* **1**. University Park, Pennsylvania. 195–213. (13.4.4)

 1972a: Poisson processes in the plane and related models for clumping and heterogeneity. *NATO Advanced Study Institute on Statistical Ecology.* Pennsylvania State University, Department of Statistics. (13.4.4, 13.5)

 1972b: Analysis of spatial patterns and ecological relations: the analysis of ecological maps as mosaics. *NATO Advanced Study Institute on Statistical Ecology,* Pennsylvania State University, Department of Statistics. (13.5)

MATUI, I. 1932: Statistical study of the distribution of scattered villages in two regions of the Tonami plain, Tayama prefecture. *Japanese Journal of Geology and Geography*, **9**, 251–66. (12.3.2, 13.2.1, 13.4.1)

MEAD, R. 1967: A mathematical model for the estimation of interplant competition. *Biometrics*, **23**, 189–205. (11.4.2)
1974: A test for spatial pattern at several scales using data from a grid of contagious quadrats. *Biometrics*, **30**, 295–307. (13.7)

MEAD, W. R. 1953: *Farming in Finland*. London. (6.5.2)

MEAD, W. R., and E. H. BROWN. 1962: *The United States and Canada*. London. (3.3.2, 4.2.1)

MEDAWAR, P. B. 1969: *Induction and intuition in scientific thought*. London. (1.4.2)

MEDVEDKOV, Y. V. 1967: The concept of entropy in settlement pattern analysis. *Regional Science Association, Papers*, **18**, 165–8. (13.7)

MEIJERLING, J. L. 1953: Interface area, edge length, and number of vertices in crystal aggregates with random nucleation. *Phillips Research Reports*, **8**, 270–90. (2.7.2)

MEINIG, D. W. 1962: A comparative historical geography of two railnets: Columbia basin and South Australia. *Annals of the Association of American Geographers*, **52**, 394–413. (1.4.3, 3.2.3)

MEITZEN, A. 1895: *Siedlung und Agrarwesen der Westgermanen und Ostgermanen des Kelten, Römer, Finen und Slawen*. Three volumes; one atlas. Berlin. (4.2.1)

MEYER, J. 1963: Regional economics: a survey. *American Economic Review*, **53**, 19–54. (1.3)

MEYNEN, E. 1960: *Orbis geographicus, 1960*. Wiesbaden. (8.1)

MIEHLE, W. 1958: Link-length minimization in networks. *Operations Research*, **6**, 232–43. (3.3.1)

MIKESELL, M. W. (1960). Comparative studies in frontier history. *Annals of the Association of American Geographers*, **50**, 62–74. (7.1)

MILLS, E. S. 1969: The value of urban land. In H. S. Perloff, Editor. *The quality of the urban environment*. Baltimore. 231–253. (6.2.2, 6.6.1)

MILLS, G. 1967: The determination of local government electoral boundaries. *Operations Research Quarterly*, **18**, 243–55. (14.5.2, 15.4.3)

MINISTRY OF TRANSPORT. 1961: *Rural bus services: report of the committee*. London. (2.6.1)

MINISTRY OF TRANSPORT. 1963: *Traffic in towns: a study of the long term problems of traffic in urban areas*. London. (3.5.3)

MINSHULL, R. 1967: *Regional geography: theory and practice*. London. (14.2.1)

MITCHELL, J. B. 1954: *Historical geography*. London. (4.2.3)

MOELLERING, H., and W. R. TOBLER. 1972: Geographical variances. *Geographical Analysis*, **4**, 34–50. (12.3.1–2)

MOLLISON, D. 1972a: Possible velocities for a simple epidemic. *Advances in Applied Probability*, **4**, 233–57. (7.7.2)
1972b: The rate of spatial propagation of simple epidemics. *Proceedings of the Sixth Berkeley Symposium on Mathematical Statistics and Probability*, **3**, 579–614. (7.7.2–3)
1975: Comments on Cliff, A. D. and J. K. Ord. 1975b: *Journal of the Royal Statistical Society*, B, **37**, 334–35. (16.2.2)

MOMBEIG, P. 1952: *Pionniers et planteurs de São Paulo*. Paris. (3.3.2, 6.6.2)

MOMSEN, R. P. 1963: Routes across the Serra do Mar—the evolution of transportation in the highlands of Rio de Janeiro and São Paulo. *Revista Geografica*, **32**, 5–167. (3.2.3)

MONMONIER, M. 1974: Measures of pattern complexity for choropleth maps. *American Cartographer*, **1**, 159–69. (9.3.3)

MOORE, E. F. 1959: The shortest path through a maze. *Annals of the Computation Laboratory of Harvard University*, **30**. (3.4.2)

MOORE, P. G. 1954: Spacing in plant populations. *Ecology*, **35**, 222–27. (13.6.1)

MORAN, P. A. P. 1948: The interpretation of statistical maps. *Journal of the Royal Statistical Society, B*, **10**, 243–51. (11.3.1)

MORGENSTERN, O. 1963: *On the accuracy of economic observations*. Princeton. (8.2.1, 8.2.3)

MORRILL, R. L. 1962: Simulation of central place patterns over time. *Lund Studies in Geography, Series B, Human Geography*, **24**, 109–20. (4.2.3)

1963: The development and spatial distribution of towns in Sweden: an historical-predictive approach. *Annals of the Association of American Geographers*, **53**, 1–14. (1.4.3)

1965: The negro ghetto: problems and alternatives. *Geographical Review*, **55**, 339–361. (6.6.2)

1968: Waves of spatial diffusion. *Journal of Regional Science*, **8**, 1–18. (7.5.1)

1970: The shape of diffusion in space and time. *Economic Geography*, **46**, 259–68. (7.5.1)

MORRILL, R. L., and W. L. GARRISON. 1960: Projections of interregional trade in wheat and flour. *Economic Geography*, **36**, 116–26. (15.1)

MOSER, C. A., and W. SCOTT. 1961: *British towns: a statistical study of their social and economic differences*. Edinburgh. (5.4.4)

MOSES, L. N. 1960: A general equilibrium model of production, interregional trade and location of industry. *Review of Economics and Statistics*, **62**, 373–99. (15.4.1)

MURRAY, M. 1962: The geography of death in England and Wales. *Annals of the Association of American Geographers*, **52**, 130–49. (10.6.1)

MUTH, R. F. 1962: The spatial structure of the housing market. *Regional Science Association, Papers*, **7**, 207–20. (6.2.2)

1969: *Cities and housing*. Chicago. (6.6.2)

NAGEL, E. 1961: *The structure of science*. New York. (1.4.3)

NAGEL, S. S. 1965: Simplified bipartisan computer redistricting. *Stanford Law Review*, **17**, 863–99. (14.5.2)

NAROLL, R. 1961: Two solutions to Galton's problem. In F. Moore, Editor. *Readings in cross cultural methodology*. New Haven. (10.2)

NEAVE, H. 1972: Observations on spectral analysis of short series—a simulation study by Granger and Hughes. *Journal of the Royal Statistical Society, A*, **135**, 393–405. (12.4.4, 12.5.3)

NEFT, D. S. 1966: *Statistical analysis for areal distributions*. Philadelphia. (13.7)

NEWLING, B. 1969: The spatial variation of urban population densities. *Geographical Review*, **59**, 242–52. (6.2.2, 6.6.1)

NEYMAN, J. 1939: On a new class of 'contagious distributions' applicable in entomology and bacteriology. *Annals of Mathematical Statistics*, **10**, 35–57. (13.2.4)

NEYMAN, J., and E. L. SCOTT. 1952: A theory of the spatial distribution of galaxies. *Astrophysical Journal*, **116**, 144–63. (13.4.4)

1958: Statistical approach to problems of cosmology. *Journal of the Royal Statistical Society, B*, **20**, 1–29. (13.4.4)

1972: Processes of clustering and applications. In P. A. W. Lewis, Editor. *Stochastic Point Processes*. New York. 646–81. (13.4.4)

NIEDERCORN, J. H., and E. F. R. HEARLE. 1964: Recent land use trends in 48 large American cities. *Land Economics*, **40**, 105–10. (6.2.4)

NISHIOKA, H. 1975: Location theory in Japan. *Progress in Geography*, **7**, 133–200. (1.1)

NORCLIFFE, G. B. 1969: On the use and limitations of trend surface models. *Canadian Geographer*, **13**, 338–48. (12.2.2)

NYSTUEN, J. D., and M. F. DACEY. 1961: A graph theory interpretation of nodal regions. *Regional Science Association, Papers and Proceedings*, **7**, 29–42. (14.6.1)

OFFICE OF STATISTICAL STANDARDS. 1958: *Criteria for defining Standard Metropolitan Areas*. Washington. (8.2.3)

OHLIN, B. 1933: *Interregional and international trade*. Cambridge, Mass. (6.4.1)

OLSSON, G. 1965: Distance and human interaction: a review and bibliography. *Regional Science Research Institute, Bibliography Series*, **2**. (2.2.2)

OLSON, J. S., and P. E. POTTER. 1954: Variance components of cross-bedding direction in some basal Pennsylvanian sandstones of the Eastern Interior Basin: statistical methods. *Journal of Geology*, **62**, 26–49. (12.3.1)

ORD, J. K. 1967: On a system of discrete distributions. *Biometrika*, **54**, 649–56. (9.7.2)

1972a: *Families of frequency distributions*. London. (10.5.2, 13.2.2, 13.2.4, 13.3.3–4, 13.4.2)

1972b: Density estimation and tests for randomness using distance methods. *NATO Advanced Study Institute on Statistical Ecology*. Pennsylvania State University, Department of Statistics. (13.6, 13.6.1)

1974: Comments of Besag, J. E. 1974: *Journal of the Royal Statistical Society, B*, **36**, 229. (16.7)

1975: Estimation methods for models of spatial interaction. *Journal of the American Statistical Association*. (11.4.2, 16.6)

ORDEN, A. 1956: The transshipment problem. *Management Science*, **2**, 276–85. (15.4.1)

O'SULLIVAN, P. M. 1968: Accessibility and the spatial structure of the Irish economy. *Regional Studies*, **2**, 195–206. (11.4.2)

PAELINCK, J. H. P. 1970: Dynamic urban growth models. *Regional Science Association, Papers*, **24**, 25–37. (5.3.3)

PAELINCK, J. H. P., and P. NIJKAMP. 1975: *Operational theory and method in regional economics*. Farnborough. (5.4.2)

PARK, R. E. 1929: Urbanization as measured by newspaper circulation. *American Journal of Sociology*, **35**, 60–79. (2.6.2)

PARR, J. B. 1970: Models of city size in an urban system. *Regional Science Association, Papers*, **25**, 221–53. (5.2.4)

PARSONS, J. J. 1949: Antioqueño colonization in western Colombia: an historical geography. *Ibero-Americana*, **32**, 1–225. (7.1)

PASSONEAU, J. R., and R. S. WURMAN. 1966: *Urban atlas: 20 American cities*. Cambridge, Mass. (10.6)

PATERSON, J. H. 1975: *North America: a regional geography*. Oxford. (5.5.3, 14.1)

PATIL, G. P., and S. W. JOSHI. 1968: *A dictionary and bibliography of discrete distributions*. Edinburgh. (13.2.2, 13.3.4)

PATTISON, W. D. 1957: Beginnings of the American rectangular land survey system, 1784–1800. *University of Chicago, Department of Geography, Research Papers*, **50**. (4.2.1)

1964: The four traditions of geography. *Journal of Geography*, **63**, 211–6. (1.2.1)

PEDERSEN, P. O. 1967: On the geometry of administrative areas. Copenhagen. Manuscript Report. (2.7.2)

1970: Innovation diffusion within and between national urban systems.

Geographical Analysis, **2**, 203–54. (7.4)

PEET, R. 1969: The spatial expansion of commercial agriculture in the nineteenth century: a von Thünen interpretation. *Economic Geography,* **45**, 283–301. (6.4.1)

— 1972: Influences of the British market on agriculture and related economic development in Europe before 1860. *Institute of British Geographers, Publications,* **56**, 1–20. (6.4.1)

PELTO, C. R. 1954: Mapping of multicomponent systems. *Journal of Geology,* **62**, 501–11. (9.4.1)

PERRING., F. H., and S. M. WALTERS. 1962: *Atlas of the British flora.* London. (1.2.2, 8.4.2, 9.8.1)

PERROUX, F. 1970: Note on the concept of growth poles. In D. C. McKee, *et al.,* Editors. *Regional economics.* New York. (15.2.3)

PERSSON, O. 1971: The robustness of estimating density by distance measurements. In G. P. Patil, *et al.,* Editors. *Statistical ecology.* University Park, Pennsylvania. 175–90. (13.6.1)

PHILBRICK, A. K. 1957: Principles of areal functional organization in regional human geography. *Economic Geography,* **33**, 299–336. (14.2.2)

PIELOU, E. C. 1957: The effect of quadrat size on the estimation of the parameters of the Neyman's and Thomas's distributions. *Journal of Ecology,* **45**, 31–47. (13.4.4)

— 1969: *An introduction to mathematical ecology.* New York. (13.1–2, 13.3.1, 13.3.4, 13.5, 13.6.5)

PLATT, R. S. 1942: *Latin America: countrysides and united regions.* New York. (8.3.)

PLATT, R. S. 1959: Field study in American geography: the development of theory and method exemplified by selections. *University of Chicago, Department of Geography, Research Papers,* **61**. (8.3, 8.3.3)

POLLACK, M., and W. WIEBENSON. 1960: Solutions of the shortest-route problem: a review. *Operations Research,* **8**, 224–30. (3.4.2)

POLYA, G. 1931: Sur quelques points de la théorie des probabilités. *Annals de l'Institut de Henri Poincaré,* **1**, 117–62. (13.2.4)

PONSARD, C. 1969: *Un modèle topologique d'equilibre économique interrégional.* Paris. (9.7.4, 14.6.2)

PORTER, P. W. 1960: Earnest and the Orephagians: a fable for the instruction of young geographers. *Annals of the Association of American Geographers,* **50**, 297–99. (13.6.5)

POSTAN, M. 1948: The revulsion from thought. *Cambridge Journal,* **1**, 395–408. (1.1)

POUNDS, N. J. G. 1959: *The geography of iron and steel.* London. (5.5.1)

PRED, A. 1964: The intrametropolitan location of American manufacturing. *Annals of the Association of American Geographers,* **54**, 165–80. (6.6.2)

PYKE, M. 1965: Spacings. *Journal of the Royal Statistical Society, B,* **27**, 395–449. (4.3.3)

PYLE, G. F. 1969: Diffusion of cholera in the United States. *Geographical Analysis,* **1**, 59–75. (4.6.1, 7.5.1)

QUANT, R. E. 1960: Models of transportation and optimal network construction. *Journal of Regional Science,* **2**, 27–45. (3.3.1, 15.4.2)

QUENOUILLE, M. H. 1949a: Problems in plane sampling. *Annals of Mathematical Statistics,* **20**, 355–75. (8.3.2)

— 1949b: A relationship between the logarithmic, Poisson and negative binomial series. *Biometrics,* **5**, 162–64. (13.2.4)

RAPOPORT, A. 1951: Nets with distance bias. *Bulletin of Mathematical*

Biophysics, **13**, 85–92. (7.3)

RAPOPORT, H., and P. ABRAMSON. 1959: An analog computer for finding an optimum route through a communications network. *Institute of Radio Engineers, Transactions on Communications Systems*, **CS-7**, 37–42. (3.4.2)

RAVENSTEIN, E. G. 1885, 1889: The laws of migration. *Journal of the Royal Statistical Society*, **48**, 52. (2.2.2)

RAVETZ, J. R. 1971: *Scientific knowledge and its social problems*. Oxford. (1.4.5)

RAYNER, J. N. 1971: *An introduction to spectral analysis*. London. (12.4.1, 12.4.3, 12.4.4)

RAYNER, J. N., and R. G. GOLLEDGE. 1972: Spectral analysis of settlement patterns in diverse physical and economic environments. *Environment and Planning*, **4**, 347–71. (4.2.1, 12.4.3)
  1973: The spectrum of U.S. Route 40 re-examined. *Geographical Analysis*, **5**, 338–50. (4.2.1, 12.4.2)

REED, W. E. 1970: Indirect connectivity and hierarchies of urban dominance. *Annals of the Association of American Geographers*, **60**, 770–85. (9.7.4)

REES, P. H. 1970: The urban envelope: patterns and dynamics of population density. In B. J. L. Berry and F. E. Horton, Editors. *Geographic perspectives on urban systems*. Englewood Cliffs, N.J. 276–305. (6.6.1)

RHYNSBURGER, D. 1973: Analytic delineation of Thiessen polygons. *Geographical Analysis*, **5**, 133–44. (13.5)

RICHARDSON, H. W. 1973: *The economics of urban size*. Lexington, Mass. (4.3.3)

RIDLEY, T. H. 1969: Reducing the travel time in a transport network. In A. J. Scott, Editor. *Studies in Regional Science*. London. 73–87. (15.4.2)

RIMMER, P. J. 1967: The changing status of New Zealand seaports, 1853–1960. *Annals of the Association of American Geographers*, **57**, 88–100. (3.5.3)

ROBINSON, A. H. 1956: The necessity of weighting values in correlation of areal data. *Annals of the Association of American Geographers*, **46**, 233–6. (10.6.1, 10.6.2)
  1961: The cartographic representation of the statistical surface. *International Yearbook of Cartography*, **1**, 53–63. (9.3)

ROBINSON, A. H., J. B. LINDBERG, and L. W. BRINKMAN. 1961: A correlation and regression analysis applied to rural farm population densities. *Annals of the Association of American Geographers*, **51**, 211–21. (8.4.2, 9.3.2, 10.6.2)

ROBINSON, A. H., and R. D. SALE. 1969: *Elements of cartography*. New York. (9.1, 9.3.1)

ROBINSON, G. 1970: Some comments on trend-surface analysis. *Area*, **3**, 31–36. (12.2.3)

ROBSON, B. T. 1973: *Urban growth: an approach*. Cambridge. (4.2.3, 4.4.1–2)

RODGERS, A. 1952: Industrial inertia: a major factor in the location of the steel industry in the United States. *Geographical Review*, **42**, 56–65. (5.4.4, 5.5.1)

ROGERS, A. 1965: A stochastic analysis of the spatial clustering of retail establishments. *Journal of the American Statistical Association*, **60**, 1094–1103. (13.2.3, 13.3.1)
  1969a: Quadrat analysis of urban dispersion: 1. Theoretical techniques. *Environment and Planning*, **1**, 47–80. (13.1, 13.2.1)
  1971: *Matrix methods in urban and regional analysis*. San Francisco. (15.5.2)
  1974: *Statistical analysis of spatial dispersion: the quadrat method*. London. (13.3.1–2, 13.3.4)

ROGERS, E. M. 1962: *Diffusion of innovations*. New York. (7.1)

ROSE, A. J. 1966: Dissent from Down Under—metropolitan dominance as the normal state. *Pacific Viewpoint*, **7**, 1–27. (4.4.1)

ROSTOW, W. W. 1960: *The stages of economic growth.* Cambridge. (3.5.3, 3.4.2)

ROSTOW, W. W., Editor. 1963: *The economics of take-off into sustained growth.* London. (5.4.2)

ROUGET, R. 1972: Graph theory and hierarchization modes. *Regional and Urban Economics,* **2**, 263–96. (14.6.2)

RUTHERFORD, J., M. I. LOGAN, and G. J. MISSEN. 1966: *New viewpoints in economic geography.* Sydney. (6.5.1)

SAARINEN, T. F. 1966: Perception of the drought hazard on the Great Plains. *University of Chicago, Department of Geography, Research Papers,* **106**. (6.5.1)

SACK, R. D. 1972: Geography, geometry and explanation. *Annals of the Association of American Geographers,* **62**, 61–78. (1.2.2)
  1974: Chorology and spatial analysis. *Annals of the Association of American Geographers,* **64**, 439–52. (1.2.2)

SAMUELSON, P. A. 1952: Spatial price equilibrium and linear programming. *American Economic Review,* **42**, 183–203. (15.1)

SANDERS, E. 1975: Urban population density function of two polar variables. *Regional Studies,* **9**, 63–8. (6.6.1)

SANDNER, G. 1961: Agrarkolonisation in Costa Rica: Siedlung, Wirtschaft und Sozialfüge an der Pioniergrenze. *Schriften des Geographischen Instituts der Universität Kiel,* **19**. (4.2.3)

SAUER, C. O. 1925: The morphology of landscape. *University of California, Publications in Geography,* **2**, 19–53. (1.2.4)
  1952: Agricultural origins and dispersals. *American Geographical Society, Bowman Memorial Lectures,* **2**. (6.6.2, 7.1)

SAUER, C. O., and D. BRAND. 1930: Pueblo sites in Southeastern Arizona. *University of California, Publications in Geography,* **3**, 415–48. (7.1)

SAVAGE, L. J. 1954: *The foundation of statistics.* New York. (1.4.3)

SCHAEFER, F. K. 1953: Exceptionalism in geography: a methodological examination. *Annals of the Association of American Geographers,* **43**, 226–49. (1.4.4)

SCHEFFÉ, H. 1959: *The analysis of variance.* New York. (12.3.1)

SCOTT, A. J. 1971a: An introduction to spatial allocation analysis. *Association of American Geographers, Commission on College Geography, Resource Papers,* **9**. (15.1–3, 15.3.2–3, 15.4.1–2)
  1971b: *Combinatorial programming, spatial analysis and planning.* London. (3.4.2, 15.4.2, 15.5.3)

SEARS, F. W., and M. W. ZEMANSKY. 1964: *University physics.* Reading, Mass. (3.2.2)

SEMPLE, E. C. 1911: *Influence of geographic environment on the basis of Ratzel's system of anthropo-geography.* New York. (1.2.3)

SEN, A. K. 1976: Large sample-size distribution of statistics used in testing for spatial correlation. *Geographical Analysis,* **8**, 175–84. (11.3.2)

SENIOR, M. L., and A. G. WILSON. 1973: Disaggregated residential location models: some tests and further theoretical developments. In E. L. Cripps, Editor. *Space-time concepts in urban and regional models.* London. 141–72. (15.5.1)
  1974: Explanations and syntheses of linear programming and spatial interaction models of residential location. *Geographical Analysis,* **6**, 209–38. (15.5.1)

SHANNON, G. W., and G. E. A. DEVER. 1974: *Health care delivery: spatial perspectives.* New York. (14.5.3)

SHERBROOKE, C. C. 1968: Discrete compound Poisson processes and tables of the geometric Poisson distribution. *Naval Research Logistics Quarterly,* **15**, 189–203. (13.3.4)

SHUMWAY, R., and J. GURLAND. 1960: A fitting procedure for some generalized Poisson distributions. *Skandinavisk Aktrarietidskrift,* **43**, 87–108. (13.2.4)

SIEGEL, S. 1956: *Nonparametric statistics for the behavioral sciences.* New York. (9.2, 10.5.3, 11.3.1)

SILK, J. A. 1965: Road network of Monmouthshire. *University of Cambridge, Department of Geography, B.A. Dissertation.* (3.3.1)

SILVA, R. C. 1965: Reapportionment and redistricting. *Scientific American,* **213**(5), 20–7. (14.5.2)

SIMON, H. A. 1955: On a class of skew distribution functions. *Biometrika,* **42**, 425–40. (4.3.4)

SINCLAIR, R. 1967: Von Thünen and urban sprawl. *Annals of the Association of American Geographers,* **57**, 72–87. (6.5.2)

SINNHUBER, K. A. 1954: Central Europe–Mitteleuropa–Europe Central: an analysis of a geographical term. *Institute of British Geographers Publications,* **20**, 15–39. (14.2.4)

SKELLAM, J. G. 1952: Studies in statistical ecology, I: Spatial pattern. *Biometrika,* **39**, 346–62. (13.6.1)
1958: On the derivation and applicability of Neyman's type A distribution. *Biometrika,* **45**, 32–36. (13.4.4)

SKILLING, H. 1964: An operational view. *American Scientist,* **53**, 388A–96A. (1.4.1–2)

SKINNER, S. W. 1964–65: Marketing and social structure in rural China. *Journal of Asian Studies,* **24**, 3–399. (5.3.1)

SMITH, D. 1971: *Industrial location.* London. (5.5, 5.6.1–2)

SMITH, W. 1955: The location of industry. *Institute of British Geographers, Publications,* **21**, 1–18. (5.6.1)

SOJA, E. W. 1968: Communications and territorial integration in East Africa: an introduction to transaction flow analysis. *East Lakes Geographer,* **4**, 39–57. (14.6.2)

SOPER, H. E. 1929: Interpretation of periodicity in disease prevalence. *Journal of the Royal Statistical Society,* **92**, 34–73. (7.7.4)

SORRE, M. 1947–52: *Les fondements de la géographie humaine.* Three volumes. Paris. (1.2.3)

SORRE, M. 1961: *L'homme sur la terre.* Paris. (1.2.3)

SPECHT, R. E. 1959: *A functional analysis of the Green Bay and Western Railroad.* Stevens Point. (3.2.2)

SPENCE, N. A. 1968: A multifactor regionalization of British counties on the basis of employment data for 1961. *Regional Studies,* **2**, 87–104. (14.4.3)

SPENCER, J. E., and R. J. HORVATH. 1963: How does an agricultural region originate? *Annals of the Association of American Geographers,* **53**, 74–92. (6.6.2)

SPOONER, R. S. 1975: Local variations in monthly unemployment series: northern England, 1927–36. *Bristol University. B.Sc. Project.* (4.6.2)

SPROTT, D. A. 1958: The methods of maximum likelihood applied to the Poisson binomial distribution. *Biometrics,* **14**, 97–106. (13.2.4)

STAFFORD, H. A., JR. 1963: The functional bases of small towns. *Economic Geography,* **39**, 165–75. (5.2.1)

STAMP, L. D., and S. W. WOOLDRIDGE, Editors. 1951: *London essays in Geography.* London. (14.2.1)

STANISLAWSKI, D. 1946: The origin and spread of the grid-pattern town. *Geographical Review,* **36**, 105–20. (7.1)

STEINER, D. 1965: A multivariate statistical approach to climatic regionalization and classification. *Tijdschrift van het Koninklijk Nederlandsche Aardrijkskundig Genootschap*, **15**, 23–35. (14.4.2)

STEVENS, B. H. 1961: Linear programming and location rent. *Journal of Regional Science*, **3**, 15–25. (15.2.3)
1968: Location theory and programming models: the von Thünen case. *Regional Science Association, Papers*, **21**, 19–34. (6.3.1)

STEWART, C. T., JR. 1958: The size and spacing of cities. *Geographical Review*, **48**, 222–45. (4.3.1)

STEWART, J. Q., and W. WARNTZ. 1958: Macrogeography and social science. *Geographical Review*, **48**, 167–84. (2.4.5, 9.6.2)

STODDART, D. R. 1967: Growth and structure of geography. *Institute of British Geographers, Publications*, **41**, 1–19. (1.4)
1975: Kropotkin, Reclus, and 'relevant' geography. *Area*, **7**, 188–90. (1.4.5)

STOKES, D. E. 1965: A variance components model of political effects. In J. M. Claunch, Editor. *Mathematical applications in political science*. Dallas. (12.3.1)

STOREY, K. J. 1972: Some structural characteristics of the Newfoundland economy. In M. A. Micklewright and P. Y. Velleneuve, Editors. *Problems of slow growth and stagnant areas in developed countries*. St John's, Newfoundland. 165–89. (9.7.4)

STOUFFER, S. A. 1940: Intervening opportunities: a theory relating mobility and distance. *American Sociological Review*, **5**, 845–67. (2.3.4, 2.6.2)

STRAUSS, D. J., and M. ORANS. 1975: Mighty sifts: a critical appraisal of solutions to Galton's problem and a partial solution. *Current Anthropology*, **16**, 573–94. (10.2)

STUART, A. 1962: *Basic ideas of scientific sampling*. London. (8.2.2, 8.3, 8.3.1)

STUDENT. 1914: The elimination of spurious correlation due to position in time or space. *Biometrika*, **10**, 179–80. (10.3.2)

SVIATLOVSKY, E. E., and W. C. EELLS. 1937: The centrographic method and regional analysis. *Geographical Review*, **27**, 240–54. (9.6.2)

TAAFFE, E. J., Editor. 1970: *Geography*. Englewood Cliffs, N.J. (1.2.1)

TAAFFE, E. J., R. L. MORRILL, and P. R. GOULD. 1963: Transport expansion in underdeveloped countries: a comparative analysis. *Geographical Review*, **53**, 503–29. (3.5.2, 3.5.3)

TANNER, J. C. 1967: Layout of road systems on plantations. *Ministry of Transport, Road Research Laboratory Report*, **LR68**. (3.3.2)

TARRANT, J. R. 1973: Comments on the Lösch central place system. *Geographical Analysis*, **5**, 113–21. (5.2.4)

TAYLOR, P. J. 1975: *Distance decay models in spatial interaction*. Norwich. (2.3.1)

THEIL, H. 1965: The analysis of disturbances in regression analysis. *Journal of the American Statistical Association*, **60**, 1067–79. (11.4.1)
1971: *Principles of econometrics*. New York. (10.6.2)

THEODORSON, G. A., Editor. 1961: *Studies in human ecology*. Evanston. (2.6.1)

THOMAS, D. 1963: *Agriculture in Wales during the Napoleonic Wars: a study in the geographical interpretation of historical sources*. Cardiff. (9.4.2)

THOMAS, E. N. 1960: Maps of residuals from regressions: their characteristics and uses in geographic research. *State University of Iowa, Department of Geography, Report*, **2**. (3.3.2)
1961: Towards an expanded central place model. *Geographical Review*, **51**, 400–11. (4.5.2)
1962: The stability of distance–population size relationships for Iowa towns

from 1900 to 1950. *Lund Studies in Geography, Series B, Human Geography*, **24**, 13–30. (4.5.2)

THOMAS, E. N., and D. W. ANDERSON. 1965: Additional comments on weighting values in correlation analysis of areal data. *Annals of the Association of American Geographers*, **55**, 492–505. (10.6.2)

THOMAS, F. H. 1960: The Denver and Rio Grande Western Railroad: a geographic analysis. *Northwestern University, Studies in Geography*, **4**. (3.3.2)

THOMAS, M. 1949: A generalization of Poisson's binomial limit for use in ecology. *Biometrika*, **36**, 18–25. (13.2.4, 13.4.1)

THOMAS, W. L., JR., Editor. 1956: *Man's role in changing the face of the earth.* Chicago. (1.2.4, 2.4.4, 2.6.1, 4.2.1, 6.6.2)

THOMPSON, J. H., S. C. SUFRIN, P. R. GOULD, and M. A. BUCK. 1962: Toward a geography of economic health—the case of New York state. *Annals of the Association of American Geographers*, **52**, 1–20. (14.4.3)

THOMPSON, W. R. 1957: The coefficient of localization: an appraisal. *Southern Economic Journal*, **23**, 320–25. (9.3.4, 10.6.2)

THOMPSON, D'ARCY W. 1917; abrid. edit. 1961: *On growth and form.* Cambridge. (1.2.4, 2.2.1, 2.7.1)

THOMPSON, W. R. 1957: The coefficient of localization: an appraisal. *Southern Economic Journal*, **23**, 320–5. (9.3.4)

THORNGREN, B. 1970: How do contact systems affect regional development? *Environment and Planning*, **2**, 409–27. (5.5.2)

THÜNEN, J. H. VON. 1826, 1875: *Der Isolierte Staat in Beziehung auf Landwirtschaft und Nationalökonomie.* Hamburg. (1.2.2, 6.3, 6.3.2)

TINKLER, K. J. 1972: The physical interpretation of eigenfunctions of dichotomous matrices. *Institute of British Geographers, Publications*, **55**, 17–46. (9.7.4)

1973: The topology of rural periodic market systems. *Geografiska Annaler*, **55, B**, 121–33. (5.3.1)

TINLINE, R. R. 1971: Linear operators in diffusion research. In M. D. I. Chisholm, A. E. Frey, and P. Haggett, Editors. *Regional forecasting.* London. 71–91. (7.6.2, 16.2.2)

1972: *A simulation study of the 1967–8 foot-and-mouth epizootic in Great Britain.* University of Bristol. Unpublished Ph.D. dissertation. (7.1, 13.3.1)

TOBLER, W. R. 1963: Geographic area and map projections. *Geographical Review*, **53**, 59–78. (2.7.3)

1965: Computation of the correspondence of geographical patterns. *Regional Science Association, Papers*, **15**, 131–42. (7.6.2)

1967: Of maps and matrices. *Journal of Regional Science*, **7**, 275–80. (16.2.2)

1969a: The spectrum of U.S. 40. *Regional Science Association, Papers*, **23**, 45–52. (6.2.1, 12.4.2)

1969b: Geographical filters and their inverses. *Geographical Analysis*, **1**, 234–53. (16.2.2)

1970: A computer movie simulating urban growth in the Detroit Region. *Economic Geography*, (Supplement) **46**, 234–40. (10.2, 11.2.1, 16.2.2)

TOBLER, W., and S. WINERBURG. 1971: A Cappadocian speculation. *Nature*, **231**, 40–1. (9.8.2)

TROXEL, E. 1955: *Economics of transport.* New York. (6.4.2)

TUKEY, J. W. 1961: Discussion emphasizing the connection between analysis of variance and spectrum analysis. *Technometrics*, **3**, 191–219. (12.3.1)

1962: The future of data analysis. *Annals of Mathematical Statistics*, **33**, 1–67. (11.4.2, 16.4.1)

TURNER, F. J. 1920: *The frontier in American history*. New York. (7.1)

TYLOR, E. B. 1889: On a method of investigating the development of institutions, applied to laws of marriage and descent. *Journal of the Royal Anthropological Institute of Great Britain and Ireland*, **18**, 245–72. (10.2)

ULLMAN, E. L. 1949: The railroad pattern of the United States. *Geographical Review*, **39**, 242–56. (3.3.2)

1957: *American commodity flow: a geographical interpretation of rail and water traffic based on principles of spatial interchange*. Seattle. (2.6.1)

ULLMAN, E. L., and M. F. DACEY. 1962: The minimum requirements approach to the urban economic base. *Lund Studies in Geography, Series B, Human Geography*, **24**, 121–43. (5.2.1, 5.4.4)

UNSTEAD, J. F. 1933: A system of regional geography. *Geography*, **18**, 175–87. (14.2.2)

VAJDA, S. 1961: *The theory of games and linear programming*. London. (5.6.3, 6.5.1)

VALKENBURG, S. VAN, and C. C. HELD. 1952: *Europe*. New York. (6.4.1)

VANCE, J. E., JR. 1960: Labor-shed, employment field, and dynamic analysis in urban geography. *Economic Geography*, **36**, 189–220. (2.6.1)

1961: The Oregon Trail and the Union Pacific Railroad: a contrast in purpose. *Annals of the Association of American Geographers*, **51**, 357–79. (3.2.3)

1962: Emerging patterns of commercial structure in American cities. *Lund Studies in Geography, Series B, Human Geography*, **24**, 485–518. (2.6.2)

1970: *The merchant's world: the geography of wholesaling*. Englewood Cliffs, N.J. (5.3.2)

VIDAL DE LA BLACHE, P. 1917: *La France de l'est*. Paris. (1.2.3)

1922: *Principes de la géographie humaine*. Paris. (1.2.3)

VINING, R. 1955: A description of certain spatial aspects of an economic system. *Economic Development and Cultural Change*, **3**, 147–95. (5.2.4)

VON NEUMANN, J., and O. MORGENSTERN. 1944: *Theory of games and economic behaviour*. Princeton, N.J. (1.4.3)

WAGNER, H. M. 1959: Linear programming techniques for regression analysis. *Journal of the American Statistical Association*, **54**, 206–12. (11.4.2)

1962: Non-linear regression with minimal assumptions. *Journal of the American Statistical Association*, **57**, 572–78. (11.4.2)

WAIBEL, L. 1958: *Capitulos de geografia tropical e do Brasil*. Rio de Janeiro. (6.3.2, 6.5.2, 6.6.2)

WALTERS, S. M. 1957: Mapping the distribution of plants. *New Biology*, **24**, 93–108. (8.4.2)

WARD, J. H. 1963: Hierarchical grouping to optimize an objective function. *Journal of the American Statistical Association*, **58**, 236–44. (14.4.2)

WARNES, A. M. 1975: Commuting towards city centres: a study of population and employment density gradients in Liverpool and Manchester. *Institute of British Geographers, Publications*, **64**, 77–96. (6.6.1)

WARNTZ, W. 1959: *Toward a geography of price*. Philadelphia. (2.4.1, 9.3)

1961: Transatlantic flights and pressure patterns. *Geographical Review*, **51**, 187–212. (3.1)

WARNTZ, W., and D. NEFT. 1960: Contributions to a statistical methodology for areal distributions. *Journal of Regional Science*, **2**, 47–66. (9.6.2)

WARREN, W. G. 1962: Contributions to the study of spatial point processes.

University of North Carolina, Institute of Statistics Mimeo Series, **337.** (13.4.4)

WATSON, G. S. 1971: Trend surface analyses. *Mathematical Geology,* **3,** 215–26. (12.2.2)

— 1972: Trend surface analysis and spatial correlation. *Geological Society of America, Special Paper,* **146,** 39–46. (12.2.2)

WEAVER, J. B., and S. W. HESS. 1963: A procedure for non-partisan districting: development of computer techniques. *Yale Law Journal,* **73,** 288–308. (14.5.2)

WEAVER, J. C. 1954: Crop combination regions in the Middle West. *Geographical Review,* **44,** 175–200. (9.4.2)

— 1956: The county as a spatial average in agricultural geography. *Geographical Review,* **46,** 536–65. (8.4.2)

WEBB, W. P. 1927: *The Great Plains.* New York. (4.2.3, 7.1)

WEBBER, M. J. 1972: *Impact of uncertainty on location.* Cambridge, Mass. (1.2.2, 5.2.3)

WEBER, A. 1909: *Über den Standort der Industrien.* Tübingen. (1.2.2, 5.5, 5.6.1)

WELLINGTON, A. M. 1886: The American line from Vera Cruz to the city of Mexico, via Jalapa, with notes on the best methods of surmounting high elevations by rail. *American Society of Civil Engineers, Transactions,* **20.** (3.2.1)

— 1887: *The economic theory of the location of railways.* New York. (3.2.1)

WERNER, C. 1968: The law of refraction in transportation geography: its multivariate analysis. *Canadian Geographer,* **12** (1), 28–40. (3.2.2)

WETHERILL, G. B. 1967: *Elementary statistical methods.* London. (10.1)

WHITE, R. R. 1972: Probability maps of leukaemia mortalities in England and Wales. In N. D. McGlashan, Editor. *Medical geography: techniques and field studies.* London. (9.5.2)

WHITTEN, E. H. T. 1974: Scale and directional field and analytical data for spatial variability studies. *Mathematical Geology,* **6,** 183–98. (12.2.2)

WHITTLE, P. 1954: On stationary processes in the plane. *Biometrika,* **41,** 434–49. (10.3.2, 11.2.2, 11.4.2)

WILLIAMSON, E., and M, H. BRETHERTON. 1963: *Tables of the negative binomial probability distribution.* New York. (13.3.4)

WINTERS, P. R. 1960: Forecasting sales by exponentially-weighted moving averages. *Management Science,* **6,** 324–42. (16.3.3)

WHITEHAND, J. W. R. 1972: Building cycles and the spatial pattern of urban growth. *Institute of British Geographers, Publications,* **56,** 39–55. (6.6.1)

WHITTLESEY, D. 1956: Southern Rhodesia: an African compage. *Annals of the Association of American Geographers,* **46,** 1–97. (14.2.2)

WHITWORTH, W. A. 1934: *Choice and chance.* New York. (4.3.3)

WILLIAMS, W. T., and J. M. LAMBERT. 1959–62: Multivariate methods in plant ecology. *Journal of Ecology,* **47,** 83–101; **48,** 689–710; **49,** 717–29; **50,** 775–802. (14.4.1)

WILSON, A. G. 1967: A statistical theory of spatial distribution models. *Transportation Research,* **1,** 253–69. (2.5.2)

— 1970: *Entropy in urban and regional modelling.* London. (1.2.4, 2.5, 2.5.1–2)

— 1972: Theoretical geography: some speculations. *Institute of British Geographers, Publications,* **57,** 31–44. (1.4.2)

— 1974: *Urban and regional models in geography and planning.* London. (Postscript)

WILSON, A. G., and M. J. KIRKBY. 1975: *Mathematical methods for geographers and planners.* Oxford. (Preface, 1.1)

WINSBOROUGH, H. H. 1961: A comparative study of urban population densities. *University of Chicago, Ph.D. Thesis.* (6.2.2)

WISE, M. J. 1949: On the evolution of the jewellery and gun quarters in Birmingham. *Institute of British Geographers, Publications,* **15**, 57–72. (5.5.2)

WOLFE, R. I. 1963: *Transportation and politics.* Princeton. (3.2.3)

WOLPERT, J. 1964: The decision process in spatial context. *Annals of the Association of American Geographers,* **54**, 537–58. (6.5.3)

WOOD, W. F. 1955: Use of stratified random samples in land use study. *Annals of the Association of American Geographers,* **45**, 350–67. (8.3.2)

WOODWARD, V. H. 1971: Review of *Optimal Patterns of Location,* J. Serck-Hanssen, Amsterdam: North-Holland 1970: *The Economic Journal,* **81**, 396. (15.4.1)

WRIGLEY, N. 1973: The use of percentages in geographical research. *Area,* **5**, 183–86. (16.5.2)

WYNNE-EDWARDS, V. C. 1962: *Animal dispersion in relation to social behaviour.* Edinburgh. (2.7)

YAPA, L. 1976: On the statistical significance of the observed map in spatial diffusion. *Geographical Analysis,* **8**, 255–68. (7.6.2)

YATES, F. 1960: *Sampling methods for censuses and surveys.* London. (8.3, 8.3.1, 8.3.5)

YEATES, M. H. 1963: Hinterland delimitation: a distance minimizing approach. *Professional Geographer,* **15** (6), 7–10. (2.4.2, 14.1, 14.5.1, 15.4.3)

1974: *An introduction to quantitative analysis in human geography.* New York. (10.1)

YEATES, M. H., and B. J. GARNER. 1971, 1976: *The North American city.* New York. (6.3.4)

YUILL, R. S. 1965: A simulation study of barrier effects in spatial diffusion problems. *Michigan Inter-University Community of Mathematical Geographers, Discussion Papers,* **5**. (7.5.1)

YULE, G. U., and M. G. KENDALL. 1957: *An introduction to the theory of statistics.* (Thirteenth edition) London. (10.6.1, 10.6.2)

ZIPF, G. K. 1949: *Human behaviour and the principle of least effort.* Cambridge, Mass. (2.2.1, 2.2.2, 4.3.1)

ZOBLER, L. 1958: Decision making in regional construction. *Annals of the Association of American Geographers,* **48**, 140–8. (14.4.3)

Further reading

To add a section on further reading to an extended list of references (given on pages 556–88) may appear to be gilding the lily. Nonetheless it is arguable that a list which derives from the reasonable need to document the many and varied sources from which the notes for this book were assembled is not likely to be very helpful to the reader who is looking for some more limited or basic reading or wishes to keep up to date on current trends.

(a) *Basic reading.* If we may assume that the student is already familiar with the traditional literature of regional and human geography then a very good starting point is provided by ABLER, ADAMS, and GOULD (1971)* over the whole range of locational theory and by CHISHOLM (1962) and by SMITH (1971) over agricultural and industrial location respectively. BUNGE (1962) also remains a lively, stimulating and unusual approach to locational analysis from a strongly geometrical viewpoint. Students unfamiliar with more conventional geographical writing will find that HARVEY (1969) and AMADEO and GOLLEDGE (1975) give scholarly reviews of the aims, methods, and problems of the discipline. THOMAS (1956) and HAGGETT (1975a) give examples of substantive studies in human geography.

(b) *Advanced reading.* A number of the classic studies in locational theory—notably those of LÖSCH (1954), CHRISTALLER (1966), von Thünen (HALL, 1966) and HÄGERSTRAND (1967)—are available in translation. Most of the early contributions have been summarized and greatly extended by ISARD (1956) in what is still among the most useful textbooks in the field. WILSON (1974) provides a more rigorous contemporary account with special emphasis on spatial interaction models.

There is no single source for methods in locational analysis, although that by ISARD (*Introduction to Regional Science*, Englewood Cliffs, N.J., 1975) comes nearest. There is a variety of texts on statistical analysis of varying degrees of difficulty and relevance to spatial analysis: that by KING (1969) probably remains the best for geographers. Standard mathematical procedures are outlined clearly in WILSON and KIRKBY (1975). Probably the most important reading here for student geographers is concerned with the whole strategy of scientific method rather than the tactics of individual tests: HANSON (1958) and HARVEY (1969) provide excellent introductions to this field.

* Full titles are given only where books have not been previously mentioned in the text.

(c) *Current research.* The rapid rate of evolution of locational studies and the introduction of wholly new methods (e.g. entropy maximizing methods) means that journals are as important as textbooks if a student is to retain a reasonably contemporary view of the subject. Most of the more traditional geographical journals now carry papers of direct importance in locational analysis. However the key journals, as judged on their content to 1975, are the *Annals of the Association of American Geographers* (Quarterly), *Geographical Analysis* (Quarterly), the *Lund Studies in Geography, Series B and C* (Occasional), the Regional Science Association's *Papers and Proceedings* (Annual), *Regional Studies* (Quarterly), and *Environment and Planning Series A* (Quarterly). In addition to these formal periodicals a few universities publish research theses (the Chicago and California Departments of Geography have outstanding series) and most produce informal discussion papers which are important sources of ideas. (The latter are regularly listed in *Geographical Analysis.*) Most difficult to keep track of are the Contract Reports of research done for government bodies (e.g. the Office of Naval Research in the United States) although these often emerge later as papers in the standard journals. *Progress in Geography* (Vols. 1–9) draws together findings from many of these research sources in regular reviews of developments within the field.

(d) *Research 'readers'.* For the student without access to a periodicals library one useful substitute is the research 'reader'—a collection of research papers on a specific topic drawn from a wide range of journals. Many items of locational interest are included in FRIEDMANN and ALONSO (*Regional development and planning: a reader,* 1975). Urban geography is covered in BERRY and HORTON (1970), economic geography in SMITH, TAAFFE and KING (*Readings in economic geography,* Chicago, 1968), industrial location in KARASKA and BRAMHALL (*Locational analysis for manufacturing: a selection of readings,* Cambridge, Mass., 1969), and transport geography in HURST (1974). Many of the methods of analysis described in the second part of this book are illustrated in BERRY and MARBLE (1968).

Subject index

Subject index